The Latest on the Best

The Latest on the Best

Essays on Evolution and Optimality

edited by John Dupré

A Bradford Book
The MIT Press
Cambridge, Massachusetts
London, England

This book was set in Palatino by Asco Trade Typesetting Ltd., Hong Kong, and printed and bound by Halliday Lithograph in the United States of America.

Library of Congress Cataloging-in-Publication Data

The Latest on the best.

"A Bradford Book"
Bibliography: p.
Includes index.
1. Evolution. 2. Evolution—Miscellanea. 3. Adaptation (Biology). I. Dupré, John.
QH371.L38   1987   575   86-27226
ISBN 0-262-04090-5

Contents

List of Contributors

John Beatty
Department of Ecology and
   Behavioral Biology
University of Minnesota
Minneapolis, Minnesota 55455

Robert Boyd
Department of Anthropology
Emory University
Atlanta, Georgia 30322

Leda Cosmides
Department of Psychology
Stanford University
Stanford, California 94305

John Dupré
Department of Philosophy
Stanford University
Stanford, California 94305

John M. Emlen
Department of Fisheries and
   Wildlife
and
The Agora: Center for Creative
   Thought
Oregon State University
Newport, Oregon 97365

Jack Hirshleifer
Department of Economics
University of California
Los Angeles, California 90024

Philip Kitcher
Department of Philosophy
University of California at San
   Diego
La Jolla, California 92093

Richard C. Lewontin
Museum of Comparative Zoology
Harvard University
Cambridge, Massachusetts 02138

John Maynard Smith
School of Biological Sciences
University of Sussex
Falmer, Brighton, United Kingdom

Peter J. Richerson
Institute of Ecology
University of California
Davis, California 95616

Roger N. Shepard
Department of Psychology
Stanford University
Stanford, California 94305

Eric Alden Smith
Department of Anthropology
University of Washington
Seattle, Washington 98195

Elliott Sober
Department of Philosophy
University of Wisconsin
Madison, Wisconsin 53706

John E. R. Staddon
Department of Psychology
Duke University
Durham, North Carolina 27706

John Tooby
Department of Psychology
Stanford University
Stanford, California 94305

Acknowledgments

This anthology derives from a Conference on Evolution and Information held at Stanford University in April 1985, at which versions of all but two of the papers in the collection were discussed. Neither the conference nor the book would have been possible without the support and generosity of two Stanford institutions. The Center for the Study of Language and Information provided the bulk of the funding for the conference, and did so in a way that not only saved me personally from lost sleep over the finances, but also enabled the conference to be held in an extremely pleasant and comfortable manner. I would also like to thank personally the center's then director, John Perry, for his support and encouragement of the project. This adds to a long list of debts to him that I cannot imagine I shall ever be in a position to repay.

Equally indispensable was the support of the Stanford Humanities Center, which not only provided a major contribution to the funding of the original conference, but also gave me a year's leave as a Humanities Center fellow during the time that the book was heading toward publication. The pleasant surroundings, stimulating intellectual environment, and release from other responsibilities that this entailed enabled me, among other things, to devote my energies far more effectively to the progress of the volume than would otherwise have been possible. I am also very grateful to the Pew Memorial Trust for support during the period when I was working on my own contribution to the collection.

I am also indebted to all of the participants in the Stanford conference for suggestions, advice, information, and stimulation. One contributor requires very special mention. Philip Kitcher has been a constant source of advice and encouragement from the moment the conference was first conceived. I could not begin to list the contributions he has made to the final result over many hours of discussion and pages of correspondence. I shall only say that whatever the project finally achieved, it would have been a great deal less without his help.

One person who should certainly be mentioned is Betty Stanton, who has been as tolerant and supportive a publisher as one could hope for. I must also thank Joanna Bujes for her indefatigable efforts in the production of the index.

Finally I would like to thank Regenia Gagnier. Uncountable hours of conversation on innumerable topics, including many discussed in this book, have helped maintain my intellectual enthusiasm and, much more important, my sense of humor.

J.A.D.
November 1986

The Latest on the Best

Introduction

John Dupré

It is a commonplace that for the last century the theory of evolution by natural selection has been the centerpiece of biology. It is another commonplace within biology, and one that long antedates Darwin's theory of evolution, that biological organisms are extraordinarily adapted to the environments in which they live. The relationship between two commonplaces, however, may be anything but obvious, and this is the case with these two. This relationship is the unifying theme of the essays in this book.

Much of the success of the theory of evolution by natural selection can be attributed to the fact that it is a theory that explains adaptation without appeal to any intentional agency. This virtue of the theory is not disputed by any of the contributors to this volume. It should be mentioned, however, that what exactly constitutes an explanation remains a matter of heated debate among philosophers of science. But without going into this thorny issue—and few, if any, philosophers deny that evolutionary theory is an excellent source of explanations—explanation is not generally considered a sufficient basis for a theory's scientific credentials. What have often been suggested as the true virtues of science are its capacities for providing prediction and control. But insofar as evolutionary theory is seen simply as a historical account of how life on earth came to achieve the forms it currently displays, it is hard to see how it could offer anything like prediction or control.

Few, if any, biologists imagine that evolutionary theory can enable us to predict the long-term future of life. What species will exist in ten million years' time is a question we must leave to our descendants—if, indeed, they prove to be included in the answer to that question. However, biologists do use evolutionary theory in ways that, if not quite so ambitious, should certainly be considered predictive. Most simply, evolutionary processes can be observed on a small scale in the laboratory, and sometimes the upshot of such processes can be predicted. Occasionally it is possible

I am very grateful to Philip Kitcher for detailed comments, on everything from stylistic infelicities to substantive philosophical objections, on an earlier draft of this introduction.

to observe evolutionary processes in the field in great detail, as for example with Kettlewell's (1973) famous studies of industrial melanism in the Peppered Moth. Given the sort of detail involved in that, and a few comparable cases, quite precise predictions are possible. But such ideal examples are rare. In general, practical problems severely limit the direct investigation of evolutionary processes in nature.[1]

There is a classical philosophical view that claims that explanation and prediction are essentially identical operations: An explanation that we give after the fact is logically identical to the prediction that we could, in principle, have given before the fact. This derives from the deductive-nomological conception of explanations, which treats them as deductions from universal laws and specified initial conditions (Hempel, 1965). It makes no important difference, in this picture, when the deduction is carried out. But, without going into the numerous philosophical objections that have been leveled against this position, it is clear that for fields such as evolutionary biology, which address phenomena of extreme complexity, there is an enormous pragmatic asymmetry. The initial conditions that would have to be specified for an evolutionary prediction may typically be far beyond our epistemological grasp. Indeed, in evolutionary theory it seems that we are much more likely to infer the initial conditions from the plausibility of a particular explanation. A process of runaway sexual selection, for example, strikes us as by far the most plausible account of the origin of the peacock's tail. On the basis of theoretical analysis of such a process, we can then retrodict a good deal about the conditions that must have obtained among the ancestors of peacocks.

But there is a rather different, and perhaps much more important, sense in which evolutionists may be said to deploy a predictive science. This is where the idea of optimality takes on central significance. Evolution, it may be argued, is a process by which organisms have come to adopt the best available strategy for dealing with the exigencies of their environment. (All evolutionists admit that this claim must be qualified; the relevant qualifications will figure largely in the papers in this volume.) If this claim is correct, then all kinds of predictive possibilities are created. In the first place, we can predict that whatever features organisms possess are, when suitably understood, optimal responses to features of their environment. This statement is open to numerous powerful criticisms, of which universal scope and vagueness are only the most obvious. But it is also possible to employ the assumption of optimality in much more specific and interesting ways. In general, we may try to analyze the problems that organisms face in survival and reproduction, and make claims of the following kind: If an organism has certain capacities and faces certain environmental problems, it will evolve a particular optimal adaptation. This is clearly a predictive claim; we need only look for organisms that satisfy the antecedent, and determine whether they also satisfy the consequent of such a conditional.

In considering the prospects for this approach, it is useful to distinguish between morphologogical and behavioral adaptation. On the whole, if one wants to investigate the morphology of an organism, one will resort to observation, dissection, and other more sophisticated experimental techniques. It is true that a lot of ingenuity has been expended in hypothesizing selective advantages for morphological features, particularly where the advantage in question is far from immediately obvious. However, reasonable doubts about whether this really adds anything to the understanding of such questions have precisely provided the foundation of skeptical attacks on the scientific usefulness of evolutionary theory. Such speculations are almost always subsequent to investigation of morphological and physiological properties by other means; and it certainly seems plausible that once a feature has been identified, sufficient ingenuity will always enable one to produce several plausible hypotheses about its adaptive advantage.

For a variety of reasons, the possible relevance of optimality theory to animal behavior is a lot more interesting. The most basic reason for this is that, in contrast with most aspects of morphological questions, it is seldom a simple matter to move from observation to an uncontroversial account of what an animal is doing. To go from a description of an animal's movements to a correct account of its behavior requires some degree of interpretation. And a very promising methodological possibility is that the best way of guiding such interpretation is by appeal to an evolutionarily based analysis of optimality.

The need for interpretation in correctly describing behavior is very familiar in philosophical discussions of human action. To take a very simple example, suppose we see someone raising an arm and making a series of horizontal motions with it. A few of the many possible interpretations might be that she is making a parting gesture to a friend, brushing flies away from her eyes, or restoring the circulation to a numb limb. Choosing between these interpretations requires further information about the context of the action and, above all, about the motives, beliefs, and intentions of the agent. In the nonhuman case, though there is a reasonable assumption that the behavioral repertoire and the repertoire of possible motives and intentions will be smaller, access to the latter cannot be attained by the most obvious means in the human case, viz., interrogation. Thus optimality analysis has seemed to many to provide an extremely promising means of circumventing this problem.

An additional factor is that in recent years great insights have been achieved in the techniques for analyzing optimality—in particular, through the study of the theory of games.[2] The basic problem about evolution addressed by this latter theory is that what behavioral strategy is selectively advantageous depends crucially on the strategies adopted by other actors in a competitive situation. In general, for evolutionary contexts such problems can be tackled by searching for what has been called an "evolutionarily stable strategy." Roughly, this is a behavioral strategy such that no alternative strategy will be able to invade a population in which the former is prevalent. Needless to say, the application of optimality analyses in general, and game theory in particular, to evolution raises numerous difficulties and has drawn many critics. It is, however, widely suggested that evolutionary game theory will avoid many of the difficulties inherent in the more straightforward optimality approach (see Philip Kitcher, this volume, and Eric Smith, this volume, for some of the salient points of contrast). The prospects, difficulties, and criticisms of both approaches, it is to be hoped, will emerge in the course of the various contributions to this volume.

The papers in this collection represent a number of very different disciplines, reflecting the extent to which evolutionary ideas have appeared relevant to a wide variety of inquiries. The book is divided into four parts. The first contains three papers that, while addressing very different issues, are all of a broadly methodological character. The second part contains a number of papers more exclusively concerned with the strictly biological issues surrounding evolution and optimality. (I should perhaps note, however, that the differentiation between these parts is not especially sharp. Both biological and methodological issues arise in both. I have divided them only in response to my own judgment of emphasis.) The two papers in the third part address the possibility of applying evolutionary ideas in two particularly crucial domains: evolutionary ecology and learning theory. The final part contains a number of papers with direct relevance to the heated current debate about the application of evolutionary theory to the human sciences.

Methodological Questions

As mentioned above, a fundamental problem underlying many of the methodological and philosophical disputes in biology is the sheer complexity of most biological, and particularly evolutionary, phenomena. Theoretical studies of evolutionary processes in such disciplines as population genetics and evolutionary game theory rely heavily on the construction of models that, while by no means necessarily simple, are acknowledged to be immensely simplified in comparison to the phenomena that they are intended to illuminate. Such an assessment could probably be made of every single model discussed in this book. It is thus appropriate to begin the book with the general defense of the use of simple models offered by Peter Richerson and Robert Boyd.

Their defense is presented in relation to their ground-breaking work on cultural evolution (Boyd and Richerson, 1985), which is briefly introduced and summarized at the beginning of their paper. While acknowledging the possibility of trading simplicity for increased realism (see Levins, 1966), they claim that for many scientific purposes simpler models are to be preferred. More complex models will tend to be less intelligible, obscuring the causal structure of the processes primarily under investigation, they will be more difficult to analyze, and they may result in little or no gain in empirical adequacy.

It should be noted here that it is possible to take the opposite position on the relation between mathematical tractability and causal structure. Elliott Sober, in particular, has been arguing for some time that mathematical tractability should not be used as an argument for employing models that sacrifice a realistic account of the causal structure of the processes in question (Sober, 1984). This issue is explicitly addressed in John Maynard Smith's contribution to this volume, and underlies an important part of the ensuing debate between Maynard Smith and Sober.

Boyd and Richerson, at any rate, suggest that the best way to approach a complex domain is to construct a diverse set of fairly simple and readily intelligible models that aim to illuminate the various processes that interact within that domain. In addition, they propose that generalized versions of such models, "generalized sample theories," which aim to capture the essential features of sets of models with more specific applications, may play a crucial role in organizing the scientist's cognitive grasp of the field in general.

It is relevant here to recall my remarks above about explanation and prediction. Complexity, especially with respect to the initial and background conditions affecting an evolutionary process, may reasonably be seen as an overwhelming obstacle to a predictive science of evolution. Insofar as one insists that science must aim at prediction, the only reaction to this problem must be to attempt to construct a sufficiently complex model to incorporate all these conditions. If one aims only at explanation, on the other hand, one may be satisfied merely with the assumption that these conditions were such as to permit the occurrence of the process the result of which is being explained. As part of their defense of simple models, Richerson and Boyd take the somewhat provocative position that explanation is, in general, a more fundamental goal of science than prediction.

Richerson and Boyd's basic idea is surely a very attractive one. Given that we are interested in phenomena the complexity of which make detailed realistic models unattainable, it seems sensible to attempt to isolate particular processes that we think may be important, and analyze them in abstraction from the morass of distinct processes that may also be taking place. It does seem, however, that this depends on an empirical belief that the causal factors involved interact in a relatively straightforward way. If two causal factors interact to produce a result that is qualitatively different from either acting alone, then the attempt to abstract either from the actual causal nexus may be seriously misleading. In this context it is worth considering how far Sober's discussion in "What Is Adaptationism?," which specifically addresses the problems with modeling the interactions of different evolutionary processes, presents obstacles of this kind to the methodology suggested by Richerson and Boyd.

Richerson and Boyd conclude with some illuminating remarks on the way that the "plausibility arguments," which provide epistemological support for classes of models, should be evaluated. They also discuss what they consider to be common but illegitimate lines of attack on such arguments, and thus on the types of models that the plausibility arguments are intended to legitimate. Rejection of these premature attacks on what they take to be worthwhile scientific exercises leads them, finally, to a plea for scientific pluralism. In the context of their discussion, what this means is the development of various sets of models underpinned by competing plausibility arguments.

The second paper in this part, by John Beatty, raises issues in evolutionary biology, in methodology, and, finally, about the overall rationality of science. One of the central issues in recent evolutionary theory, and the issue that provides the focus for Beatty's paper, is the relative importance of selection and drift in the course of evolution. Beatty does not attempt to offer a judgment on the concrete issue. Rather, he is interested in how we should understand the relation between evolutionary explanations of these two kinds, and how scientific resources should be allocated between the pursuit of hypotheses of these kinds. As Beatty points out, in science as elsewhere, we often find what we are looking for. Thus our view of the relative importance of two possible evolutionary forces will depend heavily on the amount of effort we expend on looking for explanations of the relevant kinds.

Beatty's ultimate conclusion is that if we are genuinely interested in deciding on the relative importance of drift and selection, we must try to ensure that comparable amounts of energy are expended on looking for instances of each kind of process. The heart of the paper is devoted to exposing a misconception about the relation between these investigations that may appear to subvert this conclusion.

A prominent notion in recent discussions of scientific methodology is that of the null hypothesis. Very simply, when we are investigating a causal hypothesis, what we frequently try to do is compare the probabilities that a certain kind of result (paradigmatically that of a controlled experiment) is the result of chance or the result of a causal influence that we are investigating. The former hypothesis is what is generally called the null hypothesis. For reasons that Beatty clearly delineates, it is tempting to think that a drift hypothesis is implicitly the null hypothesis in the investigation of a claim about a process of selection. Thus the advocates of selectionism, or adaptationism, can claim that the pursuit of their favored research program is implicitly also an investigation of the importance of evolutionary drift. Beatty convincingly exposes the flaws in this position. The logic of hypothesis testing, he argues, tells us nothing about the relative importance of investigating these different evolutionary processes. If Beatty is correct, his conclusions have profound significance for the socially rational conduct of investigations in evolutionary biology.

Philip Kitcher's contribution to the collection brings us closer to the specific focus of the volume. His paper is an exemplary case study in the application of ideas from the philosophy of science to a concrete theoretical problem in science. As briefly mentioned above, when we come to deal with behavior rather than morphology in either animal or human studies, the problem is often not so much one of explanation, but of interpretation. We cannot even begin to *explain* behavior, until we are confident that we have adequately *described* it; and an adequate description requires the interpretation of the purely physical action in some kind of teleological terms. An obvious possibility for exploiting ideas of optimality is then precisely as a guide to the interpretation of behavior. The question Kitcher poses is the following. Suppose we have various interpretations of an aspect of the behavior of an animal. Suppose also that one such interpretation accords with an analysis of what, from an evolutionary perspective, would be the optimal pattern of behavior for that animal. Then to what extent does this justify us in accepting that interpretation?

Kitcher approaches the problem from the perspective of Bayesian decision theory. The question is, How does the existence of an optimality analysis backing a functional description of behavior affect the prior probability that that description is correct? Kitcher answers this question in terms of a function of the following probabilities: that one of the descriptions we are considering is correct; that one of these descriptions identifies the best available ancestral type; and that evolution has produced the best available type. Clearly if all these probabilities are certainties, a correct optimality analysis will generate certainty as to the correct description. The question then concerns how doubts about each of these propositions affects the optimality analyst's strategy. This provides a framework in which the practical significance of the various and numerous objections that have been raised to optimality assumptions can be pragmatically evaluated in a highly original and illuminating way. For those not familiar with the recent history of this debate, this discussion incidentally provides a very useful survey of the major difficulties that *have* been proposed with the uncritical use of adaptationist assumptions. While making very clear the potential hazards involved in the use of optimality assumptions, Kitcher ends on a note of cautious optimism. His analysis certainly does provide a description of circumstances under which an optimality analysis *would* lend additional credence to a behavioral hypothesis. A skeptic might nevertheless wonder whether, if Kitcher's analysis is accepted, there are really likely to be many optimality analyses that would be acceptable. Eric Smith, in his contribution, reacts just this way, but argues that Kitcher's conditions are unreasonably stringent.

Evolution and Optimality

This part begins with a paper by Elliott Sober that directly addresses the question what adaptationism, as a thesis about evolution, means. Sober suggests, to begin with, that adaptationism is the thesis that selection has been the most powerful cause of evolution. He then considers how this thesis could be interpreted in relation to various other forces that are often taken to compete with selection.

Sober begins with the simplest case, that in which selection is opposed by directional mutation. Selection operates to increase the frequency of a certain gene, but the tendency of that gene to mutate operates to decrease it. In this case it is straightforward to compare the strengths of the two forces involved. In the two other cases he considers, drift and pleiotropy, however, the situation is much less simple. Since evolutionary drift is a stochastic process, we cannot evaluate its force as compared with selection simply by looking at what happens in a single population. To do this, or the nearest equivalent thing to this, we need to consider a large ensemble of populations undergoing identical selection, and subject to the same probabilities of drift. We can then roughly equate the claim that adaptation is the most powerful force at work, at least in this population type, with the claim that the dispersal of the results in this ensemble is relatively small. It should be clear that Sober's analysis reinforces Beatty's thesis that investigating drift hypotheses cannot simply be an inevitable corollary of investigating the efficacy of selection.

Pleiotropy is the phenomenon of two or more different characters being controlled by the same gene. Since there could be two pleiotropic characters of which one was advantageous and the other deleterious, and the deleterious character might be selected by "hitchhiking" on the advantageous one, pleiotropy has often been proposed as a serious obstacle to adaptationism. Sober again shows that this cannot be seen as a case of two opposing forces, selection favoring, and pleiotropy opposing, adaptation— or at any rate not in the simple way described for directional mutation. In this case, the relevant question is the overall extent to which pleiotropy prevents optimal adaptation. To assess its "force" we need to look at a variety of different traits within a single population, and investigate the extent to which pleiotropy prevents their optimization.

Sober concludes by revising the original proposal for defining adaptationism. To achieve a general picture of how the various phenomena discussed relate, it is more useful to consider adaptationism as a thesis about the general accuracy of a class of models of evolutionary processes. Adaptationism certainly should not deny that forces other than selection occur in evolutionism; it may claim, and such a claim is surely empirical, that simple models of selection will give reasonably accurate predictions despite ignoring these other factors.

The next contribution, by John Maynard Smith, addresses two main issues. First, in natural sequence to Sober's question as to what adaptationism is, Maynard Smith considers the problem, What is liable to exhibit it? A great deal of recent debate has concerned what has come to be known as the "units of selection problem," very roughly, Among what entities—genes, gene complexes, genomes, organisms, groups of organisms, populations, species—does natural selection select?[3] Much of the interest in this debate derives from the question whether entities at these levels will evolve adaptations, and it is natural to suppose that this question will turn on whether there is selection among entities of the kinds in question. Maynard Smith argues that this connection between the units of selection problem and adaptation is mistaken. He draws a distinction between units of selection and units of evolution, and argues that the latter are the only kinds of entities that can evolve adaptations. Units of evolution are entities that, in addition to being subject to selection, also possess heredity. A type of entity may be a unit of selection, in the obvious sense that there is differential survival and fecundity between entities of that type that reflects differences in fitness, but, Maynard Smith argues, unless offspring resemble their parents there will be no evolution of adaptations. One controversial issue to which this has major relevance is the question of group selection, specifically, whether the fact that there may be selection between groups of organisms licenses the expectation that groups will evolve adaptations. Maynard Smith's proposal provides a condition that must be satisfied for this to occur. His distinction is also relevant to another controversial issue, that of genic selectionism. Since organisms clearly do evolve numerous adaptations, they must be units of evolution; and moreover, a condition of their being units of evolution is also that genes are not, typically, units of evolution.

The second issue that Maynard Smith raises again concerns the use of different models. But whereas Sober's concern is with models representing processes of different kinds, Maynard Smith is interested here in the possibility of providing different models of the same process. His reaction is to advocate pluralism of approaches. Different models may offer different insights into the same process; they may also vary in significant pragmatic respects, such as computational manageability. There is no need, he urges, to choose between them, although, like Richerson and Boyd, he does maintain that such pragmatic advantages are significant. Despite major differences, Maynard Smith, Sober, and Richerson and Boyd all agree, at least, that it is important to illuminate evolutionary phenomena from different perspectives, employing different kinds of models.

In a response to Maynard Smith's paper, Sober offers a critique of Maynard Smith's views on the first set of issues. Sober argues that to be a unit of evolution is neither a necessary nor a sufficient condition for an entity to evolve adaptations. As both Maynard Smith and Sober agree, this disagreement reflects a fundamental difference about the nature of the debate about group selection that has taken place over the last twenty years. Sober uses a hypothetical example to assert one major disagreement with Maynard Smith, his denial that group heredity is necessary for group adaptation. In this example, altruism, conceived as a group adaptation, evolves although there are no hereditary relations between groups. In barest outline, what makes this possible is that groups in each generation are formed by like associating with like; altruistic individuals form groups together, as do selfish individuals. Since the altruistic groups do better than the selfish groups, there are more altruistic individuals when the time comes for the next generation to form into new groups. Here there is selection between groups but, as the example is constructed, no group heredity.

Sober also finds certain aspects of Maynard Smith's pluralism objectionable. Although he agrees that different models should be explored, he wants to make a fundamental distinction within possible models. Some of them do, and some of them do not, correctly represent the causal structure of the processes that are taking place. In particular, genic selectionism, an approach to model building, at least, with which Maynard Smith is highly sympathetic, according to Sober is generally misleading about the causal facts. That causal structure is what we must try and elucidate in getting an adequate picture of the evolutionary process is a thesis that Sober has argued at length in his book *The Nature of Selection*.

Maynard Smith, in a brief rejoinder to Sober, shows himself unconvinced on both issues. Maynard Smith insists that Sober's example (and a somewhat more complicated case concerning sex ratios, discussed in both their previous contributions to the debate) can, and should, be interpreted in terms of individual adaptation. For Maynard Smith, the propensity of like to consort with like is simply part of the environment that determines the optimal strategy for individuals; the environment is one constructed to favor altruistic individuals.

Maynard Smith is also unpersuaded by the conclusions that Sober wants to derive from his conception of causation. Exploration of the philosophical issues involved here would be beyond the scope of this introduction. Very briefly, Sober relies on the development of a view of causality that has emerged in a recent philosophical debate on probabilistic causality. Here I must leave the interested reader to examine the exchange between Sober and Maynard Smith, and the very interested reader to follow up further references on the subject.[4]

This part concludes with a paper by Richard Lewontin, who has been one of the most prominent critics of adaptationism in evolutionary theory (see Gould and Lewontin, 1979; Lewontin, 1978). The present paper extends the critique in important new directions. Lewontin begins with a crucial point about the structure of optimization arguments. This is that use of an optimality model always requires a mapping from a state space of alternatives to a metric scale; the optimum must be translated into a maximum or minimum. This simple point leads to a number of much less simple questions that are not generally addressed in discussions of optimization.

The obvious response to this point is merely that the range of alternatives in question should be mapped onto Darwinian fitnesses. But for reasons that Lewontin states very clearly, this will not do. One fundamental problem, which has been much discussed in the relevant literature, is that fitness is always in danger of being defined tautologically; we must avoid saying that organisms survive and reproduce because they are fitter, and that fitness is the property of surviving and reproducing. To avoid this, it seems that we must identify characters of organisms that *cause* fitness. Thus, as Lewontin concludes, if we want to analyze the optimization of a particular character, we need a criterion that is to be maximized, which, in turn, must be both a *consequence* of the character in question and a *cause* of fitness.

This way of stating the problem shows very graphically how severe will be the problems raised by the complexity of causal relations in biology. A typical criterion used in an optimality argument is rate of energy acquisition. But this rate is unlikely to be solely a function of the character we are investigating, and it is unlikely to be the only consequence of the character relevant to fitness. Moreover, analogous complexities are likely to bedevil the causal relation between this criterion and fitness. Lewontin graphically illustrates these difficulties with a simple example. In a sense this can be seen as a very lucid presentation of a fundamental difficulty that emerged from Lewontin's earlier critiques of optimality: It is very doubtful how much sense can be made of an optimality analysis that abstracts one particular character from the vast set of characters that are functionally integrated in the organization of an organism. The abstraction of a particular causal path from one character to consequences on fitness provides a particularly striking perspective on the nature of this difficulty.

Assuming, for the sake of argument, that these problems can be solved, Lewontin then discusses another major problem. There is, of course, no such thing as the Perfect Animal. Optimality arguments require some set of constraints that define a particular problem. These constraints will include some facts about the organism and about the environment in which it finds itself. Two serious problems then arise. First, supposing that we can select the appropriate constraints and fully describe the consequent adaptive topography, this topography may well include a large number of distinct maxima. An organism that evolves to one such maximum may well be unable to evolve from there to an alternative higher maximum, since the only evolutionary paths will be through points of lower fitness.

The second problem concerns how we decide on the appropriate constraints, specifically those that have to do with what is given about the organism. When, to take Lewontin's example, we analyze the most efficient way for *Drosophila* to discover and consume yeast colonies, why do we assume that *Drosophila* are condemned to eat yeast rather then, say, carrion or blood? How, in general, do we determine the range of possibilities accessible to a particular organism?

What unites these two difficulties is their emphasis on the role of historical contingency in evolution. Historical accident may very well determine which of alternative optima an organism happens to reach; and historical accident may determine which morphological or behavioral possibilities become available to an organism in its evolutionary history. This leads to a problem that is also discussed in Kitcher's paper. Is there any way of including a possibly indefinitely large set of historical contingencies as constraints on the optimizing scenarios that we construct without reducing the project to vacuity? Lewontin concludes with a challenge. If we incorporate every accident of history as a constraint on our maximization problem, so that every deviation from the optimum we expect is describable as historical accident, optimality theory is vacuous. If we deny the importance of historical contingencies, it is patently false. Can a satisfactory middle way be found?

Applications

The papers in the preceding two parts, while not constituting a systematic treatment of all the issues that could be raised about the theoretical grounding of evolutionary optimality theory, should give a very good sense of the problems and prospects involved, and of the relation between this issue and other relevant areas of evolutionary biology and the philosophy of science. These papers have, on the whole, stayed at a fairly abstract level.

The papers in the remaining parts will be more concrete, focusing on the possible fruits to be harvested from the use of optimality analysis in various areas of scientific enquiry.

It would be far beyond the scope of such a volume to attempt to survey the kinds of uses to which optimality arguments have been put within biology. The most that can be hoped is that the preceding papers (and the one following) should put the reader in a good position to make a sophisticated assessment of the virtues and vices of particular applications. The aim of the remaining papers is rather to review the prospects for applying evolutionarily grounded optimality theory in areas beyond biology. In part because of the high degree of controversy surrounding this issue, not to mention the potential importance of its correct resolution, the remaining papers are mainly concerned with possible applications to the study of humans. However, before turning to that question, the third part will present the perspectives of two scientists working in fields not directly concerned with human problems, but fields for which optimality theory has great prima facie relevance.

The first of these papers, by John Emlen, remains within biology proper. Evolutionary ecology, the field that Emlen considers, would appear to be a particularly crucial area of biology in this context. One way of seeing ecology is as evolution writ small, or anyway small enough to allow genuine empirical investigation of the processes that we postulate as producing, in the long term, evolutionary change. It is not surprising, therefore, that the use of optimality analyses has figured largely in recent ecological work.

Emlen begins by discussing some problems involved in presenting a practically applicable definition of adaptedness. He emphasizes the additional complications to such a definition posed by environmental fluctuations and by density dependence of fitness. He then makes the point that, whereas optimality analyses function by identifying a putative end point of the evolutionary process, evolutionary ecologists treat these analyses as describing a process rather than a state; we do not expect organisms to exhibit optimal states, but these states do define the direction in which we expect the population to be moving. This point should certainly be important in deterring naive empirical dismissals of optimality.

The bulk of Emlen's paper is then concerned with describing some fundamental objections to seeing optimality as strictly true of organisms in real environments. These divide into two kinds. The first type of problem is genetic. As also discussed in Kitcher's paper, phenomena such as pleiotropy and epistasis may make optimal adaptations inaccessible. But second, even if we had complete genetic knowledge, it is questionable whether adaptive maxima could be defined ecologically. The discussion here reinforces Lewontin's critique: first, there is no a priori way of deciding what is an appropriate range of behavioral possibilities for an organism; and second, there is no way of identifying *the* function of a type of behavior, since behavior will generally have many consequences relevant to the fitness of an organism. These two difficulties are discussed in some detail.

While the above leads Emlen to a very skeptical position on the possible truth of an adaptationist position, his paper is framed in a philosophical context that leads him to greater optimism. He suggests that although from a perspective of scientific realism optimality analysis is quite untenable, from a more pragmatic point of view it may nevertheless be defensible. Optimality analysis, he suggests, can provide understanding and explanation, and should be evaluated on the basis of its coherence and usefulness. From this perspective, optimality begins to look much more promising.

While Emlen does cite influential advocates of the kind of antirealism he proposes (see especially van Fraassen, 1980), it should be noted that the position he espouses is a highly controversial one. Moreover, it is not clear that, even from this philosophical perspective, the problems he describes are wholly defused. His description of the genetic limitations on optimal adaptation suggest that the assumption of optimality may *not* be coherent with our best view of genetics; and his remarks on the ecological problems raise the question whether adaptationism is even a coherent, let alone a true, view of ecology. On the other hand, Emlen's reflections do certainly raise one issue fundamental to a debate of this kind: What relative importance should one attach to the claims of practitioners in a field that a particular approach is useful and fruitful, and to the claims of theoreticians that the approach is philosophically untenable? This is a question that should confront the reader of this collection at several points.

John Staddon's contribution evaluates the usefulness of optimality to behavioral psychology. Staddon, with a qualification that will be mentioned shortly, is generally optimistic about this project. The position he defends is that behavior, specifically learned behavior of various kinds, will, under specified conditions, maximize some proxy for fitness such as energy intake. His essay is structured round three possible objections to this position: that optimality analyses are not causal, and hence unscientific; that they are teleological rather than teleonomic (which means adequately buttressed by an evolutionary explanation of the apparent teleology); and that they do not work.

Staddon has a number of replies to the first objection. Optimality analysis explains and unifies a wide range of phenomena; it does so more successfully than any competing approach; it generates predictions that can be tested empirically; and even the failures of some such predictions have led to further insights into the processes involved. Certainly these are good grounds for the claim that the approach is scientifically respectable. In response to the second objection Staddon gives a summary of the sorts of things that we do now know about the mechanisms of conditioned learning and the kinds of factors that determine its effects. Despite major gaps in our understanding of the relation between behavior and the underlying physical mechanisms, Staddon argues convincingly that we know quite enough to see, first, that there is nothing inherently mysterious about the sort of mechanisms that produce adaptive learning, and second, that the types of biases that favor particular kinds of behavior are plausibly related to likely selective forces.

Staddon responds to the question of whether optimality analyses work in the obvious way by describing some of its successes. He describes in some detail a range of results from foraging experiments, which appear to confirm quite impressively optimality models of this class of behavior. He also describes one rather more complex experimental setup in which the optimal behavior is not produced. This anomalous case leads him to an intriguing concluding suggestion. Whether an animal produces an optimal response to a particular kind of problem may be used as a way of determining whether this kind of problem is a "natural" one for the animal. That is, from an evolutionary perspective we should expect optimal behavior if, and only if, the kind of situation we contrive is sufficiently analogous to situations to which the organism was exposed in its evolutionary history. Staddon even suggests that the greatest use of optimality analysis may be as a source of insight into features of the niche in which an animal evolved. One might worry whether this suggestion involves a vicious circularity—the niche gives rise to particular forms of optimal behavior, and the behavior tells us what were the salient features of the niche. At the very least, the cogency of this kind of reasoning must depend heavily on an independent grounding for the assumption of optimality.

It will be clear from this brief summary that Staddon is a good deal more optimistic than Emlen about the justification of applying optimality analysis to his field. It is worth a moment's thought whether there are any obvious differences of subject matter that might account for this. One suggestion is the following. The phenomena that Staddon describes, learning in relatively simple experimental situations, are fairly simple in their consequences, but their peculiarities are often functionally obscure. The ecological phenomena considered by Emlen may or may not be functionally straightforward—presumably they often are—but their consequences are typically enormously complex. Optimality analysis will always be an attractive approach for investigating function. But as the consequences of a behavioral feature become more complex, the force of hypothesizing its selective significance becomes more debatable. At least one-half of the complexities that Emlen describes do not arise in the cases Staddon discusses. The genetic difficulties are of course equally pressing; but it is at least an empirical possibility that such constraints have somehow not proved too serious an obstacle to optimal results. With this cautious optimism about the prospects for optimality in these relatively simple psychological domains, the final section will provide some assessment of the possibility of illuminating the human domain from this direction.

Applications to Human Behavior

The final part of the book begins with a perspective from an ecological anthropologist, Eric Smith. Smith provides a very lucid summary of some of the major attempts at anthropological applications of optimality analysis, and some thoughtful reflections on the underlying theoretical issues.

Smith begins his paper with a brief discussion of models in general that suggests an approach very similar to that described by Richerson and Boyd, and then briefly describes the main features of optimality models in particular. He next considers and contrasts the sources of optimality models in neoclassical economics and evolutionary theory, and gives a short account of their recent introduction into anthropology. He suggests several reasons for the appeal of the optimality approach to ecological anthropologists: theoretical unification both within anthropology and externally with evolutionary biology and economics; the provision of a general theory from which hypotheses can be generated; and the possibility of empirical, quantitative predictions. He illustrates the potential value of the approach with four detailed case studies from hunter-gatherer socioecology: systems of land tenure, foraging-group size, reciprocal food sharing, and birth-spacing intervals.

I shall not attempt to summarize any of the details of the theoretical and empirical results Smith describes. I think it would be hard to dispute that in certain clear respects the approach is shown to be remarkably fruitful. The theoretical predictions are, in many cases, well supported by the data, and the ability of the optimality approach to generate plausible and testable predictions from a theoretically unified vantage point is clearly illustrated. It is perhaps worth noting, however, that, as Smith remarks, the causal interpretation of this success remains debatable. The first three cases, at least, could be viewed as standard economic logic as readily as evolutionary adaptation.

Smith then discusses in some detail the major critiques that have been directed against the optimality approach he has been describing. In this second part of his paper he provides the most detailed general defense of the optimality approach that appears in this collection. First, he addresses objections to the thesis that evolution produces optimal phenotypes. While treating these objections sympathetically, Smith maintains that, provided we recognize the relativity of optimization to an appropriate fitness currency, design problem, and set of constraints, the objections can be met. He does, however, emphasize that the development of game theory, by implying optimal strategies that do not lead to optimal individual behavior, does lead to a radically revised conception of optimality. (This is nicely illustrated by part of his earlier discussion of foraging-group size.)

Smith next considers the difficulty, mentioned briefly above, that optimal adaptation does not entail an evolutionary origin of the optimal feature. While he is sympathetic to this claim, he contends that it is not a methodologically damning point. Identification of an optimal phenotype does not settle the question of its origin, but rather invites further research on that question. Recognition of this limitation, he contends, in no way contradicts the claim that optimization theory has greatly improved our understanding of important aspects of human behavior. He is also sympathetic to a more specific version of this critique, that evolution can only optimize the mechanisms that are proximate causes of behavior, not the behavior itself. Again, Smith maintains that our ignorance of the entire causal chain by which adaptation is achieved is no reason to abandon the use of optimality analysis, but only reason to abandon naive assumptions about its etiology. (The relation between behavior and proximate mechanisms is discussed in more detail in Cosmides and Tooby's contribution below.)

Third, Smith takes up the issue of the lack of realism in optimality models. Once again, he concedes the point, but suggests that its importance tends to be overstated. In outline, he takes a similar position to that defended at length by Richerson and Boyd: Simple models are *not* realistic, but they can be highly valuable scientific tools nonetheless.

Finally, he discusses what is probably the most widely voiced objection within anthropology, that optimality analysis fails to take account of the central role of culture in determining human behavior. To begin with, Smith is willing to concede at least that genetic programs do not specifically encode behavior. There are, nevertheless, a number of extant hypotheses about how they might direct behavior toward fitness-maximizing forms, the specific content of which could be culturally variable. Against more ambitious cultural determinists, however, he expresses skepticism about where cultural forces are supposed, ultimately, to originate. It does seem a reasonable complaint that to treat culture purely as an unexplained explainer is somewhat unproductive from a scientific point of view. In conclusion, he suggests that there may be a way beyond this impasse provided by recent work on cultural evolution. I consider one way of pursuing this suggestion in my own contribution to this collection.

With the next two papers we move from evolutionary anthropology to evolutionary psychology. A number of the papers in the second half of this volume emphasize the importance of the possibilities for theoretical unification of a scientific field by evolutionary optimality theory (especially those by Smith, Emlen, and Staddon). Perhaps the most ambitious such proposal is outlined in the contribution by Roger Shepard. As his title suggests, Shepard is concerned to propose a general evolutionary tendency toward convergence between the way organisms represent the world and crucial and pervasive features of the way the world is. He suggests not only that such convergence may constitute a general trend in animal evolution, but even that the existence of such a trend might give rise to laws of a completely general applicability governing psychological processes.

The thesis is illustrated with reference to four features of the world that can reasonably be taken to be both spatially and temporally uniform: the constant period of circadian revolution; the degrees of freedom in the variation of natural illumination; the three-dimensional Euclidean structure of terrestrial space; and what he calls the "metric of functional equivalence." This last means, roughly, the natural tendencies of organisms to make judgments of similarity in extrapolating from past experience to more or less different current stimuli. The last two cases are discussed in more detail with reference to recent psychological explorations of these issues, many of them by Shepard himself.

The last case is, perhaps, the most controversial. The appropriateness of judgments of similarity, and hence the tendency of principles determining them to evolve, is surely to some extent a function of the specific needs of the organism in question. Nevertheless, Shepard presents an intriguing theory of this phenomenon, at a very high level of generality, with impressive empirical support. One thing that is clear, and which is also brought out in Staddon's paper, is that the existence of an appropriate similarity metric is an essential ingredient in any adequate theory of animal learning, and is certainly a plausible candidate for illumination from an evolutionary perspective.

Whereas Shepard's concern is with very general aspects of the ways in which information about the world is acquired and processed, Cosmides and Tooby directly address the question of an evolutionary approach to human behavior. Their starting point is one also discussed in Smith's paper: Evolution can only produce behavior indirectly by producing cognitive mechanisms that are the direct causes of behavior. To emphasize this point they remark that, contrary to one naive criticism of the evolutionary approach to behavior, it is a prediction of, rather than a problem for, evolutionary psychology that human behavior is variable. A cognitive mechanism produces behavior in response to contingencies of the environment; given the variability of the environment, we would expect behavior to vary even if the underlying cognitive mechanisms are (approximately) constant throughout the species.

After this preliminary, Cosmides and Tooby present a forceful argument that evolutionary considerations can in fact give us a great deal of insight into the nature of these cognitive mechanisms, and can even do so in a way that will tell us a good deal about the behavior that they will tend to generate. Their starting point for this project is the observation that one is unlikely to get very far in understanding a cognitive mechanism, or information-processing system, if one does not know what its function is. This observation is not by itself sufficient to show that evolutionary analysis will give any very useful information about this function. On the one hand, the extreme skeptic about the relevance of evolutionary analysis may claim that the mind is simply a general-purpose calculating device. Its possible functions will then be essentially infinite, and everything will depend on the present exigencies of the environment. Alternatively, a naive sociobiologist might suppose that the mind was a general-purpose fitness-maximizing calculator. Then behavior could be calculated solely by analysis of fitness, and the structure of the mind would be immaterial.

The central thesis of Cosmides and Tooby's paper, contrary to both these positions, is that the mind is composed of a number of domain-specific Darwinian algorithms. What this means is, first, that the correct functional analysis of the mind shows it to comprise a number of content-specific information-processing devices, and second, that the way to identify these "mental modules" is by analysis of the crucial selective factors that existed during the Pleistocene, when most relevant human evolution occurred.

They offer two distinct lines of argument that converge on this position. First, against the position I ascribed to the "naive sociobiologist" they argue that direct calculations of inclusive fitness are seldom possible; and even if they were, specific mechanisms for dealing with crucial problems would be vastly more efficient, and therefore favored by selection. Such specific mechanisms are the Darwinian algorithms. (The reader will evidently want to consider, in the light of the general discussions, especially of Kitcher and Lewontin, whether this adaptive argument is legitimate.)

Against the believer in the mind as a quite general-purpose information processor, they appeal to some general results from psychology and artificial intelligence. As illustrated by Chomsky's early arguments about language learning, without a good deal of cognitive architecture, it is very difficult to describe an information processor that can do, or learn to do, anything. In general it seems necessary to start out with some cognitive structure that provides the general framework that will organize the treatment of problems of particular kinds. This is what computer scientists sometimes refer to as the "frame" problem. Combining these critical lines of thought suggests an obvious positive synthesis. Domain-specific Darwinian algorithms, they suggest, provide just the cognitive structure required as a solution to the frame problem. This hypothesis can in principle provide a powerful tool for functional analysis of the mind.

Jack Hirshleifer's paper provides an extremely elegant example of theoretical optimality analysis at work. It has very widely been assumed that, from the point of view of individual self-interest that provides the starting point for both economic and evolutionary optimality analysis, the existence of emotions is something of an anomaly. An emotional response is often contrasted with a rational one. However, the recognition of situations such as the widely discussed Prisoner's Dilemma, in which the self-interestedly rational solution to a problem is less than optimal for two parties in a situation of conflict, raises a possible alternative to this traditional view.

Hirshleifer explores the possibility that emotional, prima facie irrational, responses may actually turn out to further an agent's self-interest by helping to reach mutually advantageous, cooperative solutions to problems of this kind. It has been recognized that the ability to make credible threats or promises is one way in which the negative consequences of games such as Prisoner's Dilemma may be evaded. Hirshleifer's idea is that certain kinds of emotional response may serve to render such threats and promises effective.

Hirshleifer considers two dimensions of emotional response. The first, which consists of malevolence and benevolence, he describes as action-independent. The basic idea is that these consist simply of the attachment of negative or positive utility, respectively, to the well-being of the other party. The second kind are action-dependent, and are exemplified by anger and gratitude. In these cases the wish to inflict harm or bestow good is a function of the action performed by the other party. (For purposes of analysis, the emotional response is considered as being restricted to the second mover in the game. The first mover behaves according to the classical conception of economic rationality.)

The analysis produces some surprising results. Under certain assumptions, Hirshleifer shows that benevolence can actually prove advantageous to the agent who exhibits it. Essentially, this comes about because benevolence may, when recognized, serve to guarantee a promise. The reader will be relieved to discover that malevolence, on the other hand, is seldom advantageous; it is unlikely to encourage cooperation, since resources secured by the first mover for the second may be expended by the latter in an attempt to impoverish the former. Anger and gratitude, on the other hand, may both be effective, the one backing threats, the other promises. As Hirshleifer remarks, these emotions, in representing a kind of loss of control, represent a particularly radical departure from the traditional conception of the rational agent.

The possible implications of this kind of analysis for evolutionary theory are of course open to debate. However, it is quite clear that these results open up some fascinating possibilities. Most strikingly, the possible consequences of benevolence suggest a novel contribution to the voluminous debate about the evolution of altruism. And while it would take a much more detailed analysis of actual evolutionary scenarios and their relation to the parameters of Hirshleifer's models to present a convincing account of the evolutionary origin of real human anger or gratitude, a highly promising line of further inquiry is presented for phenomenona that are, from an evolutionary perspective, distinctly problematic.

In my own paper, finally, I take up the issue raised at the end of Smith's paper, the role of culture in human behavior, and the limitations that this might pose to evolutionary analysis of human behavior. The most virulent opposition to an evolutionary explanation of human behavior has generally come from people who want to assert the importance of cultural forces. However, their objections have frequently been put in ways that have failed to impress the evolutionists (see the remarks by Smith on this topic, and more uncompromisingly, by Cosmides and Tooby).

There are some clear reasons for the failure of communication on this topic. As mentioned in my discussion of Smith's paper, defenders of culture have not always had much of an answer to the question whence cultural forces are supposed to come. And there are many plausible routes by which cultures may be supposed to be directed by genetically evolved dispositions of the individuals who comprise them. My aim in this paper is to find a statement of the intuition behind the cultural objection to evolutionary explanations of behavior that escapes these difficulties.

As suggested in the conclusion of Smith's paper, a starting point may be provided by recent work on cultural evolution, particularly that of Boyd and Richerson. Boyd and Richerson generally present their ideas in a rather atomistic way. However, if the processes they describe are important, it seems plausible that this atomism may ultimately provide a serious limitation. The theory of genetic evolution, after all, developed from an answer to the problem of how species came to exist; pursuing the analogy between cultural and genetic evolution raises the possibility that there could be a process of cultural speciation. If this is the case, then the atomistic approach may well generate a spurious expectation of optimization, for reasons analogous to those discussed in the classic Gould and Lewontin (1979) critique for the case of genetic evolution. Culture, that is to say, may evolve into highly integrated forms that preclude any simple assumption of trait-by-trait optimization.

Clearly there will be some problems with the concept of cultural species. It would be foolish to assume that cultural diversity would exactly mimic biological diversity. Obstacles to cultural introgression will be of a quite different kind from those to genetic introgression, and may well be less effective. However, I do think the concept is useful in sharpening the intuition that there are fundamental problems in extrapolating from ways of understanding animal behavior to those appropriate for human behavior.

Much of the failure of communication between human sociobiologists, on the one hand, and cultural anthropologists and others who insist on human diversity, on the other, can be traced to the fact that for the former the (biological) homogeneity of the human species is obvious, while for the latter its (cultural) diversity is equally obvious. The idea of cultural evolution giving rise to cultural speciation may perhaps be susceptible of development in ways that make the anthropological perspective intelligible within the framework assumed by evolutionists and biologists. At any rate, I have attempted to lay the groundwork for such a development.

I shall conclude this introduction with one general comment about the overall picture that emerges from the papers here collected. A number of contributors to the earlier parts of the anthology (especially Kitcher, Lewontin, and Emlen) argue forcefully for the difficulties with any general assumption that evolution generates optimal adaptation. On the other hand, a number of the contributors involved in applications of optimality analysis are extremely enthusiastic about the potential benefits of the approach. Even within biology proper, it is much easier to find enthusiastic applications of optimality analysis than forthright defenses of the position that evolution produces, in any simple sense, an optimal result. Richerson and Boyd, for example, are clearly sympathetic to the use of optimality models, but are very far from asserting that such models straightforwardly represent reality. The second part of Smith's paper is the most thorough specific defense of the methodology; but the defense is a cautious one, and he is very careful to avoid commitments to a reliable etiology for optimal adaptation.

A number of interpretations suggest themselves for this situation. The simplest would be that it merely reflects the selection of contributors. There is no doubt some truth in this, and particularly since, as mentioned earlier, I have deliberately not tried to cover the wide range of work in biology that involves actual use of optimality arguments. A somewhat more interesting explanation would be that this disparity is exactly what one would expect for any comparable issue. When considering foundational and conceptual issues one will generally be able to find theoretical difficulties; when doing real scientific work one will generally not worry too much about foundational issues if a certain approach seems to work. This contrast may even have some validity when, as is the case with most of the contributors to this volume, the same people do both theoretical and practical research. Indeed, this is a possible basis for a general skepticism, occasionally voiced, about the value of philosophy of science. No doubt there is some truth in this explanation as well.

The most pessimistic conclusion to draw would be that there is a genuine failure of communication involved. If optimality analysis is as valuable a tool as contributors such as Smith, Staddon, Shepard, or Cosmides and

Tooby suggest, and even Emlen wants to find philosophical space to defend, the difficulties raised by Kitcher, Lewontin, and again Emlen raise a very pressing problem: Why does it work so well? This question, and the scientific activities that give rise to it, even ignoring the ethical and political disputes that have so frequently become enmeshed with it, do at least make clear why the whole issue remains such a major focus of controversy.

But perhaps a more optimistic assessment can be derived from a consideration of Kitcher's analysis. It is certainly worth considering that what this divergence reflects is a genuinely empirical difference of opinion. In terms of Kitcher's analysis, it might just be the case that optimists (or optimalists) assign much higher values to the probabilities he distinguishes than do pessimists such as Lewontin or Emlen. To analyze this dispute in this way certainly does not make its resolution trivial. It is far from obvious how we would set about evaluating the probabilities he discusses. However, it is surely a promising starting point for further research, both empirical and theoretical.

It should be evident that this book makes no pretense of providing a systematic treatment of the various issues that surround this dispute. However, I do think that the major issues involved can be seen running through the various papers here collected. The reader should, I think, be able to glean a good sense of the grounds both for enthusiasm and for skepticism about the use of evolutionary optimality models, and gain a fair picture of the issues that continue so sharply to divide those who have considered the problems that surround their use.

Notes

1. For a good description of some of types of case in which significant predictions are possible, however, see Kitcher, 1973, chapter 3, esp. pp. 78–81.
2. Game theory as a recognized field of study dates from the work of von Neumann and Morgenstern (1953). For subsequent applications to evolutionary theory, see Maynard Smith (1982).
3. For good discussions of this issue see, e.g., Wimsatt (1980), Sober and Lewontin (1982), and Sober (1984).
4. See Cartwright (1979) and Eells and Sober (1983) for discussion, and Sober (1984) for the development of this view in the present context. The theory of causality developed in these papers has been criticized by Dupré (1984) and Dupré and Cartwright (1987).

Bibliography

Boyd, R., and P. J. Richerson (1985). *Culture and the Evolutionary Process.* Chicago and London: University of Chicago Press.

Cartwright, N. (1979). Causal Laws and Effective Strategies. *Nous* 13 : 419–437.

Cartwright, N. (1983). *How the Laws of Physics Lie.* Oxford and New York: Oxford University Press.

Dupré, J. (1984). Probabilistic Causality Emancipated. *Midwest Studies in Philosophy* 9: 169−175.

Dupré, J., and N. Cartwright (1987). Probability and Causality: Why Hume and Indeterminism Don't Mix. *Noûs.*

Eells, E., and E. Sober (1983). Probabilistic Causality and the Question of Transitivity. *Philosophy of Science* 50:35−57.

Gould, S. J., and R. C. Lewontin (1979). The Spandrels of San Marco and the Panglossian Paradigm: A critique of the Adaptationist Program. *Proceedings of the Royal Society of London* 205:581−598.

Hempel, C. G. (1965). *Aspects of Scientific Explanation and Other Essays in the Philosophy of Science.* New York: Free Press.

Kettlewell, H. B. (1973). *The Evolution of Melanism.* Oxford: Oxford University Press.

Kitcher, P. (1973). *Abusing Science: The Case against Creationism.* Cambridge, MA: M.I.T. Press.

Levins, R. (1966). The Strategy of Model Building in Population Biology. *American Scientist* 54:421−431.

Lewontin, R. C. (1978). Adaptation. *Scientific American* 239:159−169.

Maynard Smith, J. (1982). *Evolution and the Theory of Games.* Cambridge: Cambridge University Press.

Sober, E. (1984). *The Nature of Selection.* Cambridge, MA: Bradford Books/M.I.T. Press.

Sober, E., and R. C. Lewontin (1982). Artifact, Cause, and Genic Selection. *Philosophy of Science* 47:157−180.

van Fraassen, B. C. (1980). *The Scientific Image.* Oxford: Clarendon Press.

von Neumann, J., and O. Morgenstern (1953). *Theory of Games and Economic Behavior.* Princeton: Princeton University Press.

Wimsatt, W. (1980). Reductionist Research Strategies and Their Biases in the Units of Selection Controversy. In T. Nickles (ed.), *Scientific Discovery*, pp. 213−259. Dordrecht: Reidel.

I
Methodological Questions

1

Simple Models of Complex Phenomena: The Case of Cultural Evolution

Peter J. Richerson and Robert Boyd

A great deal of the progress in evolutionary biology has resulted from the deployment of relatively simple theoretical models. Staddon's, Smith's, and Maynard Smith's contributions to this volume illustrate this point. Despite their success, simple models have been subjected to a steady stream of criticism. Emlen's, Sober's, and Kitcher's papers here are good examples. The complexity of real social and biological phenomena is compared to the toylike quality of the simple models used to analyze them, and their users charged with unwarranted reductionism or plain simplemindedness.

This critique is intuitively appealing—complex phenomena would seem to require complex theories to understand them—but misleading. In this paper we argue that the study of complex, diverse phenomena like organic evolution requires complex, multilevel theories, but that such theories are best built from toolkits made up of a diverse collection of simple models. Because individual models in the toolkit are designed to provide insight into only selected aspects of the more complex whole, they are necessarily incomplete. Nevertheless, students of complex phenomena aim for a reasonably complete theory by studying many related simple models. The neo-Darwinian theory of evolution provides a good example: fitness optimizing models, one and multiple locus genetic models, and quantitative genetic models all emphasize certain details of the evolutionary process at the expense of others. While any given model is simple, the theory as a whole is much more comprehensive than any one of them.

Our argument is not very original; the conscious use of the strategy of using simple models to study complex phenomena goes back at least as far as Weber's (1949) use of "ideal types" to study human societies. Good modern expositions include those by Levins (1966, 1968), Liebenstein (1976), Wimsatt (1980), and Quinn and Dunham (1983). If we can contribute anything useful to the case for simple models, it is because our work has involved extending standard evolutionary theory to a particularly

We thank D. T. Campbell, J. M. Diamond, J. M. Emlen, G. Macey, A. Rosenberg, E. A. Smith, J. Staddon, and S. Vail for comments on drafts of this paper, We also benefited from conversations with J. Quinn and J. Griesemer.

troublesome complexity, cultural inheritance of humans (and in rudimentary form, of some other organisms). This work makes a variety of uses of starkly simple evolutionary models, including models based on the assumption of fitness optimization. Yet one of our concerns has been to determine the conditions under which fitness optimization models will fail to account for human behavior. Perhaps we have acquired a self-conscious awareness of some of the tactical details of the simple-model strategy that will be of some use to others.

1 The Complexity and Diversity of Evolutionary Processes

Evolutionary processes are both extremely complex and extremely diverse. On this count, those who are skeptical of simple models are certainly on solid ground. Every evolving population has a complex history in which many processes have contributed to its evolution, including perhaps drift, migration, mutation, and many other things besides selection. Further, each of these processes can be broken down into a series of interacting subprocesses, each encompassing many varieties. Take selection. There is selection on genes with large effects, selection on quantitative characters, selection on correlated characters and pleiotropic genes, frequency and density dependent selection, selection on sex-limited and sex-linked characters, sexual selection of a couple of kinds, and so on. Aside from viruses, all organisms have an intimidatingly large number of interacting genes and phenotypic characters. Environments vary in space and time with large effects on migration and selection. Age, sex, and social organization structure populations and affect their response to evolutionary processes. Developmental processes are complex, although poorly understood, and perhaps affect evolution in fundamentally important ways. Organisms affect their environments as they evolve. In the case of cultural evolution, additional complexities are introduced. We must understand the details of how individuals acquire and modify attitudes and beliefs, how different attitudes and beliefs interact with genes and environment to produce behavior, and how behavior and environment interact to produce consequences for individual lives. Obviously, the study of evolutionary processes must somehow cope with this complexity.

Evolutionary processes are diverse because different populations are quite different from one another in terms of their biology and the environments to which they are and have been exposed. Discoveries about the concatenation of processes affecting the evolution of one population or species do not necessarily say very much about those in others. In the case of cultural evolution, the details of the cultural transmission process vary appreciably from culture to culture. In some, fathers are more important in childhood socialization; in others, less. Modern societies depend on formal teachers, in traditional societies members of the extended family are often important, and so on. Our models of cultural evolution suggest that such structural differences can be quite important to understanding what cultural traits might evolve.

2 Culture and the Evolutionary Process

In this section, in order to provide a body of detailed examples for use in the later sections, we shall sketch some theoretical results from our own work on the complexities in the evolutionary process caused by culture. Other kinds of complexities of the evolutionary process could be used instead, but we know this one best.

In the last few years, a number of scholars have attempted to understand the processes of cultural evolution in Darwinian terms. Social scientists (Campbell, 1965, 1975; Cloak, 1975; Durham, 1976; Ruyle, 1973) have argued that the analogy between genetic and cultural transmission is the best basis for a general theory of culture. Several biologists have considered how culturally transmitted behavior fits into the framework of neo-Darwinism (Pulliam and Dunford, 1980; Lumsden and Wilson, 1981; Boyd and Richerson, 1983). Other biologists and psychologists have used the formal similarities between genetic and cultural transmission to develop theory describing the dynamics of cultural transmission (Cavalli-Sforza and Feldman, 1973, 1981; Cloninger, Rice, and Reich, 1979; Eaves et al., 1978).

The idea that unifies all this work is that social learning or cultural transmission can be modeled as a system of inheritance; to understand the macroscopic patterns of cultural change we must understand the microscopic processes that increase the frequency of some culturally transmitted variants and reduce the frequency of others. Put another way, to understand cultural evolution we must account for all of the processes by which cultural variation is transmitted and modified. This is the essence of the Darwinian approach to evolution. We (Boyd and Richerson, 1985) have been particularly interested in the question of the origin of cultural transmission. Under what circumstances might selection on genes favor the existence of a second system of inheritance based on the principle of the inheritance of acquired variation?

Cultural and genetic transmission are similar in some respects. For example, the skills and dispositions transmitted during enculturation of children by parents create patterns of behavior that are very difficult to distinguish empirically from patterns resulting from genetic influences.

In other respects, cultural and genetic transmission differ sharply. First, culture is transmitted by an individual observing the behavior of others or by the naive being taught by the experienced. This means that behavior modified by trial-and-error learning can subsequently be transmitted; culture is a system for the inheritance of acquired variation. Second, patterns of cultural transmission are quite different from patterns of genetic transmission. Models other than biological parents are often imitated, including peers, grandparents, and so forth. The cultural analogues of generation length and the mating system are different from, and more variable than, the genetic case. Finally, the naive individual acquiring an item of culture is a more or less active decision-making participant in the transmission process. To some extent, we choose what traits we learn from others, but a zygote cannot choose its genes.

The goal of the Darwinian approach to cultural evolution is to understand cultural change in terms of the forces that act on cultural variation as individuals acquire cultural traits, use the acquired information to guide behavior, and act as models for others. What processes increase or decrease the proportion of people in a society who hold particular ideas about how to behave? We thus seek to understand the cultural analogues of the forces of natural selection, mutation, and drift that drive genetic evolution. These are divisible into three classes: random forces, decision-making forces, and natural selection operating directly on cultural variation.

The random forces are the cultural analogues of mutation and drift in genetic transmission. Intuitively, it seems likely that random errors, individual idiosyncrasies, and chance transmission play a role in behavior and social learning. For example, linguists have documented a good deal of individual variation in speech, some of which is probably random individual variation (Labov, 1972). Similarly, small populations might well lose rare skills or knowledge by chance, for example due to the premature death of the only individuals who acquired them (Diamond, 1978).

Decision-making forces result when naive individuals evaluate alternative behavioral variants and preferentially adopt some variants relative to others. Naive individuals may be exposed to a variety of models and preferentially imitate some rather than others. We call this force biased transmission. Alternatively, individuals may modify existing behaviors or invent new ones by individual learning. If the modified behavior is then transmitted, the resulting force is much like the guided, nonrandom variation of classical "Lamarckian" transmission.

The decision-making forces are derived forces (Campbell, 1965). Decisions require rules for making them, and ultimately the rules must derive from the action of other forces. These decision-making rules may be acquired during an earlier episode of cultural transmission, or they may be genetically transmitted traits that control the neurological machinery for acquisition and retention of cultural traits. The latter possibility is the basis of the various sociobiological hypotheses about cultural evolution (Alexander, 1979; Lumsden and Wilson, 1981). These authors, among others, argue that the course of cultural evolution is determined by natural selection operating indirectly on cultural variation via the decision-making forces.

Natural selection may also operate directly on cultural variation. Selection is an extremely general evolutionary process (Campbell, 1965). Darwin was able to formulate a clear statement of natural selection in the absence of a correct understanding of genetic inheritance because it is a force that will operate on any system of inheritance with a few key properties. There must be heritable variation, the variants must affect phenotype, and the phenotypic differences must affect individuals' chances of transmitting the variants they carry. That variants are transmitted by imitation rather than sexual or asexual reproduction does not affect the basic argument, nor does the possibility that some of the variants were originally acquired under the guidance of individual decisions. Darwin had no problem in imagining that random variation, acquired variation, and natural selection all acted together as forces in organic evolution. In the case of cultural evolution, we see none either.

We have attempted to construct a series of models that represent all of the processes sketched in the previous section. One interesting general result is that the processes of cultural evolution can easily lead to the evolution of behaviors that reduce Darwinian fitness, especially when non-parental individuals are important in cultural transmission. In the simplest model we have analyzed (Richerson and Boyd, 1984) natural selection acting on cultural variation transmitted by a parent and a "teacher" may cause the trait favoring transmission via teachers to go to fixation at a cost in terms of the number of children produced by parents. Some Darwinian students of humans (Alexander, 1979; Lumsden and Wilson, 1981; Durham, 1976) argue that such effects are unlikely to be important because a system of cultural inheritance with such properties would not be favored by selection on genes. Selection, the argument would run, ought to have acted to prevent such distorted cultural adaptations by either (1) the creation of decision-making forces that counteract the effect of selection on nonparentally transmitted cultural variation or (2) preventing nonparental individuals from becoming important in cultural transmission.

We believe this argument is incomplete because it ignores the fact that individual decision-making may be costly compared to social learning. If the costs of using individual decision-making processes are high, selection may not favor decision-making forces that would completely compensate for the maladaptive effects of nonparental transmission. Similarly, if non-parental pattern of cultural transmission offer advantages to individuals of economy in information acquisition, selection on the genes that underlie a capacity for asymmetric transmission may be favored.

For example, nonparental individuals may be more useful models than parents because they may be more skilled or knowledgeable than parents.

The effort in decision-making required to discriminate exactly among the adaptive skills and maladaptive inclinations of teachers and other non-parental models may require extensive, costly, empirical checks of each element of the teacher's behavior. In contrast, the use of relatively simple, low-cost decision-making rules to bias the choice of models or which of their behaviors to imitate may substantially increase a naive person's skills at a tolerable cost of imitating some maladaptive behaviors. We have analyzed the evolutionary consequences of a variety of simple bias rules. These models suggest that nonparental transmission may often be adaptive despite the cost of selection, especially in spatially variable environments (Boyd and Richerson, 1982, 1985—chapters 7 and 8). In essence, humans may accept the cost of imitating maladaptive cultural traits because the alternatives are a high frequency of random errors or extreme decision-making costs. Even when a cultural system of inheritance optimizes genetic fitness when averaged over all the traits it transmits, many traits taken individually may be quite far from those that would optimize fitness.

Even more extreme violations of the genetic fitness optimizing model are conceivable. For example, if rules of mate choice are transmitted culturally, human genes might be "domesticated" to serve cultural functions. On the other hand, perhaps the critics of these models are correct, and the abstract possibilities demonstrated by such models are empirically unimportant. The essential point is that, like many bits of genetic realism, adding culture to the evolutionary process might make a qualitative difference in the behavior we expect to observe compared to that expected from the simple fitness optimizing caricature of evolution.

3 Why Families of Simple Models

Disadvantages of Complex Models

In the face of the complexity of evolutionary processes, the appropriate strategy may seem obvious: to be useful models must be realistic; they should incorporate all factors that scientists studying the phenomena know to be important. This reasoning is certainly plausible, and many scientists, particularly in economics (e.g., Hudson and Jorgenson, 1974) and ecology (Watt, 1968), have constructed such models, despite their complexity. On this view, simple models are primitive, things to be replaced as our sophistication about evolution grows.

Nevertheless, theorists in such disciplines as evolutionary biology and economics stubbornly continue to use simple models even though improvements in empirical knowledge, analytical mathematics, and computing now enable them to create extremely elaborate models if they care to do so. Theorists of this persuasion eschew more detailed models because

(1) they are hard to understand, (2) they are difficult to analyze, and (3) they are often no more useful for prediction than simple models. Let us now consider each of these points in turn.

(1) Complex, detailed models are usually extremely difficult to understand. As more realism is added, the myriad interactions within the model become almost as opaque as the real world we wish to understand. When a set of not-so-complex parts is linked into an interacting complex, it is often impossible to understand why the results behave as they do. To substitute an ill-understood model of the world for the ill-understood world is not progress. In the end, the only way to understand how such a model works is to abstract pieces from it or study simplified cases where its behavior is more transparent. Even when complex models are useful, they are so because we understand how they work in terms of simple models abstracted from them.

Costly, complex models are most likely to be scientifically justified when phenomena are complex but not diverse. It is worth studying the complexities of atoms in great detail because there are only a few kinds, and they all obey the same basic laws. The generality of such laws makes them worth knowing even if the task is difficult. The equivalent sophistication in a model of the evolution of a given society or species is possible, perhaps, but unlikely to be justified on scientific grounds because of limited generalizability to other species or societies.

(2) The analysis of complex models is also expensive and time consuming. The complexity of a recursion model is roughly measured by the number of independent variables that must be kept track of from generation to generation. It usually is not possible to analyze nonlinear recursions involving more than a handful of variables without resorting to numerical techniques. Until the advent of digital computers, obtaining numerical solutions was impractical. Since then, however, there have been many attempts to make computer simulation models of complex social and biological processes. These projects have generally been quite costly. As the number of variables in a model increases, the number of interactions between variables increases even faster. This means that even with the fastest computers, it is not practical to explore the sensitivity of a model to changes in assumptions about very many of its constituent interactions. Considerations of economy of effort in scientific practice dictate that we should be satisfied with much simpler models than we could build in principle.

Complex, realistic models are sometimes employed when prediction rather than understanding is the main goal. Numerical weather prediction models and economic forecasting models come to mind. In both cases the gains in *understanding* of atmospheric and economic phenomena are mostly attributable to the constituent simple submodels of particular processes that are individually not much good for prediction. The marginal increase in understanding relative to cost in the large predictive models is so small that only their practical application justifies their expense; scientific discovery would be better served by more attention to the simpler models. As Dupré observes in his introduction, explanation differs from prediction in being easier to achieve (leaving aside statistical models that make no pretentions to explanation). We would argue in addition that explanation or under-standing is scientifically far more fundamental than prediction as well. This is most clearly evident in examples such as the simple deterministic models of economic and population processes that can exhibit chaotic behavior (Day, 1982; May, 1976). If these models prove to apply in the real world, they will guarantee that only short-range predictions are possible with less than perfect specification of initial conditions, but they also give a quite satisfactory explanation of why this is so. The problem is well under-stood in the context of a purely physical problem, weather prediction (Smagorinsky, 1969).

(3) Detailed models of complex social or biological systems are often not much more useful for prediction than are simple models. Detailed models usually require very large amounts of data to determine the various para-meter values in the model. Such data are rarely available. Moreover, small inaccuracies or errors in the formulation of the model can produce quite erroneous predictions. The temptation is to "tune" the model, making small changes, perhaps well within the error of available data, so that the model produces reasonable answers. When this is done, any predictive power that the model might have is due more to statistical fitting than to the fact that it accurately represents actual causal processes. It is easy to make large sacrifices of understanding for small gains in predictive power. Contrari-wise, although evolutionary processes are inherently complex and diverse, models with a few variables may capture enough of the really important processes in a given case or class of cases both to explain and to predict with tolerable accuracy, as Smith's, Staddon's, and Maynard Smith's papers in this volume show.

The Utility of Simple Models

In the face of these difficulties, the most useful strategy will usually be to build a variety of simple models that can be completely understood but that still capture the important properties of the processes of interest. Liebenstein (1976—chapter 2) calls such simple models "sample theories." Students of complex and diverse subject matters develop a large body of models from which "samples" can be drawn for the purpose at hand. Useful sample theories result from attempts to satisfy two competing desiderata: They should be simple enough to be clearly and completely grasped, and at the same time they should reflect how real processes actually do work, at least to some approximation. A systematically constructed population of sample theories and combinations of them constitutes the theory of how the whole complex process works.

The synthetic theory of evolution provides a good example. Each of the basic processes (e.g., selection, mutation, drift) is represented by a large variety of simple models, some specific to a particular population, and others quite general. These models are combined in different ways to represent interesting phenomena, (e.g., sexual selection, speciation). This whole family of models, together with a knowledge of which models are appropriate for what kinds of situations, constitutes the theoretical system of population biology.

A theoretical system so constituted from simple sample models is a complicated and diverse collection of knowledge; it cannot be legitimately labeled simpleminded. Still, every tactical deployment of models to study a question of interest will be quite simple compared to the phenomena that they are intended to represent. The sample models are caricatures. If they are well designed, they are like good caricatures, capturing a few essential features of the problem in a recognizable but stylized manner, and with no attempt to represent features not of immediate interest.

Wimsatt (1980, 1981) provides good general discussions of tactical considerations in the deployment of simple models. To Wimsatt, all sample models of evolutionary phenomena should be viewed as "heuristics" rather than universally applicable laws. This terminology has the virtue of emphasizing that all sample models have defects. They usefully apply only over a limited range of phenomena, and even over the range where they are useful they are almost certain to have biases. Even the very best scientific heuristic (or sample model) will fail and possibly mislead if pushed too far or in the wrong direction. It is in attention to details of the use of simple sample theories that these problems are minimized and the maximum understanding gained. The user attempts to discover "robust" results, conclusions that are at least qualitatively correct, at least for some range of situations, despite the complexity and diversity of the phenomena they attempt to describe.

Note that simple models can often be tested for their scientific content via their predictions even when the situation is too complicated to make practical predictions. Experimental or statistical controls often make it possible to expose the variation due to the processes modeled, against the background of "noise" due to other ones, thus allowing a ceteris paribus prediction for purposes of empirical testing. Simple models, in other words, are the formal theoretical parallel of the experimental and comparative methods so widely used in biology and the social sciences.

Generalized Sample Theories

Generalized sample theories are an important subset of the simple sample theories used to understand complex, diverse problems. They are designed to capture the qualitative properties of the whole class of processes that they are used to represent, while more specialized ones are used for closer approximations to narrower classes of cases. Generalized sample theories are useful because we do not seem to be able to construct models of social and biological phenomena that are general, realistic, and precisely predictive (Levins, 1966, 1968). That is, evolutionary biologists and social scientists have not been able to satisfy the epistemological norm derived from the physical sciences that holds that theory be in the form of universal laws that can be tested by the detailed predictions they make about the phenomena considered by the law. This failure is probably a consequence of the complexity and diversity of living things. Basic theoretical constructs like natural selection are not universal laws like gravitation; rather they are taxonomic entities, general classes of similar processes that nonetheless have a good deal of diversity within the class. A theoretical construct designed to represent the general properties of the class of processes labeled natural selection must sacrifice many of the details of particular examples of selection. On the other hand, a model tailored to the details of a particular case is unlikely to have much relevance beyond that case. Further, the most precise predictions may be obtained by statistical models that sacrifice realism and hence are useless as explanatory devices.

One might agree with the case for a diverse toolkit of simple models, but still doubt the utility of *generalized* sample theories. Fitness maximizing calculations are often used as a simple caricature of how selection ought to work most of the time in most organisms to produce adaptations. Does such a generalized sample theory have any serious scientific purpose? Some might argue that their qualitative kind of understanding is, at best, useful for giving nonspecialists a simplified overview of complicated topics and that real scientific progress still occurs entirely in the construction of specialized sample theories that actually predict. A sterner critic might characterize the attempt to construct generalized models as loose speculation that actually inhibits the real work of discovering predictable relationships in particular systems.

These kinds of objections implicitly assume that it is possible to do science without any kind of general model. All scientists have mental models of the world. The part of the model that deals with their disciplinary specialty is more detailed than the parts that represent related areas of science. Many aspects of a scientist's mental model are likely to be vague and never expressed. The real choice is between an intuitive, perhaps covert, general theory and an explicit, often mathematical, one.

It seems to us that generalized sample models such as fitness optimizing models do play an important role. Well chosen to represent the stripped-down essence of a much larger set of more specialized models, generalized sample theories serve important functions in scientists' cognitive organization of complex-diverse subject matters and in communication between specialists. For example, we are concerned with the details of how cultural transmission occurs, a subject studied by psychologists (Boyd and Richerson, 1985—chapter 3). Social learning theorists have made many, but not all, of the kinds of measurements that are necessary for specifying good sample theories of cultural transmission. Crucial unknowns include the mechanisms by which variation and covariation are maintained in cultural traits. These properties have important implications for the process of cultural evolution because the selection and bias forces depend on the maintenance of variation for their effectiveness. These deficiencies of social learning theory are not at all apparent in the absence of a theory linking the psychology of enculturation with the macroscopic phenomena of social institutions and long-run outcomes. It seems unlikely that a sensible psychologist would be motivated to make the arduous and costly experiments necessary to determine such processes without a general theoretical argument justifying their importance. This is an example of a common situation: constructing models that make such links, even if they are simple caricatures, often shows that processes with small, relatively hard to measure, effects can produce major results.

The relationship between a generalized sample theory and empirical test or prediction is a subtle one. To insist upon empirical science in the style of physics is to insist upon the impossible. However, to give up on empirical tests and prediction would be to abandon science and retreat to speculative philosophy. Generalized sample theories normally make only limited qualitative predictions. The logistic model of population growth is a good elementary example. At best, it is an accurate model only of microbial growth in the laboratory. However, it captures something of the biology of population growth in more complex cases. Moreover, its simplicity makes it a handy general model to incorporate into models that must also represent other processes such as selection, and intra- and interspecific competition. If some sample theory is consistently at variance with the data, then it must be modified. The accumulation of these kinds of modifications can eventually alter general theory, either by compelling the abandonment of some sample models or by systematizing knowledge about the variation of processes. In extreme cases, major discoveries in some of the components of a general theory can compel the reorganization of the entire edifice, as exemplified by the impact of Mendelian genetics on Darwinian theory in biology. No one nowadays would think of using Karl Pearson's models of the inheritance of acquired variation as a sample theory of genetic inheritance, although they might have some specialized uses in the study of cultural evolution.

A generalized model is useful so long as its predictions are qualitatively correct, roughly conforming to the majority of cases. It is helpful if the inevitable limits of the model are understood. It is not necessarily an embarrassment if more than one alternative formulation of a general theory, built from different sample models, is more or less equally correct. In this case, the comparison of theories that are empirically equivalent makes clearer what is at stake in scientific controversies and may suggest empirical and theoretical steps toward a resolution.

4 Some Remarks on the Strategy of Building Simple Models

One of the main points of the preceding discussion is that the analysis of evolutionary problems using simple models depends very much on the appropriate choice of those models. How does one go about making such choices? Evolutionary biologists and social scientists use a variety of methods to accomplish this task that, we believe, can be collected under three main headings, corresponding to idealized analytical steps: (1) the choice of problem, (2) the modularization of analysis, and (3) the construction of synthetic hypotheses that we shall call "plausibility arguments."

Choice of Problem

When one uses simple models to understand complex and diverse problems, the choice of the problem to be analyzed exerts a strong influence on the kinds of simplifications one chooses. The idea is to simplify most drastically those aspects that are not centrally related to the problem at hand in order to retain the maximum feasible detail in the features of most direct interest. In the case of our models of cultural evolution, we have been concerned with the evolution of cultural organisms from acultural ancestors. This required us to represent the processes of ordinary organic evolution in most of our modeling efforts. Still, we were also interested in trying to develop preliminary general models of the important structural features and forces that affect cultural evolution. Given this choice of problem, it seemed advisable to use very simple models of genetic processes to represent the evolution of genetic capacities for culture in order that the models of cultural transmission could be made a bit more elaborate. Thus, we frequently asked what parameter value of a model controlling the propensity to acquire culture in a certain way would cause fitness to be optimized. Those models that included specific genetics used only the simplest haploid one locus or quantitative models of genetic transmission.

Models emphasizing cultural detail at the expense of genetic detail accept the risk that some particular complexity of the human genetic system plays a direct role in the coevolution of genes and culture. For example, if genes affecting the behavior toward relatives are transmitted on the Y chromosome, as Hartung (1976) suggested, the models we constructed might turn out to be seriously misleading. The opposite risk, however, seemed more serious to us in the context of the problem; in models that are too complex the important details of culture itself might be obscured or lost. Several commentators (Maynard Smith and Warren, 1982; Boyd and Richerson, 1983; Kitcher, 1985) have remarked that the analysis that led Lumsden and Wilson (1981) to their "thousand year rule" is dubious because key properties of culture disappear as a result of simplifying assumptions. The general formulation of their model is conceptually satisfactory, but its complexity appears to have dictated misleading simplifications in the interests of successful analysis.

Modularization of Analysis
Most interesting evolutionary problems involve the interaction of evolutionary processes and a particular pattern of genetic transmission and gene expression. For example, the interaction of selection and mutation at a diploid locus is a classic problem of the synthetic theory. The sample models of the parts of this problem are less interesting than the combination of them in a model that can help us understand how the two basic forces interact with genetically inherited variation. Similar problems are of interest in cultural evolution. How does learning, acting as an evolutionary force because learned variants can be imitated, interact with selection, both selection on the cultural variants and on the underlying senses of reward and punishment that guide learning? Such combinations of processes inevitably make for relatively complex models. To make any headway, relatively difficult mathematical and experimental procedures have to be introduced, and many simplifying assumptions have to be made. Difficult choices between analytical tractability, comprehensibility, generality, and realism have to be made. Is a fitness optimization representation of the genetic process a reasonable simplification, or can some additional genetic realism be usefully retained in the context of the problem?

The answers to such questions are sought by breaking the problem down first into its constituent sample models and then reassembling them step by step into more complex combinations. This tactic is obvious, but easily misunderstood and misused. In the long run, the simple models strategy leads to large families of well understood sample models, some of which will be relatively complex, specialized, and difficult to understand. Also, relatively complex combinations of models are often useful. However, such relatively complicated models depend on a thorough understanding of the simplest models of each family and of the constituent submodels of compound models. The possibility for artifactual results increases with the complexity of the analysis unless one can be reasonably confident that the constituent sample models are empirically reasonable and mathematically well behaved. It is relatively much easier to conduct experiments and detailed mathematical analysis on processes when they are isolated than when they are imbedded in a complex system. In population biology, both history and pedagogic practice suggest that one must begin with an understanding of the elementary constituents of the theory.

While building models of complex processes composed of simpler modules may be second nature to evolutionary biologists, in our experience it sometimes confuses social scientists who read the present body of theory in cultural evolution. The modularization of complex problems seems reductionistic; even after the parts are reassembled it seems to some readers as if the models are attempting to deduce the properties of wholes from properties of parts. The tactical "reductionism" used to understand a problem does not imply that the interaction of parts might not produce irreducible effects. For example, some models of culture built using this tactic suggest that group selection might be especially likely under some plausible forms of cultural transmission (Boyd and Richerson, 1985—chapter 7).

Sometimes, evolutionary biologists (and social scientists who use similar methods, such as economists) contribute to the confusion by failing to distinguish between the heuristic use of tactical reductionism from a real belief that some particular simple model is true description of a complex process. Indeed, the relative ease with which interesting, even approximately correct, results can be obtained for intrinsically rather complex processes with simple models can lead the unwary to conclude that successful tactical reduction implies the adequacy of a philosophical reductionist stance. Those who are so tempted should consult the papers of Wimsatt cited above. Most users of simple models know better. For example, Dawkins (1982), a prototypical genetic reductionist by some accounts (Sober, 1984), begins his discussion (pp. 1–2) by asking the reader to take his idea of selfish genes with extended phenotypes as a heuristic model. Later (by p. 7), Dawkins does express the hope that it may prove more fundamental than a mere heuristic, but the distinction between the two interpretations is clear, and the reader is left the choice.

The development of a formal theory of cultural evolution is in its infancy, and attention has properly concentrated on quite elementary models. This means that the theory to date appears quite reductionistic. For example, most models consider only one cultural trait. On the one hand, an overenthusiast might claim that these models are relatively successful in explaining human behavior and hence that human cultures really can be atomized into traits. On the other hand, a critic might complain that they are completely bankrupt because they do not take account of the fact that cultural traits must interact in complex ways. The fact is that such preliminary models are silent about what complexities might flow from the interaction of multiple traits. That is a difficult question in its own right, but one whose analysis must be deferred until we understand the simpler theoretical elements we might use in such an analysis.

The thorough study of simple models includes pressing them to their extreme limits. This is especially useful at the second step of development, where simple models of basic processes are combined into a candidate generalized model of an interesting question. There are two related purposes in this exercise.

First, it is helpful to have all the implications of a given simple model exposed for comparative purposes, if nothing else. A well understood simple sample theory serves as a useful point of comparison for the results of more complex alternatives, even when some conclusions are utterly ridiculous.

Second, models do not usually just fail; they fail for particular reasons that are often very informative. Just what kinds of modifications are required to make the initially ridiculous results more nearly reasonable? For example, the failures of the logistic model of population growth suggest the amendments needed to make better models. In the case of culture, models that include only faithful cultural transmission suggest that culture is generally inferior to genes as a mode of inheritance (Cavalli-Sforza and Feldman, 1983). If the evolution of culture in the hominid line was favored by natural selection, there must be more to the story than just the acquisition of behavior by imitation. We have suggested that the ability of culture to couple individual learning to a transmission mechanism, thus to generate a system for the inheritance of acquired variation, could cause capacities for culture to evolve (Boyd and Richerson, 1983a, 1985—chapter 4). However, this analysis also fails because it suggests that the advantages of culture are quite general, and hence that many organisms ought to have "Lamarckian" systems of inheritance. This failure in turn suggests that there are other costs to the inheritance of acquired variation that must be accounted for.

In both of these respects, human sociobiology has made a major contribution by showing what must be true if the genetic fitness optimizing model generally holds when behavioral variation is proximally transmitted by culture. For example, Alexander (1979; see also Flinn and Alexander, 1982) argues that decision-making forces are powerful enough to constrain cultural variation to maximize fitness in most circumstances. Important qualitative predictions flow from this argument. If strong, accurate decision-making is possible, then humans need not depend on relatively passive imitation; they can easily invent or choose those behaviors appropriate to the environments they find themselves in. If so, culture will behave more like ordinary mechanisms of phenotypic flexibility than like an inheritance system. Empirically, behavioral variation will be largely explicable, even in the short run, in terms of environmental variation rather than the variation in what traits are available for imitation. This argument also implies that costs of making decisions are low relative to any economies that might result from imitation. In our judgment (Boyd and Richerson, 1985—chapter 5), theory and the available data suggest that Alexander's argument is incorrect in general, although it may well be roughly correct for those traits for which accurate decision-making is easy. Regardless of whether we or Alexander ultimately prove more nearly correct, his contribution is substantial; work on the complexities of culture is much aided by having the implications of the simplest genetic fitness maximizing model incorporating culture cogently developed.

The exhaustive analysis of many sample models in various combinations is also the main means of seeking robust results (Wimsatt, 1981). One way to gain confidence in simple models is to build several models embodying different characterizations of the problem of interest and different simplifying assumptions. If the results of a model are robust, the same qualitative results ought to obtain for a whole family of related models in which the supposedly extraneous details differ. Although he makes a slightly different point, Maynard Smith's discussion in this volume of the use of multiple models of the same general process is a good example. The fact that genetic and game theoretic models of altruism usually lead to similar conclusions reassures us that general results like Hamilton's $k = 1/r$ rule are robust. Similarly, as more complex considerations are introduced into the family of models, simple model results can be considered robust only if it seems that the qualitative conclusion holds for some reasonable range of plausible conditions. Thus, quantitative genetic (Boyd and Richerson, 1982) and multiple-locus models (Uyenoyama and Feldman, 1980) suggest that Hamilton's rule is approximately correct when a variety of complications are introduced. Complications substantially affect the exact form of the rule, but do preserve the qualitative result that kin cooperation can evolve and the propensity to cooperate should be a function of relatedness under most circumstances that seem empirically reasonable. Nevertheless, it is slow and difficult work to make reasonably certain that particular results can be treated as robust (Wimsatt, 1980).

In the case of cultural evolution, we make the tentative claim that the costly information argument is a robust result. In all of the models we have constructed of the novel structural properties of culture and the evolutionary forces that result from them, it seems that optimizing the genetic fitness of a capacity for culture generally leads to a situation in which many individual cultural traits can easily evolve to values quite distant from those that would maximize fitness, so long as decision-making is costly. These results do not depend on whether cultural traits are imagined to be discrete characters or continuous quantitative variables, for example. The tentativeness of the claim must be emphasized because the whole corpus of models of cultural evolution is still so small.

Plausibility Arguments
We believe that "plausibility argument" is a useful term for a scientific construct that plays much the same role in the study of complex, diverse phenomena that mutually exclusive hypotheses are supposed to play in the investigation of simpler subject matters. A plausibility argument is a hypothetical explanation having three features in common with a traditional hypothesis: (1) a claim of deductive soundness, of in-principle logical sufficiency to explain a body of data, (2) sufficient support from the existing body of empirical data to suggest that it might actually be able to explain a body of data as well as or better than competing plausibility arguments, and (3) a program of research that might distinguish between the claims of competing plausibility arguments. The differences are that competing plausibility arguments (1) are seldom mutually exclusive, (2) can seldom be rejected by a single sharp experimental test (or small set of them), and (3) often end up being revised, limited in their generality or domain of applicability, or combined with competing arguments rather than being rejected. In other words, competing plausibility arguments are based on the claims that a different set of submodels is needed to achieve a given degree of realism and generality, that different parameter values of common submodels are required, or that a given model is correct as far as it goes, but applies with less generality, realism, or predictive power than its proponents claim. Most frequently, the empirical program suggested by competing plausibility arguments is an arduous series of measurements of the relative strengths of several known processes in a wide range of organisms.

The reason for these differences is that quantitative questions are at the crux of debates about evolutionary processes. For example: How strong is selection among individuals relative to selection among groups? Theoretical analysis suggests that selection among groups must be commonplace, and laboratory experiments (Wade, 1977) demonstrate that it could have important effects. However, it is not at all clear whether selection among groups is important in nature. Sex ratio provides another example. Clear examples of sex ratio distortion exist (Hamilton, 1967), and theory suggests that it should be favored under a wide variety of ecological conditions (Charnov, 1982). Yet this process seems to be relatively rare— at least weak enough to neglect in most cases. Even if we are willing to be content with qualitative knowledge of complex processes, the term "qualitative" must be taken in the sense of rough estimates of quantitative variables, not in the sense of simple acceptance or rejection of mutually exclusive hypotheses. This feature of evolutionary problems is the basis for Quinn and Dunham's (1983) rejection of Popperian falsification as a proper epistemological model in ecology and evolution (See also Rapoport's, 1967, claim that many scientific paradoxes have been resolved when the polar positions were shown to be only opposite ends of a continuum).

Human sociobiology provides a good example of a plausibility argument. The basic premise of human sociobiology is that fitness optimizing models drawn from evolutionary biology can be used to understand human behavior. Many social scientists have objected to this enterprise on the grounds that evolutionary theory does not account for the existence of culture. As we have already noted, Alexander (1979), Lumsden and Wilson (1981), Durham (1976), and others have defended the fitness optimizing approach not by denying the importance of culture but by proposing various means by which decision-making forces could evolve under the guidance of selection to constrain cultural evolution so as generally to produce fitness optimizing behavior. These authors have supported their plausibility argument by constructing an array of simple models that predict the details of human behavior in various circumstances—for example, patterns of adoption, unilineal descent, and child abuse—and compared the results of these simple models with empirical data.

The sociobiological explanations of human behavior and those derived from explicit models of cultural evolution provide an example of competing plausibility arguments. As Flinn and Alexander (1982) argue, there is wide agreement among Darwinian students of the problem of human evolution that culture is important, and that the processes of cultural evolution may sometimes fail to keep cultural variation "on track" of genetic fitness (e.g., Alexander, 1979—p. 142). Disagreements revolve around the relative strength of decision-making forces compared to natural selection on cultural variation, the degree to which cultural transmission acts like an inheritance system rather than an ordinary mechanism for phenotypic flexibility, the importance of nonparental transmission, and so forth. For example, we have argued that decision-making is frequently costly, and that this allows culture a certain autonomy, while Durham (1976) argues that cultural evolution will be constrained to produce behaviors that approximately maximize fitness most of the time.

We think that the clearest way to address the controversial questions raised by competing plausibility arguments is to try to formulate models with parameters such that for some values of the critical parameters the results approximate one of the polar positions in such debates, while for others the model approximates the other position. If the parameters that produce these contrasting results capture some real features of the processes of cultural and genetic coevolution, it may be possible to understand at least what is at stake in the controversy. In the models we have constructed, several parameters control the extent to which a typical cultural trait will be at the fitness optimum. If decisions about what cultural behaviors to adopt or invent can be made easily and accurately, and the rules that guide choices are ultimately transmitted genetically and subject to selection, culture will be very strongly constrained to maximize genetic fitness. Similarly, if important cultural traits are transmitted mostly from biological parents to offspring, cultural variation will act much like an extra chromosome of a biochemically odd kind. Even if decision-making forces are weak, selection on cultural variation will favor individual (inclusive) reproductive success, subject only to the same kinds of qualifications that obtain for a genetic locus. This result seems to approximate Durham's (1976) argument. As decision-making costs and nonparental transmission are allowed to become more important, cultural evolution becomes less directly constrained by selection on genes that control culture and it is possible to approximate positions like the group-functionalism of many social scientists and the afunctional position of Sahlins (1976).

As primitive as our own models are in this regard (see also Pulliam and Dunford, 1980; Werren and Pulliam, 1981; Pulliam, 1982, 1983), we think they are a promising step. The costs of decision-making and the extent to which important items of culture are transmitted by nonparental individuals are empirical issues that can be resolved. Indeed, data already exist on these points (Boyd and Richerson, 1985 chapters 3 and 5). It would be overenthusiastic to claim that any of the controversial questions surrounding the application of Darwinism to human culture are resolved, but we do believe that the modest body of formal theory so far developed, and empirical argument derived from the theory, has clarified the issues to the extent that rapid progress is now possible.

A well developed plausibility argument differs sharply from another common type of argument that we call a programmatic claim. Most generally, a programmatic claim advocates a plan of research for addressing some outstanding problem without, however, attempting to construct a full plausibility argument. Programmatic claims can be exceedingly useful; the development of a Darwinian theory of culture was greatly stimulated by mostly programmatic essays such as those by Campbell (1965), Ruyle (1973), and Cloak (1975). However, they are useful only insofar as they indicate the possibility of, or need for, new plausibility arguments. An attack on an existing, often widely accepted, plausibility argument on the grounds that the plausibility argument is incomplete is a kind of programmatic claim. Critiques of human sociobiology are commonly of this type. Burden-of-proof claims are another variant. For example, sociobiologists often seem to imply that the general success of adaptive reasoning in biology means that the existence of any prima facie plausible adaptive interpretation of human behavior is a sufficient counter to anything but a perfect case for a nonadaptive explanation.

Programmatic attacks and burden-of-proof claims can be positively harmful when taken, by themselves, as sufficient substitutes for a sound plausibility argument. We have argued that theory about complex-diverse phenomena is necessarily made up of simple models that omit many details of the phenomena under study. It is very easy to criticize theory of this kind on the grounds that it is incomplete (or defend it on the grounds that it one day will be much more complete). Such criticism and defense is not really very useful because all such models are incomplete in many ways and may be flawed because of it. What is required is a plausibility argument that shows that some factor that is omitted could be sufficiently important to require inclusion in the theory of the phenomenon under consideration, or a plausible case that it really can be neglected for most purposes. Thus, for example, it is not enough to attack a purportedly general plausibility argument with a few special cases, for it is (or ought to be) stipulated that generalized models are always likely to account more or less poorly for many special cases. Contrariwise, the success of genetic fitness maximizing theory in biology cannot be used to defend that generalized model in the face of plausible arguments that cultural evolution is a divergent special case.

It seems to us that until very recently, "nature-nurture" debates have been badly confused because plausibility arguments have often been taken to have been successfully countered by programmatic claims. It has proved relatively easy to construct reasonable and increasingly sophisticated Darwinian plausibility arguments about human behavior from the prevailing general theory. It is also relatively easy to spot the programmatic flaws in such arguments; conventional Darwinian models do not allow for human culture. The problem is that programmatic objections have not been taken to imply a promise to deliver a full plausibility claim. Rather, they have been taken as a kind of declaration of independence of the social sciences from biology. Having shown that the biological theory is in principle incomplete, the conclusion is drawn that it can safely be ignored. Sahlins's (1976) objections to human sociobiology seem to us to have been as much in this tradition as Tarde's (1903—pp. xxi–xxii) very early one. Both arguments ignore that Darwinian plausibility arguments ordinarily contain a serious rationale for accepting their claims despite the unique aspects of the human species. Certainly this is the case with contemporary human sociobiology, and explains why it has attracted support by social scientists like van den Berghe (1979, 1981) who cannot be accused of simpleminded hereditarianism.

5 *The Importance of Scientific Pluralism*

Jared Diamond (personal communication) has drawn the following useful lesson from his experience as both a physiologist and a community ecologist: In physiology, controversial issues are ordinarily settled quickly by definitive experiments. As a result, debate over contending hypotheses is quite restrained and polite. One or the other contending claim is almost certain to turn out wrong in short order, and any grandiose pronouncements, ad hominem attacks, or similar departures from polite scientific discourse can be held against the loser. As long as scientists know that they can easily be proven wrong by a few critical experiments in the next few years, they will refrain from such departures. In ecology, major controversies last much longer because the issues are more complex and testing contending plausibility arguments is a long-drawn-out affair. The result is that individual claimants are often unlikely to be proven cleanly right or wrong, at least during their own lifetimes. Rhetorical excesses thus cannot be clearly proven as such by the failure of the programmatic claim or plausibility argument to which they are attached, and consequently the motivation to avoid them is reduced.

Perhaps differences between these two disciplines can be understood in terms of Campbell's (1979) general discussion of scientific honesty (see also Beatty's contribution to this volume). According to Campbell, scientists are more honest in their occupational behavior than other professionals, but not because they are morally superior as individuals. Rather, they are careful to present honest work because other scientists are very discriminating consumers. Scientists frequently replicate crucial experiments, and can gain prestige by detecting errors. In a controversy, many members of the community will act as relatively unbiased judges of the acceptability of contending hypotheses because their own work depends on using the correct result—say, to make a more accurate measurement instrument. Such acceptors (to borrow Beatty's term) have an interest in the resolution of the controversy, but not a vested interest in any particular outcome. It seems likely that this mechanism will work much more effectively when controversial issues are resolved quickly, and consumer/acceptors can confidently use secure results in their own work. In the case of evolutionary and ecological problems, ambiguity lasts longer, and consumers may be forced to choose among plausibility arguments, thus coming to have a vested interest in the controversy. The extensive empirical program of the complex-diverse disciplines reduces the incentive to replicate individual experiments directly because they make so small a contribution to the total program.

Campbell (1969, 1986) contributed an insightful analysis of another potentially serious problem in the study of complex-diverse subject matters:

the social complexity of the sciences that study them. Specialization is obviously demanded by complexity and diversity. But there is no guarantee that disciplines will not evolve what Campbell characterized as parochial "tribal" norms and customs that impede scientific progress. His argument is illustrated with reference to the arbitrary disciplinary boundaries, schools within disciplines, and the resulting "ethnocentrism" within the social sciences. Our impression is that the scientific endeavor becomes more prone to "ethnocentrism" as problems become more complex and diverse; certainly evolutionary biology, despite the unifying value of Darwinism, is not immune. As the enforcement of the universalistic norms of scientific discourse weaken, very human motives, such as a desire for collegial relations within one's discipline, a tendency to find that one's extrascientific ideology can be squared one way or another with one's science, career considerations, and a need to economize on information, can easily lead the social structure of science in directions that reduce its collective ability to solve complex-diverse problems. The mental effort of keeping multiple, partly conflicting, plausibility arguments in mind, the ambiguous relationship of these to ideas and norms derived from other roles, and the need to have some knowledge of several unfamiliar disciplines might be psychological motivations that encourage the formation of independent disciplines and schools with little communication between them. Nevertheless, it seems inescapable that complex-diverse subjects demand free communication between specialists and a wide tolerance for the pursuit of temporarily divergent plausibility claims.

Deriving norms from this diagnosis is by no means straightforward. Perhaps new disciplines and new ideas need a measure of isolation, which the development of ethnocentric and sectarian attitudes affords (Campbell, 1985). Beatty's argument in this volume that the pursuit of hypotheses is a useful enterprise is very well taken. On the other hand, unchecked this process can result in a declaration of independence for a mature discipline, such as Sahlins offers for anthropology, which may be wholly harmful. There may be an optimal amount of disciplinary and research program "ethnocentrism" for maximizing scientific progress at any given time.

Nonetheless, we think that the following two norms would, if adopted, improve scientific debate surrounding complex, diverse subjects.

Ad hominem attacks on particular positions and the use of self-serving programmatic claims should be viewed as tacky. Given the deep importance of human behavior to humans, the weakness of the consumer/acceptor mechanism for regulating academic discourse, and the fact of the evolution of "ethnocentric" norms within disciplines, it is utopian to expect that the temptation to behave in such ways will always be resisted, particularly by those who are legitimately pursuing a position. Widespread agreement that

Campbell, D. T. (1975). On the Conflicts between Biological and Social Evolution and between Psychology and Moral Tradition. *Amer. Psychol.* 30:1103–1126.

Campbell, D. T. (1979). A Tribal Model of the Social System Vehicle Carrying Scientific Knowledge. *Knowledge: Creation, Diffusion, Utilization* 1:181–201.

Campbell, D. T. (1985). Science Policy from a Naturalistic Sociological Epistemology. In *PSA 1984*, Vol. 2, P. D. Asquith and P. Kitcher (eds.). East Lansing, MI: Philosophy of Science Association: 14–29.

Campbell, D. T. (1986). Science's Social System of Validity-Enhancing Collective Belief Change and the Problems of the Social Sciences. In *Metatheory in the Social Sciences: Pluralisms and Subjectivities*, D. W. Fisk and R. A. Shweder, eds. Chicago: University of Chicago Press: 86–105.

Cavalli-Sforza, L. L., and M. W. Feldman (1973). Cultural versus Biological Inheritance: Phenotypic Transmission from Parents to Children (a Theory of the Effect of Parental Phenotypes on Children's Phenotypes). *J. Human Genetics* 25:618–637.

Cavalli-Sforza, L. L., and M. W. Feldman (1981). *Transmission and Evolution: A Quantitative Approach*. Princeton, NJ: Princeton University Press.

Cavalli-Sforza, L. L., and M. W. Feldman (1983). Cultural versus Genetic Adaptation. *Proc. Natl. Acad. Sci. USA* 80:4993–4996.

Charnov, E. (1982). *A Theory of Sex Allocation*. Princeton, NJ: Princeton University Press.

Cloak, F. T., Jr. (1975). Is a Cultural Ethology Possible? *Human Ecology* 3:161–182.

Cloninger, C. R., J. Rice, and T. Reich (1979). Multifactorial Inheritance with Cultural Transmission and Assortative Mating. II. A General Model of Combined Polygenic and Cultural Inheritance. *Amer. J. Hum. Genet.* 31:176–198.

Dawkins, R. (1982). *The Extended Phenotype: The Gene as the Unit of Selection*. San Francisco: Freeman.

Day, R. H. (1982). Irregular Growth Cycles. *Amer. Econ. Rev.* 72:406–414.

Diamond, J. (1978) The Tasmanians: The Longest Isolation, the Simplest Technology. *Nature* 273:185–186.

Diamond, J. (1986). Overview: Laboratory Experiments, Field Experiments, and Natural Experiments. In *Community Ecology*, J. Diamond and T. J. Case, eds. New York: Harper and Row, pp. 3–22.

Durham, W. H. (1976). The Adaptive Significance of Cultural Behavior. *Human Ecology* 4:89–121.

Eaves, L. J., K. A. Last, P. A. Young, and N. G. Martin (1978). Model-Fitting Approaches to the Analysis of Human Behavior. *Heredity* 41:249–320.

Flinn, M. V., and R. D. Alexander (1982). Culture Theory: The Developing Synthesis from Biology. *Human Ecology* 10:383–400.

Hamilton, W. D. (1967). Extraordinary Sex Ratios. *Science* 156:477–488.

Hartung, J. (1976). On Natural Selection and the Inheritance of Wealth. *Current Anthropology* 17:607–622.

Hudson, E. A., and D. W. Jorgenson (1974). *The Long Term Interindustry Transactions Model: A Simulation Model for Energy and Economic Analysis*. Washington, DC: Federal Preparedness Agency, General Services Administration.

Kitcher, P. (1985). *Vaulting Ambition: Sociobiology and the Quest for Human Nature*. Cambridge, MA: MIT Press.

Labov, W. (1972). *Sociolinguistic Patterns*. Philadelphia: University of Pennsylvania Press.

Levins, R. (1966). The Strategy of Model Building in Population Biology. *Amer. Scient.* 54:421–431.

Levins, R. (1968). *Evolution in Changing Environments: Some Theoretical Explorations*. Princeton, NJ: Princeton University Press.

Liebenstein, H. (1976). *Beyond Economic Man: A New Foundation for Microeconomics*. Cambridge, MA: Harvard University Press.

Lumsden, C., and E. O. Wilson (1981). *Genes, Mind and Culture*. Cambridge, MA: Harvard University Press.

May, R. M. (1976). Simple Mathematical Models with Very Complicated Dynamics. *Nature* 261:459—467.

Maynard Smith, J., and N. Warren (1982). Models of Cultural and Genetic Change. *Evolution* 36:620—627.

Pulliam, H. R. (1982). A Social Learning Model of Conflict and Cooperation in Human Societies. *Human Ecology* 10:353—363.

Pulliam, H. R. (1983). On the Theory of Gene-Culture Co-Evolution in a Variable Environment. In *Animal Cognition and Behavior*, R. L. Mellgren, ed. Amsterdam: North-Holland.

Pulliam, H. R., and C. Dunford (1980). *Programmed to Learn: An Essay on the Evolution of Culture*. New York: Columbia University Press.

Quinn, J. F., and A. E. Dunham (1983). On Hypothesis Testing in Ecology and Evolution. *Am. Nat.* 122:602—617.

Rapoport, A. (1967). Escape from Paradox. *Sci. Am.* 217 (July):50—56.

Richerson, P. J., and R. Boyd (1984). Natural Selection and Culture. *BioScience* 34:430—434.

Ruyle, E. E. (1973). Genetic and Cultural Pools: Some Suggestions for a Unified Theory of Biocultural Evolution. *Human Ecology* 1:201—215.

Sahlins, M. (1976). *Culture and Practical Reason*. Chicago: University of Chicago Press.

Smagorinsky, J. (1969). Problems and Promises of Deterministic Extended Range Forecasting. *Bull. Amer. Meterol. Soc.* 50:286—311.

Sober, E. (1984). *The Nature of Selection: Evolutionary Theory in Philosophical Focus*. Cambridge, MA: MIT Press.

Tarde, G. (1903/1962). *The Laws of Imitation*. Gloucester, MA: Peter Smith.

Uyenoyama, M., and M. W. Feldman (1980). Theories of Kin and Group Selection: A Population Genetics Perspective. *Theoret. Pop. Biol.* 17:380—414.

van den Berghe, P. L. (1979). *Human Family Systems*. New York: Elsevier.

van den Berghe, P. L. (1981). *The Ethnic Phenomenon*. New York: Elsevier.

Wade, M. J. (1977). An Experimental Study of Group Selection. *Evolution* 31:134—153.

Watt, K. E. F. (1968). *Ecology and Resource Management*. New York: McGraw-Hill.

Weber, M. (1949). *The Methodology of the Social Sciences*. Glencoe, IL: The Free Press.

Werren, J. H., and H. R. Pulliam (1981). An Intergenerational Model of the Cultural Evolution of Helping Behavior. *Human Ecology* 9:465—483.

Wimsatt, W. C. (1980). Reductionistic Research Strategies and Their Biases in the Units of Selection Controversy. In *Scientific Discovery*, II: *Case Studies*, T. Nickles, ed. Dordrecht: D. Reidel, pp. 213—259.

Wimsatt, W. C. (1981). Units of Selection and the Structure of the Multi-Level Genome. In *PSA-1980*, Vol. 2, R. Giere and P. Asquith, eds. East Lansing, MI: The Philosophy of Science Assn., pp. 121—183.

2

Natural Selection and the Null Hypothesis
John Beatty

[The evolutionary biologist] must first attempt to explain biological phenomena and processes as the product of natural selection. Only after all attempts to do so have failed, is he justified in designating the unexplained residue tentatively as a product of chance. (Mayr, 1983, p. 326)

All of our work begins with tests of the null hypothesis that variation in allele frequencies generated by random genetic drift is the primary cause of molecular evolutionary change. This is the logical point of departure .... In our view, natural selection should be invoked only when the stochastic model is rejected. (Selander, 1985, pp. 87–88)

1 Introduction

Evolution by natural selection is one of many modes of evolutionary change. That much we know for sure. What we do not know for sure is its relative "importance" among the various modes. One hears often enough that its importance is overestimated. How would we ever know?

Consider, for starters, the difficulty of deciding how to distribute our scientific resources in order to find out. Here are two different strategies: either (1) we fund *all* evolutionary biologists to look for evolution by natural selection, or (2) we fund *half* the evolutionary biologists to look for evolution by natural selection, and *half* to look for other modes of evolution. Do you think we would end up attributing the same relative importance to evolution by natural selection in both cases? Here are two more contrasting strategies: either (1) we fund all evolutionary biologists to look *first* for evolution by natural selection, and only to look for other modes of evolution when no evidence for selection can be found, or (2) we fund all evolutionary biologists to look *concurrently* for evolution by natural selection *and* other modes of evolution. Again, do you think we would end up

I am very grateful for the help I received from Peter Abrams, Mark Crimmins, Kendall Corbin, John Dupré, Marcus Feldman, Ronald Giere, Deborah Gordon, Richard Jeffrey, Jonathan Roughgarden, Peter Sloep, and Elliott Sober.

attributing the same relative importance to evolution by natural selection in both cases?

I shall be considering such distributional and scheduling problems particularly as they relate to determining the relative importance of evolution by natural selection versus evolution by "random drift." I shall discuss the differences between these two modes of evolution in detail later. Suffice it for now to say that evolution by random drift is a "matter of chance" in a sense in which evolution by natural selection is not. We attribute the increase in frequency of a particular gene or trait to natural selection when the possessors of that gene or trait, *because of the possession of that gene or trait*, leave a greater average number of offspring than possessors of alternative genes or traits. We attribute the same change to random drift, on the other hand, when the change is simply a *matter of chance*, having nothing to do with the ability of possessors of the gene or trait to survive and reproduce.

Of all the modes of evolution besides evolution by natural selection, evolution by random drift has been accorded the highest priority. If the scientific resources available for determining the importance of evolution by natural selection were to be divided between the search for that mode of evolution and any other mode of evolution in particular, it would be evolution by random drift. Should there be any division of labor in this respect? If so, should the search for selection precede the search for drift? Or should the search for selection go hand in hand with the search for drift? There are interesting suggestions in this regard in the literature of evolutionary biology. I am especially interested in a suggestion, based on a particular conception of hypothesis testing, to the effect that drift hypotheses are the appropriate "null" hypotheses alongside which, and hence *concurrently* with which, selection hypotheses should be investigated. I hope to show that the case for this proposal is, at best, very messy. Of course, that is not to say that the case for any other particular proposal is any neater.

2 *Selectionist Pursuits and the Evolutionary Community*

First, I would like to restate the problem, taking into account two important distinctions. The first is the distinction between the "pursuit" (or the "entertainment") of a hypothesis and the "acceptance" of a hypothesis. The second is the distinction between "individual rationality" and "community rationality." Let us start with the distinction between pursuit and acceptance.

To pursue (or entertain) a hypothesis is to seek evidence for or against it. To accept a hypothesis is to assert its truth on the basis of evidence already gathered in its behalf. Clearly, what makes a hypothesis worthy of pursuit is not the same as what makes it worthy of acceptance. What makes any hypothesis worthy of acceptance (if anything does) is a high degree of evidential support. A hypothesis need not, however, have a high degree of evidential support in order to be worthy of pursuit. Presumably, for instance, it would be rational to pursue a hypothesis in order to determine *just how much* evidential support it has. It is not my concern here to elaborate upon the criteria appropriate for determining whether a hypothesis is worthy of pursuit. I only want to point out that these criteria are different from those for determining whether a hypothesis is worthy of acceptance (see L. Laudan, 1977, and R. Laudan, 1987).

An example of a pursuit that is all too often misconstrued as an accepted hypothesis is "selectionism." Selectionists (when they are being selectionists) are pursuing particular selection hypotheses. They have not necessarily made up their minds about the truth of those particular hypotheses, nor about the general evolutionary importance of natural selection. That is what they are trying to determine. And they are trying to determine it by *pursuing* particular selection hypotheses.[1] One might also try to determine the overall importance of natural selection by pursuing particular drift hypotheses, but one would not be a selectionist in that case. Dobzhansky referred to himself on occasion as an "old drifter."[2] For want of a better term, then, let us distinguish "selectionists" from "drifters" as people who are pursuing particular selection hypotheses versus people who are pursuing particular drift hypotheses.

It is worth noting, with regard to the pursuit "selectionism," that selectionists come in all shapes and sizes. Some selectionists are only part-time selectionists. Others are full-time, pursuing one after another selection hypothesis, so that when one selection hypothesis fails, another is tried in its place. The common term "panselectionist" is apt for the latter sort of selectionist.

The problem of deciding how best to distribute scientific resources in order to determine the evolutionary importance of natural selection is a problem about what hypotheses to pursue, not necessarily about what hypotheses to accept. Should all evolutionary biologists be panselectionists? Should all be selectionists half the time? Should half be selectionists all the time? Should all be selectionists first, and only after that pursue alternatives like drift?

The second distinction that I wanted to raise before getting on with the issues is the distinction between "individual rationality" and "community rationality." Again, my purpose is just to point out that there are differences, without going into those differences in detail. To see that there is a diference, it helps to consider the following. One scientist might be entirely justified in pursuing a particular hypothesis. But there may be alternative hypotheses worth pursuing as well, in which case it might not be reasonable for *all* scientists to pursue that same hypothesis. It might be more reasonable, as far as the scientific community is concerned, for *some* scientists to pursue the alternatives to the hypothesis in question. After all, it might be one of the alternatives that turns out to be true, in which case the community might regret not having "covered more bases" earlier on. And, from a purely methodological point of view, the simultaneous pursuit of alternative hypotheses might improve the standards of assessment otherwise applied to each hypothesis individually (Feyerabend is the usual source for such pluralistic appeals in science—e.g., Feyerabend, 1975; see also Sarkar, 1982).

The problem of deciding how best to distribute scientific resources in order to determine the evolutionary importance of natural selection is, at least as I shall construe it here, as much a matter of community rationality as of individual rationality. I am not only concerned with whether any individual scientist is justified in being a selectionist all of the time (or just some of the time), but also with whether it is reasonable to devote all (or just some) of the efforts of the community of evolutionary biologists to selectionism.

These distinctions lend themselves to different interpretations—some more compelling, some less so—of Gould and Lewontin's influential critique of panselectionism (Gould and Lewontin, 1979). On one interpretation, the charge they are leveling is that too many biologists are *pursuing* selection, without looking for evidence relevant to the occurrence of alternative modes of evolution like random drift. This is very different from the charge that too many biologists *accept* as proven the all-importance of selection. The latter charge would, after all, be difficult to substantiate: not many biologists have been so careless as to assert such a general thesis as proven. The almost exclusively selectionist pursuits of many biologists, on the other hand, are more easily substantiated by their actions.

Furthermore, when Gould and Lewontin complain about the prevalence of selectionist pursuits in evolutionary biology, the target of their complaints may reasonably be interpreted to be the *community* of evolutionary biologists. On this interpretation, *individual* evolutionary biologists are not so much Gould and Lewontin's targets, but are instead the only kinds of instances to which Gould and Lewontin have recourse in order to point out the selectionist excesses of the evolutionary biology community.[3] Gould and Lewontin's point, in this case, is not that it is unreasonable for an individual scientist to be a stalwart selectionist, but that it is unreasonable for the community of evolutionary biologists to put all its eggs into the selectionist basket.

3 The Priority of Natural Selection

Gould and Lewontin's critique of panselectionism is a good point from which to take off. Is such an overwhelming investment in the pursuit of natural selection hypotheses—i.e., as overwhelming an investment as Gould and Lewontin attribute to the present community of evolutionary biologists—a bad way to solve the problem of the overall importance of evolution by natural selection? Should there also be some investment in the search for alternative modes of evolution like random drift? If the answer to the latter question is yes, then *when* should drift hypotheses be pursued—after, before, or concurrently with the pursuit of selection?

I know of no stronger answer to these questions than Mayr's recent answer: "[The evolutionary biologist] must first attempt to explain biological phenomena and processes as the product of natural selection. Only after all attempts to do so have failed, is he justified in designating the unexplained residue tentatively as a product of chance" (Mayr, 1983, p. 326). The reason, according to Mayr, that evolutionary biologists should first pursue selection is that they cannot hope to demonstrate random drift anyway. Selection is at least demonstrable. So we should first try to demonstrate selection, and "only after all attempts to do so have failed" can we "tentatively" invoke drift.

What could have prompted Mayr to take such an extreme position in this regard? A little history might be helpful here. The sort of panselectionist position that Mayr advocates became generally acceptable among evolutionary biologists during the Forties and Fifties. During that time, a number of the most celebrated cases of random drift were more or less successfully reinterpreted in terms of natural selection. Selectionists of that period succeeded in finding evidence of selection where such evidence was previously overlooked. Buoyed by these successes, selectionists of the Fifties and Sixties began to wonder whether any purported case of drift would stand up to rigorous investigation. Invocations of drift seemed to them to be just admissions of ignorance regarding the subtle selective mechanisms actually at work in the cases at issue. Cain, perhaps the most vocal of these panselectionists, put the point as follows: "This is the real basis for every postulate of random variation or (more recently) genetical drift. The investigator finds that he, personally, cannot see any [evidence of selection], and concludes that, therefore, there is none" (Cain, 1951a, p. 424). "This procedure is wrong. They have not proved drift to be acting, but have failed to prove that selection is acting, and invoked drift to cover the failure. An explanation which depends for its success on the failure of the investigator cannot be regarded as satisfactory." (Cain, 1951b, p. 1049; see also Cain, 1964, pp. 47–51).

From our perspective today, when drift hypotheses are somewhat more respectable, it sounds rather incredible to charge an investigator with *failure* for having invoked drift. Just as incredible, from our perspective, is to hear Cain denounce Mayr, whom we now consider one of the great selectionists, as having once been a great failure in this very regard (Cain,

1951a, p. 424). In fact, Mayr had earlier supported the celebrated cases of drift, and was later forced to retract his support in light of the reinterpretations of those cases as cases of evolution by natural selection (Mayr, 1942, p. 75; Mayr 1963, pp. 203–214; see also the discussion of this in Provine, 1986). Thereafter, to Mayr, as to Cain, it became increasingly questionable whether selection could *ever* be ruled out, hence whether drift was *ever* demonstratable.[4]

Past failures at demonstrating drift should not, however, be confused with the in-principle impossibility of its demonstration. This is where Cain and Mayr have gone too far—at least, too far beyond the grounds that they themselves provide for believing that drift cannot be demonstrated.[5] Mayr, for instance, treats this issue very briefly: "Almost any change in the course of evolution might have resulted by chance. Can one ever prove this? Probably never" (Mayr, 1983, p. 326). Cain also went too far beyond the past failures at demonstrating drift in concluding that "those characters or variation patterns that have been described as non-adaptive or random should properly be described as uninvestigated" (Cain, 1951a, p. 424). The consequence of following Mayr's and Cain's advice in this regard would be to abandon the pursuit of drift. Why pursue drift if there is ("probably") no degree of investigation that can demonstrate it?

Perhaps what Mayr and Cain really meant to discourage is not the pursuit of drift, but the pursuit of drift *alone*: drift should be pursued only in conjunction with the pursuit of selection. Since selection can, in one form or another, mimic the expected results of drift, drift should never be pursued independently of an investigation of end-equivalent forms of selection. This sort of approach to drift might have prevented premature invocations of drift such as those celebrated cases on which Mayr himself had to reverse his position.

Mayr and Cain may, then, have just been encouraging the pursuit of drift hypotheses in conjunction with end-equivalent selection hypotheses, and never alone. But what of the pursuit of selection hypotheses alone? Is that another matter altogether? Is that OK?

4 The Priority of Random Drift

One of the most interesting proposals for making the pursuit of a drift hypothesis a necessary concomitant to the pursuit of any selection hypothesis is the suggestion that drift hypotheses play the role of "null hypotheses" in any proper investigation of selection. I shall discuss the nature and importance of null hypotheses shortly. Suffice it for now to say that, if drift hypotheses are to be construed as null hypotheses relative to selection hypotheses, that means that investigators will have to come up with grounds for rejecting drift before they can claim to have established selection. Were this the case, then a selection hypothesis could not be tested without testing, at the same time, an alternative drift hypothesis. This suggestion would, for all practical purposes, rule out the difference between pursuing a selection hypothesis and pursuing a drift hypothesis. It would make pluralists of individual evolutionary biologists (at least those that subscribe to the conception of hypothesis testing in question), and not just of the evolutionary community.

The suggestion that a drift hypothesis is indeed the appropriate null hypothesis in any test of a selection hypothesis is a suggestion that has been "in the air" longer than it has been in print, and is still more frequently voiced than written. It is not uncommon to hear claims to the effect that "I don't know whether random drift is very important, but it's sure a good null hypothesis." Leading drifters like Kimura and Nei now refer to drift hypotheses as null hypotheses relative to selection hypotheses (e.g., Kimura, 1983, p. 272; Nei, 1983, p. 170; Nei and Graur, 1984).[6] Selander strongly discourages the pursuit of selection hypotheses independently of a null, drift hypothesis (Selander, 1985, pp. 87–88):

> All our work begins with tests of the null hypothesis that variation in allele frequencies generated by random genetic drift is the primary cause of molecular evolutionary change. This is the logical point of departure, because alleles at all loci are potentially subject to the action of genetic drift in equal degree. The advantage of this basically demographic approach over those based on more complex models of population structure in which natural selection is the predominant factor is that the stochastic model makes a number of specific, quantitative predictions, whereas more complex models generate no predictions that cannot be explained away if expectations are not met by the data. In our view, natural selection should be invoked only when the stochastic model is rejected. In adopting this approach, we do not blindly subscribe to the neutral theory of protein polymorphism or to recent modifications of it—the theory of effectively neutral mutations. Nor do we in any way exclude natural selection as a factor determining population structure and mediating evolutionary change at the molecular level. There is no need for an either/or attitude. It is simply that we prefer to begin with the simplest model, determining, as a baseline for further analysis and interpretation, the degree to which existing geographic (and, in the case of bacteria, clonal) structure matches expectations of a stochastic model. Deviations from this model are a source of new hypotheses for further analysis.

In passing, it is worth noting that a somewhat similar line of reasoning has been employed in the ecological literature in order to discourage the exclusive pursuit of interspecific competition accounts of community structure. Simberloff, Connor, Strong, and others who are concerned about the overemphasis on competition in ecology have suggested construing random-process hypotheses as the most appropriate null hypotheses in investigations of community structure, and have argued further that this consideration counts against the pursuit of competition hypotheses alone (e.g., Strong et al., 1979, and Connor and Simberloff, 1979). There are some difficulties with this line of reasoning, as has been pointed out by Roughgarden and others (see, e.g., Roughgarden, 1983).[7] I shall not rehearse Roughgarden's and the others' criticisms here. They do not exactly apply to the evolutionary issue in question. But one of Roughgarden's main concerns is the same as mine: namely, the concern that the logic of hypothesis testing in question not be misinterpreted as providing simple answers to difficult problems about the priority of scientific pursuits.

Is a random drift hypothesis really the obvious choice for a null hypothesis in any test of a selection hypothesis? Drift hypotheses do indeed bear a resemblance to the standard sort of null hypothesis discussed in the literature of hypothesis testing. The most evident similarity, and the one, I think, that most accounts for the identification of drift hypotheses as the obvious null hypotheses, is that both sorts of hypotheses are associated with assumptions about "sampling error." There are important differences, though, that count against any straightforward identification of drift hypotheses with the standard sort of null hypothesis. Let us consider the apparent similarities between null hypotheses and drift hypotheses, though, before considering their differences in detail.

'Null hypothesis' literally means "hypothesis that there is no difference." More precisely, the standard sort of null hypothesis states that there is no difference between two populations under investigation (generally a "test" population and a "control" population) with respect to some property of interest. For instance, the standard null hypothesis in a test of the carcinogenic effects of smoking among males is that the incidence of cancer among males who smoke is no different from the incidence of cancer among males who do not smoke.[8]

To test the null hypothesis, one "indiscriminately" samples each of the populations under investigation (indiscriminately, that is, with respect to any physical differences between members of each population) and compares these sample populations. Although the standard sort of null hypothesis rules out differences between the populations under investigation, it does not rule out differences between the sample populations. Even if there is no difference between the populations under investigation, some degree of difference between the sample populations is expected as a result of chance alone, i.e., entirely as a result of "sampling error." A null hypothesis is associated with probability distributions of sample differences—one probability distribution for each combination of sample sizes.

These distributions specify the probabilities of differences between sample populations that would result from sampling error alone.

On the conception of hypothesis testing at issue here, null hypotheses play a very special role in the testing of "alternative" hypotheses. The standard sort of alternative hypothesis states that there *is* a difference between the two populations under investigation (the test population and the control population) with respect to the property of interest, the reason for the difference having to do with some other respects in which the test and control populations differ. So, for instance, the standard sort of alternative hypothesis in a test of the carcinogenic effects of smoking among males is that the incidence of cancer among males who smoke is different from the incidence of cancer among males who do not smoke, the difference having to do with smoking.

To test the alternative hypothesis, one indiscriminately samples each of the populations under investigation and compares the samples. Clearly, not just any magnitude of difference between the samples with respect to the property of interest can be considered strong support for the alternative hypothesis. As already noted, the null hypothesis is compatible with a range of differences between the sample populations. Any differences within this range are attributed by the null hypothesis to chance. Only large enough differences—differences very unlikely to be the result of sampling error alone—count strongly in favor of the alternative hypothesis. The null hypothesis must thus be rejected as unlikely before the alternative hypothesis can be established. Null hypotheses clearly play an important role in this scheme of hypothesis testing. Supposedly, drift hypotheses play just as important a role in the testing of selection hypotheses.

Now let us consider how the standard sort of null hypothesis compares to drift hypotheses, and how the relation between the standard null hypothesis and the standard alternative hypothesis compares to the relation between a drift hypothesis and a selection hypothesis.

Random drift is a biological sort of sampling error. Since the basis for the identification of drift hypotheses with the standard sort of null hypothesis seems to be that they are both associated with assumptions about sampling errors, it is perhaps worth considering in some detail what is meant by "sampling error" in each case. Sampling error as usually construed, and as understood in the context of discussions of the standard sort of null hypothesis, has its source in the intentional indiscriminacy practiced by the person who takes samples from the populations under investigation. The frequency of a property of interest within a sample population taken by an indiscriminate sampler is likely to differ from the frequency of that property within the sampled population precisely because the indiscriminate sampler did not *try* to get a representative sample.

There are primarily two sources of sampling error involved in random drift: indiscriminate parent sampling and indiscriminate gamete sampling. By "parent sampling," I mean *the process of determining which organisms of one generation will be parents of the next, and how many offspring each parent will have.* This sort of sampling might be "indiscriminate" in the sense that any physical differences between the organisms of one generation might be irrelevant to differences in their offspring contributions. A forest fire, for instance, might so sample parents—killing some, sparing some—without regard to physical differences between them. Such sampling is indiscriminate in the same sense in which sampling for the purpose of hypothesis testing is indiscriminate—that is, any physical differences between the members of the population sampled are irrelevant to whether or not they are sampled.

If a biological population is so maintained at a particular finite size—i.e., by sampling parents indiscriminately—its gene and genotype frequencies will "drift" from generation to generation. The reason is that the genotype frequencies of the parents, weighted according to their reproductive success, may by chance not be representative of the genotype frequencies of the parents' generation. There is no form of discrimination to ensure that the genotype frequencies *are* representative. To the extent that a parent sample is unrepresentative, and to the extent that the gene and genotype frequencies of the next generation reflect the appropriately weighted gene and genotype frequencies of their parents, the next generation's gene and genotype frequencies may diverge from those of the previous generation —i.e., an evolutionary change may occur.

Indiscriminate sampling in nature might also take the form of indiscriminate gamete sampling. By "gamete sampling," I mean *the process of determining which of the two genetically different types of gametes produced by a heterozygotic parent is actually contributed to each of its offspring.* This sort of sampling might be indiscriminate in the sense that any physical difference between the two types of gametes produced by a heterozygote might be irrelevant to whether one or the other is actually contributed to any particular offspring. According to Mendel's law, there is no physical basis for a bias in the proportion of the two genetically different types of gametes *produced* by a heterozygote. What we are now considering is that there is also no physical basis for a bias in the proportions of gametes that are actually *contributed* to a heterozygote's offspring.

If a biological population is so maintained at a particular finite size—i.e., by sampling the gametes of heterozygotes indiscriminately—the gene and genotype frequencies of the population will drift from generation to generation. For the gene frequencies of the gametes that are contributed to a generation of offspring may by chance not be representative of the gene frequencies of the parents' generation. Again, there is no form of discrimination to ensure that they *are* representative. Thus, indiscriminate gamete sampling, either together with indiscriminate parent sampling or alone, can result in an evolutionary change, a so-called "random drift" of gene and genotype frequencies.

Like drift, selection is also a sampling process. Unlike drift, however, it is a *discriminate* form of sampling. For instance, we attribute the increase in frequency of a particular gene or trait to natural selection when the possessors of that gene or trait, *because of the possession of that gene or trait,* leave a greater average number of offspring than possessors of alternative genes or traits.[9]

Investigators may invoke random drift and/or natural selection to explain differences in gene or trait frequencies between different generations of the same population or species (as in figure 2.1a), or to explain differences in gene or trait frequencies between related populations or species (as in figure 2.1b).

Inasmuch as drift hypotheses explain differences between biological populations, or differences between generations of the same population, in terms of some sort of sampling error, they may look like the usual sort of null hypothesis. The difference is, however, apparent enough. One way of expressing the difference is to point out that investigators invoke random drift hypotheses in order to *account for differences* between the groups under investigation, while investigators invoke the standard null hypothesis in order to *deny differences* between the groups under investigation.

Generation 1

Generation 2

(a)

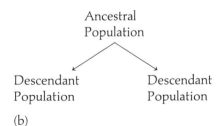

Ancestral
Population

Descendant   Descendant
Population   Population

(b)

Figure 2.1
(a) Evolutionary change due to discriminate and/or indiscriminate sampling. (b) Difference in evolutionary outcomes due to discriminate and/or indiscriminate sampling.

That is, according to the random drift hypothesis, the groups under investigation (either the related populations or the different generations of one population) differ as a result of evolutionary changes—evolutionary changes due to biological sampling error. According to the standard null hypothesis, on the other hand, there is no real difference between the groups under investigation (i.e., the test and control groups). Apparent evidence of a difference—in the form of a difference between samples of those groups—is *explained away* by defenders of the null hypothesis as being due to sampling error.

In this respect, drift hypotheses, together with selection hypotheses, are more like the standard sort of alternative hypothesis than the standard sort of null hypothesis. The standard sort of alternative hypothesis, just like a drift hypothesis, and just like many selection hypotheses, assumes that there are *real* differences between the populations under investigation, differences that it seeks to explain.

Actually, to turn the matter on its head, there are some situations for which *no differences* between the populations under investigation would be good evidence for *selection*, while *differences* would be better evidence for *drift*. If, for instance, the frequencies of the various alleles at one locus did not differ significantly among geographically isolated populations of a species, then one might infer that there are identical selection pressures operating on each of the various populations. On the basis of such strong similarities between the populations, one might reject the hypothesis that the alternative alleles are being indiscriminately sampled from generation to generation in each population. For instance, Ayala (1974) presented the data in table 2.1 in support of the hypothesis that selection, not drift, maintained the allele frequencies at the loci in question.

To repeat the point being made, while the standard sort of null hypothesis assumes no difference between the populations under investigation, drift hypotheses assume real evolutionary differences. The "deeper" distinction that underlies this one is that drift hypotheses are themselves sampling hypotheses, whereas null hypotheses are not. At least one of the populations described by a drift hypothesis is a sample population, in the biological sense of "sample" (refer back to figure 2.1). Null hypotheses are about test and control groups. They can be brought to bear upon similarities or differences between test and control *samples* only in conjunction with hypotheses about how the samples were taken. So, for instance, one might argue that smoking does not cause cancer on the basis of an investigation that shows that there is only a very small difference in frequency of cancer between sampled smokers and sampled nonsmokers. But that argument relies for its strength on the further assumption that the samples were taken randomly (e.g., that the healthiest smokers were not preferentially chosen for purposes of the investigation). The null hypothesis in-

Table 2.1

Allele frequency variation at the *Est-7* locus in 8 natural populations of *Drosophila tropicalis*

Locality	Genomes sampled	Allele frequencies				
		96	98	100	102	105
Catatumbo	50	0.04	0.08	0.48	0.32	0.04
Barinitas	100	0.02	0.14	0.64	0.18	0.02
Caripito	110	0.00	0.11	0.47	0.35	0.05
Tucupita	44	0.05	0.09	0.77	0.09	0.00
Santiago	75	0.00	0.15	0.43	0.35	0.05
Santo Domingo	90	0.01	0.11	0.46	0.30	0.09
Mayaguez	57	0.02	0.16	0.51	0.28	0.04
Barranquitas	32	0.00	0.06	0.34	0.41	0.16

Allele frequency variation at the *Ald-1* locus in 8 natural populations of *Drosophila tropicalis*

Locality	Genomes sampled	Allele frequencies		
		98	100	102
Catatumbo	50	0.00	0.90	0.10
Barinitas	100	0.00	0.76	0.24
Caripito	98	0.01	0.84	0.15
Tucupita	24	0.00	0.58	0.42
Santiago	90	0.01	0.49	0.48
Santo Domingo	116	0.01	0.76	0.22
Mayaguez	64	0.00	0.77	0.22
Barranquitas	46	0.02	0.87	0.11

Allele frequency variation at the *Adk-1* locus in 8 natural populations of *Drosophila tropicalis*

Locality	Genomes sampled	Allele frequencies		
		100	106	112
Catatumbo	42	0.52	0.36	0.12
Barinitas	100	0.38	0.52	0.10
Caripito	56	0.48	0.46	0.04
Tucupita	24	0.33	0.54	0.08
Santiago	90	0.30	0.59	0.11
Santo Domingo	104	0.25	0.67	0.07
Mayaguez	64	0.52	0.42	0.06
Barranquitas	52	0.35	0.58	0.06

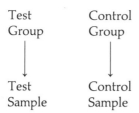

| Test | Control |
| Group | Group |

Figure 2.2
The null hypothesis concerns the similarities between the test and control groups. The sample hypothesis concerns the procedure for taking the test and control samples.

voked in the argument is distinct from the sampling hypothesis invoked (figure 2.2). Of these two sorts of hypotheses, drift hypotheses are more like sampling hypotheses than the null hypothesis.

One might argue that there is a standard null hypothesis still lurking undiscovered in this discussion of drift. It involves an assumption implicit in invocations of the sort of biological sampling error that we have been discussing. That is (or so the argument goes), gene or trait frequencies drift randomly when the alternative genes or traits in question are selectively "neutral," in the sense of selectively equivalent. When alternative genes or traits are equal in their selective values, there can be no selective discrimination among them, which means that they must be indiscriminately or randomly sampled from generation to generation, giving rise to a random drift in their frequencies. The standard null hypothesis involved in invocations of drift is thus that there is *no difference* between the alternative genes or traits in question as far as their selective advantages or disadvantages are concerned.

This suggestion is, however, unhelpful. The reason has to do with the fact that in small enough populations, the frequencies of even selectively nonequivalent genes or traits can change considerably by random drift (e.g., as a result of indiscriminate gamete sampling—see the discussion of this process above). Taking this into account, many biologists who profess to pursue neutral gene hypotheses (e.g., Kimura, 1983, pp. 29–49) suggest broadening the meaning of 'neutral' from strict selective neutrality to "effective" selective neutrality. By "effectively neutral" genes, they mean genes that behave evolutionarily just like strictly neutral genes—i.e., their frequencies drift randomly to the same extent as would the frequencies of strictly neutral genes.[10] As Nei and Graur note, "In population genetics . . . , the definition of neutrality of a gene depends on whether the behavior of the gene in a population is dictated by random drift or not" (Nei and Graur, 1984, p. 91).

Technically, effectively neutral genes are those whose relative selective advantage or disadvantage is small in comparison with the reciprocal of the effective population size (where effective population size is the number of parental organisms in the population). That is, a gene is effectively neutral when $s \ll 1/N_e$ (where s is the coefficient of selection and N_e is the effective population size). So there can be a selective difference in magnitude as great or greater than 10 between two alleles, and yet, if the population in question is very small, the frequencies of those alleles will drift just as if the magnitude of the selective difference was 0.0.

Inasmuch as neutrality accounts of evolutionary change, as they are understood by many of those most interested in pursuing them, are really just drift accounts, and inasmuch as they do not deny selective differences after all, they are really not like the standard null hypothesis.

The case for construing drift hypotheses as examples of the standard null hypothesis does not look good. I said earlier, though, that I thought the case was messy, not that it was entirely without merit. All I have argued so far is that drift hypotheses (and neutral gene hypotheses) are not *themselves* formally identical to the standard null hypothesis. There are, however, some *predictions* based on drift hypotheses that do bear a formal resemblance to standard null hypotheses. One might, for instance, predict that if evolution with respect to a particular protein has been primarily a matter of random drift, then the rate of evolution of that protein should be the *same* from species to species (see, e.g., Fitch, 1976). After all, why *should* the relevant allele frequencies change faster in one species than another in this case? Or one might predict that if evolution with respect to a number of loci of one species has been in each case primarily a matter of random drift, then the variance in allele frequencies between the populations of that species should be the *same* for each of those loci (see, e.g., Cavalli-Sforza, 1966).[11] After all, why *should* populations differ more with respect to one such locus than another?

These predictions clearly resemble no-difference null hypotheses. That is in part because I have stated them oversimplistically. Just as the random drift of allele frequencies from generation to generation in one population is associated with a *probability distribution* of outcomes (as one would expect from a random sampling process), so too the evolution by random drift of a particular protein in different populations or species leads to a probability distribution of evolutionary rates, and so too evolution by random drift at a number of different loci of one species leads to a probability distribution of between-population variances per locus. Inasmuch as evolution by random drift is a stochastic process, one can only talk about the probabilities of its outcomes. To posit the "same" outcome of random drift in different species, or at different loci, or in different generations, etc., is, then, just a shorthand way (and a misleading way at that) of positing the same *probability* of a particular outcome, or the same probability distribution of outcomes.

That these predictions posit no difference between probability distributions of evolutionary outcomes (rather than just no difference between outcomes) does not render them any less like the standard null hypothesis. So some predictions based on drift hypotheses are indeed formally like null hypotheses. But not all predictions of drift hypotheses resemble the standard null hypothesis. For instance, one might predict that if changes in gene frequencies at a particular locus of a species are primarily a matter of drift, then the variance with respect to that locus among small subgroups of the species should be larger than the variance among large subgroups, the sampling error in the larger "sample" groups being smaller (see, e.g., Cavalli-Sforza, 1966).

So drift hypotheses are not, themselves, instances of the standard null hypothesis, and while some predictions based on drift hypotheses have the form of the standard null hypothesis, some do not. Thus, even the best case for construing drift hypotheses as instances of the standard null hypothesis is limited.

5 Priority Problems of a Different Sort

Of course, the *standard* sort of null hypothesis is not the only *legitimate* sort of null hypothesis. The *function* of a null hypothesis can be served by hypotheses that are not *literally* "null" hypotheses. Functionally speaking, the job of the null hypothesis—as that job was discussed above—can be accomplished by any hypothesis formulated precisely enough to be associated with a probability distribution of sample differences for each combination of sample sizes.[12] Hypotheses that claim specific real differences between the populations under investigation can accomplish this task as well as hypotheses that claim no difference. So although drift hypotheses are not identical to the standard sort of null hypothesis, they may serve as null hypotheses in tests of selection hypotheses anyway.

But now a different problem arises. Suppose we are testing a selection hypothesis against a null drift hypothesis, and suppose we have drawn sample populations of some particular size. We can then say what differences between the sample populations are unlikely on our null hypothesis, and what differences are likely. If the actual differences between the sample populations are very unlikely, we can consider those differences as strong negative evidence against the null drift hypothesis, and, if selection is the only plausible alternative to drift, as strong positive evidence in favor of the occurrence of selection. But how likely must the differences be in order to be considered strong positive evidence for the null drift hypothesis? In order to determine that, the selection hypothesis being tested must be formulated precisely enough to have definite probability distributions of test outcomes associated with it. One must be able to compare the probability distributions associated with the selection hypothesis with the probability distributions associated with the null drift hypothesis. The reason for this is that a very likely test outcome on the null hypothesis may also be a very likely (and perhaps even more likely) test outcome on the selection hypothesis. The sort of difference that supports the null drift hypothesis over the selection hypothesis is one that is not only likely given the drift hypothesis, but also *less likely* (and better yet, *unlikely*) given the selection hypothesis.[13]

To determine this, one needs to formulate the selection hypothesis precisely enough so that it will have associated with it specific probability distributions of test outcomes. But what if it is not possible or practical to formulate selection hypotheses so precisely that such probability distributions follow from them? "Broad" selection hypotheses, which state no more than that selection is responsible for differences in frequencies of a gene or trait, do not seem specific enough to be associated with definite probability distributions.

There is a real problem here. There would, in this case (i.e., the case where a drift hypothesis is being tested alongside a broad selection hypothesis that is associated with no definite probability distributions of test outcomes), be a fundamental asymmetry plaguing the pursuit of selection and drift hypotheses. With a sufficiently precise null drift hypothesis, we would be able to decide when that hypothesis was very negatively supported by the evidence, and also when the alternative broad selection hypothesis was very positively supported. But with an insufficiently precise selection hypothesis, we would not be able to decide when the null drift hypothesis was strongly supported. We might then say that we were pursuing drift and selection hypotheses concurrently, but it would be less misleading to say that we were looking for evidence *against* drift hypotheses at the same time that we were looking for evidence *for* selection hypotheses.

Critics of panselectionism would, I think, like to see drift hypotheses pursued concurrently with selection hypotheses. But most likely not just any sort of joint pursuit will satisfy them. Critics of the selectionist excesses of the evolutionary community want their colleagues to pay attention to drift as well as selection. But they do not want them to divide their attention between *negative* cases of drift and *positive* cases of selection!

One might propose solving this problem by testing drift hypotheses against very specific selection hypotheses—selection hypotheses so specific with respect to selection intensities, and with respect to the genetics of the trait in question, etc., that they are associated with specific probability distributions of test outcomes. But this proposal would not solve the problem after all. For even if one could specify a selection hypothesis so precisely that it could be associated with a definite probability distribution of test outcomes, and even if its distribution was sufficiently distinct from the distribution associated with the drift hypothesis, and even if the actual outcome fell well within the range of outcomes expected on the basis of the drift hypothesis and well outside the range expected on the basis of the selection hypothesis, it might still be possible to come up with another, equally plausible selection hypothesis whose associated distribution of outcomes had sufficient overlap with the drift hypothesis that the outcome in question was equally likely on both hypotheses. The point is that a drift hypothesis may never receive strong overall confirmation in a test along-side any one *particular* selection hypothesis, because there may always be an alternative selection hypothesis that gives the drift hypothesis a better run for its money. Strong support for a drift hypothesis only comes when the actual evolutionary outcome is unlikely on *any* plausible selection hypothesis, i.e., on a very broad selection hypothesis. But, as just discussed, such broad selection hypotheses are going to be difficult to state in such a way as to determine what probability distributions of test outcomes to associate with them. And without knowledge of those distributions, we do not know what outcomes are unlikely on those hypotheses.

Of course, by similar reasoning, no *particular* selection hypothesis will receive strong support in a test alongside a drift hypothesis. An outcome of a test between a drift hypothesis and a particular selection hypothesis may be more likely on the selection hypothesis than on the drift hypothesis, but the outcome may be even likelier on other particular selection hypotheses.

When it comes to testing a *particular* selection hypothesis, there is no more reason, on the conception of hypothesis testing in question here, to test it against a drift hypothesis than against another particular selection hypothesis, as long as the selection hypothesis playing the part of the null hypothesis has specific probability distributions of test outcomes associated with it. A particular selection hypothesis can only be shown to be improbable, never highly probable, in a test against a null drift hypothesis. The same is true of any test of that hypothesis against a null selection hypothesis. The outcome of a test of a particular null selection hypothesis versus a particular alternative selection hypothesis may be more likely on the latter than on the former hypothesis. But it may be likelier still on innumerable other particular selection hypotheses. The point here is not just that particular selection hypotheses are difficult to prove on the conception of hypothesis testing in question, but that, as far as that conception of hypothesis testing is concerned, there is no more reason to test a particular selection hypothesis against a drift hypothesis than to test it against another particular selection hypothesis.[14] And that gets us to the conclusion.

6 Conclusion

Gould and Lewontin strongly criticize panselectionists for their stubborn pursuit of one after another selectionist account of nature. The basic dictum of panselectionism, they complain, is (Gould and Lewontin, 1979, p. 586),

> If one adaptive argument fails, try another. Zig-zag commissures of clams and brachiopods, once widely regarded as devices for strengthening the shell, become sieves for restricting particles above a given size .... A suite of external structures (horns, antlers, tusks) once viewed as weapons against predators, become symbols of intraspecific competition among males .... The eskimo face, once depicted as 'cold engineered'..., becomes an adaptation to generate and withstand large masticatory forces .... We do not attack these newer interpretations; they may all be right. We do wonder, though, whether the failure of one adaptive explanation should always simply inspire a search for another of the same general form, rather than a consideration of alternatives to the proposition that each part is 'for' some specific purpose [i.e., the product of natural selection].

Mayr retorts, "Gould and Lewontin ridicule the research strategy: 'If one adaptive argument fails, try another one.' Yet the strategy to try another hypothesis when the first fails is a traditional methodology in all branches of science" (Mayr, 1983, p. 326). As Mayr seems quite aware, within the context of the logic of hypothesis testing, two different selection hypotheses are just as much alternatives with respect to each other as are a selection hypothesis and a drift hypothesis. Within the context of the logic of hypothesis testing *alone*, then, there is no more reason for dividing the resources of the evolutionary community between the pursuit of selection hypotheses and drift hypotheses than for dividing those resources completely among different selectionist pursuits. For instance, why not emphasize the difference between selection for homozygous traits and selection for heterozygous traits, and make *these* the alternatives of most concern?[15] Our problem would then be to divide up the resources of the evolutionary community between the pursuit of accounts based on selection for homozygotes and the pursuit of accounts based on selection for heterozygotes.

How we distribute the resources of the evolutionary community is no straightforward matter of the logic of hypothesis testing. It has to do with the questions we pose for ourselves. It is only upon posing for ourselves the question of the overall relative importance of natural selection versus random drift, without any concern for the particulars of the various occurrences of selection, that the choice with regard to any particular evolutionary outcome becomes *selection versus drift*. There would be no point in making *that* the choice if we were trying to determine the particulars of each and every evolutionary change (or if, as above, we were most interested in the relative importances of selection for homozygotes versus selection for heterozygotes).

If the relative overall importance of selection versus drift *is* really an issue we want to resolve, then we really *must* give serious thought to distributing the resources of the evolutionary community between the pursuit of selection and drift hypotheses. Again, the logic of hypothesis testing alone will not help us here. Other sorts of considerations will be relevant. Those other considerations are well worth our thought. For the division of labor we settle on will most certainly bias the answer we get.[16]

Notes

1. In their selectionist account of insect mating strategies, Thornhill and Alcock (1983) are careful to distinguish between selectionism as a "working" hypothesis and selectionism as an accepted hypothesis. They prefer the former interpretation. The distinction between "working" hypothesis and "accepted" hypothesis is another way of marking the distinction between what I have called the "pursuit" (or "entertainment") of an hypothesis and its acceptance.

2. Dobzhansky to J. L. King, March 27, 1973. Dobzhansky's correspondence and papers are at the American Philosophical Society Library in Philadelphia.

3. For instance, Lewontin (1972, p. 182) elsewhere applauds the stalwart selectionism of specific individuals like Phillip Sheppard.

4. For more detailed discussions of this episode in the history of evolutionary biology, see Gould (1980, 1982, 1983), Provine (1983, 1986), and Beatty (1986, 1987).

5. I shall return to this issue later.

6. Kimura and Nei actually refer to "neutral mutation" hypotheses as null hypotheses. The similarities between neutral mutation hypotheses and drift hypotheses will be discussed later in the text.

7. See also Quinn and Dunham (1983), Case and Sidell (1983), Colwell and Winkler (1984), Gilpin and Diamond (1984), and Sloep (1986). See, in response to some of the early criticisms, Simberloff (1983) and Strong (1983).

8. When I say that the "standard" sort of null hypothesis has a particular form, I mean, for instance, that textbooks in statistics and experimental design most always illustrate the notion of null hypothesis with hypotheses of this form. Fisher invoked hypotheses of this form in introducing the notion of null hypothesis in his groundbreaking text, *The Design of Experiments* (Fisher, 1937, pp. 18–19, and Fisher, 1971, pp. 15–16). And he has been followed in this respect by textbook writers since (e.g., Snedecor and Cochran, 1980, pp. 11–12; Wilson, 1952, p. 59; Box et al., 1978, pp. 21–22, 83).

   Although the term "null" hypothesis indeed suggests hypotheses of this form, there are actually deeper criteria for what constitutes a null hypothesis. These criteria are generally satisfied by the "no-difference" form of hypothesis, but are satisfied by other forms of hypotheses as well. So, for instance, while Fisher did indeed label null hypotheses "null," he also proposed criteria for qualifying as a null hypothesis that had nothing to do with the no-difference criterion (see note 13).

   Nonetheless, I strongly suspect that the notion of null hypotheses as no-difference hypotheses, reinforced by the terminology "null" hypothesis, and by the standard form of null hypotheses encountered in the literature, has played a considerable (though ultimately misleading) role in the conception of drift hypotheses as null hypotheses. And I want to make that role clear from the beginning. Later in the paper, I consider the consequences of relaxing the no-difference criterion.

9. For more detailed discussions of the differences between evolution by natural selection and random drift, see Beatty (1984), Sober (1985), and Hodge (1987).

10. For example, effectively neutral genes have the same probabilities of fixation as strictly neutral genes (see Nei, 1975, pp. 97–98).

11. This particular test design was refined considerably by Lewontin and Krakauer (1973).

12. Fisher already made this point in 1935 (see Fisher, 1937, pp. 19, 198–199, and Fisher, 1971, pp. 16, 187). This criterion renders the terminology "null" hypothesis rather misleading. Some writers thus avoid the term, e.g., Neyman (1950, p. 259 and note). See Sokal and Rohlf (1969, p. 155) for a valiant attempt to reconstrue the meaning of "null" so as to reduce the tension between the old term and the new criterion.

13. The possibility of testing one selection hypothesis against another "null" selection hypothesis is explored in detail by Endler (1986, see especially pp. 86–93).

14. Mark Crimmins pointed out to me a hidden assumption lurking in my analysis. That is, I am assuming here (at least, I *should* be assuming here) that the plausibilities (Bayesian prior probabilities) of the null and alternative hypotheses are equal. For reasons that Bayes's theorem (appropriately interpreted) makes clear, an outcome that is very likely on the alternative hypothesis and very unlikely on the null will not lend much overall support to the alternative if the alternative is initially very implausible. Kitcher, in his contribution to this volume, discusses the role of plausibility considerations in assessing selection hypotheses.

15. In the late Fifties and Sixties, when the overarching importance of natural selection was generally assumed, the only issue remaining with regard to the relative importances of the various modes of evolution had to do with the relative importances of the various kinds of selection. For instance, the so-called "balance" school championed the importance of selection in favor of heterozygotes. The so-called "classical" school championed the importance of selection in favor of homozygous pairings of optimal alleles. For a detailed discussion of the classical/balance controversy, see Lewontin (1974).

16. It is worth pointing out in passing (although this is really rather scandalous since it deserves much more than passing notice) that all this talk about null drift hypotheses and alternative selection hypotheses is beside the point for many evolutionists. For many, the issue of the relative importance of drift vs. selection is not a matter of whether selection *or* drift occurs more frequently. Many assume that evolutionary changes are almost always matters of drift *and* selection (and not just negligibly one or the other). The issue for these evolutionists is the relative magnitudes of the concurrent influences of selection and drift. Neither the null, pure drift hypothesis, nor any pure selection hypothesis is among the alternatives pursued by them. Wright is preeminent among the evolutionary biologists who have discouraged the either/or attitude to selection versus drift (see, e.g., Wright, 1976, pp. 443–473). Sober, in his contribution to this volume, discusses the conceptual difficulties of assessing the relative importances of drift and selection in evolutionary changes that involve both (see also Beatty, 1984, pp. 192–196).

References

Ayala, F. J. (1974). Biological Evolution: Natural Selection or Random Walk? *American Scientist* 62 : 692–701.

Beatty, J. (1984). Chance and Natural Selection. *Philosophy of Science* 51 : 183–211.

Beatty, J. (1986). Pluralism and Panselectionism. In P. Kitcher and P. Asquith (eds.), *PSA 1984*, Proceedings of the 1984 Meetings of the Philosophy of Science Association, Volume 1. East Lansing, Michigan: Philosophy of Science Association.

Beatty, J. (1987). Dobzhansky and Drift: Facts, Values, and Chance in Evolutionary Biology. In L. Krüger (ed.), *The Probabilistic Revolution*. Cambridge: MIT Press (Bradford Books).

Box, G. E. P., et al. (1978). *Statistics for Experimenters*. New York: Wiley.

Cain, A. J. (1951a). So-Called Non-Adaptive or Neutral Characters in Evolution. *Nature* 168:424.

Cain, A. J. (1951b). Non-Adaptive or Neutral Characters in Evolution. *Nature* 168:1049.

Cain, A. J. (1964). The Perfection of Animals. *Perspectives in Biology* 3:36–63.

Case, T. J., and R. Sidell (1983). Pattern and Chance in the Structure of Model and Natural Communities. *Evolution* 37:832–849.

Cavalli-Sforza, L. L. (1966). Population Structure and Human Evolution. *Proceedings of the Royal Society* B164:362–379.

Colwell, R. K., and D. W. Winkler (1984). A Null Model for Null Models in Biogeography. In D. R. Strong et al. (eds.), *Ecological Communities: Conceptual Issues and the Evidence*. Princeton: Princeton University Press.

Endler, J. A. (1986). *Natural Selection in the Wild*. Princeton: Princeton University Press.

Feyerabend, P. (1975). *Against Method*. London: NLB.

Fisher, R. A. (1937). *The Design of Experiments* (2nd ed.; 1st ed. 1935). Edinburgh: Oliver and Boyd.

Fisher, R. A. (1971). *The Design of Experiments* (6th ed.; 1st ed. 1935). Edinburgh: Oliver and Boyd.

Fitch, W. M. (1976). Molecular Evolutionary Clocks. In F. J. Ayala (ed.), *Molecular Evolution*. Sunderland, Massachusetts: Sinauer.

Gilpin, M. E., and J. M. Diamond (1984). Are Species Coocurrences on Islands Nonrandom, and Are Null Hypotheses Useful in Ecology? in D. R. Strong et al. (eds.), *Ecological Communities: Conceptual Issues and the Evidence*. Princeton: Princeton University Press.

Gould, S. J. (1980). G. G. Simpson, Paleontology, and the Modern Synthesis. In E. Mayr and W. B. Provine (eds.), *The Evolutionary Synthesis*. Cambridge: Harvard University Press.

Gould, S. J. (1982). Introduction. In Columbia Classics in Evolution Series reprint of the first edition of T. Dobzhansky's *Genetics and the Origin of Species* (1937). New York: Columbia University Press.

Gould, S. J. (1983). The Hardening of the Synthesis. In M. Grene (ed.), *Dimensions of Darwinism*. Cambridge: University of Cambridge Press.

Gould, S. J., and R. C. Lewontin (1979). The Spandrels of San Marco and the Panglossian Paradigm: A Critique of the Adaptationist Programme. *Proceedings of the Royal Society* B205:591–598.

Hodge, M. J. S. (1987). Natural Selection as a Causal, Empirical, and Probabilistic Theory. In L. Krüger (ed.), *The Probabilistic Revolution*. Cambridge: MIT Press (Bradford Books).

Kimura, M. (1983). *The Neutral Theory of Molecular Evolution*. Cambridge: Cambridge University Press.

Kitcher, P. (1987). Why Not the Best? In J. Dupré (ed.), *The Latest on the Best: Essays on Evolution and Optimality*. Cambridge: MIT Press (Bradford Books).

Laudan, L. (1977). *Progress and Its Problems*. Berkeley: University of California Press.

Laudan, R. (1987). The Rationality of Entertainment and Pursuit. In M. Pera and J. Pitt (eds.), *Modes of Progress: Theories and Episodes of Scientific Rationality*. Dordrecht: Reidel.

Lewontin, R. C. (1972). Testing the Theory of Natural Selection. *Nature* 237:181–182.

Lewontin, R. C., and J. Krakauer (1973). Distribution of Gene Frequency as a Test of the Theory of Selective Neutrality of Polymorphisms. *Genetics* 74:175–195.

Mayr, E. (1942). *Systematics and the Origin of Species*. New York: Columbia University Press.

Mayr, E. (1963). *Animal Species and Evolution.* Cambridge: Harvard University Press.

Mayr, E. (1983). How to Carry Out the Adaptationist Program. *American Naturalist* 121:324–334.

Nei, M. (1975). *Molecular Population Genetics and Evolution.* Amsterdam: North Holland.

Nei, M. (1983). Genetic Polymorphism and the Role of Mutation in Evolution. In M. Nei and R. K. Koehn (eds.), *Evolution of Genes and Proteins.* Sunderland, Massachusetts: Sinauer.

Nei, M., and D. Grauer (1984). Extent of Protein Polymorphism and the Neutral Mutation Theory. *Evolutionary Biology* 17:73–118.

Neyman, J. (1950). *Probability and Statistics.* New York: Holt.

Provine, W. B. (1983). The Development of Wright's Theory of Evolution: Systematics, Adaptation, and Drift. In M. Grene (ed.), *Dimensions of Darwinism.* Cambridge: Cambridge University Press.

Provine, W. B. (1986). *Sewall Wright and Evolutionary Biology.* Chicago: University of Chicago Press.

Quinn, J. F., and A. E. Dunham (1983). On Hypothesis Testing in Ecology and Evolution. *American Naturalist* 122:602–617.

Roughgarden, J. (1983). Competition and Theory in Community Ecology. *American Naturalist* 122:583–601.

Sarkar, H. (1982). *A Theory of Method.* Berkeley: University of California Press.

Selander, R. K. (1985). Protein Polymorphism and the Genetic Structure of Natural Populations of Bacteria. In T. Ohta and K. Aoki (eds.), *Population Genetics and Molecular Evolution.* Tokyo: Japan Scientific Societies.

Simberloff, D. (1983). Competition Theory, Hypothesis-Testing, and Other Community Ecological Buzzwords. *American Naturalist* 122:626–635.

Sloep, P. B. (1986). Null Hypotheses in Ecology: Toward the Dissolution of a Controversy. In A. Fine and P. Machamer (eds.), *PSA 1986*, Proceedings of the 1986 Meetings of the Philosophy of Science Association, Volume 1. East Lansing, Michigan: Philosophy of Science Association.

Snedecor, G. W., and W. G. Cochran (1980). *Statistical Methods* (7th ed.; 1st ed. 1937). Ames: Iowa State University Press.

Sober, E. (1985). *The Nature of Selection.* Cambridge: MIT Press (Bradford Books).

Sober, E. (1987). What is Adaptationism? In J. Dupré (ed.), *The Latest on the Best: Essays on Evolution and Optimality.* Cambridge: MIT Press (Bradford Books).

Sokal, R. R., and F. J. Rohlf (1969). *Biometry.* San Francisco: Freeman.

Strong, D. R. (1980). Null Hypotheses in Ecology. *Synthese* 43:271–285.

Strong, D. R. (1983). Natural Variability and the Manifold Mechanisms of Ecological Communities. *American Naturalist* 122:636–660.

Strong, D. R., et al. (1979). Tests of Community-Wide Character Displacement Against Null Hypotheses. *Evolution* 33:897–913.

Thornhill, R., and J. Alcock (1983). *The Evolution of Insect Mating Systems.* Cambridge: Harvard University Press.

Wilson, E. B. (1952). *An Introduction to Scientific Research.* New York: McGraw-Hill.

Wright, S. (1976). *Evolution and the Genetics of Populations*, Volume 3: Experimental Results and Evolutionary Deductions. Chicago: University of Chicago Press.

3

Why Not the Best?

Philip Kitcher

In the natural constitution of an organized being, i.e., one suitably adapted to life, we assume as an axiom that no organ will be found for any purpose which is not the fittest and best adapted to that purpose. (I. Kant)

Introduction

What Kant took as an axiom, many contemporary students of behavior regard as a Darwinian theorem. Behavior, as well as anatomy and physiology, is the product of the evolutionary process. Because the chief agent of evolutionary change is natural selection, evolution bequeaths to us the patterns of behavior that are fittest and best. Our understanding of behavior can thus be greatly enhanced by analyzing the conditions under which animals find themselves and discovering which behavioral strategies are optimal for them.

The sophisticated are aware that appeals to optimality must be treated with caution. Michael Posner views optimality analysis as a potentially useful tool for the functional dissection of human behavior, but he is quite explicit in proposing that it should be employed in conjunction with other psychological techniques (1978, p. 23). John Krebs and Robin McCleery note that there are complications in the use of optimality models, and they offer a brief account of "the logical basis for using optimality arguments in biology" (1984, p. 91). As they note, more extensive comments have been provided by others (for example, Maynard Smith, 1978, and Oster and Wilson, 1978). But, in my judgment, none of these authors has focused the methodological issues involved: all agree that there is a danger of going wrong, but nobody has tried to measure the risk. My aim is to achieve a

I am grateful to a large number of people who read or heard earlier versions of all or parts of this paper. In particular, I would like to thank Peter Abrams, John Beatty, Jack Hirshleifer, Craig Packer, Peter Richerson, and Elliott Sober for helpful suggestions that have enabled me to improve the final version. Since I have not taken all the advice they gave me, it should not be assumed that any of them agrees with my conclusions. Finally, my apologies to Jimmy Carter for stealing a good title.

more precise understanding of the reliability of the tool. What exactly are the chances of going astray if we pursue the policy of relying on optimality analyses in the study of behavior?

Intended Conclusions
First, it is important to decide what kinds of conclusions proponents of optimality arguments are attempting to reach. Here the root difficulty concerns the complexity of human and animal behavior. As ethologists candidly acknowledge (Hinde, 1983, pp. 30–32), it is a major achievement to divide up the stream of animal behavior into meaningful units, to describe what the animal did. Posner makes a similar point, lamenting the fact that the complexity of the human information-processing system stands in the way of "disentangling" it (1978, p. 23). Thus the end product of the analysis is a certain kind of description of the behavior and of the mechanism that generated it. That description does not simply describe the overt bodily movements, nor does it delve into the neurophysiological processes that underlie those movements. What is wanted is a *functional* description.

Consider an example. In a famous experiment by Hans Kummer, male hamadryas baboons were described as "respecting the ownership rights of other males." Later work has shown that the original story was somewhat too simple (Bachmann and Kummer, 1978), but that story may, nonetheless, provide a paradigm of the kind of description that optimality arguments are designed to supply. In the more precise idiom of evolutionary game theory, we declare that the baboons are playing Bourgeois (Maynard Smith, 1982). Our declaration involves attributing various capacities to the animals and making claims about the ways in which these capacities are causally related to one another, to stimuli and to the overt bodily movements.

The functional description involves an interpretation of baboon bodily movements under a variety of different conditions. When the baboons are seen with bared teeth, in close proximity, when limbs are rapidly extended, and so forth, we interpret this as a fight. When the baboon simply fidgets, and watches the other male consort with "his" female, we suppose that the urge to aggression has been inhibited. We attribute to the male baboons a disposition to attack males who associate with neighboring females, coupled to two further capacities: the disposition can be inhibited by observation that the male has been associating with the female during a lengthy period of time, and it can be strengthened by observing that the female is an associate of the baboon's own. Thus we could represent the male baboon's psychology in a primitive flowchart, and we would link the psychological description to observable bodily movements by specifying the conditions under which a stimulus will trigger the capacities and dispositions (for example, the conditions under which a baboon's capacity for detecting "ownership" will be exercised) and the bodily movements that will be associated with various outcomes (for example, the ways in which attack behavior will be manifested).

Plainly, in any situation in which the actions of several different animals are involved, a full analysis of this type will have to specify the flowcharts for all the participants unless we can legitimately argue that some of them are simply treated as inanimate objects for the purposes of the interaction. Consider the phenomenon that used to be known as "agonistic buffering." A male, A, faced with a threatening male, B, picks up an infant C, and carries it toward B. Here, it is tempting to offer a functional description simply of the behavior of A and of B (e.g., "A is appeasing B," or "A is protecting C from B"). We assume that C's dispositions to behavior can be left out of the picture, on the grounds that whatever C did would make no difference to the actions of A and B. I suggest that it is always worth scrutinizing such assumptions. Even "helpless infants" may have behavioral strategies for affecting the outcome of interactions in which they are involved. Even "passive bystanders" may be exercising dispositions to behavior that are relevant to the way in which things turn out.

Hence, in an n-party interaction, the functional description consists in attributing dispositions and capacities to each of the n participants and describing the ways in which the psychological dispositions are related to stimuli and to bodily movements. Of course, any such description may be extremely coarse grained and yet be useful. A preliminary blueprint of the causal mechanisms underlying behavior may serve as something to be filled in by later studies.

Optimality arguments are supposed to help us arrive at these kinds of descriptions by offering suggestions about the ways in which natural selection would be expected to have shaped the capacities and dispositions of the animals under study. By identifying the costs and benefits of various forms of activity, an evolutionary analysis promises to lead us to see the tasks that a psychological system might have to perform and the way in which we should expect such a system to be organized.

Moreover, the optimality analysis is intended to enable us to understand the way in which the overt movements of the animals under study are the outcome of an interaction between their dispositions to behavior and the ecological constraints to which they are subject. So, for example, in under-standing the behavior of gibbons, we may hypothesize that the formation of social groups (family groups, in this case) is the product of dispositions to sexual behavior that the gibbon species share with other higher primates and the ecological constraint, the dietary habits of the females, that deter-mines that females will be spatially separated. In the case of our own species, the ecological constraints will typically involve features of our social institutions. Thus, an optimality analysis that attributes to us behavioral dispositions that are virtually never manifested in behavior might be defended on the grounds that human society imposes checks on the behavior in question.

The general point is that a functional analysis of animal or human behavior consists of a pair of hypotheses, one of which attributes dispositions to the organisms under study, while the other identifies the constraints to which the manifest behavior of those organisms is subject. It is not hard to appreciate the possibility of genuine instances of underdetermination.

Intended Force

Next, we need to be more precise about what optimality arguments might offer. Let us consider three distinct theses.

1. Achieving an optimality analysis that identifies a functional description D as optimal justifies us in accepting that description.
2. Functional descriptions that are backed by optimality analyses receive substantially higher prior confirmation than those that are not backed by optimality analyses.
3. Optimality analyses play a merely heuristic role, identifying hypotheses that are worth testing further.

I take it that (3) is not likely to be a serious subject of controversy. If optimality analyses are simply viewed as ways of jogging the scientist's imagination, then there will be little reason to fuss about their employment. On the other hand, I suspect that many proponents of the use of optimality analyses will assert that (1) is a straw man. Since everybody knows that other forces besides selection operate in evolution, nobody can maintain anything so strong as (1). However, as critics of optimality analyses complain (Gould and Lewontin, 1979), what is admitted in theory is often ignored in practice, and I think that it is worth recognizing that many practicing biologists act as if they were motivated by (1). (Examples are rife in the literature on sociobiology.) Perhaps the most interesting position is (2), a position that admits a preference for functional descriptions that are backed by optimality analyses, but that does not commit itself to accepting any such description that may be produced and does not rule out the possibility of accepting functional descriptions that are not endorsed by any such analysis. (Perhaps this is the approach of some of the most sensitive behavioral ecologists. See, for example, Emlen, 1984, and Vehrencamp and Bradbury, 1984.)

I am interested in understanding if either (1) or (2) is defensible. In light of the discussion so far, we can pose two obvious questions about the strategy of employing optimality models: How likely is it that the evolutionary process will produce the best behavioral phenotype available to the ancestral population? How likely is it that our perspective on the evolution of the animals we are studying will enable us to identify the best behavioral phenotype available to the ancestral population? My main task in this essay is to explore these questions. Before I proceed to that task I want to relate them to the versions of the optimality thesis just distinguished and to the general worry with which we began. How likely are we to be wrong if we pursue research into animal behavior by relying on optimality arguments?

When Optimality Arguments Are Useful

I suggest that optimality arguments might be useful in a situation where we have underdetermination of functional description by behavioral evidence. In situations of this kind an optimality argument can yield a resolution of the conflict among the various functional descriptions. In the extreme case, we find that there is a unique functional description that is generated by an optimality argument, and we accept this description and reject all other rivals compatible with the overt behavior. A second possibility is to use an optimality argument to decrease uncertainty in a case where we have only been able to think of one functional description that is compatible with the overt behavior. I propose the description, but I am aware that my inability to construct alternatives may reflect on my own lack of imagination rather than the inevitability of the description that I have achieved. I now discover that the description that I have given receives the backing of an optimality argument. It is tempting to think that, in a case like this, my rational confidence in the description is increased—perhaps even increased sufficiently for me to be able to accept the description. So we should consider optimality arguments as potentially useful either in screening out actual rivals or as reassuring us that we have not overlooked serious alternatives to the description that we propose to give.

Compounding and Canceling Errors

As my two questions indicate, there are potentially two ways of making mistakes in applying optimality arguments. First, we may be wrong in thinking that the evolutionary process produced the best available phenotype, and, second, we may be wrong in identifying what counts as the best for animals in the group under study. The errors are independent, and it is obviously possible that they should compound. What may be less obvious is that they may cancel. A faulty identification of what is best that overlooks strategies that were available to animals in the ancestral population may reach the right answer if the evolutionary process did not fix some superior rival strategy. So there is a chance of achieving the right result from a doubly flawed analysis.

The Strategy of the Cautious Bayesian

We can make the previous points much more precise if we introduce a rudimentary model for making scientific decisions. I shall use a simple version of a Bayesian confirmation theory that resembles most closely the approach developed by Wesley Salmon (1967, 1983). I assume that we can ascribe probabilities to hypotheses, and that our assignments of prior probabilities reflect prior judgments about what is plausible. In the case at hand, the focus of interest is the possibility of boosting the prior probability of some functional descriptions on the grounds that we have an analysis that claims that behavior meeting that description is optimal.

Imagine a cautious Bayesian. This person is engaged in studying the behavior of a group of animals and has achieved a set D of incompatible functional descriptions. For each description in D there is an associated hypothesis about ecological constraint, which renders the description compatible with the behavioral data so far obtained. I shall assume that the hypotheses about ecological constraints are all equally plausible.

Among the descriptions in D, there is a subset OD, the members of which are backed by optimality arguments. More exactly, for each description d in OD there is an analysis that purports to show that d specifies the optimal phenotype that would have been available to the ancestors of the organisms under study. I suppose that the cardinality of D is N, that of OD is n, and that $n < N$.

The Bayesian has prior assessments about the probabilities that the hypotheses so far proposed include the correct functional description and that one of the optimality analyses correctly identifies the best available ancestral phenotype. Let

p = probability that one of the descriptions in D is correct,
q = probability that one of the descriptions in OD identifies the best available ancestral phenotype,
r = probability that the evolutionary process has produced the best available phenotype.

Plainly the values $1 - p$, $1 - q$, represent the extent of uncertainty about the possibility that the search for hypotheses has so far missed the right answer and about the possibility that all of the available optimality analyses may be mistaken. For present purposes, I shall assume that $p > q$. I take it that this supposition is reasonable, in that any uncertainty about evolutionary pressures that might have been overlooked should be reflected in uncertainty about the available optimality analyses.

There are plainly important and interesting questions about the ways in which probability values for hypotheses relate to various kinds of scientific action. I suppose that when the value of p is sufficiently low, then the rational strategy is to search for alternative hypotheses. I shall not investigate in any detail the conditions under which it would be rational to pursue or to accept a hypothesis. (For classic discussions, see Carnap, 1952, and Jeffrey, 1983.) Nonetheless, it is worth noting that the relation between probability values and scientific action is not simply a question about the strategies of individuals. There are strategic considerations for the community to consider, and assignments of probabilities to hypotheses may be reflected in distributions of strategies within the community.

The cautious Bayesian adjusts the probabilities of the available functional descriptions to reflect the probability that evolution has produced the best available phenotype and that the optimality analyses given succeed in identifying the best available ancestral phenotype. I shall assume that the probability that one of D is correct, given that evolution has produced the best available phenotype, is identical to the probability that one of D is correct *simpliciter*. (The chance that the search for hypotheses has captured the correct hypothesis is independent of the question whether evolution has done the best it could.) The cautious Bayesian will also appeal to the principle of indifference when all else fails. (Of course, indifference can be applied—and misapplied—in various ways; my use of the principle will flow straightforwardly from my description of the choice situation.)

With these considerations in mind, I shall write the probability of a description d in D as follows:

$$P(d) = P(d/\text{evolution produces the best}) \cdot r$$
$$+ P(d/\text{evolution does not produce the best}) \cdot (1 - r).$$

The assumptions made above lead to the following specifications:

For d in OD:

$$P(d) = qr/n + (1 - r)\{(n - 1)pq/n(N - 1) + (1 - q)p/N\}.$$

For d^* in $D - OD$:

$$P(d^*) = (p - q)r/(N - n) + (1 - r)\{pq/N - 1 + (1 - q)p/N\}.$$

In case these assignments seem to come from thin air, let me explain. The first term in $P(d)$ reflects the possibility that evolution produces the best available phenotype and that d describes that phenotype: the chance of the former is r; that of the latter, by the assumption of indifference, is q/n. The other terms represent the possibilities that d is correct even if evolution has not produced the best. This may come about in one of two ways: either because one of the descriptions in OD identifies the optimal phenotype and d is not it (first term) or because none of the descriptions in OD identifies the optimal phenotype. Once again, in these cases, all the candidate hypotheses are taken to be on a par. The value of $P(d^*)$ is computed in a similar way: The first term representing the possibility that d^* is correct if evolution produces the best, the latter two representing two ways in which d^* might be right if evolution fails to produce the best (one case in which some member of OD picks out the optimal phenotype and one in which no member of OD identifies the optimal phenotype). Perhaps some of the assumptions involved in generating these values may seem artificial, but it is reassuring to note that similar points to those adduced below can be obtained from a different model in which one starts with the probability that one of the candidate hypotheses is correct and considers the conditional probability of one of the members of OD picking out the optimal phenotype, given that one of the candidates is correct. I shall not pursue the alternative approach here.

To assess the impact of optimality analyses, it is helpful to consider two quantities: the absolute value of $P(d)$ [where d is in OD] and the ratio of $P(d^*)$ to $P(d)$. The latter provides an index of the extent to which the provision of optimality analyses boosts the probability of a description that receives the backing of such an analysis. However, it is possible that the value of $P(d^*)/P(d)$ should be quite low—so that optimality analyses make a significant difference to the assignment of probabilities—and yet that the absolute value of $P(d)$ should also be small. Evidently, the value of $P(d)$ will only be high if q is appreciable, that is, if the uncertainty about the optimality analyses is relatively small. As we might expect, optimality analyses have the greatest impact when q is close to p and r is close to 1. For a large range of cases, the $P(d^*)/P(d)$ ratio is minimal when q is approximately equal to p, and it then attains the value

$(1 - r)/r.$

While this value is very small when r is close to 1, it is important to see that a cautious Bayesian will not reject descriptions in $D - OD$ (i.e., assign them zero probability) if $r < 1$.

The practice of the cautious Bayesian can best be understood by focusing on the case in which $n = 1$, $N = 2$. Here we are comparing the rival merits of two functional descriptions, one of which is backed by an optimality analysis and the other of which is not. The probabilities are

$P(d) = qr + (1 - r)(1 - q)p/2,$
$P(d^*) = (p - q)r + (1 - r)\{pq + (1 - q)p/2\}.$

The ratio becomes

$P(d^*)/P(d)$
$\quad = \{p + pq(1 - r) - r(2q - p)\}/\{p - pq(1 - r) + r(2q - p)\}.$

From these formulas it is easy to derive the following conclusions:

A. If r is close to 1, q is close to p, then optimality analyses are very powerful.

B. If $r > 0.9$, p is about 0.9, q is about 0.8, then optimality analyses are powerful though not completely decisive. (The critical ratio is about 0.22.)

C. If $r < 0.75$, $q < 0.75$, p is about 1, then optimality analyses are surely not decisive. (The ratio is greater than $13/19$.)

D. If r is close to 1, p is about 1, $q < 0.6$, then optimality analyses are also not decisive. (The ratio is greater than $2/3$.)

I do not mean to suggest that we can achieve reliable, precise estimates of the probabilities p, q, and r. The point is to reinforce qualitative assessments of the merits of optimality analyses. As the four special conclusions indicate, the conditions for optimality analyses to settle issues about functional descriptions are rather stringent. Indeed, we can rule out the idea of eliminating all hypotheses that are not backed by optimality analyses and accepting a hypothesis that is backed by an optimality analysis (in the case where there is a unique such hypothesis), unless $r = 1$, and p and q are equal and close to 1. Thus position (1) considered above is likely to be overly optimistic about the power of optimality analyses. Moreover, conclusions (C) and (D) reveal that uncertainty with respect to the reliability of optimality analyses may operate alone to diminish the power of such analyses [as in (D)], or may interact with the probability that evolution has failed to produce the best available phenotype [as in (C)]. Finally, we can envisage the possibility that there should not be a blanket dismissal of or enthusiasm for all optimality analyses. It is eminently possible that our assessments of the parameters should differ from group to group or from phenotypic character to phenotypic character.

Critics may protest that these points are academic. Why are we worried about the extent to which functional descriptions receive a boost from optimality analyses, when, given sufficient time, the empirical data will settle the issue for us? And, in any case, what alternatives do we have for starting with an optimality model and refining it in the light of the evidence? Both challenges are serious. I reply to the first that critics of the adaptationist program (e.g., Gould and Lewontin, 1979) are worried about our ability to escape from the confines of a false commitment to the idea that there is a *correct* optimality analysis to be found. They see the danger of adding epicycles in the manner beloved of medieval astronomy. The obvious reply is that the danger is very slight, and that the way of optimality analyses is the yellow brick road of behavioral biology (in John Staddon's happy phrase). However, we shall not *know* whether or not we are treading the yellow brick road or a primrose path unless we do the kind of analysis that I am recommending.

Similarly, the second objection (forcefully presented to me by Craig Packer) either supposes that there are *no* other ways of investigating behavior systematically, a view that I take to be belied by the ethological tradition and by the possibility of starting with a statistical analysis of the behavior under study, or that the strategy of generating hypotheses using optimality analyses is a decided improvement over other approaches. But, of course, the latter complaint leads directly to the question I have asked. To what extent are descriptions that are backed by optimality analyses more likely to be true, *in virtue of that fact alone*? Thus, I suggest, the investigation of this section answers the fundamental question of the logic of optimality analyses, albeit by giving a specific development of a specific approach to confirmation. If this is right, then those who seek to resist my conclusions ought to investigate alternative Bayesian models for appraising the credentials of optimality analyses or offer a different (non-Bayesian) account of confirmation that can be applied to this special case.

Spencer's Slogan
At this point, I want to take up the main questions that were distinguished above: What is the probability that evolution produces the best available phenotype? What is the chance of our being right in identifying the best available phenotype? The point of the previous discussion has been to argue that these are the main questions. We need to identify likely values for the parameters r and q. I shall begin with the former, taking up an issue that has surely already occurred to many readers. What do we mean when we claim (or deny) that evolution produces the best available phenotype?

The idea of "the survival of the fittest" exercises a profound influence in many popular discussions of Darwinism, and may lurk behind the relatively sophisticated allusions to evolution that are found in the behavioral sciences (or even in philosophy; cf. Quine, 1969, pp. 126–127). The phrase is Spencer's, not Darwin's, and should be adopted at the user's risk. But is there a refined version of the slogan that will underwrite the idea that evolution produces the best?

Optimality arguments are typically concerned with the fitness relationships among individuals, so I shall ignore interpretations of the slogan that appeal to the idea that selection maximizes population mean fitness (Fisher, 1930; Crow and Kimura, 1970; Roughgarden, 1979). The simplest version is to suggest that if P is the fittest phenotype available in a population, then the evolutionary process will lead to the fixation of that phenotype in the population. [Note: I assume, without argument, that fitness is to be understood as a propensity, as in the treatment of Mills and Beatty, 1979. However, it is important to understand that this commitment leaves open many distinct possibilities. For one may take different views about the entities to which fitness is to be ascribed, about the entities in terms of which reproductive success is to be counted, and about the time at which the counting is to be undertaken. To explore all the relationships among various propensity interpretations of fitness would require another paper. For present purposes, 'fit' and cognate terms can be understood as systematically ambiguous, subject only to the constraint that fitness is some sort of propensity for leaving descendants.]

It hardly takes much thought to see that the naive proposal of the last paragraph is wrong: an accident might eliminate the bearers of the optimal phenotype, or a mutation producing something better might arise. So let us narrow the scope of the claim. If we abstract from the action of other evolutionary forces, considering a population evolving under selection alone, should we expect that the fittest phenotype antecedently present in the population will be fixed?

Again, it takes little thought to answer the question. If the fittest phenotype is coded by a heterozygote, then it is inevitable that individuals with alternative phenotypes (those coded by the homozygotes) must exist in the population for at least some part of each generation. [Except in the unusual case where both homozygotes are lethal, they will be around for longer.] Very well, then, let the fittest phenotype be directed by a homozygote. Even this will not rescue the Spencerian tag. For imagine that there are three alleles at a locus and that the fitness relationships for the phenotypes correspond to the allelic fitness relationships

$$CC > AS > AA > AC > CS > SS.$$

What happens in a random mating population in which A alleles are vastly predominant, but in which there are a few mutant individuals with each of the above genetic combinations? Answer: the C allele is eliminated under selection and the population forms a stable polymorphism between A and S. The case is no model builder's idle fancy, but the story of evolution at the sickling locus in some African populations (see Templeton, 1982.)

It is not hard to see why the C allele is driven out. Even though superanimal (CC) is, *ex hypothesi*, right there from the start, most C alleles are doomed to appear in poor combinations. Most will be found in AC individuals who are less fit than the predominant AA individuals. By contrast, S remains, because it turns up in a context that produces fit individuals. The random-mating requirement is obviously important. Were there to be some propensity for individuals to mate with individuals carrying the same alleles, then C would stand a higher chance of finding itself in the fit homozygous condition, while S would have greater probability of occurring in the unfit homozygous condition.

The example is the second simplest instance of a general problem. Let us say that a phenotype has a trajectory problem in a population when (i) it is the fittest phenotype found in that population, (ii) even if the population evolves under selection alone, the phenotype will not become fixed in the population. The very simplest trajectory problem is the case of the phenotype that is coded by a heterozygote. The next simplest is the case in which the qualitative fitness relationships among the alleles at a locus do not always correspond to the course of selection at that locus, because the allele that is superior in homozygotes fares badly in heterozygous condition; such cases can occur when there are three or more alleles at a locus.

Further trajectory problems arise when we consider more than one locus, either with simple additive effects or with interactions among the loci. A classic example is the evolution of chromosome polymorphisms in *Moraba scurra* (Lewontin and White, 1960; Lewontin 1974, chapter 6). Since everything we know about the molecular basis of heredity suggests that interactions among genes are inevitable, we might expect trajectory problems to be rampant in nature.

The only hope for defending Spencer's slogan, even when we focus on evolution under selection alone, is so to gerrymander the concept of availability that we guarantee that the fittest available phenotype is always fixed. Champions of the slogan must declare that a genotype is available to selection only if selection is able to fix it in the population under study.

Now we reach an abyss of vacuity from which the most prudent users of optimality analyses have hoped to draw back (see Oster and Wilson, 1978, p. 301). As we are considering selection, it is a deterministic process. Given the initial state of a population, the end state is fixed. Hence, if a population *can* become fixed for a particular phenotype, then it *must* become fixed for that phenotype. The slogan reduces to the claim that selection fixes the best available phenotype, that is, the best phenotype that can be fixed in the population, that is, the best phenotype in a collection with exactly one member, the single phenotype that selection inevitably fixes in a population starting from the pertinent initial state. I should note that my defense of a result of crushing triviality has been predicated on the assumption that there is a unique fittest phenotype and that it is coded by a homozygote.

Construed in this way, Spencer's slogan is entirely useless for the purposes of defending the power of optimality analyses. Suspending worries about heterozygote superiority or the possible impact of drift, let us grant that we can find an interpretation on which evolution produces the best available phenotype, so that r is set at 1. The notion of "availability" that has been forced on us in developing this interpretation sets obvious problems for the proponent of optimality analyses. Claims that a particular phenotype was the best available must be defended by detailed understanding of the genetic basis of the phenotype and by knowledge of gene interactions during development. In effect, a high value for r is obtained by making it extraordinarily difficult to attain rational confidence about proposed optimality analyses. The cost is a dramatic lowering in the value of

q, and, as we have seen, this suffices to lower the power of optimality analyses. "What you gains on the swings you loses on the roundabouts."

However, matters are even worse than a narrow focus on selection might suggest. As every biologist knows, chance effects can play a large role in the evolution of small populations. Imagine a small population, with three alleles initially present at a locus. The fitness ordering of the genotypes is

$$CC > BC > AC > BB > AB > AA.$$

Under these circumstances, given an initial prevalence of A alleles and small frequencies of the B and C alleles, selection will work to fix the C allele. Suppose, however, that a flood destroys all the organisms that possess the C allele before they mate. Under these conditions, the subsequent *immediate* course of selection will be different: the intermediate B allele will be fixed.

Assume further that the molecular constitution of the alleles makes direct mutation from B to C highly improbable. (This could occur if, for example, both B and C are obtainable from A by different single base substitutions, so that they differ from one another by two base substitutions.) Because of an extraneous event—the flood—a population that would have become fixed for the best available allele is diverted from the optimum to which it is initially closest. (Similar results are possible for populations of *Moraba scurra* studied by Lewontin and White. At certain initial mixtures of the relevant chromosomes, a minute perturbation can change the outcome of the evolutionary process.)

Friends of optimization can make two responses. First, one may claim that the occasions on which extrinsic accidents enter the evolutionary picture are too rare to take seriously. Second, one may contend that the perturbations only have a temporary effect, so that, while a population may be diverted for a short time, selection will ultimately take it to the optimum that it would have reached without the perturbation. In both cases, I think that the response is overconfident.

The general question of how likely populations are to be temporarily diverted is almost impossible to answer. Plainly, there are enormous numbers of ways in which accidents of birth, death, and mating might operate. We can address certain specific issues. If, for example, a small population loses some of its members to an accident (for example, a flood), what is the probability that an allele that would have reached fixation is eliminated? Elementary combinatorial considerations show that, for a haploid population of size 10, in which one individual bears the B allele and one the C allele, the probability of eliminating the C allele and retaining the B allele, given that a flood occurs and wipes out some individuals, is about 0.18. Hence, when we consider marginal populations that are exposed to recurrent hazards, I suggest that the effects of extrinsic factors are nonegligible. Of course, there are reasons to think that much of the evolutionary action occurs in such marginal populations.

However, it may still seem that these disruptions of the smooth working of selection are only temporary. Sooner or later the population will have another opportunity to find the optimum that it previously missed—either because of the possibility of mutation at the locus where selection occurred or because the phenotype is the result of additive effects from a number of different loci. In response, we should note that the second chance may come too late. For the characteristics of the genetic environment may be critically altered by the fixation of an alternative allele, and, in the novel context, the allele that was originally superior may no longer be favored.

Wright argued that, properly understood, stochastic factors work in harmony with selection, enabling populations to "explore the adaptive topography" and to find optima that they would otherwise have missed (see Wright, 1968, and Templeton, 1982). However, the argument is critically dependent on the assumption that selection pressures be relatively constant. If the environment changes rapidly enough or if selection pressures are frequency-dependent, then the local maxima at which populations arrive may leave their mark on subsequent evolution. Thus, if the alleles that are fixed at certain loci affect the fitnesses of alleles at other loci, a freak accident can make a permanent mark on evolutionary history.

I conclude that we are not entitled to believe that $r = 1$, even if we gerrymander the concept of availability in the interests of preserving Spencer's slogan. Hence position (1) cannot be maintained. The genuinely interesting question is whether there is a defensible interpretation of the idea that evolution tends to produce the fittest available phenotypes that will allow for relatively high confidence about the optimality analyses that we are able to provide. I have argued, in effect, that the value of r is reduced unless we place conditions on the notion of "available phenotype," and that these conditions impose limits on our ability to make justified claims to the effect that certain phenotypes are the best that were available to an ancestral population. The upshot is that the increase in r is purchased by diminishing q, except in those cases in which we have considerable knowledge of the genetics and development of the organisms that are being studied.

Evolutionarily Stable Strategies

The discussion of the previous section was predicated on the idea that optimality analyses endeavor to show that a particular phenotype would have been maximally fit. Although there are numerous examples in which optimization techniques are employed in just this way (see, for good cases,

Heinrich, 1979, and Oster and Wilson, 1978), one of the most important theoretical advances in evolutionary studies of behavior uses quite a different approach to optimization. In a series of seminal papers, and in a recent monograph (1982), Maynard Smith has applied game-theoretic notions to animal interactions. His central concept, the notion of an *evolutionarily stable strategy* (ESS), captures the idea that a form of behavior may be *maintained* in a population under selection provided that rival forms of behavior cannot gain advantages in interactions with it. More precisely, *I* is an ESS with respect to a set of rival strategies R just in case there is no strategy in R that would be able to invade a population playing *I*. Writing E(*I*, *J*) for the expected payoff to an individual playing *I* in an encounter with an individual playing *J*, Maynard Smith derives the following condition for *I* to be an ESS with respect to *J*:

For each *J* in R, either
$$E(I, I) > E(J, I) \quad \text{or}$$
$$E(I, I) = E(J, J) \quad \text{and} \quad E(I, J) > E(J, J).$$

I want to ask whether demonstrations that a strategy *I* satisfies this condition with respect to some collection of strategies R avoids some of the problems encountered in the last section.

There are parallel difficulties. As Maynard Smith is well aware, claims that an ESS will be maintained in a population under selection depend on the assumption of perfect heritability. Were the ESS coded by a heterozygote, mating would produce in each generation individuals who did not play the ESS. Results about evolutionary stability go through smoothly for haploid populations, but we need to take care in extrapolating to cases in which the organisms under study are sexually reproducing diploids. Provided that the ESS is coded by a homozygote at a single locus (in the ur-Mendelian fashion), there is little trouble. However, it is not hard to see that there will be troubles if the ESS depends on the presence of at least m alleles in homozygous condition at n critical loci. In such cases, matings between organisms having the important alleles at different loci will produce offspring that do not play the ESS. When the ESS requires the presence of some number m in the interval $[k, s]$, where $1 < k < s < n$, then the problem is parallel to that of the simple case in which the ESS is produced by a heterozygote.

Another source of trouble for the Spencerian slogan was the possibility of multiple alleles at a single locus with fitness relationships that prevented the incorporation of the fittest (homozygous) combination. Similarly, unless we place a condition on the set of alternatives, it is possible that a strategy that cannot be invaded by a single type of mutant can be invaded by a combination of invading strategies. The appropriate condition is that the set of rivals be closed under mixtures. For, if *I* is an ESS with respect to a set R of alternatives such that any mixture of members of R is included in R, then any situation in which a number of distinct alternative strategies arise within a population playing I is equivalent to a situation in which a group of mutants playing an appropriately chosen mixed strategy arise within I, and since I is able to resist all such mixed strategies, it can resist the multiple invasion. (Maynard Smith, 1982, in appendix D, notes the point in a somewhat different context.) Hence, so long as ESS results are formulated with respect to suitably chosen collections of alternatives, there need be no concerns about multiple invasions.

We reach the following result: Provided that there are no genetic complications from heterozygosity or multiple loci, selection can be expected to maintain strategies that are evolutionarily stable with respect to the strategies available to the organisms in the population (and with respect to all mixtures of such strategies). However, it is entirely possible that a strategy that fails to meet this stringent condition might be kept in an evolving population. For an extrinsic accident might prevent some strategy that could invade from arising, or might check its career once it did arise. Historical contingencies can allow for the maintenance of strategies that are not ESSs.

An example is furnished by one of the most interesting ESS analyses, the study of cooperative behavior in iterated encounters (Axelrod and Hamilton, 1981; Axelrod, 1984). It is frequently claimed that TIT FOR TAT is an ESS with respect to any rival strategy for playing iterated Prisoner's Dilemma (Axelrod, 1984; Maynard Smith, 1982). This is almost —but not quite—true. Since TIT FOR TAT has the same expected payoff as the strategy of pure cooperation, provided that the population is initially composed of individuals playing any nice strategy, it is possible for a population playing TIT FOR TAT to be clandestinely invaded by CO-OPERATE (or any other nice strategy). The snag is that, were CO-OPERATE to drift to fixation in a population, it could be invaded in turn by strategies that are not nice (e.g., DEFECT). Hence, historical contingencies may be crucial in maintaining a strategy that is not an ESS or in preventing a strategy that would be an ESS (such as DEFECT) from becoming fixed. (This point was also noted, independently, by Jack Hirshleifer.)

The same example enables us to appreciate another way in which the ESS may be overthrown. In discussing the original introduction of cooperation within a population of defectors, it is common to suppose that the cooperators enter as a group of individuals who are disposed to interact with one another more frequently than they do with the general population. (See Axelrod and Hamilton, 1981, and Axelrod, 1984; in effect, the proposal is similar to suppositions about nonrandom mating in standard population genetics.) Maynard Smith's conditions on the concept of an ESS are derived by supposing that, when mutants playing J with some low frequency s arise within a population playing I, the fitnesses of the strategies can be written as

$$W(I) = W_0 + (1 - s)\,E(I, I) + s\,E(I, J),$$
$$W(J) = W_0 + (1 - s)\,E(J, I) + s\,E(J, J).$$

Since s is small, the difference will be dominated by the second term. Hence, $E(I, I) > E(J, I)$ suffices for I to resist invasion by J. However, the above formulas express the idea that interactions take place at random, so that the probability of encountering a J-player is s.

However, if J players have a tendency to consort, then the analysis may go astray. We can give a coherent treatment by writing the fitnesses as

$$W(I) = W_0 + (1 + ks^2 - 2s)\,E(I, I)/(1 - s)$$
$$\qquad + s(1 - ks)\,E(I, J)/(1 - s),$$
$$W(J) = W_0 + (1 - ks)\,E(J, I) + ks\,E(J, J).$$

Here, the parameter k represents the preference for J players to interact together. I suppose that $0 < k < s^{-1}$. When k is less than 1, then J players have a disposition against interacting; when k is greater than 1, they have a preference for interacting. [It is easy to verify that, when $k = 1$, we have the Maynard Smith condition on random interaction.]

Assuming that s is small but ks is nonnegligible, Maynard Smith's condition on an ESS is replaced by

$$E(I, I) > (1 - ks)\,E(J, I) + ks\,E(J, J).$$

When ks approaches 1 this becomes

$$E(I, I) > E(J, J),$$

representing the intuitively obvious point that, if J players interact almost exclusively with one another, the appropriate comparison is between $E(I, I)$ and $E(J, J)$.

Hence, if there is preferential interaction among organisms—either as the result of an accident or because of some systematic feature of the situation—a strategy that meets the Maynard Smith conditions may not be evolutionarily stable. By the same token, strategies that fail to meet those conditions may be evolutionarily stable.

Let us now consider how the approach of the cautious Bayesian is to be understood in situations where the optimality analyses are demonstrations that certain strategies are ESSs with respect to specified sets of alternatives. The parameter r will now represent the probability that the evolutionary process has produced a phenotype that is an ESS with respect to the strategies available to the organisms under study. We can think of q as the probability that one of the ESS analyses identifies a collection of rival strategies that includes the strategies actually available. [In fact, the algebra developed in outlining the approach of the cautious Bayesian cannot be taken over unmodified because of the possibility of multiple ESSs, but, for present purposes, this complication can be safely ignored.]

The considerations advanced earlier in this section reveal that if ESSs are strategies that are subject to the Maynard Smith conditions, then there are various ways in which the evolutionary process can fail to produce an ESS. Alternatively, we can boost the value of r to 1 by insisting that a genuinely *stable* strategy must have a genetic basis that enables it to persist in a population, that it must be able to resist invasion even in cases of preferential interaction, and so forth. However, this tactic succeeds in increasing the value of one crucial parameter at the cost of making it more difficult to achieve a high value for the other. By demanding more of a stable strategy, we decrease the probability that the considerations advanced in our optimality analyses suffice to show that the strategies singled out are really stable. Thus, as before, there is a trade-off.

Educated Guesses
Whether we consider optimality analyses that attempt to show that a particular phenotype is the best available to the ancestral population or those that try to show that a particular behavioral strategy is evolutionarily stable, it is necessary to make a variety of hypotheses about the organisms under study. Critics of optimality arguments frequently complain—with some justice—that enthusiastic champions of optimization overlook alternatives. An apt response is to point out that the critics' case is made by fixing on the most egregious examples of evolutionary storytelling. Thus, Gould and Lewontin (1979) correctly point out Barash's neglect of an obvious rival to his favored hypothesis about the behavior of male mountain bluebirds. However, it is perfectly fair to respond that this is Darwinism at its most vulgar, and that behavioral ecologists frequently do much better.

If the dispute is to proceed beyond a tedious parade of favorite cases, we must have a clearer idea of the ways in which uncertainties about optimality analyses can arise. We need to know the factors that tend to decrease or increase the value of q. Let us start with analyses that attempt to identify the best available ancestral phenotype.

We have already seen that strengthening the concept of availability tends to increase the value of r while making it more difficult to achieve a high value for q. However, it should be clear that the difficulty is not insuperable. Were we to know enough about the genetic basis of the traits, then we would perhaps be able to satisfy ourselves that trajectory problems are not likely to arise. I shall now argue that knowledge of genetic and developmental details is important in overcoming other sources of uncertainty that would tend to depress q.

In their prudent assessment of the uses of optimality arguments, Oster and Wilson note that "optimization models consist formally of four components: (1) a state space; (2) a set of strategies; (3) one or more optimization criteria or fitness functions; and (4) a set of constraints" (1978, p. 297). The state space is generated by omitting from consideration many aspects of the organisms under study, and concentrating on what are taken to be the key biological variables. The set of strategies is the collection of alternatives taken to be available to selection. The optimization criteria are supposed to pick out some quantity that is correlated with fitness. Finally, the constraints may be imposed by any of a number of aspects of the organisms, their genetics, their physiological needs, their ecology, and so forth.

Mistakes are possible with respect to each component. Consider, first, the choice of state space. What we construct is an idealization of the organisms, and it is perfectly possible that this idealization should omit variables whose values are crucial to the optimization problem. Plainly, it is important that the incorporation of the extra variables should not induce dramatic changes in the solution to the optimization problem. One factor that helps to decrease the uncertainty $1 - q$ is *stability*. If we are able to show that the introduction of complicating variables into the state space, in the service of greater realism, would not perturb the result of our optimality analysis, then we can eliminate one source of doubt that would depress the value of q.

A second type of error concerns the specification of alternative strategies for the organisms. To have a clear view of the possibilities we need information about the genetics and development of the behavior in which we are interested. Ignorance of pleiotropic effects, linkage, allometry, or other forms of developmental constraint may lead us to admit as alternatives strategies that vary one aspect of the organism's behavior while leaving most of its other features substantially unaltered, or may lead us to overlook possibilities that were available to selection. Gould and Lewontin reinforce the point by offering the example of the human chin, which is formed as the result of interactions between two growth fields. Similar examples are legion. It used to be fashionable to explain the loss of the ophidian middle ear as the response to selection pressures on hypothetical burrowing ancestors. However, a simpler account of the absence of the tympanic membrane and the eustachian tubes in snakes is generated by recognizing the constraints that operate in ontogenesis. If snakes are to develop their characteristic feeding mechanism, then the jaw musculature will not leave room for the development of a complex middle ear. Snakes have to settle for a suboptimal mode of hearing as the result of pressures that initially seem quite remote—until we recognize the developmental connections (see Berman and Regal, 1967).

A third potential source of uncertainty lies in the choice of fitness functions. In many optimality analyses a quantity is introduced as a proxy for the genetic contribution to the next generation. Thus one looks for a strategy to maximize the rate of discovery of food items, or the number of copulations, and assumes that the quantity so maximized correlates directly with fitness. Such assumptions deserve scrutiny. Even when the surrogate appears closely connected with fitness—as when we count the number of surviving offspring—it is still worth asking whether there are discrepancies between the quantity maximized and the genetic contribution to descendant generations. Consider models of mate desertion (Maynard Smith, 1982; Grafen and Sibly, 1978). Although the payoffs are typically computed in terms of offspring who survive to maturity, they may nonetheless mislead us in situations in which there is pronounced competition for mates. In such circumstances, apparently trivial differences in the quality of the mature offspring may play a large role in the transmission of genes to subsequent generations.

Finally, mistakes about the constraints to which the organisms are subject may be reflected in a completely misguided optimality analysis. This is most apparent in the case of pleiotropy, allometry, developmental constraints, and so forth. Lack of information about such connections may lead us to assign wildly erroneous fitness values to certain behavioral strategies. Gould and Lewontin protest the atomization of the phenotype, and their point is readily appreciated by example. Suppose that behavior B_1 is coded by genotype aa and behavior B_2 by ab. [Of course, this supposition is highly simplistic in that we can hardly pair behaviors with pairs of alleles. It should be clear that a more realistic supposition would simply reinforce the point.] We are tempted simply to compare the merits of B_1 with B_2, but this is almost certainly shortsighted. Substitution of b for a may have profound effects on the development of the organism, and the benefit brought by achieving B_2 may be greatly outweighted by some unsuspected deficit. Even in so simple a case as the production of human (adult) hemoglobin, where the developmental story amounts to a tale of simple substitution of a different molecule in the erythrocytes, the mature phenotype is modified in two distinct ways when the S allele is present. The tendency to sickling is accompanied by resistance to malaria.

Oster and Wilson candidly admit that their models of caste structures in social insect colonies are based on "guesses," and they talk of "reconstructing evolution in ... imagination", (1978, p. 299). In defense of their procedure, one could point out that the guesses were hardly untutored and the imaginative flights were launched from the basis of unparalleled knowledge of the organisms. I have pointed to various kinds of ignorance that can adversely affect our certainty about the optimality analyses that we offer, and, as we have seen earlier, as the value of q diminishes below 0.6, optimality analyses should make little impact on our estimates of rival hypotheses. However, I am not simply concerned to amass difficulties, but to identify the kinds of information we need to rely on optimality analysis. Optimization can be a powerful tool when we are sufficiently conversant with the genetics, development, physiology, and ecology of the animals to lay to rest the kinds of doubts that I have distinguished.

Similar points apply when the optimality analysis takes the form of a demonstration that a particular strategy is an ESS with respect to a specified collection of strategies. If this demonstration is to be useful in boosting the credentials of a functional description, then we must be confident that

i. the kinds of instability described in the last section do not threaten the strategy,
ii. the strategy identified as an ESS is available to the animals,
iii. the collection of strategies identified as alternatives includes all the strategies available to the animals, and
iv. the payoffs assigned to the various strategies are correct.

Satisfying ourselves with respect to (i) will typically require some knowledge of the genetic basis of the behavior that we are interested in studying. Understanding of ontogenesis and physiology will be relevant both to (ii) and to (iii). Finally, responsible assessment of the payoffs will demand of us recognition of developmental and ecological constraints as well as sensitivity to the possibility of delayed fitness effects.

Thus, like the type of optimality analysis practiced (and pondered over) by Oster and Wilson, the appeal to demonstrations of evolutionary stability needs to be buttressed by information from genetics, development, and ecology. Moreover, the employment of Maynard Smith's fruitful concepts is supported when we provide arguments to show that the analysis given remains stable as idealizing assumptions are removed. In some of the best work in behavioral ecology (see, for example, Parker, 1978, on dungflies, and Woolfenden and Fitzpatrick, 1985, and Emlen, 1984, on helping at the nest or den), investigators take pains to show that their analyses yield conclusions that continue to hold as more aspects of the animals' behavior are considered. A striking instance of the opposite phenomenon occurs in popular discussions of gamete dimorphism and differences in sexual behavior (Dawkins, 1976; Wilson, 1978). Here it is relatively easy to show that the conclusions can be modified at will by refining the initial assumptions (Maynard Smith, 1982; Kitcher, 1985).

Quick Defenses

Although the Gould-Lewontin critique of "the Panglossian paradigm" has been very influential, I think that its real significance has not been understood. Three separate issues are involved: the possibility of confirming explanations of the presence of traits that appeal to natural selection, the issue of whether evolution inevitably produces the best available phenotype, and the question of the reliability of our guesses about best available phenotypes. As I interpret Gould and Lewontin (or, more exactly, Gould and the Lewontin of 1979; the Lewontin of the 1980s holds a more radical position about adaptation; see Lewontin, 1983), they do not deny that it is possible to confirm hypotheses about the selective benefits that traits conferred on their bearers and that were important in leading those traits to fixation. It would be a mistake to accuse Gould and Lewontin of inconsistency on the grounds that a style of explanation that they (allegedly) disavow is to be found in their writings.

The major emphasis of the Gould-Lewontin critique is on the importance of developmental constraints. Neglect of these constraints can lead us to construct faulty optimality analyses that fail to identify the genuine alternatives or that assign the wrong values to the rival fitnesses. Because we are frequently ignorant of developmental constraints, Gould and Lewontin's central point is important. However, as I have tried to show in previous sections, it is only one among many ways in which the values of two crucial parameters may be depressed. There are other considerations that affect the employment of optimality analyses, and, although Gould and Lewontin allude to many of these, their treatment seems to run together difficulties that ought to be distinguished and to be addressed separately.

If this interpretation is correct, then it is possible to resolve the dispute between Gould and Lewontin and some of the most thoughtful responses to their critique. Champions of "the adaptationist program" have replied that the search for selectionist explanations of the presence of traits is the only possible strategy for the practicing biologist (see Krebs and Davies, 1981; Mayr, 1983), that the appeal to hypotheses about drift or accidents of history is an appeal of last resort. The reply makes an incorrect contrast and misses the central point. Let us grant, for the sake of argument, the difficulty of confirming a claim about the disruption of natural selection (although such claims are sometimes very tempting—witness various proposals for explaining the extinction of the dinosaurs and the subsequent proliferation of mammals). The central thrust of the Gould-Lewontin critique concerns the behavior of scientists engaged in the search for selectionist explanations. If one proceeds on the assumption that the characteristics that first catch the eye are the direct products of selection that has worked to optimize those traits in isolation from the rest of the features of the organism, then one is very likely to go astray. Moreover, there is an obvious strategy for improving research. Increased knowledge of the genetics and development of the organisms under study can yield more reliable selectionist explanations. Phylogenetic reconstruction can gain from recapitulating ontogenetic reconstruction.

My own examination has focused on a more inclusive collection of ways in which optimality analyses can go astray, not in the interests of inducing a "forlorn skepticism," but in pinpointing the strategies that are available for improving hypotheses about selective pressures and functional significance. However, like Gould and Lewontin, I would argue that, when the work of buttressing the optimality analyses has not been done (or when it is impossible in practice to do it), then acceptance of hypotheses on the basis of such analyses is premature and misleading. Even if we concede that the search for selective explanations is the only game in town, it is reasonable to protest the naive practice of that game. Moreover, the Gould-Lewontin protest, with its main emphasis on developmental constraints, appears to be essentially in harmony with Mayr's long campaign against "beanbag genetics."

A different response to Gould's brief for investigations of development, offered by Alexander (1979, p. 203), maintains that the requisite information about ontogenesis can only be obtained on the basis of a prior understanding of the functioning of the organism. Hence, in Alexander's view, an evolutionary analysis is a prerequisite to the fathoming of the proximate mechanisms of animal behavior. To the extent that there is a sound point here, it is readily accommodated. There are surely many features of organismic development that can be investigated using the standard techniques of genetics and developmental biology, and we can expect to learn in this way some of the constraints to which organisms are subject. (It would be folly to think that evolutionary analysis somehow had to precede the Berman-Regal identification of the constraint imposed by ophidian feeding mechanisms.) Yet when ontogenetic investigation does presuppose knowledge of functional organization, it would be foolish to suppose that untutored guesses about function are prior and preferable to untutored guesses about ontogeny. Both areas of ignorance must be explored—and, with luck, conquered—together.

The Cautious Bayesian Revisited

I want to conclude by recognizing that the analysis that I have offered may not suffice to resolve all of the difficulties that attend the use of optimality arguments in the confirmation of hypotheses about the function of animal behavior. I have imagined that the force of an optimality analysis is evaluated by a cautious Bayesian, who assigns values to the crucial parameters p, q, and r. The assessment involves attending to a number of sources of doubt that tend to diminish the values of the parameters. Is it possible to be confident that there have been no trajectory problems? That the analysis given is stable under the incorporation of factors that make it more realistic? That the alternatives available to the animals have been adequately delineated? That the fitnesses or payoffs are correct? And so forth. [One problem that I have not explored is the independent confirmation of the hypothesis that is used to square the functional description with the actual behavior. Familiar methodological issues lurk here, and, because they are familiar, I have assumed that they do not need to be treated explicitly. Hence the initial assumption that the rival hypotheses linking rival functional descriptions to overt behavior are equally satisfactory].

The cautious Bayesian ponders all these factors and reaches a judgment about the values of p, q, and r. These values are assigned by using our best available knowledge about the group of animals under study. Much of the literature on optimality arguments has witnessed a dispute between those who recite a catalog of complications—as I have done above—and announce that the complications devastate the use of optimality analyses, and those who admit the complications but suppose that they are too infrequent to prove troubling. The central suggestion of this paper is that we can advance beyond this standoff. Provided that we can obtain values for certain probabilities—the probabilities that various kinds of complications will occur—we can insert those probabilities into a calculus to weigh the merits of an optimality argument that has been proposed within a particular context of investigation. Instead of alternately shouting "Rare exceptions!" and "Common complications!" at one another, we can try to investigate how frequently the perturbations I have mentioned actually occur—and we may receive different answers for different animal groups or for different classes of phenotypic traits.

So I conclude with cautious optimism. Vulgar Darwinizing has given the use of optimality analyses a bad name. But many behavioral ecologists believe that critics have overreacted, and that a valuable tool may be dismissed as worthless. If I am right, the central issue can be formulated precisely, and, using empirical information about the frequency with which certain kinds of situations occur in nature, we can achieve a clear view of the strength of particular optimality analyses. Vulgar Darwinism is only for the vulgar, but it is possible to aspire to something more sensitive.

References

Alexander, R. (1979). *Darwinism and Human Affairs*. Seattle: University of Washington Press.

Axelrod, R. (1984). *The Evolution of Cooperation*. New York: Basic Books.

Axelrod, R., and W. Hamilton (1981). The Evolution of Cooperation. *Science* 211:1390–1396.

Bachmann, C., and H. Kummer (1980). Male Assessment of Female Choice in Hamadryas Baboons. *Behavioral Ecology and Sociobiology* 6:315–321.

Berman, R., and P. Regal (1967). The Loss of the Ophidian Middle Ear. *Evolution* 21:641–643.

Carnap, R. (1952). *Logical Foundations of Probability*. Chicago: University of Chicago Press.

Crow, J., and M. Kimura (1970). *Introduction to Population Genetics Theory*. New York: Harper and Row.

Dawkins, R. (1976). *The Selfish Gene*. Oxford: Oxford University Press.

Emlen, S. T. (1984). Cooperative Breeding in Birds and Mammals. In Krebs and Davies (1984).

Fisher, R. A. (1930). *The Genetical Theory of Natural Selection*. Oxford: Oxford University Press.

Gould, S. J., and R. C. Lewontin (1979). The Spandrels of San Marco and the Panglossian Paradigm: A Critique of the Adaptationist Programme. Reprinted in Sober (1984).

Grafen, A., and R. Sibly (1978). A Model of Mate Desertion. *Animal Behaviour* 26:645–652.

Heinrich, B. (1979). *Bumblebee Economics*. Cambridge, MA: Harvard University Press.

Hinde, R. (1983). *Ethology*. Oxford: Oxford University Press.

Jeffrey, R. (1983). *The Logic of Decision*, 2nd ed. Chicago: University of Chicago Press.

Kitcher, P. (1985). *Vaulting Ambition: Sociobiology and the Quest for Human Nature*. Cambridge, MA: MIT Press.

Krebs, J. R., and N. B. Davies (1978). *Behavioral Ecology: An Evolutionary Approach*. Sunderland, MA: Sinauer.

Krebs, J. R., and N. B. Davies (1981). *An Introduction to Behavioral Ecology*. Oxford: Blackwell.

Krebs, J. R., and N. B. Davies (1984). *Behavioral Ecology: An Evolutionary Approach*, 2nd ed. Sunderland, MA: Sinauer.

Krebs, J. R., and R. McCleery (1984). Optimization in Behavioural Ecology. In Krebs and Davies (1984).

Lewontin, R. C. (1974). *The Genetic Basis of Evolutionary Change*. New York: Columbia University Press.

Lewontin, R. C. (1983). Organism as Subject and Object of Evolution. *Scientia* 118:65–82.

Lewontin, R. C., and M. J. D. White (1960). Interaction between Inversion Polymorphisms of Two Chromosome Pairs in the Grasshopper, *Moraba scurra*. *Evolution* 14:116–129.

Maynard Smith, J. (1978). Optimization Theory in Evolution. Reprinted in Sober (1984).

Maynard Smith, J. (1982). *Evolution and the Theory of Games*. Cambridge: Cambridge University Press.

Mayr, E. (1983). How to Carry Out the Adaptationist Program. *American Naturalist* 121:324–334.

Mills, S., and J. Beatty (1979). The Propensity Interpretation of Fitness. Reprinted in Sober (1984).

Oster, G., and E. O. Wilson (1978). *Caste and Ecology in the Social Insects*. Princeton: Princeton University Press.

Parker, G. (1978). Searching for Mates. In Krebs and Davies (1978).

Posner, M. (1978). *Chronometric Explorations of the Mind*, Hillsdale, NJ: Lawrence Erlbaum Associates.

Quine, W. V. (1969). Natural Kinds. In *Ontological Relativity*, New York: Columbia University Press.

Roughgarden, J. (1979). *Theory of Population Genetics and Evolutionary Ecology*. New York: Macmillan.

Salmon, W. C. (1967). *Foundations of Scientific Inference*. Pittsburgh: University of Pittsburgh Press.

Salmon, W. C. (1983). Carl G. Hempel on the Rationality of Science. *Journal of Philosophy* 80:555–562.

Sober, E. (ed.) (1984). *Conceptual Issues in Evolutionary Biology.* Cambridge, MA: Bradford Books/MIT Press.

Templeton A. (1982). Adaptation and the Integration of Evolutionary Forces. In R. Milkman (ed), *Perspectives on Evolution.* Sunderland, MA: Sinauer.

Vehrencamp, S., and J. Bradbury (1984). Mating Systems and Ecology. In Krebs and Davies (1984).

Wilson, E. O. (1978). *On Human Nature.* Cambridge, MA: Harvard University Press.

Woolfenden, G., and J. Fitzpatrick (1985). *The Florida Scrub Jay: Demography of a Cooperative Breeding Bird.* Princeton: Princeton University Press.

Wright, S. (1968). *Evolution and the Genetics of Populations,* Vol. 1. Chicago: University of Chicago Press.

II
Evolution and Optimality

4

What Is Adaptationism?

Elliott Sober

1 Introduction

A standard formulation of the view called "adaptationism" says that natural selection is the overwhelmingly most powerful force of evolution. Adaptationists do not deny the existence of mutation, migration, drift, and systems of mating, for example, but tend to downplay the importance of these causal factors.

A standard criticism of adaptationism is that it is unfalsifiable. If you observe a character in a species, you can always invent a story that shows how natural selection drove it to fixation, once it was introduced by mutation. If subsequent observation shows that this adaptive scenario is untenable, you can always tinker with the details or invent another selectionist story. This means that adaptationism fails to rule out any possible observation. It therefore commits the cardinal Popperian sin. The problem is not that adaptationism is *mistaken* science; the problem is that adaptationism isn't science at all.

Before moving on to the real topic of this paper, I shall say a few words about this familiar methodological criticism. It does not seem to me that adaptationism, properly understood, is guilty of any a priori defect. This is not to say that all is well in evolutionary theory. Particular evolutionary hypotheses have not always received the critical scrutiny they deserve. However, the defects of adaptationism are to be found in its practice, not in its theory. Adaptationism is as testable a generalization as the pluralism that some see as adaptationism's more plausible competitor.

Like other *isms* that guide a scientific research program, adaptationism is not refutable by a single, isolated observation. But repeated failures in a variety of contexts can gradually undermine adaptationism. It is true that a new adaptationist scenario can be invented if an old one fails; but this does not mean that it is always plausible to do so. Adaptationism is testable, and potentially disconfirmable, by observation. And as always, an old outlook is more quickly discarded when an alternative perspective is available that succeeds where the old one fails.[1]

My thanks to the National Endowment for the Humanities for financial support.

When we imagine ourselves explaining a characteristic found in a single population, it can be quite easy to dream up a new adaptationist story, if the old one is disconfirmed. However, this is less easy to do when one works with comparative data. Rather than explaining a single trait in a single population, let the unit of inquiry be a pattern of character diversity in a group whose common ancestry (monophyly) is antecedently known. This does not guarantee that the one true adaptationist explanation must shine through. However, this kind of data clearly counts as *better* data; it provides a check (though not a foolproof prophylactic, as if there could be such a thing) against idle speculation.

So, in my view, the charge of "unfalsifiability" is doubly misplaced. First, the criticism it implies is often wrongly levelled against propositions, rather than against persons. It is not the thesis of adaptationism that is defective, so much as the way some scientists have uncritically depended upon it. Second, it is a mistake to think that a scientific proposition must be crisply refutable by a single observation. The testing of broad-gauge propositions is not in harmony with the Popperian model. But that shows that there is something wrong with Popperianism, not with adaptationism.

The real subject of this paper, however, is not the methodology of testing adaptationism. I want to get clear on what it means. My point of departure is the formulation that has adaptationism asserting that selection has been the most powerful cause of evolution. What might "most powerful cause" mean here? Is this a fully adequate way of characterizing the implied comparison between selection and other causes of evolution?

In the next section, I shall discuss a simple model in which selection and mutation pressure are the only evolutionary forces described. This provides a clear context in which we know what it means to say that selection is more influential than another evolutionary force. In section 3, I examine what it might mean to compare the impact of selection and drift on an evolutionary outcome. In section 4, I discuss the idea that pleiotropy can limit the power of natural selection. In the conclusion, I shall try to generalize from these cases and say what adaptationism really is.

2 Selection and Mutation

No evolutionist can hold that natural selection is the *only cause* of a population's exemplifying a given trait. The trait must have been introduced by mutation. And random genetic drift—the sort of sampling error induced by finite population size—*must* have played some role. Moreover, it is plausible to think that other evolutionary forces, like linkage, pleiotropy, and the system of mating played some role. Perhaps, then, adaptationism ought to be understood as holding that selection is the most important—the most powerful—force at work.

To see whether this formulation makes sense, we must examine what it means to compare the magnitudes of various evolutionary forces. I begin with a relatively simple case, one in which it is possible to compare the impact of selection and mutation pressure on the frequency of an allele.

If there are two alleles A and a at a locus, then mutation can cause evolution when the rate of mutation from A to a differs from the rate of mutation from a to A. Let u denote the net mutation rate from A to a. Where q is the frequency of an allele, the rate of change in frequency (Δq) when mutation is the only force at work is $(u)(1 - q)$ per generation. Similarly, when there is selection with complete dominance, the allele will decrease in frequency approximately at the rate of $-sq^2(1 - q)$ per generation.

A simple model of mutation and selection views their joint impact as an additive effect of what would happen if each occurred alone. Hence, the equation for change in gene frequency takes the form

$$\Delta q = u(1 - q) - sq^2(1 - q).$$

This equation allows us to apportion causal responsibility between mutation and selection in much the way that Newtonian physics allows us to say how much of a particle's acceleration is due to gravity and how much is due to electricity. We can use this equation to examine the single population under study and thereby determine which contributing cause made the larger difference in the observed change in gene frequency.

The above equation allows us to determine the equilibrium frequency of the allele ($\hat{q}$) by setting $\Delta q = 0$. It is

$$\hat{q} = \sqrt{u/s}.$$

This equation tells us that the mutation rate and the selection coefficient play the same mathematical role in determining the equilibrium value of the gene. Wilson and Bossert (1971, p. 62) conclude from this that "since most mutation rates are on the order of 10^{-4} per generation, or less, it is clear that mutation pressure can hold sway only if the selection pressure is very weak—far weaker than has been found to be true in the majority of cases of microevolution to date." Of course, one might object that the failure to detect weak selection is not a strong argument for its nonexistence. However, the point here is that the model just sketched makes it quite clear how one can compare the magnitudes of two evolutionary forces.

The reason we are able to do this is that mutation and selection are understood in terms of a *common currency*; each is a directional force, describable in terms of the way it will change gene frequencies. Causal contributions can be decomposed in the way that component forces can be disentangled in the case of an accelerating Newtonian particle. The change in gene frequency effected by mutation and selection is just the sum of what each would have produced if it had acted alone.

In addition to stressing the importance of mutation and migration as possible significant causes of evolution, critics of adaptationism also mention drift, allometry, and pleiotropy. Adaptationists downplay the import of these factors, while their critics criticize them for deemphasizing those factors without sufficient reason. To get clear on what this issue amounts to, we first must see that comparing selection with drift or pleiotropy is fundamentally different from comparing selection with mutation, as we did above. Drift is characterized in terms of its effects on gene frequencies, but it is not a directional force. Assessing the importance of pleiotropy, on the other hand, requires that we describe selection in a finer-grained way than is customary and, also, that we recognize that it involves issues beyond that of the "power" of natural selection.

3 Drift

Chance enters evolutionary theory via the concept of random genetic drift.[2] We can understand the way it interacts with selection by considering a locus in a diploid population at which two alleles can occur. By assigning fitness values that represent differences in viability to the three genotypes, we thereby describe the average probability that an individual of given genotype has of surviving the passage from zygote to adult. It is a simple fact of probability theory that the average per capita probability of surviving need not exactly coincide with the proportion of individuals that survive. If there were infinitely many individuals, we might invoke Bernoulli's theorem as a reason to think that probability and actual frequency will differ only infinitesimally. But in the real world of finite populations, this need not be true. The theory of random genetic drift describes how sampling error can lead frequencies to depart from probabilities.

If there are ten zygotes of each genotype, and the fitnesses of AA, Aa, and aa are, respectively, 0.9, 0.8, and 0.7, then probability theory tells us how to calculate a probability distribution for each genotype; we can describe the probability that 0 AA individuals will survive, that 1 AA will survive, and so on, for each possible number of survivors and for each genotype. The expected number of survivors for the three genotypes, of course, is 9.0, 8.0, and 7.0, respectively. But, if I may put it this way, there is no absolute assurance that the actual values will be identical to the expected values.

In this example, "sampling error" affects survivorship. However, drift is more standardly construed as affecting the other part of the life cycle—namely, reproduction. Before saying something about models that describe the joint effects of selection and drift in this sense, I should say a little about how drift is understood when it acts alone. Let us imagine a diploid locus with two alleles that have the same frequency independent fitness values.

Suppose that the population begins with the two alleles at a given frequency and maintains a certain constant census size.[3] When a generation of organisms reaches the adult stage they reproduce and then die. Since the organisms do not vary in fitness, each has the same expectation of reproductive success. However, in view of the constant population size, the parents produce gametes that are far more numerous than the lucky $2N$ gametes that produce the N offspring of the next generation. Each gamete has an equal chance of being chosen; the sampling of gametes that occurs to construct zygotes permits sampling error to play a role. The offspring of the next generation then grow to adulthood and the process begins again.

What happens to the frequencies of the A and a genes in this process? Suppose that the population begins with each at 50% representation and that there are 100 organisms in the population. Since the organisms are diploid, there are 200 copies of the genes in total. The theory of random drift describes what will happen when 200 gametes are drawn at random from a gigantic gamete pool containing equal proportions of the two genes. This is represented as a probability distribution of possible gene frequencies.

What happens when the sampling procedure is repeated in the next generation? The following figure (figure 4.1) represents the probabilistic consequences of the multigeneration process of random drift. As the process procedes, the probability distribution of possible gene frequencies becomes more dispersed. If a population drifts to either 100% or 0%, it remains there, since the model does not allow mutation to reintroduce the lost variant. Hence, 100% and 0% are absorbing states. A population that starts at 50% representation of the two alleles will do a random walk that eventually leads to one of these absorbing states.

Hence, as time proceeds, the chance of ending up at 100% or 0% increases. The bell curve becomes more dispersed and flattened out. It eventually becomes trimodal—as the probability of reaching an absorbing state goes up and the intermediate frequencies approach a flat distribution. Yet throughout this process there is something that has not changed. The expected value of the gene at the beginning of the process is its starting frequency, whether the process proceeds for one or for many generations. What changes is the distribution of outcomes that together comprise this expectation.

So far I have mentioned one variable that affects the dynamics of this process; it is *time*. For a population of any fixed size—100 organisms, say—the more generations, the more dispersion of the probabilities. But *population size* is itself a variable. If we fix the number of generations through which the process will proceed, we shall get more dispersion, the smaller the population. Gamete sampling to form a population of 1,000 individuals is more likely to yield a next generation whose gene fre-

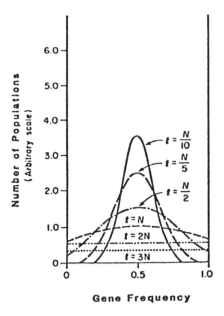

Figure 4.1
Predicted results of random genetic drift in a population whose initial gene frequency is 0.5. Areas under the curves represent the proportion of populations yet to reach fixation. The amount of time elapsed (t) and the effective population size (N) both influence the amount of dispersion of the probability distribution. See text for discussion (adapted from Crow and Kimura, 1970).

quencies resemble its parents than is gamete sampling to form a population of 10 individuals. The contributions of time (t) and population size (N) to the evolution of the probability distribution are shown in the figure.

So much for drift when it acts alone. What would a model look like that represents the joint effects of selection and drift? The basic change is to convert a deterministic prediction about gene frequencies into a probability distribution. Again, the expected value is the point value of the deterministic prediction. That is, if selection acts alone, we can deduce the gene frequencies from the starting frequencies. If sampling error intrudes, we cannot deduce a point value; rather, we have to view the point value that selection alone implies as the expected value of a probability distribution.

A coin-tossing analogy loses some of the details but clarifies the essential point. Consider a fair coin that is tossed some number of times. What will be the frequency of heads and tails? Roughly speaking, the law of large numbers says that as we make the number of independent tosses large without limit, the probability approaches unity that the observed frequency will be arbitrarily close to 0.5, which is the coin's probability of landing heads on any toss. The smaller the number of tosses, the more chance there is for the actual frequency to depart significantly from 0.5.

A coin-tossing analogue of the multigenerational process of iterated sampling is as follows: We toss a coin some fixed number of times and then bend the coin so as to alter its probability of heads. In particular, the frequency of heads in a run dictates the new probability of heads that the coin is to be given. We flip 10 times, then bend the coin, then flip 10 more times, and so on. Figure 4.1, reinterpreted appropriately, shows how the coin's probability of heads will evolve.

Just as an adaptationist or a critic of adaptationism might wish to compare the importance of selection and mutation in the explanation of a character in a particular population, so it might be of interest to compare the importance of selection and drift. Which, we might ask, has been the more powerful force in influencing the frequency of a character found in some population?

This question about selection and drift sounds like the question we posed in the previous section about selection and mutation. But there is a difference. Not to put too fine a point on it, the difference is that the question about selection and drift makes no sense. Let us go back to coin tossing to see why.

When a fair coin lands heads 7 out of the 10 times it is tossed, how are we to explain this? Well, the probability of heads on each independent toss is 0.5. This plus the sample size allows us to compute the probability of getting 7 heads. But which was the stronger determiner of the outcome—the probability of heads or the sample size? This question is nonsense.

In this case, we can pose some questions that relate to the impact of the two "factors." If the sample size were not 10, but 1,000, how would this affect the chance of getting roughly 70% heads, given that the coin is fair? And given that the coin was tossed 10 times, how would the probability of obtaining 7 heads have been different if the probability of each toss had been, not 0.5, but, for example, 0.6? We can see how varying one factor while holding fixed the other affects the probability of the outcome. But this leaves the question of causal contribution as unanswerable as it was before: we still have not been able to make sense of the question of which contributed more—sample size or probability—to the outcome in this single experiment.

To compare the relative importance of selection and drift, it is useful to shift from a single population to an ensemble of populations that begin with the same initial gene frequency and are subject to identical selection pressures and have identical effective population sizes. Since this last factor allows chance to intrude, the populations (probably) will come to display different gene frequencies after several generations.

In this ensemble of populations, we can say that there (probably) will be more variation among gene frequencies at the end of some fixed number of generations to the degree that sampling error has played a larger role. If each population were infinite, they would arrive at the same final gene frequency. If each were tiny, then the dispersal of final values would be quite large. Perhaps this offers us a measure of the importance of random genetic drift. The larger the percentage of populations whose gene frequencies are "close" to the expected value, the smaller the difference that drift makes to the evolutionary dynamics.

The present proposal is that drift makes little difference to the variation found within a set of similarly prepared populations, if taking it into account does not greatly improve the accuracy of a deterministic model's predictions about that set. But this "global" method of assigning a magnitude to the importance of drift does not allow one to say anything "local" about one population in the ensemble as opposed to another. One cannot compare two populations, one of which ends up further from the expected value than the other, and say that the former was more influenced by drift. The two populations, after all, were affected by the very same pair of causal factors. Nor, as I have said, can one look at a single population and say whether drift or selection contributed more to its evolution.

This contrasts with what we can say about a model in which mutation and selection are the only forces at work; here it is local facts about the single population under study that determine which causal factor contributed more to the change in gene frequency.[4]

4 Pleiotropy

I now turn to another problem for making sense of the adaptationist claim that natural selection is the most powerful force of evolution. It is posed by the phenomenon of pleiotropy. A gene or cluster of genes may have more than one phenotypic consequence. Suppose that one of these phenotypes is good (G) and the other bad (B) for the organisms in which they occur. Since they are consequences of a common cause, they will be correlated. Because of this correlation, both the good and the bad phenotypes may evolve and be maintained in the population. If the advantages associated with the good phenotype outweigh the disadvantages imposed by the bad, selection will be powerless to eliminate the disadvantageous phenotype; and if the bad outweighs the good, selection will eliminate the good trait along with its deleterious correlate.

If the two phenotypes are perfectly correlated, then every individual in the population will have either both G and B, or neither G nor B. If G is highly advantageous whereas B is mildly deleterious, then organisms with both will be fitter on average than individuals with neither. We therefore may expect, ignoring complications extraneous to the point here at issue, that both G and B will evolve.

How does pleiotropy affect the plausibility of adaptationism? Intuitively, it seems to diminish the power of natural selection. The phenotype B, I said, is disadvantageous; yet, because of its pleiotropic connection with G, selection cannot eliminate it. On the surface, it may appear that we have here a situation akin to the opposition between selection and mutation pressures discussed initially. Selection pushes to decrease the frequency of B; pleiotropy pushes to increase or maintain it. The net result of these component forces is an intermediate equilibrium.

However, just as in the case of selection and drift, a second look reveals that this interpretation poses a problem. A population of the sort we have just described, in which selection and pleiotropy combine, is represented by a single set of parameters—namely, fitness values. The fitness of a phenotype is simply the average fitness of the organisms possessing it. Since G and B are perfectly correlated, they must be identical in fitness. Examining the two types of organisms—those that have both and those that have neither—reveals that G is fitter than not-G *and* that B is fitter than not-B.

This latter result may seem paradoxical—how can B be *bad*, if it is fitter than its alternative not-B? I shall return to this puzzle in a moment. So far, my point is that the standard way of assigning fitnesses to characters has the effect of representing what we initially though of as two forces— selection and pleiotropy—by a single set of parameters, namely fitness values. If fitness assignments provide the quantitative representation of this system, that representation does not allow us to compare the relative importance of selection and pleiotropy. Notice that here we are in a fundamentally different situation from the one we faced in the mutation and selection case, in which we could assess the relative "power" of natural selection and mutation by comparing *two* parameter values.

There is a way out of this paradox. It requires that we give up the idea that the selection processes acting in a population can be exhaustively represented in terms of the fitness values of traits.[5] Fitnesses are probabilities; if we are concerned with fitness differences that reflect differential viabilities, these probabilities represent the average per capita chance of surviving from the egg to the adult stage, say. We then can represent the way in which selection and pleiotropy interact via a set of probabilistic inequalities.

Let us begin by saying what it means for G to be advantageous. This will be true if,[6] no matter what other traits an organism has, its chance of surviving would be better if it had G than it would be if it lacked G. Similarly, B will count as deleterious if, no matter what other suite of characters an organism possesses, it would be worse off with B than without B. In each of these cases, we consider different possible sets (S) of background characters—i.e., other total suites of characters an organism might have apart from the one of interest—and see how the presence/absence of the character in question affects the chance of surviving:

$$\text{Pr}(\text{surviving}/G \& S) > \text{Pr}(\text{surviving}/\text{not-}G \& S), \text{ for all } S, \tag{1}$$

$$\text{Pr}(\text{surviving}/B \& S) < \text{Pr}(\text{surviving}/\text{not-}B \& S), \text{ for all } S. \tag{2}$$

That is, a trait is advantageous if it counts as a positive causal factor for surviving, in the sense of the probabilistic theory of causality developed by Good (1961–2), Suppes (1970), Cartwright (1979), Skyrms (1980), Eells and Sober (1983), and Sober (1984).

Note that we have not yet compared the *overall* chance of surviving, conditional on G alone, or conditional on B alone. To compare the fitnesses of G and not-G, for example, we need to reach a conclusion like the following:

$$\text{Pr}(\text{surviving}/G) > \text{Pr}(\text{surviving}/\text{not-}G). \tag{3}$$

It is essential to realize that this claim is independent of (1) and (2).

Statement (3), of course, is true in the example we are discussing. But so is the following inequality pertaining to the bad character B:

$$\text{Pr}(\text{surviving}/B) > \text{Pr}(\text{surviving}/\text{not-}B). \tag{4}$$

The overall chance of surviving among individuals who have the bad character is greater than the overall chance of surviving among those who lack it. The reason, again, is that B and G are correlated.

Notice that the inequality sign is reversed as we move from (2) to (4). Each individual in the population would have its chance of surviving reduced if it had B. Yet individuals with B have a higher average chance of surviving than individuals without B. This phenomenon, in which inequalities within "subpopulations" are reversed in the population as a whole, is sometimes called Simpson's paradox. It offers us some hope for representing, in the case considered, the relative importance of selection and pleiotropy.[7]

Inequalities (1) and (2) represent the fact that there is selection *for* trait G and selection *against* trait B. I stress the prepositions "for" and "against" to contrast how (1) and (2) differ from (3) and (4). These latter two inequalities say only that G and B are both *correlated* with survival. (3) tells us that there is selection *of* trait G; this inequality compares the fitness *of* G with the fitness *of* not-G. Statement (4), finally, tells us that there will be selection *of* trait B; it will increase under selection. Notice that there is selection *of* B, but no selection *for* it (Sober, 1984). Simpson's paradox in the guise of pleiotropy has made this possible.

This approach does not compare selection and pleiotropy by asking "how much" of an evolutionary outcome was caused by selection and "how much" was caused by pleiotropy. This is as meaningless as the comparable question about selection and drift. Rather, the strategy has been to abandon the representation of selection in terms of overall fitness differences; that representation collapses the effects of selection and pleiotropy. Instead, I have chosen a finer-grained technique for representing the idea that traits can be selected for and against. This mode of representation, embodied in (1) and (2), may be thought of as giving the "component" selective forces. The "net" effect under selection is given by the overall fitnesses of (3) and (4). Pleiotropy bridges the gap between component and net:

component selective forces + pleiotropy = net fitness values.

Although this way of formulating the issue explains how pleiotropy can "reverse" the effects of selection—by maintaining characteristics that are selected against, or by eliminating characteristics that are selected for—we still have no quantitative representation of "how much" selection and pleiotropy contribute to the evolution of a single character. Perhaps this question must be handled in the way we approached the comparable question about selection and drift. It is meaningless when asked of a single trait. In the drift case, we looked at an ensemble of populations, each subject to the same evolutionary forces and beginning at the same initial gene freqeuency. However, this is the wrong ensemble to look at in the case of selection plus pleiotropy, since this deterministic problem will imply that all the identically prepared populations will have the same end state. Rather, we might better examine many different traits in a single population and ask *how often* a trait is maintained by pleiotropy even though it is selected against, or is eliminated by pleiotropy even though there was selection for it. This is a far cry from looking at a single trait whose presence in a population is the joint product of selection and pleiotropy and asking which contributed more to its evolution.

I shall make one final remark on what pleiotropy means to adaptationism. Gould and Lewontin (1979) stressed the importance of pleiotropy and linkage[8] as modulators of the effects of natural selection. Adaptationists have sometimes responded that natural selection has the power to break the correlations that, as it were, get in its way. For example, Dawkins (1982, p. 35) asserts that "[i]f a mutation has one beneficial effect and one harmful one, there is no reason why selection should not favour modifier genes that detach the two phenotypic effects, or that reduce the harmful effect while enhancing the beneficial one."

Indeed, no evolutionist can deny that this is possible in principle. The gene in the present example has two phenotypic effects, one good (G) and one bad (*B*). It will sweep to fixation if the good outweighs the bad. However, as Dawkins says, there is no a priori barrier to a new mutation arising that allows the initial gene to produce *G* and not-*B*. This modifier gene could then evolve and the pleiotropic connection of *G* and *B* would thereby be severed. Dawkins's scenario is certainly possible. The question, however, concerns how often such fortuitous mutations will break the ties that bind.

Here we must see that the issue concerns not the power of natural selection, but, as it were, the power of mutation. Whether or not *G* and *B* are correlated, it is true that the best combination of traits would be *G* and not-*B*. The issue of whether they are correlated does not concern what would be advantageous, but whether the variation on which selection acts includes this combination.

5 Concluding Remarks

What, then, is the unifying idea behind adaptationism? As I have discussed it so far, there are a variety of issues, only some of which can really be said to concern the question of how much selection, as opposed to other causes, contributed to the evolution of a given trait in a given population. In the simplest case of the joint effects of selection and mutation, we have two forces whose quantitative representation allows us to say which was the more powerful determiner of an evolutionary outcome. But in the cases of drift and pleiotropy, it is unclear what this comparative judgment would even mean.

When we considered drift and pleiotropy, we had to consider an ensemble of populations. There is no way to apportion causal responsibility by consulting intrinsic facts about the evolution of a single trait in a single population. Rather, we compared a number of identically prepared populations, in the case of selection and drift, and a set of different traits within a single population, for the case of pleiotropy and selection. Whereas the relative contributions of selection and mutation to the evolution of a single trait are locally determined, apportioning causal responsibility between selection and drift, or between selection and pleiotropy, is not a local matter.

Nevertheless, there is a general issue here that ties some of these examples together. Adaptationism concerns the power of certain simple models *of* selection; it is not a claim about the power of selection *in* evolution. What is the difference between these two formulations? To talk about the power of natural selection in a particular circumstance, we must consider a model in which the true values of all evolutionary forces are represented. We then must compare the value associated with selection with the values associated with the other evolutionary forces of interest.

This is how we made sense of comparing the contributions of selection and mutation in section 2. To talk of the power of a simple model of natural selection, on the other hand, we consider a model in which the true selective values are the only ones represented. We then compare the predictions of this simplified model with the predictions of a model that is ideally complete. The first approach compares the *parameter values* specified within a single ideally complete model. The second approach compares the *predictions* made by an ideally complete model with the ones generated by a simple model.

Let me briefly apply this suggestion to the case of selection and drift. Suppose we compare the predictions of a model that posits selection alone with the predictions of a model that posits the same selection coefficients, but with drift acting as well. As noted in section 3, the former model will predict a point frequency; the latter will predict a probability distribution, whose dispersion is a function of generation time and effective population size.

Let us imagine that we are applying these two models, not to a single population, but to a large number of populations. The predictive accuracy of the deterministic model can be measured by how often the members of this ensemble of populations exhibit frequencies that are close to the predicted point frequency. The more dispersed these observed frequencies are, the less accurate the deterministic model will be said to be. The point is that we do not compare the selection coefficient with the effective population size, whatever that might mean, but that we compare the predictions of one model with the predictions of another. Because one of the models is stochastic, we must compare the two models not with respect to what they imply about the frequency exhibited in a single population, but with respect to the distribution of frequencies in a large number of populations.

Adaptationism is the thesis that certain simple models are good predictive approximations. It does not deny that other forces were at work. Nor should it even pretend that there is an intelligible way to compare the magnitudes of all the factors that contribute to an evolutionary outcome. Rather, adaptationism holds that the predictions that follow from simple selectional models, in which the true selection coefficients are recorded, would not be much perturbed by taking other factors into account.[9]

It is a truism that every model must provide an incomplete account of the causal factors that impinge on the system it describes. Every model, therefore, must include a *ceteris paribus* disclaimer, whether this is given explicitly or implicitly. The idea of *ceteris paribus* is best understood to mean *ceteris absentibus*.[10] What matters is not that the other factors be equal in magnitude, but that they be absent. Adaptationism poses the question of whether selection *ceteris absentibus* yields predictions that closely approximate those that would follow from that ideally complete "model" in which no factors are ignored.

Notes

1. Adaptationism has an epistemological status within evolutionary theory that is similar to that of behaviorism and mentalism within psychology, on which see Sober (1985).
2. Sober (1984, Chapter 4) provides a philosophical treatment of what chance means in evolutionary theory.
3. Actually, we need to assume that the effective population size is constant, where this quantity takes into account not just the census size but the relative numbers of males and females.
4. The difference between local and nonlocal approaches to apportioning causal responsibility is discussed in Sober (1987).
5. There are ample independent reasons for doing this, which I develop in Sober (1984).
6. I shall not say "only if" here, since this would raise questions about the necessity of the condition I suggest that are extraneous to the present point.
7. In Sober (1984), I argue that Simpson's paradox is crucial for an understanding of what it means for an altruistic character to evolve under group selection.
8. Linkage can be given the same probabilistic treatment as the one provided for pleiotropy.
9. The requirement that the simple selection model should contain the true selection coefficients is important. Without this constraint, adaptive values could be invented so that the model will inevitably fit the phenomenon being modeled.
10. An observation I owe to Geoffrey Joseph.

References

Cartwright, N. (1979). Causal Laws and Effective Strategies. *Nous* 13:419–437.

Crow, J., and M. Kimura, (1970). *An Introduction to Population Genetics Theory*. Minneapolis: Burgess.

Dawkins, R. (1982). *The Extended Phenotype*. San Francisco: W. H. Freeman.

Eells, E., and E. Sober, (1983). Probabilistic Causality and the Question of Transitivity. *Philosophy of Science* 50:35–57.

Good, I. (1961–2). A Causal Calculus I and II. *British Journal for the Philosophy of Science* 11:305–318, 12:43–51, 13:88.

Gould, S., and R. Lewontin, (1979). The Spandrels of San Marco and the Panglossian Paradigm: A Critique of the Adaptationist Programme. *Proc. R. Soc. London* 205:581–598. Reprinted in E. Sober (ed.), *Conceptual Issues in Evolutionary Biology*, Cambridge, MA: Bradford/MIT Press, 1984, pp. 252–270.

Skyrms, B. (1980). *Causal Necessity*. New Haven: Yale University Press.

Sober, E. (1984). *The Nature of Selection: Evolutionary Theory in Philosophical Focus*. Cambridge, MA: Bradford/MIT Press.

Sober, E. (1985). Methodological Behaviorism, Evolution, and Game Theory. In J. Fetzer (ed.), *Sociobiology and Epistemology*. Dordrecht: Reidel, pp. 181–200.

Sober, E. (1987). Apportioning Causal Responsibility (unpublished).

Suppes, P. (1970). *A Probabilistic Theory of Causality*. Amsterdam: North-Holland.

Wilson, E., and W. Bossert, (1971). *A Primer of Population Biology*. Sunderland, MA: Sinauer.

5

How to Model Evolution

John Maynard Smith

---

1 Introduction

In recent years, a number of arguments have occurred between evolutionists about the best way of modeling various evolutionary processes. There is agreement about the basic biology of the situation, and about the results to be expected. The disagreements concern such questions as whether a particular process is best seen as a case of individual selection, gene selection, group selection, or kin selection, or whether inclusive or classical fitness is the appropriate measure. Perhaps these arguments are trivial: if the deductions from the different models are the same, there can be no empirical choice between models, and a good Popperian can regard the whole matter as pseudoscience.

I do not think we can avoid the problems quite that easily, for the following reason. When confronted with a biological phenomenon, one first attempts to fit it into one of the categories with which one is familiar. For example, one might think such things as "This is a case of heterosis," or "Starling roosts are selfish herds," or "This biased sex ratio arises from local mate competition." Any such first idea is quite likely to be wrong. Further investigation would require a more precise formulation of the hypothesis, a search for alternatives, and an attempt to decide between them empirically. However, one does start out with a set of formal categories in terms of which one attempts to interpret phenomena. In the absence of such categories, one could not hope either to explain phenomena in terms of existing theory or, more important, to recognize that some phenomenon does not fit existing theory.

I think that, for most of us, phrases such as "group selection" or "mixed ESS" represent the causal structure of an explanation, rather than the

An earlier draft of this paper has been modified in the light of two sets of written comments. In response to Elliot Sober, I have tried to clarify why I think that causes can be context-dependent in their effects. In response to Richard Dawkins, I have explained the difference between the distinction I make here between units of evolution and units of selection, and his distinction between replicators and vehicles. I thank them both for forcing me to be more explicit.

algebraic details. If so, our choice of models, and to some extent our choice of words to describe them, is important because it affects how we think about the world. In saying this, I am agreeing with a view recently expressed by Sober and Lewontin (1982), who argue that what matters about a model is that it should have the correct causal structure, and that computational convenience is secondary. To give an example where I think this is true, consider the statement that light passes from one point to another by that path that minimizes the passage of time. This is correct and mathematically convenient, but it would be causally misleading if it led one to suppose that the light beam computed an optimal path. In physics, no one is likely to be misled, but the dangers are much greater in biology. As against this, if a model leads to mathematical simplicity, that implies that it is easy to reason about, which is greatly in its favor. I am uncertain about the importance of computational simplicity, but I do not think it can be rejected as confidently as do Sober and Lewontin.

In this essay, I aim to do the following. First, by discussing the term "adaptation," I shall illustrate how our choice of model decides what phenomena we regard as readily explicable, and which need further investigation. Second, I shall illustrate how two alternative methods of modeling the same process may be available, by giving two examples—heterozygous advantage and the sex ratio in subdivided populations. Finally, I shall discuss how far "gene selection" models of evolution are appropriate, and contrast several approaches to the modeling of interactions between relatives.

2 Adaptation

The problem solved by Darwin was not only to suggest a mechanism whereby populations would change in time—that is, would evolve; he also explained a particular characteristic of evolution, which was overwhelmingly apparent to him, as to all naturalists. This is the fact that organisms have a structure and behavior that adapts them to survive and reproduce. For Darwin, the task was not to prove that organisms are well adapted to particular ways of life: it was to explain how they came to be so.

The explanation he offered was, in effect, that if there is a population of entities with multiplication, variation, and heredity, and if some of the variations alter the probability of multiplying, then the population will evolve. Further, it will evolve so that the entities come to have adaptations in the sense of the last paragraph. For Darwin, the relevant entities were individual organisms. Hence his theory provided an explanation of adaptations ensuring the survival of individuals. He knew nothing of genes, and was clear that his theory did not predict species-level adaptations. He slipped up at least once, but later corrected himself. In the first edition of

The Descent of Man, he explained the 1 : 1 sex ratio by arguing that such a ratio would benefit the population. By the second edition, he had seen his error, and wrote, "I formerly thought that when a tendency to produce the two sexes in equal numbers was advantageous to the species, it would follow from natural selection, but I now see that the whole problem is so intricate that it is safer to leave its solution to the future." It is intriguing that his greatest nineteenth-century follower, August Weismann, had a similar experience. As is widely known, he interpreted senescence as a species adaptation, arguing that only if individuals died could the population evolve. However, he too saw this mistake, and later offered an explanation of the evolution of senescence that is not too far from the theory (Williams, 1957) that most of us today would accept.

Thus Darwin's theory predicts certain kinds of adaptation, but not others. For example, the statement "The emargination of the primary feathers of birds evolved because it has the effect of producing wing slots that reduce the stalling speed" is compatible with the Darwinian model, whereas "Earthworms eat dead leaves because this releases nutrients into the soil that nourish plants" is not. Note that I am not saying that the former statement is correct and the latter not, but only that Darwin's theory predicts adaptations of the former kind, but not of the latter. Note also that there is nothing in the theory to predict that adaptations will be perfect.

Today, we are asking whether there are entities other than individuals with the properties of multiplication, heredity, and variation, and that therefore evolve adaptations by natural selection. In particular, are genes, or populations, or species, such entities? I shall refer to such entities as "units of evolution." To qualify as a unit of evolution, it is not sufficient that an entity be selected for or against: it must have heredity. In contrasting units of evolution with units of selection, I am making a distinction different from that drawn by Dawkins (1976) between a "replicator" (i.e., an entity whose structure and information content is copied more or less precisely in the process of reproduction) and a "vehicle," whose structure is not replicated, but that is the object upon which selection typically acts. Thus organisms are units of evolution, but they are not replicators. What makes organisms into units of evoluion is that

> i. they have heredity, in the sense in which Darwin would have used the word—that is, offspring resemble their parents—and
>
> ii. the replicators, or genes, that are responsible for heredity behave in a way that, typically, does not permit within-individual, between-replicator selection; thus in typical cell division one copy of each gene present in the mother cell is transmitted to each daughter cell, and in meiosis each member of a pair of genes is equally likely to be transmitted.

There are, of course, exceptions to the second condition—for example, in "meiotic drive." However, if meiotic drive were the rule, organism-level adaptations would not have evolved, and there would be no organisms to qualify as units of evolution.

Thus whether an entity qualifies as a unit of evolution depends on the relationship between that entity and the replicators that are ultimately responsible for heredity. In this sense, the distinction between units of evolution and selection is less fundamental than that between replicators and vehicles. Nevertheless, it is important to distinguish between objects we can expect to evolve adaptations and those we cannot. In particular, selection may act between groups of organisms, but it does not follow that group adaptations will evolve.

Consider, for example, the following imaginary scenario. Each generation of a large, random-mating population breaks up into groups of 100 individuals. These groups are then selected according to some criterion—for example, their ability to defend themselves against predators—some groups being wiped out and others surviving. The members of the surviving groups then reenter the random mating pool. In this example, there is no question that selection is acting on the groups. But it would be dangerous to think of the groups as units of evolution. If we did, we would expect the groups to evolve adaptations ensuring their survival—for example, the existence of some individuals that sacrifice their lives to ensure the survival of the rest. Once we appreciate that the groups do not (at least, in the usual sense) have heredity, we shall be cautious about assuming that such suicidal individuals will evolve: if we observe them, we shall suspect that there is something about the situation we do not know. If we want to know whether self-sacrificing behavior will evolve, we shall treat the individuals as the units of evolution (while accepting that selection acts on the groups), and ask whether individuals with a genotype that makes them sometimes sacrifice themselves are on average more or less likely to survive—or, and I shall return to this later, we may prefer to treat the genes as the units of evolution.

The point made in the last two paragraphs is illustrated in table 5.1. I suppose that there are two kinds of individuals—S ("selfish") and A ("altruistic"). Groups of two are formed randomly, and individuals contribute numbers of offspring to the next generation as shown in the table. In table 5.1a, both altruism and selfishness are ESSs: that is, a population of altruists would be stable against invasion by selfish mutants, and vice versa. We might be tempted to argue that the stability of altruists is guaranteed by the fact that groups of altruists are, as groups, fitter than other groups (combined output of 8 offspring, as opposed to 4 offspring from AS and SS groups). However, this would be a mistake, as shown by table 5.1b. Here, selfishness, S, is the only ESS, although again groups of altruists are, as

Table 5.1
Fitnesses of "altruistic" (A) and "selfish" (S) individuals interacting in pairs

	Case (a)			Case (b)			Case (c)		
Group fitness	A,A	A,S	S,S	A,A	A,S	S,S	A,A	A,S	S,S
	4,4	1,3	2,2	4,4	1,5	2,2	4,4	3,5	2,2
		A	S		A	S		A	S
Payoff matrix	A	4	1	A	4	1	A	4	3
	S	3	2	S	5	2	S	5	2

groups, fittest. Hence selection between groups does affect the course of evolution, but it is better to think of such group selection as acting by altering individual fitnesses, because it is individual and not group fitness that is maximized. However, if groups had heredity, and produced groups like themselves, then altruism would evolve for the fitnesses of table 5.1b. For completeness, table 5.1c shows fitnesses for which neither altruism nor selfishness is an ESS, and a stable polymorphism results.

There has been some semantic confusion about the phrase "group selection," for which I may be partly responsible. For me, the debate about levels of selection was initiated by Wynne-Edwards's book, *Animal Dispersion* (1962). He argued that there are group-level adaptations—for example, "epideictic displays"—which inform individuals of the size of the population so that they can adjust their breeding for the good of the population. He saw clearly that such adaptations could evolve only if populations were units of evolution in the sense that I have used the term here. Perhaps unfortunately, he referred to the process as "group selection." As a consequence, for me and for many others who engaged in this debate, the phrase came to imply that groups were sufficiently isolated from one another reproductively to act as units of evolution, and not merely that selection acted on groups.

The importance of this debate lay in the fact that group-adaptationist thinking was at that time widespread among biologists. It was therefore important to establish that there is no reason to expect groups to evolve traits ensuring their own survival unless they are sufficiently isolated for like to beget like. It is, I think, not an accident that the present interest in evolution of sex, recombination, and breeding systems generally was initiated by Williams (1975) and myself (Maynard Smith, 1971, 1978), both of whom had been engaged in the attempt to correct group-selection thinking.

When Wilson (1975) introduced his trait-group model, I was for a long time bewildered by his wish to treat it as a case of group selection, and doubly so by the fact that his original model (which permitted only additive fitness interactions) had interesting results only when the members of groups were genetically related, a process I had been calling kin selection for ten years. I think that these semantic difficulties are now largely over, with the use of the terms "intrademic group selection" and "trait-group selection" for the process envisaged by Wilson, and "interdemic selection" and "species selection" for that envisaged by Wynne-Edwards (according to whether the "groups" are demes or species).

There remains the question whether it is really true, in the trait-group model, that there is no heredity. What is required for the Darwinian process is that there should be different kinds of entities, A's, B's, C's, etc., and that when these replicate, A's should give rise to A's, B's to B's, and so on. For the imaginary example of trait groups of 100, a group with, say, 60 A's and 40 B's does not give rise to a group of the same composition. Instead, the individuals enter a random-mating pool and contribute genes to many different groups in the next generation. However, the same objection holds for individuals in a sexual population. Consider, for simplicity, changes in the frequency of a pair of alleles at a locus. Individuals can be thought of as a kind of trait group of two genes, upon which selection acts, before the genes reenter the gene pool, and pair up with new partners in the next generation. On this model, the entities with heredity are the genes: individuals are merely temporary trait groups.

There are two possible replies to this. One, made by Williams (1966) and Dawkins (1976), is to accept that the genes are indeed the units of evolution. To quote Dawkins, "I shall argue that the fundamental unit of selection, and therefore self-interest, is not the species, nor the group, nor even, strictly, the individual. It is the gene, the unit of heredity." (Note that Dawkins is using the term unit of selection in the sense that I am here using unit of evolution.) There is much to be said for this point of view, although it does not wholly solve the difficulty of identifying the unit of heredity. How small is a gene? If we think of the gene as the unit of function, it can be broken up by recombination. If we insist on a unit that is never broken up, we are left with the absurdity of a single base pair. Dawkins, following Williams, says, "A gene is defined as any portion of chromosomal material which potentially lasts for enough generations to serve as a unit of natural selection."

The alternative is to stick to the individual organism as the unit of evolution, on two grounds. First, with only two alleles at a locus, the correlation between parent and offspring is high (one-half, if we ignore environmental variance and non-additive gene effects). Second, and more fundamental, there is typically no analogue of within-group, between-individual selection, because the two alleles at a locus have equal chances of passing on a gamete. In our imaginary example of trait groups of 100, the reason why group adaptations could not readily evolve is that there was within-group selection: self-sacrificing individuals are less likely to survive. As soon as Mendelian rules break down (as in meiotic drive, or transposable elements), the basis for the evolution of individual adaptation breaks down also.

Although there are two alternatives, I do not think we have to choose between them. In developing evolutionary game theory, I have adopted the individual as the unit, but there are many problems for which a gene's eye view is more appropriate. Since Dawkins wrote enthusiastically of game theory, I take it that he accepts that it can be useful to think of individuals as the units. I suspect, however, that he would argue that a gene-centered view is in some sense more fundamental, and I agree with him.

3 *Alternative Models of Evolution*

At this point, it will be useful to look at two examples of biological processes that can be viewed in different ways. I repeat that in neither case is there any argument about the biological facts, or about the results to be expected: it is simply an argument about viewpoints.

The first, used by Sober and Lewontin (1982), is sickle cell anemia, the classic example of heterozygous advantage. There are, in human populations, two allelic genes, A and S, coding for the β chain of hemoglobin. S/S homozygotes usually die from anemia. A/A homozygotes do not suffer from anemia, but may die from malaria if that disease is prevalent. The A/S heterozygotes do not die either from malaria or anemia: thus they are fitter than either homozygote. As a consequence, both alleles are maintained in populations at high frequency in malarial regions. Sober and Lewontin argue that it would be absurd to regard this as an example of selection at the genic level, although they concede that the approach has some computational advantages. Obviously, selection acts on the individual. The "fitness" of a gene depends on which other gene it finds itself with: an S gene is fit if it unites with an A gene, but unfit if with another S gene. Since Sober and Lewontin regard causal appropriateness as a more important feature of a model than computational convenience, they insist that the individual selection model is the right one.

At first, I was persuaded by this argument, but now I am less certain. Let me start with the computational side. The classic, individual selection approach is to ascribe fitnesses—say $1 - s$, 1, $1 - t$, respectively—to the three genotypes AA, AS, SS. If one wishes to find the equilibrium frequency, say p, of allele A, one writes down an equation for p', the frequency in the next generation, as a function of p, s, and t, and then solves the equation $p' = p$. The result is a cubic. This is not as bad as it sounds, because the equation can be factorized. However, I have seen generations of biology undergraduates discouraged by the messy algebra.

Let us now approach the problem by ascribing fitnesses to the alleles A and S. The fitness W(A) of allele A can be written as (probability that A unites with A) × (fitness of AA) + (probability that A unites with S) × (fitness of AS): that is, $W(A) = p(1 - s) + 1 - p = 1 - ps$. By a similar argument, the fitness of the S allele $= W(S) = 1 - t + pt$. Hence, at equilibrium, $1 - ps = 1 - t + pt$, or $p = t/(s + t)$.

This is computationally so much nicer than the textbook method that one is tempted to seek a causal justification for it. Such justification is not hard to find. After all, the A and S genes do cause the appearance of specific chains, and these in turn cause the death or survival of their carriers. This implies that the fitnesses of the A and S alleles depend on which other allele they find themselves with, and hence are frequency-dependent. It might be objected that the genes themselves cannot be thought of as the causes of fitness differences, because a given gene substitution is sometimes associated with an increase of fitness, and sometimes with a decrease. I do not think this objection is valid. If I put a flame under a beaker of water, the water will expand if it is above 4°C, and contract if it is between 0°C and 4°C, yet in both cases I would wish to say that the flame caused the changes in density. Similarly, melanic moths are fitter in industrial areas, and less fit in rural areas, yet I want to say that the color difference causes the fitness difference. Indeed, it is often the case that individual fitnesses are frequency-dependent. Evolutionary game theory was developed to analyze such when detailed genetic information is lacking. By analogy, I am tempted to say that the best way of representing the sickle cell problem is in the form of a payoff matrix to genes as follows:

	A	S
A	$1 - s$	1
S	1	$1 - t$

This is an example of the Hawk-Dove game: the ESS is given by $p = t/(s + t)$.

My second example, recently reviewed by Harvey, Partridge, and Nunney (1985), concerns the sex ratio with local mate competition (Hamilton, 1967). There is a choice of at least three methods: classical population genetics, a game-theoretic approach based on individual fitnesses, and intrademic group selection (Colwell and Wilson). Hamilton sought the stable sex ratio when the offspring of several females mate among themselves before dispersal. Using a game-theoretic approach, he showed that, if the offspring of n females interbreed, the stable proportion of males is $(n - 1)/2n$. The essence of the problem can be understood from the case $n = 2$. Consider two kinds of females, Hamilton (H) females, producing 1♂:3♀, and Fisher (F) females, producing 1♂:1♀. There are three possible groupings (table 5.2). The "fitnesses" in the table are the expected values of "number of genes passed on to grandchildren." From the payoff matrix, it is clear that, if H and F are the only possible strategies, then H is the only

Table 5.2
The sex ratio game, assuming four offspring per female

Type of female	H	H	H	F	F	F
Number of offspring	3♀, 1♂	3♀, 1♂	3♀, 1♂	2♀, 2♂	2♀, 2♂	2♀, 2♂
Grandchildren per child	4, 12	4, 12	4, 20/3	4, 20/3	4, 4	4, 4
Total grandchildren	12 + 12	12 + 12	12 + (20/3)	8 + (40/3)	8 + 8	8 + 8
	24	24	18.7	21.3	16	16

Payoff matrix		H	F
	H	24	18.7
	F	21.3	16

ESS. It is not difficult to show that the ratio $(n - 1)/2n$ is stable against any other ratio.

This is the individual selection model. There are two alternatives. The first is to recognize that the above definition of "fitness" is unorthodox and potentially misleading, particularly when the genetic system is haplodiploid (as in the parasites considered by Hamilton). The classic population genetics approach is to consider a population with two alleles, determining the sex ratios S and s, respectively, and write down the recurrence equations for their frequencies (Maynard Smith, 1978). One then seeks a sex ratio allele S such that no alternative allele s can invade an S population. This is a kind of hybrid between classical population genetics and game theory: fortunately, it yields the same stable sex ratio as Hamilton's more intuitive approach.

The other possible departure (Wilson and Colwell, 1981) is to note that, in mixed groups, F females do better than H females, and that the success of the H phenotype arises because all-H groups do better than all-F or FH groups. This is the intrademic group selection approach. It is worth noting that in this example the fitnesses of groups are constant but of individuals frequency-dependent, whereas in the sickle cell example the fitnesses of individuals were constant but of genes frequency-dependent.

It would be easy to multiply examples from evolutionary genetics in which a variety of different approaches are possible. Is there any sense in which one of these is best? I am inclined to think not. Classical population genetics models, in which fitnesses are ascribed to genotypes (or to genotypes in specific environments), and recurrence equations for gene frequencies written down, have the virtues of clarity and correctness, but are often algebraically messy and lacking in perspicuity, as will become clearer when I discuss models of the evolution of altruism. Game-theoretic models are often algebraically simpler, and lend themselves to a kind of strategic thinking—"If I were an animal—or a gene—what would I do?" They have an obvious justification in analyzing the evolution of traits of whose genetics we know little or nothing. But they can be misleading, and may need checking by more formal genetic models. The intrademic group selection model has the virtue of emphasizing that those factors that increase between-group genetic variance relative to within-group will favor the spread of altruistic traits, but seem needlessly tied to cases in which the population has a group structure, and not merely neighbors.

4 The Evolution of Altruism

One virtue of the trait-group model is that it brings out particularly clearly that there are two contexts in which traits that are advantageous to the group but disadvantageous to the individual may spread: the first is when fitnesses combine nonadditively, and the second when interactions are between relatives. It is the second of these possibilities that has been the greatest stimulus to the development of a gene-centered view of evolution. Before discussing this approach in detail, however, I want to meet an objection to it that has a political and philosophical origin rather than a biological one. This is the objection to "genetic determinism." It has been argued that to base a biological model on the idea that gene A causes an animal to do X leads too easily to the assumption that the economic backwardness of Africa, the low pay of women, or the small proportion of working class children entering Oxford has a genetic rather than a social cause. I think this is a red herring. All that is needed in a gene centered view of evolution is the assumption that an animal with allele A, rather than a, is more likely to do X in environment E. If this were not so, it is hard to see how behavior could evolve. It does not follow that the human inequalities listed above have a genetic cause, and I do not think that they do. Those who do hold hereditarian views about racial, sexual, and class inequalities usually imagine that heredity is carried in the blood: I doubt if they are much encouraged by the knowledge that altruism requires $B/C >$ $1/r$. Finally, it does not follow that biologists who espouse gene-centered models also think that genetic differences are more important in our species than environmental ones: for example, Dawkins is clearly not a genetic determinist.

There are, I think, three main approaches to the evolution of traits that have different effects on individual and group survival:

(i) Classical or "Neighbor-Modulated" Fitness

Let us consider a gene A causing its carriers, which we shall call type X, to be more likely to perform an altruistic act. If we want to know whether A will increase in frequency, all we need to know is whether X individuals are "fitter"—that is, produce more offspring—than others (if there is dominance, there are three types whose relative fitnesses must be known). What happens to relatives of X individuals is irrelevant. However, when we calculate the fitness of X, we must remember that X individuals are more likely to have A-carrying relatives than are non-X, and hence are more likely to receive help. If we allow for this, we shall obtain what Hamilton (1964) called neighbor-modulated fitnesses, which will correctly predict genetic change.

(ii) "Inclusive Fitness"
Hamilton (1964) defined the inclusive fitness of type X as the expected number of offspring to X, not including any additional offspring to X because of help from others, plus any additional offspring to others because of help from X, weighted by the appropriate coefficient of relationship. He showed that the direction of genetic change, and its approximate rate, predicted if genotypes were given their inclusive fitnesses, correspond to the correct values predicted by neighbor-modulated fitnesses.

Cavalli-Sforza and Feldman (1978) have argued that, since the neighbor-modulated approach is exact, it is pointless to use inclusive fitness, which is hard to define, easily misunderstood (for an analysis of some misunderstanding, see Dawkins, 1979, and Grafen, 1984), and can in any case be applied only when fitnesses combine additively. Further, if intuitive ideas are going to be checked by computer simulation, there is no need to calculate inclusive fitnesses: the approach has to be classical (see, for example, Seger, 1983, which is the closest approach yet to an analysis of the relation between eusociality and haplodiploidy).

The short answer is that the classical approach is unusable except as a way of checking an insight gained in other ways. For example, I suspect that Seger, when thinking about the relations between bivoltine life histories, distorted sex ratios, and eusociality, used inclusive fitness as a guide, although this does not appear from his simulations. There are two reasons why neighbor-modulated fitnesses are hard to use. The less important is computational; one has to calculate, for all interacting relatives of X, the probabilities that they have particular genotypes, and not merely the gene frequencies in relatives (an example of how difficult this can be is given by Maynard Smith, 1982). The more serious difficulty is that one has to think causally backward. One has to say, "The reason why this bird is giving an alarm note is that the gene that is causing it to do so is likely to be present in other members of the flock, so those other members are also likely to give alarm notes, thus ensuring the survival of the gene we started with." I doubt whether many people can think that way.

(iii) Gene-Centered Models

In *The Extended Phenotype*, Dawkins argues that Hamilton's concept of inclusive fitness was a last-ditch attempt to treat the individual as the unit of evolution, and that he would have been wiser to abandon the attempt in favour of a fully gene-centered view. Grafen (1984) takes the same position, arguing that Hamilton's condition, $Br > C$, for the spread of a gene is a more useful approach than the calculation of inclusive fitnesses. In effect, one asks, for some allele A: "If allele A is expressed, and causes some action (or, more generally, some phenotype), are there as a result more or fewer copies of A than there would have been if A had not been expressed?" Such an intuitive approach can, in critical cases, be supported by a classical population genetics model, analytically or by simulation.

5 Conclusion

The issues discussed in this essay are conceptual rather than empirical. The most important distinction I have made is between what I have called "units of evolution," which must possess heredity, and "units of selection," which need not. The distinction is important because we can expect units of evolution to have complex properties ensuring their survival and reproduction. Since it is genes rather than individuals that replicate, how does it happen that most adaptations seem to be properties of individuals rather than of genes? The answer is that, so long as genes do not multiply horizontally, only those genes survive that ensure the survival of the individuals in which they find themselves. If gene selection within individuals (as in meiotic drive and transposition) were the rule rather than the exception, complex organisms would not evolve. Since, in higher level groups (demes, species, communities), there is pervasive between-individual, within-group selection, we cannot expect complex population-level adaptations.

The same biological process can often be modeled in more than one way. Different models may make the same predictions, yet give different insights: in such cases, we are not obliged to choose between them. There is much to be said for looking at a problem from different points of view. This plea for pluralism, however, differs from that recently made by Gould (1980). I am recommending a plurality of models of the same process: he is emphasizing a plurality of processes, and in particular selection at different hierarchical levels. His claim is in part an empirical one; for example, it includes the claim that differential survival and splitting of species as determined by species-level properties has been important in evolution. In the past, confusion between conceptual and empirical issues has generated needless heat. For example, the argument between Wynne-Edwards and others about "group selection" was ultimately empirical: are populations sufficiently isolated, and free of intragroup selection, to evolve complex group adaptations? In contrast, my disagreements with D. S. Wilson have been partly semantic (what shall we mean by "group selection"?), and partly concerned with whether intrademic group selection is a useful way of modeling a process that we agree happens, but that can be modeled in other ways. Let us hope that similar confusions will not needlessly exacerbate the debates now taking place about selfish DNA, concerted evolution, and species selection.

References

Cavalli-Sforza, L. L., and M. W. Feldman (1978). *Theor. Pop. Biol.* 14:268.

Dawkins, R. (1976). *The Selfish Gene*. Oxford: Oxford University Press.

Dawkins, R. (1979). *Z. Tierpsychol.* 51:184.

Gould, S. J. (1980). *Palaeobiology* 6:119.

Grafen, A. (1984). In *Behavioural Ecology*, 2nd ed. J. R. Krebs and N. B. Davies, eds. Oxford: Blackwell.

Hamilton, W. D. (1964). *J. Theor. Biol.* 7:1.

Hamilton, W. D. (1967). *Science* 156:477.

Harvey, P. H., L. Partridge, and L. Nunney (1985). *Nature* 313:10.

Maynard Smith, J. (1971). *J. Theor. Biol.* 30:319.

Maynard Smith, J. (1978). *The Evolution of Sex*. Cambridge: Cambridge University Press.

Maynard Smith, J. (1982). In *Current Problems in Sociobiology*. Cambridge: Cambridge University Press.

Seger, J. (1983). *Nature* 301:59.

Sober, E. (1984). In *Minds, Machines and Evolution*. C. Hookway, ed. Cambridge: Cambridge University Press.

Sober, E., and R. C. Lewontin (1982) *Philosophy of Science* 49:157.

Williams, G. C. (1957). *Evolution* 11:398.

Williams, G. C. (1966). *Adaptation and Natural Selection*. Princeton: Princeton University Press.

Williams, G. C. (1975). *Sex and Evolution*. Princeton: Princeton University Press.

Wilson, D. S. (1975). *Proc. Nat. Acad. Sci.* 72:143.

Wilson, D. S., and R. K. Colwell (1981). *Evolution* 35:882.

Wynne-Edwards, V. C. (1962). *Animal Dispersion*. Edinburgh: Oliver & Boyd.

6

Comments on Maynard Smith's "How to Model Evolution"

Elliott Sober

1 Units of Evolution

Maynard Smith (1987) distinguishes *units of evolution* from *units of selection*. He claims that it is the first of these, not the second, that forms the conceptual center of the controversy that Wynne-Edwards (1962), Williams (1966), Hamilton (1964, 1967), Lewontin (1970, 1974), and Maynard Smith (1964, 1976) himself helped shape.

I agree that the process Wynne-Edwards postulated involves groups that exhibit heredity. David Wilson's (1975, 1980) trait groups require no such thing. Trait groups, according to Maynard Smith's proposed usage, are not units of evolution. Maynard Smith concludes that the trait group idea does not address the problem that stems from Wynne-Edwards's invocation of group selection.

My main disagreement with Maynard Smith arises here. Although Wilson's proposal is a handy example with which to distinguish Maynard Smith's way of carving up the problem from mine, our differences extend beyond the kind of process Wilson investigated. Our disagreement concerns what the biological debate of the last twenty some years has been about. It may seem more than a little odd that a philosopher should tell a biologist about the nature of a biological problem that that very biologist has done so much to illuminate. In self-defense, I can only say that it is the logic of the reasoning biologists pursue that leads me to these conclusions. Surely it is the merits of such arguments, not the disciplinary credentials of the people who put them forward, that really matter.

I take it that Maynard Smith uses the term "unit of evolution" to apply to anything that exhibits heritable variation in fitness. He also believes that an X-level adaptation requires that X's be units of evolution. This is why he says that group adaptations will be impossible if groups lack heredity. In this discussion, I shall adopt Maynard Smith's stipulation about what a unit of evolution is, but I shall question the connection he draws between this idea and the concept of adaptation. In particular, I shall claim that it is neither necessary nor sufficient for group adaptation that groups be units of evolution. Since I see group adaptation as the conceptual center of the

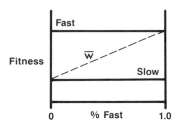

Figure 6.1
Fast deer are fitter than slow ones; the fitnesses are frequency independent. As *Fast* sweeps to fixation, the average fitness of individuals in the population, $\bar{w}$, increases.

biological controversy, I conclude that Maynard Smith's notion of a unit of evolution does not isolate the fundamental problem. This does not mean that the idea of group heredity is irrelevant, but that I assign to it a different importance.

The fundamental conceptual insight of Williams's (1966) *Adaptation and Natural Selection* was to see the difference between adaptation and fortuitous benefit. A trait of a group may be good for it, without the cause of its presence being that it is group beneficial. A group adaptation must have arisen by a process of group selection. This distinguishes group adaptations from group benefits that are artifacts of individual selection processes.

Williams (1966, p. 16) invented a simple example to illustrate this point. Suppose that speed helps deer escape from predators. Deer will therefore experience individual selection for being fast. As a result, slow deer are eliminated and the fleet survive. In this process of individual selection, the average level of speed found in the herd may increase. The process is illustrated by the frequency independent fitness function shown in figure 6.1.

Suppose for a group of deer that the slower it is, the more prone it is to extinction. If predators eat all the deer in a slow herd, the herd becomes extinct. It is therefore advantageous for a herd to be fast. Williams's point is that the survival of a fast herd is just a "statistical summation" of the facts of individual selection. Groups are benefited by containing fast deer; but it is false that groups are fast because they are so benefited.

Let us add to this picture the idea of group heredity. Imagine that groups not only go extinct but send out migrants to found new groups when the group reaches a threshold census size. Let the founders of a new group all come from the same parental population. Fast herds found more colonies and become extinct less often than slow herds. Groups thereby exhibit heritable variation in fitness. They are units of evolution, in Maynard Smith's sense. But the trait of fleetness is not a group adaptation, because it did not evolve by group selection.

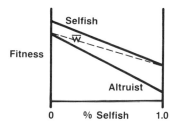

Figure 6.2
Within any group, selfish individuals are fitter than altruists, but groups of altruists will have a higher average fitness, $\bar{w}$, than groups of selfish individuals.

Slow deer are eaten while fast deer escape. As a result, slow herds survive and colonize less successfully than fast herds. But this difference between groups is just a "statistical summation" in Williams's sense. I conclude that groups can be units of evolution without there being group adaptations.

To establish the converse—that group adaptation does not require that groups be units of evolution—it is useful to think about the evolution of altruism. The relevant properties of an altruistic trait are exhibited in figure 6.2. Within any group, an altruist is less fit than a selfish individual. But groups in which altruism is common have a higher average fitness than groups in which altruism is rare.

In the kind of case I want to consider, individual and group selection will oppose each other. There will be individual selection for being selfish, but there also will be group selection for groups in which altruism is common. What will happen in this process depends on contingent properties of population structure. It cannot be determined a priori whether one trait will sweep to fixation in the ensemble of groups or selfishness and altruism will be maintained in a polymorphic equilibrium.

We can use Maynard Smith's idea of a unit of evolution to describe one way that altruism might evolve. Suppose that groups found colonies, where the founders of a daughter colony all come from the same parent. This means that we can identify for a colony in one generation its parent in the previous generation.

Let us suppose further that the organisms reproduce uniparentally, and that like always produces like. This does not imply that a daughter colony will always have exactly the same frequency of altruists as its parent. After all, the migrants from the parental colony are drawn by a sampling process; a daughter frequency may thereby differ from the parental frequency by sampling error. Nevertheless, I assume that groups have heredity in the requisite sense; although like does not always produce like, the *expected* frequency of altruists in a daughter colony (when it is founded) is just the *actual* frequency in the parental population (when sampling takes place).

Groups have heredity here just as organisms would, if the expected height of an offspring is the parent's height. So in the case before us, groups are units of evolution.[1]

The process begins with a set of populations exhibiting different local frequencies of altruism. Suppose one of these starting populations has 100% altruists. This population then founds offspring colonies, also with altruism at 100% (sampling cannot change *this* frequency). In each generation, a colony of pure altruists has a higher productivity than any other sort of colony. In the limit, we expect altruism to go to fixation in the ensemble of populations. In this group selection process, groups have heredity and a group adaptation—a trait that benefits the group at the individual's expense—thereby becomes universal. Here we have groups as units of evolution, in Maynard Smith's sense, and group adaptations as well.

For natural selection to produce evolution, heritability of some sort is essential. But for group selection to cause evolution, it is not essential that the heritability be *group* heritability.[2] Suppose that migrants are drawn by sampling from each population and then mixed in a global "migrant pool." After that, samples of ten organisms, say, are drawn from this pool, each such sample then founding a new colony. Suppose that the samples are drawn from the migrant pool, not at random, but on a principle of like associating with like. An extreme version of this procedure would have new colonies founded by either all altruists or all selfish individuals. A less extreme version might create colonies in which the ratio of altruists to selfish individuals is either 9:1 or 1:9. The point is that the distribution of local frequencies is more skewed to extreme ratios than would be expected if the sampling proceeded at random.

Altruism can increase in frequency under this regimen, even though the idea of group heritability has been destroyed. A given daughter colony may have founders drawn from many different parent colonies. Indeed, colonies do not form chains of descent (lineages) so much as densely connected webs. My point is that this does not mean that altruism—a group adaptation—cannot evolve.

A variant on this idea is Wilson's concept of trait groups. Suppose juveniles disperse into local groups, interact with each other during development from juvenile to adult, and then reassemble in a single global population to mate. If like associates with like in these local trait groups, altruism may increase in frequency. This may happen even though trait groups are entirely evanescent. A trait group in one generation cannot be said to be a parent of a trait group in the next.

In the first setup, groups have heredity—it is possible to say of a given colony, which colony in the previous generation was its parent. In the second setup, groups have many parents—conceivably the individuals in a colony may come from many (even all) of the colonies in the previous generation. In the third, the idea of group heredity has all but disappeared. Yet in all these arrangements, altruism can evolve, if the parameters are right. Altruism, I take it, is a paradigmatic group adaptation. It cannot evolve by individual selection alone, since an altruistic characteristic helps the group at the expense of the individual who possesses it. The reason that group selection can cause altruism to evolve in these systems is that altruists associate mainly with altruists and selfish individuals mainly with selfish individuals. Group heritability is one device for making sure this is true, but it is only one.

I have argued that the fundamental biological issue has been whether group adaptation is common, rare, or nonexistent. Group adaptation requires group selection. Evolution by group selection requires some mechanism of heritability. Maynard Smith has emphasized the idea of group heritability. I do not contest its importance. However, group heritability is just one way to secure the heritability needed for selection to lead to evolution. In addition, the concept of a unit of evolution glosses over the distinction between group adaptation and fortuitous group benefit. The examples discussed so far and Maynard Smith's two concepts are represented in figure 6.3. I conclude that Maynard Smith's concept separates processes that belong together and unites processes that belong apart.

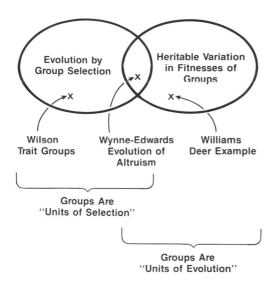

Figure 6.3
Maynard Smith's (1987) concepts of "units of evolution" and "units of selection." The controversy over group adaptation concerns whether groups are units of selection; although Wynne-Edwards's treatment required that they be units of evolution as well, this is neither necessary nor sufficient for the existence of group adaptations.

2 Causality and Context Dependence

If the difference between group adaptation and fortuitous group benefit is fundamental, then the central concept in the biological debate is the idea of a unit of selection. Maynard Smith does not characterize this concept. However, I take it that we can agree that X is a unit of selection in a given evolving system precisely when there is X selection in that system. This leaves it open whether there may be more than one unit of selection in a given biological system, whether some of those units may be more important than others, and whether different systems may have different units, depending on the details of their biology. This way of defining the idea does not mean that the kind of pluralism contemplated here is correct; it is just that the concepts should be understood in such a way that this possibility is not ruled out a priori. So the question of what a unit of selection is thereby boils down to the problem of understanding what distinguishes different sorts of selection processes.

For me, group selection is a distinctive sort of causal process. It is not definable by the existence of heritable variation in group fitness (as Williams's deer example shows); the question is not whether groups vary in fitness, but why they do so. I cannot do justice to this subject in the space of this reply, so I must refer the reader to the treatment I give of this issue in part II of *The Nature of Selection* (Sober, 1984).

Maynard Smith is quite right that Lewontin and I accorded no importance to the computational simplicity of the allelic versus the genotypic models of heterozyogote superiority (in Sober and Lewontin, 1982). This is because we wanted to say what the causal processes are that govern the evolution of this system. That question is properly answered by using some plausible account of what causality means and then consulting the biological facts. Since both the allelic and the genotypic models are correct as algebra, there is no notion of choosing between them, much less choosing between them on grounds of simplicity.[3]

Lewontin and I did not supply an explicit characterization of causality, but merely handled that sticky concept on an intuitive level. This is why I now regard some of the arguments we gave as less than conclusive. The account of causality suggested in my book underwrites the conclusions that Lewontin and I reached, but in what I think is a theoretically more satisfying way. In particular, we used the idea that context dependence can undermine a causal claim; this idea survives in the treatment of causality I develop. Maynard Smith objects to this, observing that "if I put a flame under a beaker of water, the water will expand if it is above 4°C, and contract if it is between 0°C and 4°C, yet in both cases I would wish to say that the flame caused the changes in density. Similarly, melanic moths are fitter in industrial areas, and less fit in rural areas, yet I want to say that the color difference causes the fitness differences."

To understand when context dependence is and is not relevant to the truth of a causal claim, we must distinguish two concepts of cause. There is *token causality* on the one hand and *property causality* on the other. The former describes what happens in a single unrepeated event (e.g., "Harry's smoking caused him to have a heart attack"), whereas the latter describes the causal role that properties play in some population (e.g., "Smoking is a positive causal factor in producing heart attacks among U.S. adults").

I agree that one moth may perish because it is melanic, whereas another moth, in a different area, may perish because it is nonmelanic. The fact that a trait has a given effect in one context is perfectly consistent with its having the opposite effect in another. So context dependence does not defeat claims of token causality. However, matters change when it comes to assessing the causal role that a property plays in a population. If, in a single population, melanism increases some individuals' chances of death while it decreases those of others, I do not think that the trait plays a univocal causal role in the population as a whole. Melanism is not a positive causal factor for mortality in that heterogeneous population. This does not mean that melanism is not a positive factor in one subpopulation and a negative factor in the other. Nor does it mean that melanism cannot be *correlated* with reduced mortality. This will be true if melanic individuals die less often than nonmelanic individuals.

So it is with respect to claims about the causal roles that properties play in populations that the context dependence of fitness becomes important. In the sickle cell case, having a copy of the S allele is not a positive causal factor for improved survivorship in the population as a whole. Having a copy of S on one chromosome improves fitness if there is a copy of A on the other, but it diminishes fitness if the other chromosome also has a copy of S. The real causal factors in this process are diploid genotypes; it is the pairwise gene combinations SS, SA, and AA that have determinate causal roles in the population as a whole.

Although there is no such thing as *the* causal role that melanism plays in the heterogeneous population imagined above, it is easy to divide that population in two—so that melanism is positive in one (industrial) sub-population and negative in the other (rural) one. Why not do the same thing for heterozygote superiority, thereby showing how it can be described with single genes as causal factors?

There are different ways of trying to do this, each with its special failing. For example, we could say that each gene is such that having a second copy of it counts as a negative causal factor: if you have one, you are better off without a second. But this formulation does not show that single genes are causal factors, Having a second copy of a gene, I take it, is equivalent with having two copies of the gene, so we still are talking about diploid genotypes, not single genes, as causal factors.

Another proposal might begin by labeling the two chromosomes One and Two, and then listing the causal facts for each of four "subpopulations" —(1) the individuals who have S on chromosome One; (2) the individuals who have A on chromosome One; (3) the individuals who have S on chromosome Two; (4) the individuals who have A on chromosome Two.

Here are the causal facts concerning these four groupings: (1) For individuals who have S on chromosome One, having A on chromosome Two is a positive causal factor and having S on chromosome Two is a negative causal factor. (2) For individuals with A on chromosome One, having S on chromosome Two is positive while having A on Two is negative. (3) For individuals with S on chromosome Two, having A on chromosome One is positive and having S on chromosome One is negative. (4) For individuals with A on chromosome Two, having S on chromosome One is positive while having A on One is negative. I grant that within each of these four "subpopulations," having a single gene on the relevant chromosome counts as a positive or negative causal factor. The four "subpopulations" are shown in figure 6.4.

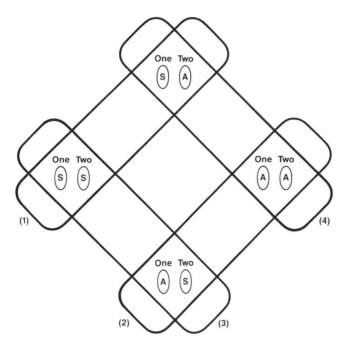

Figure 6.4
Heterozygote superiority can be analyzed so that single genes are causal factors for survival. To do so, however, requires that the population be segmented into four "subpopulations" in an entirely ad hoc way. See text for details.

Here we have heterozygote superiority from the point of view of the single gene as the unit of selection. Single genes are causal factors within "subpopulations," which in fact are four partially overlapping subsets of the single biological population under study. Notice that heterozygotes are split into two groups, depending on which allele occurs on which chromosome.

This procedure is entirely ad hoc; the "subpopulations" discerned are biologically meaningless. This creative storytelling obscures the fact that in this biological system it is entirely irrelevant whether a heterozygote has S on One and A on Two, or vice versa. Unless we deprive the word "population" of all content (so that it comes to mean any subset, no matter how arbitrary), we must grant that there is a single panmictic Mendelian population in this model, in which it is the three genotypes that are causal factors.

I conclude that genic selectionism can be formulated as a causal thesis, but at the price of inventing preposterous "subpopulations."[4] I should add that this strategy of splitting the population so that genic selectionism comes out true within artificially defined "subpopulations" will have the undesirable effect of making all selection processes cases of genic selection. Dawkins (1982) has embraced this result; for him even group selection is a kind of genic selection.[5] But this point of view deprives the group selection controversy of its empirical character. There was no need to build models or undertake detailed natural observations if the question could be dispatched so easily.

3 Cause and Correlation

In disposing of the "red herring" of genetic determinism, Maynard Smith notes that "all that is needed in a gene-centered view of evolution is the assumption that an animal with allele A, rather than a, is more likely to do X in environment E." This is entirely unobjectionable, provided that we are clear on what a gene-centered view can and cannot deliver. Maynard Smith's requirement is merely that the gene be correlated with the behavior, not that it cause it.

Whenever gene frequencies change via natural selection, there must be a correlation between genes and fitness. This is true whether the selection process occurs at the level of junk DNA, at the organismic level, or in Wynne-Edwards style group selection. In the model of heterozgyote superiority discussed before, a given allele will increase in frequency precisely when it is fitter than the alternative. Gene frequency equilibrium is reached when the allelic fitnesses are equal.

A gene-centered view of evolution, taken in this sense, is not a competitor with group selection, species selection, or with any other causal thesis about evolutionary processes. This is because the view is an algebraic truism, consistent with all possible causal stories.

I very much doubt that the idea of the selfish gene would have been so influential if it had been clearly portrayed in this uncontroversial way. The reason biologists rightly took an interest in it is that they saw it as a correction to group selectionist thinking. Here I have in mind the reception of Williams (1966) and of Dawkins (1976). But to think of the problem in this way is to conflate cause and correlation.

Once the causal and the correlational theses are separated, it is possible to see that the former is vastly overstated, while the latter is, as I have said, a truism. The idea that genes are units of selection in the causal sense has limited validity. Junk DNA and meiotic drive are plausible examples. But heterozygote superiority and inferiority, epistasis, group selection, and species selection are all counterexamples to genic selectionism. A great deal of selection proceeds without its being *single genes* that are selected for and against.

Space does not permit a full documentation of my claim that gene-centered views of evolution conflate cause and correlation. I shall, however, mention a single piece of evidence. When Dawkins (1982, p. 12) takes up the question of what it means to say that a gene "causes" a trait, he produces this analysis:

> If, then, it were true that the possession of a Y chromosome had a causal influence on, say, musical ability or fondness for knitting, what would this mean? It would mean that, in some specified population and in some specified environment, an observer in possession of information about an individual's sex would be able to make a statistically more accurate prediction as to the person's musical ability than an observer ignorant of the person's sex. The emphasis is on the word 'statistically', and let us throw in an 'other things being equal' for good measure. The observer might be provided with some additional information, say on the person's education or upbringing, which would lead him to revise, or even reverse, his prediction based on sex. If females are statistically more likely than males to enjoy knitting, this does not mean that all females enjoy knitting, nor even that a majority do.

Having said all this, I should add that I do not think the genic point of view, taken as a truism about correlation, is useless. There can be a point to seeing evolution from the gene's point of view, even when one knows that genic selectionism is false as a causal claim. As noted above in the model of heterozygote superiority, the relationship of allelic fitnesses allows one to determine how gene frequencies will change. To see whether a model process will produce evolution (here identified with change in gene frequencies) in a certain direction, it can be useful to describe it in terms of allelic fitnesses. Although these models will often be misleading as to causal processes, they may have much the same utility as the idea of a net force in Newtonian physics. Describing just the net force acting on a billiard ball will fail to capture causal information about component forces; but the net force is a simple and relevant quantity for predicting the ball's trajectory.

4   Group Selection and Female-Biased Sex Ratios

In discussing altruism in section 2, I mentioned that within each group, an altruist will be less fit than a selfish individual. If this is true within each group, how can altruism increase in frequency under selection of any sort? The answer is that altruists can have *greater* average fitness in the ensemble of groups, even though they are less fit within each group. This may happen if like lives with like. The fact that the inequality within groups is reversed when we look at the global population is an example of Simpson's paradox (Sober, 1984).

Selection can make altruism increase in frequency only if altruists are on average fitter than selfish individuals in the global population. It may sound contradictory to some biologists that altruists can be fitter on average than selfish individuals; I conjecture that this is because they define altruism in such a way that it cannot evolve at all—not even by group selection. This way of understanding altruism hardly helps make the question of group selection the empirical matter that it should be.

Fisher (1930) provided the canonical statement of how individual selection judges the way a parent determines the sex ratio of her offspring. Roughly, the best sex ratio strategy is to produce offspring of the minority sex. This leads the population to evolve by individual selection to an equilibrium 1 : 1 sex ratio. A parent producing far more daughters than sons may help augment the population's productivity; but she will be less fit within that population than a parent who follows Fisher's advice.

Let us call organisms who always produce female-biased sex ratios *Hamiltonians* and individuals who do what Fisher recommended *Fisherians*. Suppose we have an ensemble of populations, each made of a mixture of Fisherians and Hamiltonians. What will happen? Within each group, Fisherians will do better than Hamiltonians. But this does not determine whether Fisherians will be fitter on average across the ensemble of groups (Simpson's paradox again). If the parameters are right, Hamiltonianism may evolve and be maintained.

Hamiltonians are *altruists* in the sense of figure 6.2. Groups of Hamiltonians do better than groups of Fisherians, but a Fisherian in a group does better than a Hamiltonian in that same group. This is why I agree with

Colwell (1981) and Wilson and Colwell (1981) that a female-biased sex ratio is evidence of group selection. Altruism (Hamiltonianism) is counter-predicted by individual selection acting alone.

Maynard Smith follows Hamilton's (1967) treatment of female-biased sex ratios. By reparameterizing the model a little, one can show that under certain conditions, Hamiltonians will be fitter on average than Fisherians, and this explains why Hamiltonianism increases in frequency. Maynard Smith believes this shows how to account for female-biased sex ratios within the confines of individual selection. My objection here is the one I registered against genic selection before.[6] It is entirely correct that when Hamiltonianism increases in frequency under selection, Hamiltonians must be fitter on average than Fisherians. But this is a fact about correlation, and so does not address the question of whether the process involves group selection.

5 Conclusion

Hamilton's (1967) ground-breaking work on sex ratio is an example of how models can provide fruitful insights even when they are misleading about the causal facts. For this reason, I entirely agree with Maynard Smith that there is every reason to investigate a plurality of models of a single process. Each may afford its own insights, even though each may have its special limitations.

However, biology also takes an interest in whether pluralism is plausible as regards the processes themselves. Does natural selection proceed almost entirely in the Darwinian mode, or do other forms of selection also make important contributions to the diversity we observe? To assess pluralism, either positively or negatively, it is essential to become clear on how selection processes differ from one another. It is at this point that the concept of cause becomes central.

Notes

1. Michael Wade's (1976) experimental work on group selection in the flour beetle *Tribolium* has the structure described above.
2. Here I correct a careless remark on p. 276 of my book *The Nature of Selection* (Sober, 1984).
3. The argument put forward by Williams (1966) and Dawkins (1976) that genic selectionism is preferable because it is more "parsimonious" is critically evaluated in Sober (1984, chapter 7).
4. Philosophers may wish to compare this conclusion with Davidson's (1966) observation that "gred" (= "green or red") is a natural predicate provided we apply it to emeroses (= emeralds or roses).
5. This is not the view disputed in Williams (1966) or in Dawkins (1976). There the dispute between genic selectionism and its rivals was substantive and empirical.

6. Other objections to the idea, not the algebra, of "local mate competition" are developed in Sober (1984, chapter 9).

References

Colwell, R. (1981) Group Selection Is Implicated in the Evolution of Female-Biased Sex Ratios. *Nature* 290:401–404.

Davidson, D. (1966). Emeroses by Other Names. In *Essays on Actions and Events*, Oxford: Oxford University Press, 1980, pp. 225–227.

Dawkins, R. (1976). *The Selfish Gene*. Oxford: Oxford University Press.

Dawkins, R. (1982). *The Extended Phenotype*. Oxford: W. H. Freeman.

Fisher, R. (1930). *The Genetical Theory of Natural Selection*. New York: Dover.

Hamilton, W. D. (1964). The Genetical Theory of Social Behavior: I and II. *Journal of Theoretical Biology* 7:1–52.

Hamilton, W. D. (1967). Extraordinary Sex Ratios. *Science* 156:477–488.

Lewontin, R. (1970). The Units of Selection. *Annual Review of Ecology and Systematics* 1:1–14.

Lewontin, R. (1974). *The Genetic Basis of Evolutionary Change*. New York: Columbia University Press.

Maynard Smith, J. (1964). Group Selection and Kin Selection. *Nature* 201:1145–1147.

Maynard Smith, J. (1976). Group Selection. *Quarterly Review of Biology* 51:277–283.

Maynard Smith, J. (1987). How to Model Evolution. In this volume.

Sober, E. (1984). *The Nature of Selection: Evolutionary Theory in Philosophical Focus*. Cambridge, MA: Bradford–MIT Press.

Sober, E., and R. Lewontin (1982). Artifact, Cause, and Genic Selection. *Philosophy of Science* 47:157–180.

Wade, M. (1976). Group Selection among Laboratory Populations of *Tribolium*. *Proceedings of the National Academy of Sciences USA* 73:4604–4607.

Williams, G. C. (1966). *Adaptation and Natural Selection*. Princeton: Princeton University Press.

Wilson, D. S. (1975). A Theory of Group Selection. *Proceedings of the National Academy of Sciences USA* 72:143–146.

Wilson, D. S. (1980). *The Natural Selection of Populations and Communities*. Menlo Park: Benjamin/Cummings.

Wilson, D. S., and R. Colwell (1981). Evolution of Sex Ratio in Structured Demes. *Evolution* 35:882–897.

Wynne-Edwards, V. C. (1962). *Animal Dispersion in Relation to Social Behavior*. Edinburgh: Oliver and Boyd.

7

Reply to Sober

John Maynard Smith

I disagree with almost everything Sober says. But I must confine myself to essentials. I shall argue that he does not understand what the "group selection" argument was about, and that he is wrong to say that there can be group adaptations without group heredity.

First, the group selection debate. In 1962, when Wynne-Edwards published his book, biology was riddled with "good-of-the-species" thinking. Again and again, one met in the literature explanations of some trait—of behavior, breeding biology, life history, or ecological interaction—in terms of the benefit that the trait conferred on the species, or even on the ecosystem as a whole. It was quite clear to me, as it must have been clear to George Williams, that no progress would be made toward understanding the evolution of such traits until this kind of thinking was ended. It was Wynne-Edwards's great merit that he saw that the evolution of such traits did require some special explanation, even if he was, in my view, mistaken as to what that explanation should be. In effect, his book brought the whole topic out into the open. Group-selection thinking could no longer be tacit and semiconscious: it had to be explicit.

The response that I and others attempted to make was a very simple one. Entities will evolve adaptations if, and only if, they have the properties of multiplication, heredity, and variation. For example, the eye is a group of cells, but it has been able to evolve as an adaptation for seeing because the cells that form it are part of a larger group, the organism, that does have heredity. (It is also important that the possibilities of between-cell, or between-gene, within-organism selection are very limited.) It is therefore perfectly justified to study eyes (or, for that matter, ribosomes, or foraging behaviors) on the assumption that these organs adapt organisms for survival and reproduction. But it would not be justified to study the fighting behavior of spiders on the assumption that this behavior evolved because it ensures the survival of the species, or to study the behavior of earthworms on the assumption that it evolved because it improves the efficiency of the ecosystem.

This point may seem so obvious as not to need stressing. I can only say that it was not obvious to everyone twenty years ago. If Sober's way of describing the world is taken seriously, it will again cease to be obvious, and someone (not me, next time) will have the job to do over again.

But is it really true that groups without heredity do not have adaptations? Is it not the case that small groups of females whose offspring mate among themselves produce a female-biased sex ratio, which is advantageous for the group, even though, within a mixed group, "Fisher" females (producing a $1:1$ ratio) are fitter than "Hamilton" females (producing a female-biased ratio)? Of course it is true, but it is not a group adaptation. If it were a group adaptation, we would expect the sex ratio produced to be that which is optimal for the group, but it is not. For the group, the best sex ratio would be more female biased than it is. In fact, the sex ratio that evolves is the one that is optimal for the individual, in terms of the number of genes passed on to grandchildren. To see this, look at table 5.2. In a mixed group, it is true that the Fisher female does better than the Hamilton one. But, and this is the point, in such a group the Fisher female would do better still if she switched over to the Hamilton ratio (24 instead of 21.3), and the Hamilton female would do worse if she switched to the Fisher ratio (16 instead of 18.7). The Hamilton ratio is the one that maximizes individual fitness: it does not maximize group fitness.

If individuals assort in groups, but those groups do not have heredity, then the traits that evolve will be those that maximize the fitness of individuals, and not of groups. Sober discusses at some length a model in which groups are formed assortatively, with like individuals coming together. Even in this case, if you wanted to know what traits would evolve, you would have to find the trait that maximized individual fitness, allowing for the fact that the individual is likely to assort with others of the same kind. Of course, this would not be the same trait that evolved if individuals assorted randomly, but so what? It need not be the case that the same trait maximizes fitness regardless of the environment in which an individual finds itself.

As it happens, I do not think that such assortment of like with like is common in nature, although it does occur. What is common is that neighbors are genetic relatives. As Hamilton has taught us, this does affect the course of evolution. As I explained in chapter 5, there are several ways in which one can analyze such cases: by inclusive fitness, or neighbor-modulated fitness, or by a more explicitly gene-centered approach. But the one thing one cannot do is assume that the trait that evolves will be the one that maximizes the fitness of some group—even if a group exists.

My central point, then, is that entities that do not have heredity do not evolve adaptations. I shall add a few words about "causation," although I accept that I am now playing on Sober's home ground. He thinks that "... context dependence can undermine a causal claim." I agree that if all explanations must be causal, and if causes must be independent of context, then my way of seeing evolution is wrong. For a start, evolutionary game theory collapses, because it assumes that fitnesses are frequency-dependent. So much the worse, in my view, for Sober's concept of causation. Biology could not operate with context-independent causes. However, Sober does not really think that context-dependence undermines causal claims: if he did, he could not offer his explanation of sickle cell anemia. After all, AS heterozygotes are only fitter than homozygotes if the environment is malarial. His real objection, then, is to the artificiality of my explanation of sickle cell anemia as a case of gene selection. But I think this is because he chose an unnecessarily complicated way of presenting the argument. If I say, "Allele S is fitter than allele A, given that (i) the world is malarial and (ii) the allele inherited from the other parent is A," I cannot see why the first kind of context-dependence is causally permissible, but not the second. Of course, I have in this case no objection (other than algebraic messiness) to the individual-selection way of seeing things. I discussed the case only because Lewontin and Sober chose it as their example to illustrate the causal inappropriateness of gene-centered models, whereas it seems to me that a causally sensible (and algebraically elegant) gene-centered model is possible.

I conclude by emphasizing that I do think there is a difference between causation and correlation. A correlation between A and B is evidence that there is some kind of causal link between them. It may be that A causes B, or that B causes A, or that some third factor, C, causes both A and B. In the third case, I would say that there is "only" a correlation between A and B. In the case of genes, characters, and fitness, I think that (dependent, of course, on context) a gene difference can cause a character difference, and that a character difference can cause a difference in fitness. It is not merely a correlation. Hence, when I wrote ". . . an animal with allele A, rather than a, is more likely to do X in environment E," I did mean that allele A causes the animal to do X.

8

The Shape of Optimality

Richard C. Lewontin

Optimality arguments enter evolutionary biology by two routes. Primarily, they are meant to be a revelation of how things "really" are. That is, on the assumption that the direct cause of the state of living organisms is natural selection for the characteristics we see, and that sufficient heritable variation is always available to allow yet further natural selection, then it seems intuitively reasonable that organisms should be about as good as they can be in solving problems set by nature. Once we accept that organisms are, in fact, optimally designed, then optimality arguments enter by a second path into the analysis of evolution, as heuristics. Because we lack detailed knowledge of the developmental genetics and actual genetic variation of most interesting characteristics of organisms, and because we cannot measure directly the fitnesses of different genotypes in nature, the mechanical prediction or explanation of the characteristics of living beings from the principles of population genetics is impossible as a practical task. By using optimality arguments that assume a sufficiency of the underlying genetic variation and a causal efficacy of natural selection, we may argue directly about the evolution of organisms without the necessity of knowing about what is happening at the genetic and developmental level.

Arguments against optimality as either ontologically or epistemologically sufficient have pointed out that the basic assumptions of optimization theory are by no means generally to be trusted. When selection operates it may be selection "of" characters by indirect paths rather than direct selection "for" the character states themselves (Sober, 1984; Sober and Lewontin, 1982). Nor can we count on the efficacy of natural selection because the requisite genetic variation may be absent, developmental constraints may prevent the operation of selection in particular directions, and stochastic elements in both the environment and the breeding structure of real species result in nonselective outcomes to evolution (Gould and Lewontin, 1979). I do not want to rehearse those arguments here. They have theoretical force. The extent to which they disable the application of optimality arguments in evolutionary studies depends on contingent issues in each case. How small have populations been? What sorts of developmental and genetic constraints are there? How variable has the history of the environment been? How discriminating is natural selection? The answers lie in detailed analysis of particular cases. So, we know for certain that natural selection is extremely sensitive and efficacious in molding the amino acid composition of the enzyme alcohol dehydrogenase in *Drosophila melanogaster* (Kreitman, 1983), while it is at best coarse and undiscriminating for another enzyme molecule, *xanthine dehydrogenase*, in the same species (Buchanan and Johnson, 1983). But the latter molecule may be an exception to a general rule of close selective constraints. The question is, so far, unresolved.

Putting aside arguments about the efficacy of natural selection, we need to consider much more carefully the basic structure of optimality arguments, a structure that is common to such arguments irrespective of whether they are applied in evolution, political economy, physics, or the management of a basketball team. We begin with a seemingly trivial and formal distinction that nevertheless leads us a long way. That is the distinction between *optimal* and *maximal*, between *optimization* and *maximization*. Optimality is a qualitative characterization of some particular state among a list of alternatives, but without any metric. Moreover, the identification of a state as *optimal* cannot be made by reference only to the state descriptions of the alternatives. Optimality is not internally defined. So, the assertion that a birth weight of 7 pounds is optimal for a human infant cannot be made sensibly from a list of all possible birth weights, nor could 6 pounds be said to be "86% optimal." *Maximality*, on the other hand (or minimality, which is equivalent), is an internally defined characterization of a metric scale. In the range 1 to 10 pounds, 10 is the maximum. Yet maximality lies at the base of optimality, by a process of mapping. To argue that some state Y_0 is optimal among all alternatives in Y, we must map Y onto some other character X that has an associated metric scale. We then judge Y_0 to be optimal because it maps into X_M, the maximal value of X. All this seems an excessively formal way to say what we all know, but it concentrates our attention on questions that are neglected in most optimality arguments:

1. How do we decide on the *criterion scale X*?
2. What is the topology of the mapping? Is there a one-to-one correspondence of Y to X?
3. Over what range of Y does the mapping apply? That is, what alternatives are actually available?
4. As an extension of (3), what is the possible dimensionality of Y? Because it is well-ordered, the criterion scale X is necessarily one-dimensional. But what are the directions in which the characteristic Y is supposed to vary?
5. As an extension of (4), how will the mapping of Y onto X be changed by variation in yet other characteristics?

1 *The Choice of a Criterion Scale*

The necessity of choosing a criterion character whose maximization (or minimization) defines the optimality of the state that maps into it marks off ideas of optimality in the natural and social sciences, like evolution or economics, from ideas of "best" in moral philosophy or aesthetics. In this sense utilitarianism was a characteristically late eighteenth-century attempt to scientize ethics by mapping "best" in the moral sense onto a metric criterion scale, the total amount of happiness.

The first impulse for the evolutionist is to map characters on Darwinian fitness and judge that state to be optimal that maximizes fitness. After all, is it not fitness that is increased by natural selection? But for both ontological and epistemological reasons, fitness will not do. On the ontological side we need to ask, "The fitness of what?" Is it the fitness of particular genotypic or phenotypic classes or is it the mean fitness of the population (Wright's $\overline{W}$, not to be confused with the fitness of the population as a unit). To a large extent optimality theory has taken a typological view of species characters, which collapses these two senses of fitness. If there is a single morphology or behavior (or schedule of responses to environmental cues) that characterizes all the individuals in the species, then the average fitness, $\overline{W}$, is perforce equal to the fitness of the type. The optimality theorist is then free to argue that this type is optimal because it maximizes fitness, *tout court*. But if the species is polymorphic for characters, as indeed many, if not most, species are for many characters, the problem of which fitness is thought to be maximized cannot be avoided. Since different types will in general have different Darwinian fitnesses, the only thing that can be maximal is the average fitness of the ensemble, which in turn depends upon the frequency distribution of the types. This means, in turn, that it is not the original character state but the frequency distribution of states that must be said to be optimal, for it is this distribution that maps into the appropriate fitness measure. Unfortunately, there is no general evolutionary principle that guarantees the maximization of $\overline{W}$ when the population is stably polymorphic. If the observed polymorphism of characters is not a consequence of natural selection alone, but is evidence of the failure of selection to rid the population of suboptimal variants, optimality theory fails in a different way, as we shall see below. In any case polymorphism poses great difficulties to asserting that it is Darwinian fitness that is, in fact, maximized by the optimal state.

The epistemological objections to fitness as the criterion character X are, if anything, more severe. The whole purpose of optimality as a heuristic is to avoid the problem of measuring the Darwinian fitnesses of different types and of treating the full dynamical problem of changes in population composition by selection. Optimality arguments use proxies for fitness, such as energy expenditure, growth rate, territory size, and feed efficiency, precisely because these are thought to be measurable and to be in some simple relationship with the unmeasurable, fitness. If optimality theory is to be of any use at all, it must map character states onto a measurable criterion that itself is thought to be a *cause* of fitness difference. Otherwise we have nothing but an empirically vacuous definition of optimal, defining it as that state created by natural selection.

A proper criterion character stands in a special causal relation between the characteristic to be optimized, Y, and fitness, W. It must be a *consequence of Y* and a *cause of W*. This intermediate position in the causal chain flows from the theory of optimality itself, which claims that the optimal value of some trait is the cause of some other trait taking a maximal (or minimal value), which in turn leads to a higher reproductive rate of its carriers. That is, the criterion scale transforms into the selective advantage scale by an order-preserving transformation. Consider, say, the spatiotemporal pattern of flight activity of *Drosophila* from food source to food source as a character that may be optimal. We might choose calories gathered in feeding minus calories expended in flight as our criterion character, since flight pattern is obviously causally efficacious in determining this quantity, and because we reason that the greater this net caloric intake, the greater the reproductive rate of the organism. But we see immediately from the example that there are some problems. There is no one-to-one correspondence between causal traits and criterion traits. The spatiotemporal flight pattern of *Drosophila* also influences the probability that the fly will be eaten by a predator, its probability and time sequence in finding egg-laying sites, its chance of having its body temperature raised above the critical lethal level by direct solar insolation, etc., and each of these criteria has, *ceteris paribus*, a direct relation to fitness. But the mapping of Y onto X is not the same for each of these X scales, so that Y_0 from one criterion scale is not Y_0 from another. Conversely, any given criterion character is the consequence of many causal pathways, of which the character under investigation, Y, is only one. The probability of death from insolation depends, among other things, on the color of the fly, the size of the fly, the melting temperature of its cuticular wax, and so on, characters known to be variable and selectable in *Drosophila*. So the choice of a given criterion character to map onto a given primary trait necessarily assumes a restricted form of interaction between traits. The judgment that a particular flight pattern minimizes the probability of death from insolation can be made only if the other traits affecting this probability are assumed to be either constant or order-preserving in their effect on the mapping of Y onto X. Should a change in body color cause a *different* flight pattern to be optimal, then body color must be taken into account. The problem soon becomes unwieldy as the number of other traits that must be taken into account grows.

Reciprocally, because many different criterion variables are affected by a given primary trait, the value of the primary trait that is optimal on one criterion scale may not be optimal on another. So, the flight pattern that maximizes the net caloric intake, in all likelihood, is a different one than that which maximizes probability of finding a suitable egg-laying site or minimizes death from insolation. Indeed, negative correlations may minimize one criterion trait yet maximize another. Which criterion scale should we choose to determine Y? Has flight pattern evolved so as to maximize energy intake, or ease of finding a place to lay an egg, or keeping cool, or finding a mate, or avoiding a predator, or some weighted combination of all or some of these? Which are the important "problems" to be "solved" by flight pattern, and which are "solved" in some other way?

These questions bring us directly to the second mapping, that of criterion variables on fitness. Obviously, the single variable, reproductive fitness, is a consequence of many causal pathways, so that different criterion characters will be weighted more or less heavily in the determination of fitness. While it may be impossible to maximize both egg laying and predator avoidance by the same flight pattern, the quantitative relations between these characters and fitness may give a clear predominance to one or the other. Predators might be very rare, for example, or the variation in egg-laying success with different flight patterns might be very small. Just as a detailed knowledge of the mappings of primary traits onto various criterion characters is essential, so the quantitative response of fitness to variation in those criterion characters is critical. No decision can be made on the choice of criterion variable without such detailed knowledge. So, no decision about whether a primary trait is or is not optimal can be made without these details.

2 The Domain of Optima

Let us assume, for the moment, that a satisfactory choice of criterion trait has been made. Suppose that the detailed information about the biology of *Drosophila* leaves us in no doubt that fitness is almost entirely dependent upon maximizing net caloric intake, and that the way in which flies move from yeast colony to yeast colony does indeed maximize net calories per visit time. The question then arises as to whether this is the best *Drosophila* can do. Even though small perturbations of time spent on a food source, or of distance traveled from source to source, or of size of sources that will attract flies will all result in a reduction in net caloric intake, the question remains whether larger perturbations in fly biology might produce yet greater maxima of energy intake. This is the classic problem in dynamics of whether a maximum or stable point is local or global. The problem of globality is, in part, a problem of the domain in which the possible values of the state variables are assumed to lie and in part a problem of the dynamic accessibility of different regions of that domain from a given state. Both are part of the general problem of what might be called the *topology of accessibility*.

Given the species *Drosophila melanogaster* with a certain collection of genotypes and phenotypes, what are the possible ways in which net caloric intake per unit time could be increased? The answer depends upon what phenotypic states are considered accessible to the species. Optimization theorists usually take the species as given and consider only small perturbations of the primary variable, say flight pattern. That is, the domain over which optima are sought is a small neighborhood around the current state and along dimensions specified by the trait of interest. The question is how would a change in the average time spent at a yeast site and the average distance searched for a new site increase or decrease net caloric intake? But why should we limit ourselves to the neighborhood of the present search pattern? There are several levels at which alternatives need to be considered.

First, caloric intake might be increased by moving the species along a quite different dimension than the primary variable. Why is it that *Drosophila* does not stop eating yeast and start eating nectar, or pollen, or blood, or meat? Why should it not alter its mouth parts and become a chewer of plant material? The obvious answer is that the major rebuilding of the organism to allow such functions is not possible incrementally by a few mutations followed by selection. The space of evolutionary accessibility is limited for all organisms, so that optimization must be considered as *optimization under constraints*. On the one hand this answer seems right, but on the other we do not know how to make it precise enough to avoid mere *post hoc* rationalizations. After all there are insects, even *Diptera*, that chew, suck, pierce, abrade, cut, and otherwise ingest all sorts of living and dead organic material. Moreover, there are changes in adult shape, size, and even the number of wings that are mutationally accessible to *Drosophila* and have been artificially selected in the laboratory that would make major alterations in flight efficiency. One can hardly claim that two wings is the best state for a flying insect, in view of the commonness of four. Thus, a proper optimization theory must be capable of explaining why particular constraints on accessibility are regarded as absolute while others are not. My guess is that if fungus-gardening ants had never been seen, the suggestion that this was a reasonable possibility for ant evolution would have been regarded as silly.

A related possibility is to change the rules of the game. The mapping of characters onto criterion traits is a mapping of particular individual character states, with the identification of one of these states as optimal. But this leaves out of account so-called "cooperative solutions." So, a collection of behaviors each one of which maps to a nonmaximal criterion value, may, by cooperative action, increase the criterion value for all of them beyond the optimal single behavior. Such Pareto maxima certainly exist in social animals, and we would like to know why they are not more widespread. Why is it that *Drosophila* do not divide up the resources by cooperative arrangements so that net caloric intake is even greater? Again the immediate answer given is that they lack the behavioral repertoire and are constrained to optimize along other dimensions, but this is not really helpful.

Even within the dimensions already considered to be variable, there is the possibility of finding other local optima by radical shifts in the range of the character. Consider, for example, the possibility of long distance movements at certain times, taking advantage of high winds, rather than hugging the ground as *Drosophila* does in such circumstances. A free ride to regions of unexploited resource might pay off energetically. The possibility must at least be considered when calculating maxima. Again it is easy to invoke constraints, but without much specificity.

The problem with optimization theory is that a domain over which the primary character is allowed to vary must be specified a priori. The optimal state can only be the optimum over a specified set of alternatives, so it is never *the* optimum. All evolutionary reconstruction suffers in some degree from this problem. Evolutionarily Stable Strategies are stable only over the set of allowed alternatives. They may always be destablized by some as yet unspecified alternative. But the same is true even of mechanical population genetics. The stability of an allelic frequency distribution under selection can be judged only for the set of alleles actually present. There is no globally stable set, and a new allele can always be introduced that destroys the equilibrium. The difference from optimality theory (or ESS theory) is that population genetics makes this contingency explicit. Indeed, the technical literature of population genetics considers precisely this problem, for example, "Muller's ratchet" (Muller, 1964), or multiple allelic feasibility of equilibrium (Lewontin, Ginzburg, and Tuljapurkar, 1978). Optimization theory, in general, sweeps the problem under the rug, regarding what exists as defining the domain of the possible.

Finally, it is entirely conceivable that two different patterns of flight and search activities, both already possible for an insect of the size and shape of *Drosophila*, would each correspond to a local maximum of energy intake. Moreover, the species may actually be characterized by the pattern corresponding to the lower of these two local maxima. An extreme version of the optimality claim must regard this as a failure of optimization since it is the maximum of maxima that is predicted. A more reasonable claim would accept historical contingency as necessarily modifying the outcome of an evolutionary process. There are multiple maxima, and each has a domain of attraction. To which maximum the dynamic evolutionary process carries the species depends upon the initial composition of the population at the time the selective process began. The species *might* have gone to the higher local maximum except for accidental historical circumstances of initial state. The alternative maximum is now *dynamically inaccessible* because selection would have to carry the species temporarily to a less fit state in order to make the transition, and this is kinetically impossible according to the rules of gene frequency change under natural selection. The existence of alternative local maxima compromises the predictive program of optimization since it is not clear, from a knowledge of the criterion character alone, to which maximum the species will ascend, but the explanatory power of the theory is in no way weakened. Optimization theory then again takes the form of optimization subject to constraints, and in particular the constraint of historical contingency. But once historical accident is allowed as a constraint, very serious problems of confirmation arise.

3 The Actual and the Possible

All of the constraints discussed above are historical accidents. It is a historical accident that *Drosophila* cannot optimize their caloric intake by irrigated agriculture, or that humans need machines to fly. As far as we know all living organisms are connected by an unbroken chain of historical contingency. So no constraints are absolute. On the other hand, *the* optimal organism does not exist. To the extent that optimality is a property of organisms, it is optimality on extremely restricted domains of characters, which domains have been determined by globally nonoptimizing historical contingencies. The most that can be said for organisms is that they make the best of a bad situation. But do they do even that?

The problem with identifying historical contingency as a constraint within which optimization occurs is that it reduces itself to absurdity, for there is no limit to our retreat in the definition of the possible. Consider a population segregating for alternative alleles at three loci. A measurement of fitness of the various genotypes predicts that the population should reach a composition of *AABBCC* under the force of natural selection. The population is finite in size, however, and in the course of its evolution becomes fixed by chance in the early history of the population, so that only *Aa* and *Bb* are segregating. With *c* fixed, the fitnesses now predict *AAbbcc* as the selective result, and that is indeed what finally happens. In the end, when the population reaches a composition *AAbbcc*, only the first of the three loci has finally reached the selective maximum originally called for by the theory; the second locus, *b*, has reached the selective maximum contingent on the historical accident at the third locus, which has reached a composition predicted by no selective theory, but entirely by historical accident. Is this an example of the success of selective theory? In actual nature a species is unlikely to correspond to the optimal description that would have been calculated at a much earlier stage in its evolution. Indeed, because of variable environment and stochastic genetic events, it is unlikely to be exactly at the optimum predicted at *any* previous stage in its evolution. But if the historical accidents of environmental fluctuation and random genetic drift are regarded as defining the possible for the species, then no matter how far the species is from a computed optimum it is "as close as it can be." (Kitcher makes very much the same point in his paper in this volume.)

The purpose of the argument is not to refute optimality theory but to demand its nontrivial formulation. If the principle of optimality is to be useful as a description of what actually happens in evolution, it cannot swallow all accidents of history. If random genetic drift of the kind given in the thought experiment of the three loci is really at all common, then optimization is *not* a good characterization of the evolutionary process. The optimization claim must be ambitious enough to exclude a good deal of accident or it becomes empirically vacuous. It must, however, not be so ambitious as to exclude all historical contingency since then we would know it to be untrue a priori. Between these two it is not clear to me how much space is left for enlightenment.

References

Buchanan, B. A., and D. L. E. Johnson (1983). Hidden Electrophoretic Variation at the Xanthine Dehydrogenase Locus in a Natural Population of *Drosophila melanogaster*. *Genetics* 104:301–315.

Gould, S. J., and R. C. Lewontin (1979). The Spandrels of San Marco and the Panglossian Paradigm: A Critique of the Adaptationist Programme. *Proc. Roy. Soc. Lond. B* 205: 581–598.

Kreitman, M. (1983). Nucleotide Polymorphism at the Alcohol Dehydrogenase Locus of *Drosophila melanogaster*. *Nature* 304:412–417.

Lewontin, R. C., L. Ginzburg, and S. D. Tuljapurkar (1978). Heterosis as an Explanation for Large Amounts of Polymorphism. *Genetics* 88:149–170.

Muller, H. J. (1964). The Relation of Recombination to Mutational Advance. *Mutat. Res.* 1:2–9.

Sober, E. (1984). *The Nature of Selection*. Cambridge, MA: MIT Press.

Sober, E., and R. C. Lewontin (1982). Artifact, Cause and Genic Selection. *Philosophy of Science* 49:157–180.

III
Applications

9

Evolutionary Ecology and the Optimality Assumption

John M. Emlen

1 Introduction

Over the past twenty years it has become increasingly popular for ecologists to invoke the notion of optimal adaptation as an organizing principle in their field. Concurrently, there has grown up a large body of literature, contributed by both scientists and philosophers, attacking the practice as patently unscientific (see, e.g., E. Sober, this volume). The optimality approach has been reviewed several times by sympathetic researchers (Maynard Smith, 1978; Oster and Wilson, 1978; Dunbar, 1982) who have given various degrees of attention to the problems inherent in its application. Unfortunately, though, there still remains a dearth of serious published thought by practitioners about its scientific merits.

What constitutes "unscientific" practice? Science is a formal approach to explaining the real world; as scientists, we seek understanding. And most of us fall into the category of scientific realists. We believe that with the building of ever more complete and consistent pictures of the world we gradually narrow in on the "truth"—we approach an understanding of reality unblemished by the biases of our instruments, our senses, and our attitudes. It is within this context that detractors of the optimality approach have leveled their attack. In attempting to discuss the merits of the approach as science, therefore, it is necessary both to air thoroughly the various objections to it and also to examine more closely the philosophical context within which both its practice and its disparagement are couched.

When sufficiently pressed, many evolutionary ecologists avow that they do not intend testing the assumption of optimal adaptation per se. Rather they use the assumption, without necessarily believing it, as a tool for generating hypotheses (see also Oster and Wilson, 1978, p. 312). To the extent this honestly reflects their attitudes, the usual criticisms of optimality must fade in significance, for the hypotheses generated can often be made quite precise, and can be constructed in such a way as to invite falsification (see P. Kitcher, this volume). In this sense, evolutionary hypotheses are no different from those of (e.g.) physics. Unfortunately, such hypotheses as these do not provide a rationale for explaining or understanding. The hypothesis that animals choose a diet that maximizes net energy gain under certain conditions, and minimizes foraging time under others, is falsifiable, interesting, and perhaps helpful as a predictor. But it does not provide insight into the organizing principles of dietary behavior. It is the underlying assumption of optimality that provides that vital step to narrowing in on the "truth." And within the context of scientific realism, as I shall argue, the case against testability of the optimality assumption is solid; evolutionary ecology is perched precariously on a tenet with a little better support than that for faith healing.

2 Definitions

The optimality assumption states that the phenotype(s) characterizing the best adapted individuals possible in a population comes to dominate that population. What is meant here by "best adapted?" Until very recently evolutionary ecologists have spent surprisingly little effort building workable definitions (though see Ghiselin, 1966; Williams, 1966; Lewontin, 1978; Dunbar, 1982). Of that which has been done I offer a brief sketch. First, users of the optimality assumption deal with observable phenotypes. It is important that this fact be borne in mind—to the ecologist, optimal adaptation is a characteristic of phenotypes, not genotypes. If a phenotype is viewed as a compound totality of traits, then it is likely that no two individuals will fall into the same category. Therefore, it is necessary to define phenotypes on the basis of a particular, chosen subset of traits. There are two obvious definitions of "best adapted" (1) The best adapted phenotype is that whose individual members experience the greatest survival and reproductive success. (2) The best adapted phenotype is that which shows greatest persistence (survivability) over time.

Where environments are constant, definitions (1) and (2) are equivalent. Where environments fluctuate, in respect to characteristics affecting survival and reproduction, over time periods shorter than one generation, definition (2) collapses into definition (1) because individual success in surviving and reproducing can only be measured over a lifetime, whence it is the temporal mean conditions that characterize the environment. If fluctuations have long periods, then each generation may have its optimal phenotype, and phenotype frequencies (under the optimality assumption) will change in time, tracking the environment. That phenotype which approaches most closely the long-term average optimum by definition (1) is also optimal by definition (2). Here too, then, by looking at averages, definition (2) can be subsumed in definition (1). Definition (1) is tacitly adhered to in most circles, and is the one I shall consider in the following discussion.

Success in survival and reproduction can be quantified by combining the two components, usually on an age-by-age basis, into an expression that reflects total contribution to population growth. For example,

$$\text{adaptedness} = \overline{\sum_x R^{-x} l_x b_x}, \tag{1}$$

where the overbar denotes arithmetic mean over individuals of a specific phenotype, R is the population growth multiple, averaged over all phenotypes, x is age, l_x is phenotype-specific, individual survivorship to age x (1 if the individual survives, 0 otherwise), and b_x is phenotype-specific, individual fecundity (which is nonzero only if the individual in question mates). Another possibility is simply to define adaptedness as the mean of all individual contributions to R by the phenotype in question:

$$R = \overline{(p_x + p_x b_{x+1})},$$

where p_x is probability of surviving the age interval x, $x + 1$.

Still other definitions are possible, but will not be explored here; a precise quantification of adaptedness is not necessary to the following discussion.

Recently Maynard Smith and others (Maynard Smith, 1974, 1982; Maynard Smith and Price, 1973; Maynard Smith and Parker, 1976; Parker, 1974) have argued that many forms of adaptation should be investigated not as evolutionary responses to a passive environment, but as responses to interactive processes. That is, the adaptedness of a behaviorial response (of an organism that displays a certain proscribed behavioral repertoire) depends on the behavior responses of other, socially interacting individuals. Here, adaptedness can be shown to be frequency-dependent, a situation that generally does not result in maximizing mean adaptedness in a population. Such findings underscore the importance of viewing equation (1) as a mean of individual contributions.

But while agreed upon formulations of adaptedness and a definition of what is meant by the best adapted phenotype are necessary to application of the optimality assumption, they are not sufficient. For at least two reasons it is necessary to view optimality not as a state but as a process. First, regardless of what superior individuals may arise in a population, with whatever impressively high adaptedness values, as their frequency increases (a direct consequence of the optimality assumption), R rises and the population grows. Eventually density-feedback must occur and the population mean growth rate must fall to zero. At this point the (geometric) time average R for the population is one. And if the optimal phenotype has taken over the population, its adaptedness by either of the above measures is also one. The adaptedness of prevailing phenotypes in any two populations that have reached evolutionary equilibrium—i.e., optimality—are equal, regardless of their nature. To compare adaptedness between the phenotype characterizing two populations it would be necessary to mix them up and observe the subsequent process during which one or the other phenotype gained ascendancy. Also, depite the plethora of optimality models, no evolutionary ecologist actually believes his or her organisms are behaving optimally. Rather they see optimality as a process by which populations climb phenotype-adaptive peaks. The game-theoretic view does not change that perspective; it merely complicates the picture by permitting the peaks to change shape and position as the process goes forward. Optimality models exploit the putative end point of the optimization process, purporting to identify the adaptive peaks and stating that populations will indeed occupy them or their neighborhoods.

3 Are Optimality Models Scientific? Some Basic Considerations

If the purpose of science is to seek understanding, then the following analogy is appropriate. Consider a newborn baby in front of whom a chair has been placed. Viewing that chair, the baby experiences a rush of neural impulses that he or she interprets in some subjective manner. That is, in some way, the perception is organized into a mental image, a definition of the sensory experience. As the chair is moved, and viewed from new angles, new impulses that must be reconciled with the old are relayed to the brain. The mental image, the definition, may have to be altered. This is precisely how science works, except usually in a more organized fashion. The scientist continually seeks out new ways to view the chair, altering, fine-tuning, and constructing ever more elaborate definitions that are consistent with observation. Observation is, of course, nothing more than the subjective experience of neural impulses. However, though the chair itself thereby remains permanently removed from our experience, the scientific realist believes that with ever more complete definition we eventually converge on a "true" picture of that chair. In effect, as R. Levins (1966) once remarked, truth is the intersection of all independent lies (or, more accurately, all incomplete or biased views). In proposing his laws of gravitation, Newton's accomplishment was to generalize observations into a simple, mathematical form—a *definition* of gravity as a force operating between two bodies with intensity proportional to the product of their masses and inversely proportional to the square of their separation. Today, on the basis of further observations (neural impulses filtered through our instruments, our sense organs and our predispositions toward the content of truth), we "know" that Newton's definition is inaccurate; we have replaced it with a more complete, more elaborate, and quite different definition couched in terms of space-time geometry. Evolutionary ecology theory is based on the underlying basic premise that optimality, as a process, occurs. The explanation of certain events, the understanding of those events, is that they are optimal or represent behaviors in the near vicinity of a phenotype-adaptive peak. Evolutionary ecologists *define* behavior as optimal. What is at question is whether that definition is "true." As scientists, then, it is their duty to keep viewing the chair from still more angles, to see whether, in fact, that definition holds up. Let us examine some of the difficulties inherent in the task.

4 Testing Optimality Models

As in any scientific discipline, the evolutionary ecologist is charged with applying the hypotheticodeductive method. Using a deductive process, the optimality assumption, in some given context, is applied to generating hypotheses. The predictions of those hypotheses are then compared to observation. Unfortunately,

> 1. Because optimization is a (proposed) process that leads populations toward phenotype-adaptive peaks, but does not necessarily get them there, the researcher must a priori decide how far from the adaptive peak observations must lie in order to constitute falsification of (or consistency with) the hypothesis. Is a 5% error acceptable? A 20% error? Is there a defineable null hypothesis (see J. Beatty, this volume)? And if so, what is it—purely random behavior? (How can purely random behavior be defined?)
> 2. In virtually any ecological or behavioral system there is an intimidating array of physical, physiological, neurological, developmental, and genetic constraints on the adaptive process. Furthermore, all ecological and behavioral characteristics of an individual cannot possibly exist independently of one another. An optimizing process for one may occur only with concomitant adaptive deterioration in another. Any reasonable hypothesis surely must identify how such impinging constraints and trade-offs affect the position of adaptive peaks and the extent to which these peaks may be climbed, else it tells us little and provides no criterion for testing. But, inasmuch as full information on all these various constraints, or on all the complex trade-offs, can never be acquired, nor a complete picture gained of the manner in which they complicate the hypotheses, even given that information, it seems likely that positions of the adaptive peaks can be only crudely approximated, and in some cases no more than guessed at. These complications provide fertile ground for almost unrestrained and idle speculation as to why hypotheses (seem to) fail, yet do little to promote discussion of why some hypotheses (seem to) work. Gould and Lewontin's (1979) charge that a sufficiently clever mind

can eventually "explain" almost anything by the optimality assumption should not be taken lightly. When we test a hypothesis based on the optimality assumption, what are we testing? The hypothesis itself? The assumption? The adequacy with which we have identified the optimal phenotype? Our complete recognition and appropriate handling of the various constraints? If prediction matches observation, can we conclude anything at all? If it does not, can anything be concluded? In this towering babel of confusion surrounding such hypotheses (though usually the hypotheses are presented so straightforwardly that all evidence of the confusion is either unrecognized or concealed), is there any meaning at all in the terms "falsified" or "consistent with?"

The above comments are sufficiently damning to deserve further airing. I begin with a discussion of the genetic variables and constraints, then move on to problems introduced by ecological complexity.

5 Genetic Problems

Start with the simplest case, in which adaptedness is equivalent to genetic fitness—i.e., when the phenotype is determined at a single gene locus. We are taught in the first few lectures of any classical population genetics course that natural selection acts on such a system to maximize fitness of the hypothetical, mean individual. The phenotypic value of the most fit genotype in this case will have maximum adaptedness, so the optimization process should proceed. Only it does not. First, even were such ideally simple traits to exist, the most fit genotype might well be the heterozygote, in which case the very best we could hope for would be a population 50% of whose members were of the optimal phenotype. Second, it is possible that genes at the locus in question will be linked with or epistatic to other genes at other loci. In this case, as well as where pleiotropy occurs, selection at one locus might oppose realization of the optimal genotype at another. And it is now generally accepted that genes at virtually no locus act without modifying effects from genes at others, and that virtually all loci are pleiotropic. Consider, for example, two of the classical instances of purported, nonheterotic, single-locus traits. The ABO blood locus is now known to be pleiotropic, as are the loci that code for shell color and banding in Cepaea. Thus, as the alleles change frequency at a single locus they will alter the genetic background for other loci, where selection processes will also be at work. The upshot is that no single locus can be dealt with except as an integral part of the entire (or at least a sizable portion of the) genome. The importance of genetic background was dramatically demonstrated by Sokal and Taylor (1976), who measured the fitnesses of genotypes in two strains of housefly (*Musca domestica*) and their crosses and attempted vainly to use these values to predict frequency changes of a single gene. They found that properties of hybrids were not predictable from those of their parents, and that the usual expressions derived to describe gene frequency changes were useless. But if we cannot predict the progress of a single gene, or of the phenotypes it affects, can we at least examine the conditions under which a rare mutant should spread or fail to invade a population? That is, can we justify the common practice of invoking a hypothetical modifier gene to test for an evolutionarily stable strategy, a hypothetical, optimal equilibrium? The answer is no, unless we stipulate that the gene has no pleiotropic or epistatic effects—and this cannot be done for any real gene.

Quantitative genetics was developed, in part, to address the complications imposed by pleiotropy and epistasis on the genetic response to selection. It combines principles of single-locus genetics and statistics to dissect phenotypic dispersion into its various genetic and environmental components. Note that the measure analyzed is phenotype, not genotype; when genotypes are defined over all loci, every individual, in effect, becomes its own, unique genotype. When quantitative geneticists speak of fitness, what they really mean is adaptedness.

Quantitative genetics research has provided us with a body of principles that has been quite successful in animal and plant breeding programs—that is, under artificial selection regimes. Drawing on these principles, and making certain, quite reasonable assertions, Lande (1975, 1979) has derived an expression for the evolution of a set of traits $\{X\}$ under natural selection:

$$\frac{d}{dt}\overline{\mathbf{x}} = G(\nabla r)_{\overline{\mathbf{x}}},$$

where $\overline{\mathbf{x}}$ is the vector of mean trait values, G is the additive genetic variance-covariance matrix, r is fitness (adaptedness), and ∇ is the operator $(\partial/\partial x_1, \partial/\partial x_2, \cdots)$. Picking out just one trait, X_i, this expression may be written

$$\frac{d\overline{x}_i}{dt} = \sum_j \sigma_{ij}(\partial r/\partial x_j)_{\overline{\mathbf{x}}},$$

where σ_{ij} is the additive genetic covariance between X_i and X_j. Immediately we can see problems! Progress in $\overline{x}_i$ is not independent of X_i's relationship with all other traits, nor of the selection pressures, $\partial r/\partial x_j$, acting on those other traits. We can, for example, envision $\overline{x}_i$ changing in the absence of any relationship to adaptedness by virtue of selection acting on a genetically covarying trait. If the covariance is negative and of sufficient magnitude, $\overline{x}_i$ might even change in the direction of lowered adaptedness.

Do we observe such confounding covariances? Unfortunately, yes. Indeed there are reasons for suspecting that the covariances are more likely than not to be destructive of the evolution of optimality. Lerner (1954) and Falconer (1960) point out that where genes at two loci are pleiotropic and affect two traits in such a way as to increase adaptedness, both should rather quickly reach fixation. Genes that affect both traits in a detrimental way will quickly be eliminated. However, those genes that affect one trait in an adaptively positive way, the other negatively, will be fixed or eliminated much more slowly, thereby giving rise to negative additive covariance. With more than two traits involved, the covariance patterns may be expected to become exceedingly complex. Do these covariances persist in time? Can they be (are they) broken down so that evolution may proceed? In theory, yes. But in practice a number of laboratory experiments have indicated them to be remarkably resistant to change (Reeve and Robertson, 1952; Bell and Burris, 1973; Cheung and Parker, 1973). The picture that emerges, and that has been repeatedly demonstrated in laboratory experiments, is one of halting progress in a selected trait, marked by plateaus and reversals, with a final, oscillatory state that may or may not even remotely approach an ideal end point (one to be expected in the absence of confounding genetic covariances). These observations are inconsistent with the proposition that populations will gain phenotype-adaptive peaks; complexities in the genetic system virtually preclude this possibility. The assumption is salvageable, but only if we redefine the adaptive peaks—perhaps drastically—to allow for genetic constraints. And then surely we must be stretching our terminology to call the peaks phenotype-adaptive. And even then, the assumption is inapplicable without a complete knowledge of the genetic system.

By looking at the genes themselves as units of selection might these rather nasty genetic problems somehow be shown to be artificial? Dawkins (1976) writes compellingly, but manages neatly to sidestep the critical issue. Individual genes do not act independently; they do not really even assort independently. In the end it is the full, complex configuration of large, overlapping portions of the genome that determines phenotype values and mediates the evolutionary process. We must look at the genome as a whole.

There may, in some instances, be a partial escape from the ravages of obstreperous genes. For example, in the midst of high food abundance an animal equipped only with an internal calorie intake sensor and a genetically influenced disposition either to move or not to move to the next potential food item in response to information relayed from that sensor could easily achieve an optimal, energy-maximizer diet. Individuals responding inappropriately would be selected out of the population-unless the inappropriate response were beneficial in some other, unspecified manner to survival and/or reproduction. In such a case the (possible) later application of learning of food-type recognition would serve only to fine-tune slightly the response. Where a very simple mechanism, such as this, can be postulated, one might expect minimal distortion of the phenotype-adaptive space by genetic constraints. Thus, in some cases, simplistic, stripped-down models may be not only more fathomable (and perhaps, therefore, more heuristic) but, ironically, also more accurate than more complete models [Belovski's 1978, 1981, 1984a,b linear programming model, which considers only three constraints (minimal energy needs, time available for foraging and feeding, and gut capacity—and, in a few cases, minimal sodium requirements) and unrealistically assumes negligible search time, has predicted dietary behavior for a variety of animals consistently and with astonishing accuracy]. However, consistency of observation with drastically simple models of the world but not with more complete ones leaves us with mixed signals as to the "truth" of the underlying optimality assumption. If we wish to use the assumption broadly as an organizing principle, applying it to situations more complex than that described above, then we cannot escape the distortion of phenotype-adaptive peaks into perhaps quite different genotype-adaptive peaks.

6 Ecological Problems

A complete knowledge of the genetic system is necessary but still not sufficient to find adaptive peaks. Suppose we could ignore the genetic constraints. How do we identify the purely ecologically defined, phenotype-adaptive peaks?

To determine which of all alternative phenotypes is the optimum, we must take into consideration all physical, physiological, neurological, and developmental constraints on what can evolve. No one is going to predict the evolution in insects of a gigantism that subverts the capacity of the tracheal system to exchange gases, and no one expects the evolutionary emergence of street smarts in New York City cockroaches. But usually the constraints are far more subtle. Charnov (1976) has developed a "marginal value theorem" that, under certain proscribed conditions, describes optimal foraging patterns in animals. But what are the feasible mechanisms by which his subjects might realize such optimality? Can an animal make judgments regarding food quality, food density, cost of moving from one food patch to another? And how accurately? McNair (1982) and Green (1984) have shown that different modes and accuracies in judgment can lead to quite different optimality expectations. The optima we wish to identify are conditional optima, and they cannot be identified without a knowledge of the feasible mechanisms that might be mustered to meet them.

Other difficulties are still more pervasive and potentially incorrigible. Consider a meadow vole running about in a field, and ask just what that creature is accomplishing by way of being adapted. It is conceivable that it is simultaneously foraging, marking its home range, looking for or avoiding antagonists, keeping an eye open for potential mates, and giving a wide berth to predators. Can a meadow vole simultaneously optimize its behavior with respect to all of these activities? Even were its nervous system capable of such feats, we could easily imagine that patterns comprising optimal responses in respect to one activity might be maladaptive to another. And the problem is likely to be even worse for physiological or morphological traits whose status is only very slowly or not at all modifiable over time. And when addressing such a question, can we even define our terms? One critical component in optimal foraging theory is the energetic cost of moving among food patches. If, during these movements, our vole enjoys a tryst, reestablishes dominance over another individual, and relieves its bladder, can the energy expended in any way be considered a cost? If the animal does not engage in any other activities during these movements, yet the potential exists for such engagement, is there a cost?

Craig, DeAngelis, and Dixon (1979) and McNamara and Houston (1982) point out that adaptedness reflects the integration of influences throughout the lifetimes of individuals, and that one must therefore be careful in describing adaptedness based on a single portion of an organism's life in isolation from the rest. A trait that is highly adaptive in springtime may be maladaptive in winter. Even with respect to behaviors, which can change rapidly, there are potential pitfalls. For example, during any one day an animal might maximize its chances of survival by foraging in such a manner as to maximize total energy intake. But if nights were cold, overnight survival might depend on ending the day with maximum fat reserves. And the foraging pattern most efficiently meeting this latter need could be quite different from that best satisfying the first criterion. Thus a hypothesis based on daylight needs would give inaccurate predictions (even were no other constraints operative).

Fluctuating environments are a nightmare for the optimality assumption user. If the genetic machinery exists for realization of optimality, then it should be possible for populations to track very slow environmental changes. Very rapid fluctuations, according to Wiens (1984), preclude the possibility of optimal adaptation. But this view is overly sepulchral. Adaptation must in this situation be considered to apply to the arithmetic mean situation. But to conclude, therefore, that adaptation must be suboptimal is invalid—unless one wishes to change definitions. Unfortunately, fluctuations with periodicity on the order of one to a few generations are not so easily handled. We may picture, in purely teleological prose, a population scrambling to adjust its phenotypic makeup to remain de rigeur, and managing only to look hopelessly out of date. How are we to assess the optimality assumption via fit of optimum and realized phenotype when the latter forever lags the former in time?

If $\Delta \bar{x}$ gives the per generation change, due to natural selection, in the phenotypic mean value of some trait X, then we can define the evolutionary equilibrium in a fluctuating environment as $\hat{x}$ in such a way that

$$0 = E(\Delta \bar{x}) = E[\mathrm{Cov}(R, x)/R]_{\hat{x}},$$

where $R(x)$ is the population growth multiple of a phenotype defined by x (see Emlen, 1980). The quantity maximized by the process so described is

$$\left\{ \int E[\mathrm{Cov}(R, x)/R]\, dx \right\}_{\hat{x}}.$$

It is by no means clear how this horror is to be interpreted biologically; it is not mean adaptedness over time.

Tuljapurkar (1982) has attempted to model the evolutionary fate of a trait with value determined by a single gene locus in a fluctuating population with age structure. He argues that, at least under certain very simple conditions, the quantity maximized is the logarithm of $E(W)$ minus a complicated function of the time-variance structure of W, where W is fitness. This conclusion is qualitatively similar to the earlier suggestion of Real (1980) that we might profitably view selection as molding a trait, X, such that

$$E(\ln W) = \ln E(W) + (1/2)\,\mathrm{Var}(x)\,d^2 \ln W/dx^2$$

is maximized. Were it not for the genetic problems discussed above, Tuljapurkar's expression might be valid as a measure of what selection maximizes. But the genetic problems do exist; and even in their absence, the complexity of the expression makes it all but ecologically useless.

The consequences of these various ecological problems is that it is extremely difficult even to identify an optimum, virtually impossible to assert credibly that an optimum identified with respect to one activity or portion of an organism's life will translate to greater adaptedness, and impossible to define a rational criterion for inferring fit or lack of fit between predicted and observed phenotypes.

7 The Philosophical Context

The controversy over use of the optimality assumption in ecology revolves around two issues. First, antagonists argue that the assumption cannot possibly be true in any precise sense. The arguments presented above seem to me overwhelming in support of this position. The second objection is that hypotheses of optimal adaptation are nonfalsifiable. Inasmuch as we can never know that all possibilities or all constraints have been considered, and that we therefore have correctly identified the optimal phenotype, this is also undeniably so. Empirical falsification of the assumption in its precise sense is merely of academic interest since we have already conceded its falseness on other, empirical grounds, and if we attempt to bypass this fact by softening the assumption, to say that organisms approach optimality, then "falsifiability" is no longer even definable. Thus it is absurd to attempt testing the optimality assumption itself, or indeed any hypothesis of which the assumption is a part.

How then, are we to explain the rapidly growing popularity of evolutionary ecology and the growing consensus that optimality is an extraordinarily powerful tool in enabling us to understand ecology and behavior? Can we attribute the continued use of the assumption to desperation in the face of no apparent alternatives? Are the practitioners of this Popperian heresy dishonest, self-deluding, or just plain sloppy? Is the practice indeed unscientific? Kitcher (this volume), who discusses much the same issues in his paper, sees hope. Within the context of scientific realism I see no easy escape from the many criticisms. But let us return to the analogy of the baby and the chair.

To the scientific realist, the ever more finely tuned definitions arising from more and more complete information converge on a "true" picture of the chair. But what is the rationale for such a claim? Certainly it is not based on evidence—nor is it empirically falsifiable or verifiable. In the realists' context, it is a tenet of faith. But even if we grant the realists' assertion, what does it mean to converge on the "truth"? Recall that Newton defined gravity in one way, Einstein in another. What is gravity, really? Beyond our definitions of it, is that even a meaningful question? No. Truth, or our best approximation to it, is irremediably one and the same as our best definition. Let us then, as in fact we must in any case do, discard the criterion of transcendent truth as a goal of science, and instead concentrate on coherence. That is, let us build theoretical frameworks, definitions, supported solely by tests of derivative hypotheses that, by whatever criterion, adequately describe what we observe—hypotheses that, in addition, must be consistent with our world views. The results will have no necessary connection to (transcendent) truth, no claim of convergence on the "real" world. But they most certainly can be said to converge on the world as we perceive it! And just as a "true" definition, by virtue of isomorphism to the real world, explains that real world, our framework similarly explains the world we see about us. Our definitions should not, indeed cannot, be evaluated by their putative approach to transcendent truth. They can be and, for the purposes of providing understanding and explanation, should be evaluated on the basis of their coherence and usefulness (see also Laudan, 1979; van Fraassen, 1980). In this context, if the optimality assumption is internally coherent, consistent with our observations, and useful as an organizing principle, it constitutes a perfectly valid explanation for the ecology and behavior we see about us; to the selectionist it constitutes the closest present approximation to truth.

It may be argued, and from the *Weltanschauung* of the scientific realist with impeccable logic, that such easy acceptance of the optimality assumption is sloppy practice insofar as consistency or inconsistency of prediction and observation is so ill-defined. But there is no absolute criterion for consistency. Even in physics, empirical adequacy is generally a matter of consensus. And judging by the far-flung reputation of ecologists as a constantly bickering aggregate of individualists, it can hardly be claimed that they come loosely by consensus. What separates users of the optimality assumption from scientists in those fields blessed by more readily isolable subsystems, it seems to me, is not that the former, faced with unmanageable complexities, are sloppier or less scientific. Rather they are more susceptible, by virtue of unavoidable circumstances, to the forces of personal and cultural bias and more apt to err, with entirely honest intentions, in making inferences. Inasmuch as this is so, their reality may be more mutable and more polymorphic, though no less "true" than that of the physicist. This in no way makes them less effective as seekers after understanding. It is care in application of the deductive process, honesty with which data are recorded and inferences made, and willingness openly to present data that militate against an investigator's own biases that characterize or should characterize science, not one's beliefs as to the best access to metaphysical reality.

References

Beatty, J. In this volume.

Bell, A. E., and M. J. Burris (1973). Simultaneous Selection for Two Correlated Traits in *Tribolium*. *Genet. Res.* 21:29–49.

Belovski, G. E. (1978). Diet Optimization in a Generalist Herbivore, the Moose. *Theoret. Pop. Biol.* 14:105–134.

Belovski, G. E. (1981). Food Plant Selection by a Generalist Herbivore, the Moose. *Ecology* 62:1020–1030.

Belovski, G. E. (1984a). Herbivore Optimal Foraging: A Comparative Test of Three Models. *Amer. Natur.* 124:97–115.

Belovski, G. E. (1984b). Snowshoe Hare Optimal Foraging and Its Implications for Population Dynamics. *Theoret. Pop. Biol.* 25:235–264.

Charnov, E. L. (1976). Optimal Foraging and the Marginal Value Theorem. *Theoret. Pop. Biol.* 9:129–136.

Cheung, T. K., and R. J. Parker (1973). Effect of Selection on Heritability and Genetic Correlation of Two Quantitative Traits in Mice. *Can. J. Genet. Cytol.* 16:599–609.

Craig, R. B., D. L. DeAngelis, and K. R. Dixon (1979). Long- and Short-Term Dynamic Optimization Models with Application to the Feeding Strategy of the Loggerhead Shrike. *Amer. Natur.* 113:31–51.

Dawkins, R. (1976). *The Selfish Gene.* Oxford: Oxford University Press.

Dunbar, R. I. M. (1982). Adaptation, Fitness and the Evolutionary Tautology. In *Current Problems in Sociobiology* (The Kings College Sociobiology Group, eds.), Cambridge: Cambridge University Press, pp. 9–28.

Emlen, J. M. (1980). A Phenotypic Model for the Evolution of Ecological Characters. *Theoret. Pop. Biol.* 17:190–200.

Falconer, D. S. (1960). *Introduction to Quantitative Genetics.* New York: Ronald Press.

Ghiselin, M. T. (1966). On Semantic Pitfalls of Biological Adaptation. *Phil. Sci.* 33:147–153.

Gould, S. J., and R. C. Lewontin (1979). The Spandrels of San Marco and the Panglossian Paradigm: A Critique of the Adaptionist Programme. *Proc. R. Soc. Lond.* B205:581–598.

Green, R. F. (1984). Stopping Rules for Optimal Foragers. *Amer. Natur.* 123:30–40.

Kitcher, P. In this volume.

Lande, R. (1975). The Maintenance of Genetic Variability by Mutation in a Polygenic Character with Linked Loci. *Genet. Res.* 26:221–235.

Lande, R. (1979). Quantitative Genetic Analysis of Multivariate Evolution, Applied to Brain:Body Size Allometry. *Evolution* 33:402–416.

Laudan, L. (1979). *Progress and Its Problems: Towards a Theory of Scientific Growth.* Berkeley: University of California Press.

Lerner, I. M. (1954). *Genetic Homeostasis.* London: Oliver and Boyd.

Levins, R. (1966). The Strategy of Model Building in Population Biology. *Amer. Sci.* 54:421–431.

Lewontin, R. C. (1978). Adaptation. *Sci. Amer.* 239:157–169.

Lewontin, R. C. (1979). Sociobiology as an Adaptionist Program. *Beh. Sci.* 24:5–14.

McNair, J. N. (1982). Optimal Giving Up Times and the Marginal Value Theorem. *Amer. Natur.* 119:511–529.

McNamara, J., and A. Houston (1982). Short-Term Behaviour and Lifetime Fitness. In D. McFarland (ed.), *Functional Ontogeny*, Boston: Pitman Adv. Publ. Program, pp. 60–87.

Maynard Smith, J. (1974). The Theory of Games and the Evolution of Animal Conflicts. *J. Theoret. Biol.* 47:209–221.

Maynard Smith, J. (1978). Optimization Theory in Evolution. *Ann. Rev. Ecol. System.* 9:31–56.

Maynard Smith, J. (1982). *Evolution and the Theory of Games.* Cambridge: Cambridge University Press.

Maynard Smith, J., and G. A. Parker (1976). The Logic of Asymmetric Contests. *Anim. Beh.* 24:159–175.

Maynard Smith, J., and G. R. Price (1973). The Logic of Animal Conflict. *Nature* 246:15–18.

Oster, G. F., and E. O. Wilson (1978). *Caste and Ecology in the Social Insects.* Princeton: Princeton University Press.

Parker, G. A. (1974). Assessment Strategy and the Evolution of Fighting Behavior. *J. Theoret. Biol.* 47:223–243.

Real, L. (1980). Fitness, Uncertainty, and the Role of Diversification in Evolution and Behavior. *Amer. Natur.* 115:623–635.

Reeve, E. C. R., and F. W. Robertson (1952). Studies in Quantitative Inheritance. II. Analysis of a Strain of *Drosophila melanogaster* Selected for Long Wings. *J. Genet.* 57:276–316.

Sober, E. In this volume.

Sokal, R. R., and C. E. Taylor (1976). Selection at Two Levels in Hybrid Populations of *Musca domestica. Evolution* 30:509–522.

Tuljapurkar, S. D. (1982). Population Dynamics in Variable Environments. III. Evolutionary Dynamics of r-Selection. *Theoret. Pop. Biol.* 21:141–165.

van Fraassen, B. C. (1980). *The Scientific Image.* Oxford: Clarendon Press.

Wiens, J. (1984). Resource Systems, Populations and Communities. In P. W. Price, C. N. Slobodchikoff, and W. S. Gaud (eds.), *A New Ecology: Novel Approaches to Interactive systems.* New York: Wiley, pp. 397–436.

Williams, G. C. (1966). *Adaptation and Natural Selection.* Princeton: Princeton University Press.

10

Optimality Theory and Behavior
John E. R. Staddon

Why does optimality theory get into so much hot water? In biology, it has been subjected to numerous attacks (e.g., Lewontin, 1979; Gould and Lewontin, 1979), and it has been equally controversial in psychology in recent years (e.g., Mazur, 1981; Heyman, 1979; Herrnstein, 1982; Allison, 1983). Psychologists are sensitive because behaviorists and others under the influence of positivist philosophy came to believe that teleology is unscientific. Purposes, goals, objectives, and functions were OUT; mechanisms, either physiological or mechanical, were IN. The reasons for controversy in biology are similar. Pittendrigh's (1958) concept of *teleonomy* provides a respectable category for explanations that appear teleological but can in principle be reduced to mechanism via evolution through variation and natural selection. But if there are doubts about this mechanism, particularly about the part played by natural selection, optimality explanations even in biology cease to be teleonomic, and revert to teleology, to Gould's "Just-so Stories."

Optimality analyses in biology are attempts to make exact the notion that most phenotypic features are in some sense ideally designed to contribute to Darwinian fitness, the idea of *adaptation.*[1] Since the "Adaptationist program" has come under attack in recent years (e.g., Gould, 1982), optimality accounts could hardly escape. Nevertheless, it is still surprising that even *constrained optimization*—the idea that the majority of phenotypic features are optimal within limits imposed by developmental processes and physical laws (cf. Alexander, 1982; Maynard Smith, 1978)—has not been spared. Perhaps the argument is really about the relative importance for evolution of natural selection versus the internal constraints and properties of the structures and populations that have evolved. It is not so much that optimality analysis is wrong, as that it may be irrelevant to understanding many of the products of evolution.

I thank Alliston Reid, John Horner, and Peter Richerson for help and comments on earlier versions of the manuscript. Research was supported by grants from the National Science Foundation to Duke University.

1 Optimality Theory and Learning

This paper is primarily concerned with uses of, and abuses suffered by, optimality theory in the study of behavior, especially learned behavior, where the issues are slightly different. First, the role of ontogeny is more critical for behavior than for morphology: many morphological features are strongly canalized, so are little affected by variations in experience,[2] as long as these are not so extreme as to prevent the animal from attaining adulthood. Consequently, in evolutionary terms, we must speak of the adaptiveness of a given developmental *program*, rather than of a particular behavior. Much behavior is like the morphology of those corals and sponges that grow in such a way as to make the best use of available water currents: they develop a form that seems to optimize flow patterns, but what has evolved is not this form (which varies from one environment to another), but the growth program that allows it to develop. Under extraordinary conditions such programs may misfire: no doubt regimens involving varying flow patterns could be devised under which the corals would grow into inefficient forms. Doubtless such regimens are very rare in nature. Similarly, programs for learning can often be tricked, leading the animal that possesses them into bizarre, maladaptive patterns—more on this in a moment. For now, I just note that behavior is judged optimal in two senses: in the evolutionary sense that the mechanisms that underlie it yield behavior that maximizes fitness in natural environments; and in the ontogenetic sense that the behavior itself maximizes some proxy for fitness—such as energy intake—under specific conditions. Critiques of the adaptationist program are much more relevant for optimality analysis in the first than in the second sense. In this paper, I shall speak mainly of this second, ontogenetic, sense.

The objections to optimality in the ontogenetic sense are of three kinds: (a) Optimality analyses are not causal, hence not scientific. (b) Optimality analyses cannot be reduced to causal analyses even in principle; they are not even teleonomic. (c) Optimality analyses of behavior do not work. I shall deal with each of these objections in turn.

Is Optimality Analysis Scientific?

To say what is unscientific requires that we know what is scientific. Either functional (teleological) explanations are a priori unscientific, or they must be shown to lack some essential feature shared by scientific explanations. The essential feature of a scientific explanation is that it *explain*: It must describe phenomena more numerous than the assumptions of the theory. By this standard, many optimality theories do very well. For example, the marginal value theorem of optimal foraging theory (Charnov, 1976) is just the economic principle of maximizing by equating marginal rates of return.

Simple as it is, applied to rate of energy intake it nevertheless accounts for numerous results on foraging by birds, mammals, and insects (see review by Krebs and McCleery, 1984). The principle of diminishing marginal utility, applied to the contributions to fitness of particular food amounts, has been shown to account well for the foraging behavior of bees and, as I shall describe, rats and pigeons, in a variety of instrumental learning experiments (cf. Real, 1980; Real, Ott, and Silverfine, 1982; Caraco, Martindale, and Whittam, 1980; Staddon and Reid, 1987). Optimality analysis has brought under a single theoretical umbrella a wide range of behavioral data.

To achieve dominance a theory must not just explain, but explain better than competing theories. Optimality theory will be thought much less useful if other, preferably causal, theories do better. Are there such theories of foraging or choice, the areas where optimality theory has had its greatest success? Although this issue is a subject of some debate, I believe that the correct answer is, "Not really." In laboratory studies of animal choice there are descriptive theories related to the so-called *matching law* (Herrnstein, 1961; see chapters in Commons, Herrnstein, and Rachlin, 1982), and some quasi-dynamic models that account well for particular situations (e.g., Harley, 1981; Killeen, 1982; Myerson and Miezin, 1980; Myerson and Hale, 1984). But no theory accounts as well for such a wide range of natural and laboratory situations as some version of optimality theory.

The relative success of optimality analyses in behavior is not surprising. Different species certainly learn by quite different processes, and careful behavioral analysis often reveals differences even in the way individuals of the same species learn the same task. Consequently, as with analogous structures (i.e., convergent evolution), analysis in terms of function is often the only way to bring together a variety of mechanisms whose only common feature is that they accomplish the same objective.

The same argument—that the means are many, but the objectives relatively few—accounts for the almost universal reliance on optimality analysis by economists. It is hardly conceivable that economists could anticipate or even measure the varied ways that people go about satisfying their needs. Consequently, unless economists are to resort to grand theories that elevate the group above the individual—or at least assume greater lawfulness for group than individual action[3]—there is little alternative to reliance on some form of optimality analysis.

Theory serves purposes other than explanation: theories must usually predict something new that people can go out and look for; and theories often serve as aids to empirical research. In these respects also, optimality analyses of behavior have done quite well: optimality hypotheses are helpful when they fail as well as when they succeed.

Optimality hypotheses are useful even when they fail, because failures often draw attention to unsuspected causal factors. For example, disconfirmed optimal-foraging hypotheses that took no account of predation drew attention to the competing demands for predator avoidance: birds sometimes fail to maximize food intake, because they spend some time watching out for potential predators.

Optimal-foraging theory makes predictions about experiments that have been frequently confirmed (see the Krebs and McCleery review). Deriving theoretical predictions forces attention to variables whose relevance can be tested empirically.

A more technical example comes from the laboratory. Operant psychologists study a class of reward procedures known as *random-interval schedules* in which food availability is scheduled by a stochastic process. Schedule events occur at random at a given average rate. When an event occurs, the next occurrence of the specified response procures food (thus, the longer the time since the animal last responded, the more likely a schedule event will have occurred, hence the more likely a response will be effective). When animals are confronted with two possible choices, each rewarded with food according to its own random-interval schedule, they respond to both alternatives, and usually in such a way that the ratio of responses matches the ratio of obtained rewards (the matching law: Herrnstein, 1961). There is still some dispute about exactly why the animals behave in this way, but the hypothesis that they optimize on a moment-by-moment basis, always picking the alternative with the highest probability of payoff (*momentary maximizing*: Shimp, 1966), suggests that time-since-the-last-response to each alternative should have special significance: animals should always respond to the alternative with the highest weighted time-since-last-response, and this is what they tend to do (Hinson and Staddon, 1983; Silberberg, Hamilton, and Ziriax, 1978; Staddon, Hinson, and Kram, 1981). In the absence of an optimality analysis, no one would have thought to look for effects of these procedures on this rather obscure property of behavior.[4]

In a related class of procedures, animals (usually hungry pigeons) are allowed free choice between two options (*L*eft and *R*ight response keys) each of which occasionally (on a random-interval schedule) leads to a single choice associated with a given delay of reward. For example, every 60 seconds or so a peck on one of two white keys (*L* or *R*) causes it to turn red (*L*) or green (*R*), turning off the other key. The green key signifies a 10-second delay to food; the red a 20-second delay. After food, the two white keys reappear, and the cycle resumes. Reinforcement theorists at one time argued that the ratio of responses to the two white keys should match the ratio of payoff rates (2 : 1 in the example) associated with the delay components. Sometimes they do so, but optimality arguments make it obvious that the average delay in the choice component should be very important: when this time is very long, the animal has a strong interest in getting to either delay component, hence should respond equally on either key; but when this delay is short, it should attend only to the alternative leading to the shorter delay. Pigeons behave exactly as this argument suggests, "undermatching" when the initial delay is long, "overmatching" when it is short (see recent review by Fantino and Abarca, 1985).

Are Optimality Analyses of Learning Teleonomic?[5]

The second objection to optimality analyses is that they cannot be reduced, even in principle, to causal analyses. This objection seemed until recently to have more force as applied to the analysis of learned behavior than applied to any of the products of evolution (Staddon, 1973). But the recent criticisms by Gould, Eldredge, and others of the adaptationist position must make us less certain that we understand the essentials of the evolutionary process. Before these disruptive elements came on the scene, we could all take comfort in the "new synthesis" and assume that even if we lacked all the details of the evolutionary mechanism, finding them was just a matter of time and conscientious application of known methods and concepts. To the perennial uncertainty about what is selected by natural selection, we must now add substantial ignorance of developmental and population mechanisms and the constraints they place on the type and frequency of genetically induced modifications. So, even in evolution we are uncertain about how to reduce optimality accounts to causal ones.

In fact, the tables seem now to be turned: Our understanding of the causal ingredients of learning has improved greatly in recent years, so we seem now closer to an "in principle" understanding of learning processes than of evolutionary ones—although neither lies just around the corner.

This is not the place for a full-scale exposition of learning theory, but in outline a slightly biased version of the current view is roughly as follows. The function of learning is to enable the animal to do the right thing at the right time and place, where "right" means "such as to improve fitness." In practice, we can only measure proxies for fitness such as food, water, or reduction of pain—the *reinforcers* of learning theory. Thus, the function of learning is to do whatever is necessary to increase access to available reinforcers. The animal must take account of two things: the time and place to act, and the appropriate action. All learning therefore shares three common elements: (a) something to be predicted, either danger or the availability of reward (reinforcers); (b) a set of predictors: event properties and temporal relations, contextual factors, the animal's own behavior; and (c) a set of constraints that limit the animal's ability to use available information.

For example, in classical conditioning the reinforcer (unconditioned stimulus: UCS) must selectively follow (predict) the otherwise neutral CS (conditioned stimulus) if the CS is to have an effect. All potential CSs for a given UCS are not equivalent. Some have higher default values (i.e., show more conditioning following the first pairing) than others, and perhaps more rapidly acquire predictive significance as well. Many animals will sooner learn to take a sound than a light as a signal of danger, for example. Rats and people take taste over appearance as a signal of poison (some birds may do otherwise). These differences in default significances and rates of conditioning are peculiar to different species and UCSs and presumably reflect particular selection pressures and, in older and smarter animals, experiences.

Animals use two kinds of relations to gauge predictiveness; I shall term these *specific* and *general* predictors. Specific predictors reflect properties of stimuli that are endowed by an animal's phylogeny with a special significance in relation to particular to-be-predicted (target) events: Taste may have a special significance as a predictor of sickness, sound of danger, certain song elements as identifiers of species-specific song, and so on.

Temporal contiguity is the chief general predictor: no matter how specific the situation, the time between potential cause and its effect is always useful, although the shortest time need not be the best predictor. For example, when an effect is always delayed, as sickness follows poisoning with a lag, intermediate times may carry the greatest weight. Even in standard laboratory classical conditioning, the optimal CS-UCS delay is not zero but half a second or so. (Time relations are general predictors, but the specific value that is optimal may differ from system to system.)

When learning must take place rapidly, on one or a few trials, the animal has no basis for inference other than contiguity and specific predictors. When repeated opportunities for learning are available, there is in addition a second kind of general predictor, common to all recurrent experiences, namely, reliable succession, Hume's chief attribute of true causality—B always follows A and never occurs without A preceding.

The two general predictors have a special status, in that they reflect necessary properties of the world. Taste need not be the best predictor of sickness, and one can imagine worlds in which any specific predictor becomes invalid. But reliable succession, or *contingency*, as it is termed when probabilities are used [($p(A|B) > p(A|\sim B)$; degrees of succession are permitted], defines what we mean by predictiveness. Temporal contiguity has no such necessary status, but does reflect ineluctable limitations on information gathering, as well as a reliable feature of the real world: A cause remote in time from its effect will be hard to identify because intervening potential causes must first be eliminated, and most identifiable causes closely precede their effects. The only escape from the information-gathering limit is when potential causes differ in some consistent way from all intervening events—as in taste-aversion learning, where a remote taste takes precedence over intervening nontaste stimuli.

Operant (instrumental) conditioning adds to the two general factors a third, *control* by the animal that can produce a potential UCS-predictor, the response, at will and thus explore the strength of its association with a consequence (reward or punishment).

Habituation, sensitization, and classical conditioning are all situations in which an animal uses a stimulus as a signal for something of value: as a signal for safety (habituation), of danger (sensitization), or of a good or bad event (classical conditioning). Operant conditioning is a situation where the animal identifies some aspect of its own behavior as a signal for something of value. Learning of every type has implications for action. For example, once an animal has been habituated, it need no longer display protective reflexes and can get on with other necessary activities; once a stimulus has been identified as a signal for food, it can be approached and responded to in other appropriate ways. But action is intrinsic to operant conditioning: To identify an action as a possible signal for (= cause of) something, the action must occur.

How should actions be selected? The answer here seems to be the same as for the selection of "candidate" CSs in classical conditioning: in a given context there are default *activities*—activities that have high priority—and these occur first. These acts are *hypotheses*, if you like, although no conscious intent is implied thereby.[6] The set of such acts is defined by a combination of phylogenetic and ontogenetic factors. For example, for a raccoon any small object strongly associated with food elicits food-related "washing" behavior, and apparently the stronger the association, the more constrained the animal to this particular activity. A rat that has learned in one situation to press a bar for food when a tone sounds is likely to press another in a similar situation when it hears the tone. In short, both *transfer*, from other, similar situations, and built-in links between situations with motivational significance and particular activities—food situations induce food-related activities; dangerous situations, escape or agonistic activities; and so on—serve to define the set of acts that are likely to occur.

Some such restriction on the set of potential acts is necessary if animals are not to be very inefficient in settling on the appropriate action. The "search set," the set of prior acts, must be restricted in some way. Phylogeny can help with a set of initial biases—all animals have a set of activities appropriate in anticipation of feeding, drinking, flight, and so on. Ontogeny helps in two ways: by allowing transfer from other, similar situations, and by the information available from what we have been calling general predictors—temporal contiguity and correlation. Phylogeny is involved here, too, of course, in building in sensitivity to general and specific predictors, and in providing a measure of *similarity* that classifies the world in sensible ways.

Deciding on the meaning of "similar" is not a trivial problem. For example, suppose we train a hungry rat to press a black lever for food reward in a brightly lighted small wire cage. Later on, we place it, still hungry, in a large, dim enclosure with a white lever. What should it do? Since neither environment speaks much to its phylogeny, it comes with few biases, other than caution in the novel environment. Will the second lever be similar enough to the first to elicit pressing? Probably not. There are at least two things that will increase the probability the rat will behave effectively in this new environment: Put the rat in it soon after a session in the old environment; or give the rat some free food in the new environment. Temporal proximity between new and old will in and of itself induce some carryover of behavior from one situation to the other, and the presence of food will bring the two even closer. In short, time relations seem built in as useful predictors; and the presence of food, a predator, or a mate—any reinforcer—is perhaps the most important defining property of a situation. Animals classify situations primarily in terms of their motivational significance, and stimulus correlations—classical conditioning—are used for this purpose.

In operant conditioning, the inference process involves three steps (which may go on concurrently): The situation must be classified in some way—primarily, but not entirely, in terms of its motivational significance. Classical conditioning (CS-UCS relations) and similarity relations are the names we give to this first step. Once classified, the situation defines a set of default activities, each with a different priority and different sensitivity to the general predictors, contiguity and correlation, that operate in the third step. For example, a hungry pigeon faces a dark pecking key, that is occasionally briefly illuminated. Lacking prior experience with such objects, the animal may do little. But if each key illumination is followed by food (and food occurs at no other time), soon the light is classified as food related. Small food-related objects induce pecking as a high-priority activity (*autoshaping*). If the apparatus arranges that pecking produces food, the correlation between light and food is further strengthened, and in addition the general predictors—temporal contiguity and correlation between peck and food—act to favor pecking. In this way, the pigeon "learns" to peck the key.

Thus, we have a pretty good descriptive idea of the processes that underlie rewarded learning in animals: the processes that generate behavior (phylogenetic "default" activities, and transfer based on similarity) and those that selectively favor one activity over others (specific and general predictors). Much detail is lacking, and the relation between behavior and the underlying physiological mechanisms is still for the most part obscure, but it is not true now, as it was ten or fifteen years ago, that optimality accounts of learning are intrinsically teleological.

Do Optimality Accounts Work?
No theory covers all cases. Optimality accounts, like others, break down under some conditions. The failures are instructive, however. In this section, I illustrate the vices and virtues of optimality theory by describing some results from the study of operant learning in animals that are very well described in optimality terms—and contrast them with some other results where optimality fails, but a simple learning model works.

Simple optimal foraging theory assumes that animals act so as to maximize energy intake (other things being equal). Energy intake is under most conditions simply proportional to eating rate, and a number of theoretical papers have shown that eating rate is often treated as a variable to be optimized in its own right (e.g., Rachlin et al., 1976; Staddon, 1979). Moreover, the optimization has two components: diminishing marginal utility and regulation.

Data I shall describe in a moment imply diminishing marginal utility: that is, the utility function must be a negatively accelerated function of eating rate. Expressed in terms of *cost* (rather than utility), the lower the eating rate, the higher the cost, and halving the eating rate more than doubles the cost.

When animals must work for their food at a fixed "wage rate" (this is known as a *ratio schedule*), then, so long as the wage rate is not too low, they will work harder as their wage rate *decreases*. This response to increases in work requirement acts to limit decreases in feeding rate, and implies a second principle, namely, *regulation*.

These two assumptions together can be expressed by saying that animals in many foraging situations behave as if the quantity minimized is the difference between the actual and some ideal (set-point) eating rate, raised to a power greater than unity (two is handy). This is known as a *minimum-distance* model (Staddon, 1979).

This theory accounts for a number of experimental results, but I shall describe just four: molar performance on response- and time-based reward schedules, and sensitivity to risk in terms of food amount or delay.

When animals must work for food at a fixed, moderate "wage rate"—so many lever presses for each food pellet, for example—then when the wage rate is reduced (the lever-press requirement is increased), response rate typically increases so as to compensate partially for the change, as shown in figure 10.1. The figure shows two kinds of function relating work (lever presses/min) and food (pellets/min) rates: Each of the rays through the origin represents the constraint (*feedback function*) associated with a fixed wage rate (ratio schedule): the lower the slope, the higher the wage rate.

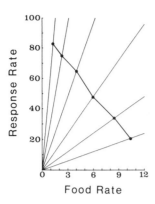

Figure 10.1
Molar (session-average) adjustment of a single rat to a series of constant-wage (ratio) food schedules. Rays through the origin denote the constraint associated with a given wage rate (i.e., food rate is forced to be proportional to lever-press—work—rate). The single line of negative slope connects points representing the animal's adjustment to each wage rate (ratio-schedule *response function*). (Redrawn from Ettinger and Staddon, 1983)

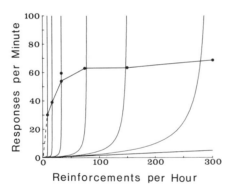

Figure 10.2
Molar adjustment of a single pigeon to a series of variable-interval food schedules. The positively accelerated functions are estimates of the feedback function for these schedules, which has a vertical asymptote at the maximum food rate, and an asymptote at the line $x = y$ (Staddon and Motheral, 1978). (The approximation works better at low reward rates—hence the off-function data points at high rates.) (Data redrawn from Catania and Reynolds, 1968, figure 1, pigeon 279)

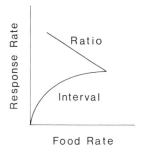

Food Rate

Figure 10.3
Schematic illustration of the difference between ratio- and variable-interval-schedule response functions.

The line of negative slope connects points representing a rat's adjustment to different wage rates: as the wage rate declines, the lever-press rate increases. This *response function* is not always linear; under slightly different conditions it has a bitonic form, with an increasing as well as a declining limb. But the declining limb is always the most stable and characteristic feature of many animals' adaptation to this kind of work schedule.

Figure 10.2 shows how animals adjust to a very different procedure, a random-interval schedule—in which (you will remember) food becomes available for a response only after a stochastic event has occurred. The figure shows the two types of function shown in the previous figure. The feedback function for random-interval schedules has the positively accelerated form shown in the figure; As response rate increases, food rate also increases, asymptotically, to a limit equal to the rate at which stochastic events occur. Pigeons and rats adjust to this procedure in quite a different way from their adjustment to fixed-rate work schedules. The response function, rather than having a negative slope over most of the range, has a positive slope, as shown in the figure. The difference between the two response functions is shown schematically in figure 10.3.

The two optimizing assumptions I have described—regulation of feeding rate plus increasing marginal cost of rate deviations—can account for these differences, which are also pretty obvious intuitively. Return is proportional to effort on the ratio schedule, so it pays to work harder. But harder work gains less and less on the random-interval schedule, so there is little point in attempting to regulate food intake. Consequently, work output is determined by the marginal benefit associated with gains in food rate (which is directly related to the maximum mean food frequency associated with the schedule, hence increases with mean food rate), compared to the marginal cost of increases in response rate (which is roughly constant at low rates). Hence, response rate increases with food rate, as the figure shows.

This same optimality approach also accounts for many results from experiments on risky choice, where the term *risk* is here used in the sense of a lottery or gamble. For example, suppose hungry pigeons are allowed to choose between two keys each of which schedules food according to a random-interval schedule. The mean rates of the two schedules are the same. The difference is that each food delivery is the same amount for one choice (left, say), whereas the amount is variable for the other. The average amount is the same for both, of course, so simple energy maximization implies no preference for one alternative over the other. But, for reasons first elaborated by Bernoulli some years ago, diminishing marginal utility implies aversion to the variable choice (*risk aversion*), and the special version of diminishing marginal utility embodied in a minimum-distance-type model implies that the degree of risk aversion should be related to the difference between actual and set-point food rate: the closer the food rate to the set point, the more risk-averse the animal should be. Although all the data are not in, both these conclusions seem to be supported (see Staddon and Reid, 1987; Krebs, Stephens, and Sutherland, 1983).

More dramatically, minimum-distance food-rate optimality predicts strong risk-*seeking* with respect to food *delay*. For example, suppose our perennial pigeon is allowed to choose between two white keys, each of which schedules a color change according to the same random-interval schedule— the same procedure described earlier in connection with unsuspected variables and optimality. One color, say red, is associated with a constant delay until food delivery, and the other, say green, with a variable delay (with the same mean). It has been known for many years that pigeons much prefer the variable-delay option, even if the mean delay on the constant alternative is much less (e.g., Herrnstein, 1964; Mazur, 1984).

Thus, minimum-distance optimality accounts for a wide range of results from experiments on reward schedules. Yet it fails equally dramatically to account for some others, as I now describe.

Suppose we give an animal a choice between two work schedules set up as a "two-arm bandit": the probability of payoff for pressing the left lever is 1/20, say, and for pressing the right lever, 1/30. Any optimality analysis would say that the animal, after sampling a bit perhaps, should eventually spend all its time working on the higher-wage alternative. Yet recent experiments (by John Horner in my laboratory, and by others reviewed in Allison, 1983) have shown that rats will very often show a stable partial preference under such conditions. When both wage rates are high, some animals (depending on their initial preference) may also fixate on the leaner of the two alternatives.

John Horner and I have shown that this pattern of results is consistent

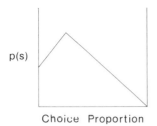

Choice Proportion

Figure 10.4

An interdependent choice schedule: Payoff probability for both choices is always $p(s)$. Dependence of $p(s)$ on choice proportion, x (averaged over the previous N choices), is shown by the triangular function.

with a reward-following process of the sort studied by Bush and Mosteller (1955) many years ago, but even simpler (Horner and Staddon, unpublished). It is necessary only to assume that a rewarded response increases the probability of responding to that alternative by some amount, while an unrewarded response decreases the probability of responding by a different, smaller, amount.[7] Moreover, this same, simple process can account for even more maladaptive results from an additional set of choice experiments by Horner. The procedure in these experiments, which used hungry pigeons, is illustrated in figure 10.4. The payoff probabilities for the two choices are always equal [$p = q = p(s)$], but the value of $p(s)$ depends on the proportion of key pecks to the two keys, s, averaged over the last N pecks (N is between 4 and 96 in different experiments). In the example shown, $p(s)$ is maximal when 75% of the previous N responses were to the left key and 25% to the right, and falls off linearly when s deviates in either direction from that value. Clearly, optimal performance on this procedure is to choose left and right in the proportion $3:1$.

This ingenious *interdependent* procedure (which was originally devised, in a more complex form, by Vaughan: Herrnstein and Vaughan, 1980) raises a general epistemological issue about behavioral theory. Testing any theory requires that we identify the terms of the theory with events in the world. The prediction that optimal choice proportion is 75/25 implicitly assumes that the relevant behavior (for the theory, hence for the animal) is not *particular choices*, left or right, but rather the *proportion* of left and right choices in the animal's recent past. Yet there is little in the voluminous literature on pigeon operant choice behavior that would lead us to assume that this particular variable enters in any way into whatever process they use to adapt to food schedules. Pigeons may be unaware—and incapable of becoming aware—of what their proportion of choices has been. Hence our pretty triangular schedule very likely looks quite different to the pigeon. Yet until we know how it looks to it—until we know more about

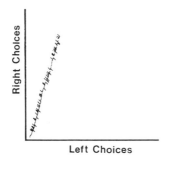

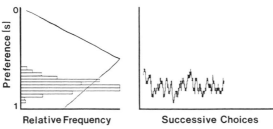

Figure 10.5
Performance of a pigeon on an interdependent schedule: (upper panel) preference trajectory—left choices plotted against right choices through a single experimental session; (right lower panel) local response rate (vertical axis) associated with successive choices; (left lower panel) histogram showing relative frequency (horizontal axis) of different choice proportions (averaged over a moving 32-choice window throughout the session). Peaked function represents the payoff probability associated with each choice proportion. (J. M. Horner, unpublished data)

the information-processing constraints to which it is subject—we cannot even apply our theory.

Surprisingly, perhaps, it is easier to apply the simple reward-following process to this procedure. The prediction is straightforward: Under most conditions, animals should show a bimodal preference pattern on these triangular reward functions. Moreover, the payoff probability, $p(s)$, at each mode (s-value) should be the same.

There are several ways to show this invariance. One is demonstrated in figures 10.5 and 10.6. Each figure shows data from a single pigeon during a single experimental session of an hour or so. The top curve is a trajectory, plotting successive left choices against right: 50:50 choice would correspond to a straight line at 45°, exclusive right choice to a vertical line, and exclusive left choice to a horizontal line. As you can see, during both sessions the animal favored the right key. The bottom right panel shows the instantaneous value of choice proportion, s (average here over

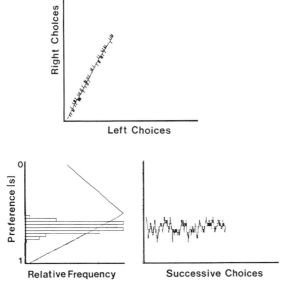

Figure 10.6
Performance on an interdependent schedule. Same animal as in figure 10.5, three days later, after three days' experience with left–right-reversed reward function. Other details as in figure 10.5.

the previous 32 choices), choice-by-choice. The bottom left panel shows the relative frequency of different choice proportions (s-values). The reward function for this procedure is superimposed on the lower left panel to show how far the animal's modal choice departed from the maximum.

Figure 10.5 shows typical preference distributions shown by a single pigeon during one experimental session under the first condition. For the session shown in figure 10.5 the right-hand limb of the reward function declines to zero at $s = 1$ (exclusive right choice). The animal shows a modal preference at $s = 0.64$. Figure 10.6 shows performance three days later, after three days' experience with a left–right-reversed version of the same reward function. The animal's response to the change is to shift the preference mode to the right, to a value of s associated with the same $p(s)$ as before.

These results seem to be typical. Pigeons on these interdependent schedules attain the maximum only by accident, when the reward-following process happens to drive them to that point. In the majority of cases, responding settles down far from the maximum, at one of the equilibria predicted by a reward-following model.

From one point of view, these nonoptimal results are not surprising. Optimal performance must always depend on specific mechanisms, and these mechanisms must fail under some circumstances. Perhaps reward-following, which easily generates the widely reported matching result (cf. Heyman, 1979), is the mechanism that underlies performance on all reward schedules? Unfortunately, reward-following fails to account for the regulatory features of performance on ratio schedules that I discussed earlier. Indeed, it is not difficult to show that it must predict a fixed relation between response and reward rate, hence cannot account for any case where response rate is higher (at a given reward rate) under one schedule than another. Figure 10.3 illustrates one such case, and there are many others (cf. Staddon, 1982). The search for a general mechanism underlying the well-established regularities of performance of many mammals and birds on reward schedules is not yet over.

2 Conclusion

The verdict on optimality theory depends on what is is to be used for. As an account of the major features of morphology it may be less useful than as an account of the details of foraging and choice. In this context, optimality theory is useful, not irredeemably teleological, and not false. It is useful because it brings together diverse phenomena by means of few assumptions; it draws attention to unsuspected variables that affect behavior; and it accounts for similar results achieved by diverse means. It is not teleological because recent developments in learning theory provide a framework within which the outline, if not the details, of potential learning mechanisms sufficient to achieve optimal results may be discerned. And it is not false because increasingly detailed experimental results can be explained by it.

Optimality analyses of behavior sharpen the distinction between "natural" and "unnatural" situations: Natural situations are (approximately) those for which an optimality analysis works; unnatural situations, those for which it fails. Unnatural situations turn out in practice to be characterized by contradictory or obscure relations between behavior and reward, as in the interdependent schedules just discussed. It seems reasonable to guess that such relations are rare in nature (or are costly to accommodate), so that learning mechanisms to detect them have not evolved. In the long run, therefore, optimality analyses may tell us more about selection pressures and developmental constraints—about the niche within which a species has evolved, and the limits on phylogenetic variation—than about psychological processes. Nevertheless, the contrast between those situations where learning mechanisms operate smoothly and lead to optimal results and those where they fail may help us discover what those mechanisms are.

Notes

1. I have not seen a precise definition of this concept of adaptation, which refers to current function rather than evolutionary origin (cf. Gould and Vrba, 1982), but it might be defined as follows: A feature is adaptive if any *slight* alteration reduces the fitness of its possessor. This reduces the problem from a conceptual one to one that is in principle (if rarely in practice) experimental. It is heuristic to speculate on exactly what kind of experiment would be necessary to assess adaptiveness in this sense. For example, a version that seems less compelling, but is slightly easier to test, is this: A feature is adaptive if any slight alteration in the environmental aspect to which it is adapted reduces the fitness of its possessor.

2. Or at least, the variations to which they are sensitive rarely or never occur under natural conditions.

3. Of course, many economists, and even more sociologists (cf. Hayek, 1952), have done just this, but the view is a minority one in economics, at least in the West. The matching law and other such "molar" principles are the behavioral equivalent of sociological and historical theories that assert greater lawfulness for the behavior of groups—nations, social classes, religious groups—than the individuals of which they are composed. Some social theorists go further and assert the essential irreducibility of group behavior to the behavior of individuals; this is the argument against reductionism. Matching-law advocates have vacillated on this point, at one time asserting the primacy of molar data, more recently arguing for a local process ("melioration") from which molar matching is derived (cf. de Villiers and Herrnstein, 1976; Herrnstein, 1982).

4. Note that momentary maximizing is an optimal decision rule, hence really a causal rather than a functional explanation. It is of course a rule that usually does maximize reward rate, and it gained attention for this reason.

5. This section is an abbreviated version of a longer paper on learning as an inference process (Staddon, 1986; see also Staddon, 1983).

6. I refer to acts as the object of selection here just out of behaviorist habit. There is of course no reason to restrict the object of selection to observable acts: "ideas," "computational elements," "representations"—pick your personal favorite mental unit— will do as well. But acts have the virtue of being observable and, fortunately, rats, pigeons, and bees seem sufficiently unreflective that giving primacy to action works surprisingly well most of the time.

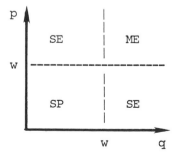

Figure 10.7
Phase-space for reward following, showing outcomes for different combinations of payoff probabilities p and q: SP = stable partial preference; ME = metastable exclusive choice; SE = stable exclusive choice. $w = b/(a + b)$.

7. The steady-state properties of the simple-reward following model in the probabilistic two-choice situation can be approximated by the "phase-space" shown in Figure 10.7: p and q are the payoff probabilities of the two alternatives, and w is the quantity $b/(a + b)$, where a is the increase in choice probability following a reward and b the decrease following a nonrewarded response. The simplified analysis shows three types of outcome: when p and q are both small, the system shows stable partial preference (SP); when both are large the steady-state outcome is fixation on one side or another depending on the starting choice probability (metastable exclusive choice, ME); when one is large and the other small, the predicted outcome is the stable exclusive choice of the majority alternative (SE). For reasons to do with the probabilistic nature of the reward schedule, none of these outcomes is truly stable, and exclusive choice of the minority alternative is in fact rare.

References

Alexander, R. McNeill (1982). *Optima for Animals*. London: Edward Arnold.

Allison, J. (1983). *Behavioral Economics*. New York: Praeger.

Bush, R. R., and F. Mosteller (1955). *Stochastic Models for Learning*. New York: Wiley.

Caraco, T., S. Martindale, and T. S. Whittam (1980). An Empirical Demonstration of Risk-Sensitive Foraging Preferences. *Animal Behaviour* 28:820–830.

Catania, A. C., and G. S. Reynolds (1968). A Quantitative Analysis of the Behavior Maintained by Interval Schedules of Reinforcement. *Journal of the Experimental Analysis of Behavior* 11:327–383.

Charnov, E. L. (1976). Optimal Foraging: The Marginal Value Theorem. *Theoretical Population Biology* 9:129–136.

Commons, M. L., R. J. Herrnstein, and H. Rachlin (eds.). (1982). *Quantitative Analyses of Behavior*, Vol. 2: *Matching and Maximizing Accounts*. Cambridge, MA: Ballinger.

Ettinger, R. H., and J. E. R. Staddon (1983). The Operant Regulation of Feeding: A Static Analysis. *Behavioral Neuroscience* 97:639–653.

Fantino, E. J., and N. Abarca (1985). Choice, Optimal Foraging, and the Delay-Reduction Hypothesis. *Behavioral and Brain Sciences* 8:315–330.

Gould, S. J. (1982). Darwinism and the Expansion of Evolutionary Theory. *Science* 216:380–387.

Gould, S. J., and R. C. Lewontin (1979). The Spandrels of San Marco and the Panglossian Paradigm: A Critique of the Adaptationist Programme. *Proceedings of the Royal Society of London* B205:581–598.

Gould, S. J., and E. S. Vrba (1982) Exaptation—a Missing Term in the Science of Form. *Paleobiology* 8:4–15.

Harley, C. B. (1981). Learning the Evolutionarily Stable Strategy. *Journal of Theoretical Biology* 89:611–633.

Hayek, F. A. (1952). *The Counter-Revolution of Science: Studies on the Abuse of Reason*. Glencoe, IL: Free Press.

Herrnstein, R. J. (1961). Relative and Absolute Strength of Response as a Function of Frequency of Reinforcement. *Journal of the Experimental Analysis of Behavior* 4:267–272.

Herrnstein, R. J. (1964). Secondary Reinforcement and Rate of Primary Reinforcement. *Journal of the Experimental Analysis of Behavior* 7:27–36.

Herrnstein, R. J. (1982). Melioration as Behavioral Dynamism. In M. L. Commons, R. J. Herrnstein, and H. Rachlin (eds.), *Quantitative Analyses of Behavior*, Vol. 2: *Matching and Maximizing Accounts*, Cambridge, MA: Ballinger.

Herrnstein, R. J., and W. Vaughan (1980). Melioration and Behavioral Allocation. In J. E. R. Staddon (ed.), *Limits to Action: The Allocation of Individual Behavior*, New York: Academic Press.

Heyman, G. M. (1979). Matching and Maximizing in Concurrent Schedules. *Psychological Review* 86:496–500.

Hinson, J. M., and J. E. R. Staddon (1983). Hill-Climbing by Pigeons. *Journal of the Experimental Analysis of Behavior* 39:25–47.

Horner, J. M., and J. E. R. Staddon (unpublished). Simple Dynamic Choice.

Killeen P. R. (1982). Incentive Theory: II. Models for Choice. *Journal of the Experimental Analysis of Behavior* 38:217–232.

Krebs, J. R., and R. H. McCleery (1984). Optimization in Behavioural Ecology. In J. R. Krebs and N. B. Davies (eds.), *Behavioural Ecology: An Evolutionary Approach*, Sunderland, MA: Sinauer.

Krebs, J. R., D. W. Stephens, and W. J. Sutherland (1983). Perspectives in Optimal Foraging. In *Perspectives in Ornithology. Essays Presented for the Centennial of the American Ornithologists' Union*, Cambridge: Cambridge University Press, pp. 165–216.

Lewontin, R. C. (1979). Fitness, Survival and Optimality. In D. J. Horn, R. D. Mitchell, and G. R. Stairs (eds.), *Analysis of Ecological Systems*, Columbus: Ohio State University Press.

Maynard Smith, J. (1978). Optimization Theory in Evolution. *Annual Review of Ecology and Systematics* 9:31–56.

Mazur, J. E. (1981). Optimization Theory Fails to Predict Performance of Pigeons in a Two-Response Situation. *Science* 214:823–825.

Mazur, J. E. (1984). Tests for an Equivalence Rule for Fixed and Variable Reinforcer Delays. *Journal of Experimental Psychology: Animal Behavior Processes* 10(4):426–436.

Myerson, J., and S. Hale (1984). Transition-State Behavior on CONC VR VR: A Comparison of Melioration and the Kinetic Model. Unpublished manuscript.

Myerson, J., and F. M. Miezin (1980). The Kinetics of Choice: An Operant Systems Analysis. *Psychological Review* 87:160–174.

Pittendrigh, C. S. (1958). Adaptation, Natural Selection, and Behavior. In A. Roe and G. G. Simpson (eds.), *Behavior and Evolution*, New Haven: Yale University Press.

Rachlin, H., L. Green, J. H. Kagel, and R. C. Battalio (1976). Economic Demand Theory and Psychological Studies of Choice. In G. Bower (ed.), *The Psychology of Learning and Motivation*, Vol. 10, New York: Academic Press.

Real, L. A. (1980). On Uncertainty and the Law of Diminishing Returns in Evolution and Behavior. In J. E. R. Staddon (ed.), *Limits to Action: The Allocation of Individual Behavior*, New York: Academic Press.

Real, L. A., J. Ott, and E. Silverfine (1982). On the Tradeoff between the Mean and the Variance in Foraging: An Experimental Analysis with Bumblebees. *Ecology* 63:1617–1623.

Shimp, C. P. (1966). Probabilistically Reinforced Choice Behavior in Pigeons. *Journal of the Experimental Analysis of Behavior* 9:443–455.

Silberberg, A., B. Hamilton, J. M. Ziriax, and J. Casey (1978). The Structure of Choice. *Journal of Experimental Psychology: Animal Behavior Processes* 4:368–398.

Staddon, J. E. R. (1973). On the Notion of Cause, with Applications to Behaviorism. *Behaviorism* 1:25–63.

Staddon, J. E. R. (1979). Operant Behavior as Adaptation to Constraint. *Journal of Experimental Psychology: General* 108:48–67.

Staddon, J. E. R. (1982). On the Dangers of Demand Curves: A Comment on Lea and Tarpy. *Behaviour Analysis Letters* 2:321–325.

Staddon, J. E. R. (1983). *Adaptive Behavior and Learning*. Cambridge: Cambridge University Press.

Staddon, J. E. R. (1986). Learning as Inference. In R. C. Bolles and M. D. Beecher (eds.), *Evolution and Learning*, Hillsdale, NJ: Erlbaum.

Staddon, J. E. R., and S. Motheral (1978). On Matching and Maximizing in Operant Choice Experiments. *Psychological Review* 85 : 436—444.

Staddon, J. E. R., and A. K. Reid (1987). Adaptation to Reward. In A. C. Kamil, J. R. Krebs, and H. R. Pulliam (eds.), *Foraging Behavior*, New York: Plenum.

Staddon, J. E. R., J. M. Hinson, and R. Kram (1981). Optimal Choice. *Journal of the Experimental Analysis of Behavior* 35 : 397—412.

Villiers, P. A., de, and R. J. Herrnstein (1976). Toward a Law of Response Strength. *Psychological Bulletin* 83 : 1131—1153.

IV

Applications to Human Behavior

11

Optimization Theory in Anthropology: Applications and Critiques

Eric Alden Smith

1 Introduction

Optimization theory has found increasing use within anthropology, where it is employed to generate explanatory hypotheses concerning cross-cultural and intracultural variation in ecological, economic, and reproductive aspects of human behavior. As is true in other disciplines (e.g., evolutionary biology, economics, psychology), the optimization approach has generated both enthusiasm and criticism. This paper reviews, at an introductory level, some representative applications of optimization models in anthropology, the sources from which these models have been drawn, and the criticisms and possible limitations associated with this mode of explanation.

The Logic of Optimization Theory

In order to grasp what the various anthropological applications of optimization models have in common, as well as to establish some basis for evaluating criticisms of these analyses, it is useful to specify the analytical properties characteristic of explanatory models in general, and optimization models in particular. Since optimization research is in a nascent stage of development within anthropology, the rather elementary discussion that follows is perhaps more representative of the way anthropologists use these models than a more sophisticated exposition would be.

I begin with the assumption that all models are necessarily caricatures of the real world. Although the degree of complexity in a model may vary as a function of several factors (including the goals of the research, the state of empirical knowledge, and the historically given level of theory development), the instrumental purpose of model building *is* simplification of the real world to some manageable or desirable level. This simplification allows

For direct comments on an earlier version of the manuscript, I thank Steve Froemming, Stefan Harrell, Kim Hill, Jack Hirshleifer, Hillard Kaplan, Pete Richerson, Gail Smith, and Bruce Winterhalder. In addition, I thank the participants at the Conference on Evolution and Information at Stanford University, where this paper was first presented, for their congenial and spirited discussion.

research to proceed with a reductionist or "piecemeal" (Krebs, Stephens, and Sutherland, 1983) approach to greater understanding of complex realities. Obviously, then, models are not complete explanations for any complex phenomena, or phrased another way, they do not satisfy our frequent longing for holistic or synthetic accounts of the real world. To carry out this larger task, models must be linked to each other and to additional theoretical constructs (as well as to empirical data) in some way. That is, models must be embedded in some larger *theory*.[1]

Optimization models share in this dual characteristic of explanatory models: individually they offer handy ways of breaking complex explanatory problems into manageable chunks, and usually they are linked to some more general theory or research program. That is, particular optimization models can be useful tools for piecemeal analysis, and they are often easily linked to larger frameworks—both methodological ones (such as the mathematical techniques common to optimization analyses) and explanatory ones (such as theories of economic rationality or natural selection).

All optimization models exhibit certain defining features: (1) an *actor* that chooses or exhibits alternative states; (2) a *strategy set* (the range of options an actor chooses from or exhibits); (3) a *currency* (the cost-benefit measure that is maximized or minimized); and (4) a set of *constraints* (all those factors that determine the feasible strategy set and the payoff to each option).[2]

In considering this set of features, we must keep in mind that their identities in any particular case are not necessarily obvious. That is, in order to decide who the actor is, what the feasible set of strategies consists of, and what the currency and payoff to each strategic option might be, one must consult both theory and data relevant to the case at hand. Furthermore, the relative importance of theory versus data varies from one element to another. The identification of the actor and of the currency can often be derived deductively from theoretical principles, whereas the content of the strategy set and the relevant constraints must be arrived at more inductively or intuitively. As Maynard Smith (1978) has emphasized, when any optimization model is subjected to empirical test, one necessarily tests the validity of one's assumptions about the identity of these component factors.

Sources of Optimization Theory
Anthropologists have drawn primarily on two existing research traditions as sources for optimization models: neoclassical economics and evolutionary biology. In terms of formal logical structure, analytical methods, and even in many cases terminology, it is becoming increasingly clear that there is little difference between models drawn from these two sources. This conclusion is supported by evidence indicating independent con-

vergence, direct borrowing, and a growing amount of cross-disciplinary research.[3]

However, there *is* a difference between economic and evolutionary optimization models in terms of their substantive referents and theoretical scope. Substantively, while both frameworks generally focus on individual actors/phenotypes as the locus of alternative strategies, the justifications provided are quite different. Neoclassical economics assigns causal primacy to rational choice (the efficient allocation of available means to arbitrary ends), but it does not attempt to offer an explanation for the primacy of individual actors as the locus of optimal decision-making. Nor, except in the special case of profit-maximizing firms, do economists account for the *content* (i.e., optimization currency) of actors' ends; instead, these goals are taken as "givens" to be explained by other theories, and the only truly general currency—utility—is a subjective construct derived inductively from an actor's "revealed preferences" (Wong, 1978)—that is, behaviorally realized choices.

In contrast, neo-Darwinian theory assigns causal primacy to a historical process of evolution, and especially (as concerns the design features of organisms) to the process of natural selection of genotypes via the differential survival and reproduction of the phenotypes they (help) produce. The role of the individual phenotype as the locus of strategic design is justified by the contingent relation between gene replication and individual action (Dawkins, 1978). As a consequence the optimization currency can be defined in terms of this contingent relation. That is, theory provides fairly good grounds for assuming that selection has designed actors to choose, or exhibit, the alternative strategy with the greatest positive effect on the replication rate of the genes coding for this strategy, or for the capacities or values producing this strategy. This deduction from general theory then requires that one decide on the appropriate measure of gene replication; this may be inclusive fitness, individual (classical) fitness, or often some proxy for fitness that the researcher—and the actor—can actually hope to monitor as an outcome of alternative strategies.[4]

One consequence of these substantive contrasts between economic and evolutionary optimization theory is in their differing explanatory scope. Because evolutionary theory seeks to account for the *content* as well as the form of actors' strategies, it is considerably more ambitious than economics, even within the confines of particular optimization models or hypotheses. Indeed, it can be argued that the capacity for rational choice, and the form of actor's utility functions, are necessarily products of evolution—cultural and genetic—and thus that evolutionary theory is necessary to provide closure to economic theory (e.g., Hirshleifer, 1977; Richerson, 1977).[5]

Table 11.1
Comparison of economic and evolutionary/ecological optimization models

Theoretical and methodological variables	Economics	Evolutionary biology
Model components		
(1) Actor	Individual or firm	Individual phenotype
(2) Strategy set	Range of feasible choices	Range of feasible phenotypes
(3) Currency	Utility, monetary profit	Individual or inclusive fitness, proximal correlates (e.g., energy efficiency)
(4) Constraints	Payoff structure, information, cognitive abilities	Same, plus constraints on design and genetic variation
Analytical methods	Graphical and mathematical maximization (extremum), game theory	Same (but less advanced?)
Ultimate design force	Human nature and culture (exogenous)	Natural selection (locally variable)
Proximate causal forces	Rational choice, survival in a competitive marketplace	Genetic programming, learning, decision-making, social transmission
Primary decision sets	Commodity production, exchange rates, consumption choices (in monetized economies)	Foraging strategies, reproductive strategies, spatial organization, social interactions

A second consequence of the differences between these two sources of optimization models is found in the differing uses anthropologists have made of them. For the most part, optimization models drawn from economics have been used to study production and exchange in peasant economies, whereas models from evolutionary biology and ecology have been employed in analyzing human strategies of foraging, reproduction, and land use. (See table 11.1 for a summary of the contrasts between these two sources of optimization models.)

In this review, I focus primarily on evolutionary/ecological models, for three reasons: (1) as argued above, neo-Darwinian theory offers the more general explanatory framework; (2) the focus of this volume is on the evolutionary basis of optimization arguments; (3) I am more familiar with evolutionary/ecological models and applications than with economic ones. But if the boundary between economic and evolutionary theory continues to blur, we can expect that future anthropological uses of optimization models will reflect this, and become increasingly synthetic in character.

2 Anthropological Applications

Anthropological applications of optimization models have a rather short history. This is perhaps due to several factors, including the qualitative mode of argument frequently favored in a discipline with one foot in the humanities and the other in the social sciences, and the bias in most of the social sciences against reducing social institutions and processes to the action of self-interested individuals [which dates at least to Durkheim's (1938/1895) dictum that social facts can only be explained by social facts, and that individual psychology is subservient to "collective representations"]. Nevertheless, the cross-cultural and evolutionary perspectives of anthropology have led to repeated attempts to establish lawful regularities governing human behavioral variation (Harris 1968), and in recent years growing interest in economic, ecological, and evolutionary theory has seen increased numbers of anthropologists making some use of formal models from these fields.[6]

Several factors have contributed to this recent growth of anthropological interest in optimization models. One is simply that only recently were such models available treating ecological and evolutionary topics, as opposed to narrowly economic ones. But equally important is the frustrating state of conventional research programs in ecological anthropology, which are characterized by a paucity of formal theory, testable hypotheses, and rigorous tests (Johnson 1978). This has led to a failure to articulate theory and data in a productive fashion, and as a result the field has been dominated by narrowly particularist or inductive studies on the one hand, and unresolvable polemical debate on the other (e.g., Sahlins 1978 vs. Harris 1979, Harris and Sahlins 1979; Friedman 1974, 1979 vs. Rappaport 1968, 1984). In the absence of much progress in theory building, the advantages of optimization models, especially when based in general evolutionary ecological theory, are considerably magnified.

In the current context, then, optimization models offer specific advantages over conventional anthropological approaches to understanding human behavioral variation. First, they provide a relatively rigorous basis for generating hypotheses from general theory. Second, most such models provide explicit, quantitative predictions, which facilitate empirical tests. While critics might not feel that optimization models actually deliver on all these promises, I believe I have fairly characterized their advantages *as perceived by anthropologists who utilize them*. The examples discussed below can serve to evaluate these assertions, as well as to illustrate the kinds of uses to which these models have been put by anthropologists.

Rather than a cursory review of a large number of anthropological optimization studies, this paper will illustrate the approach as it has developed thus far in the area of hunter-gatherer socioecology, via examination of four topics: (1) optimal systems of land tenure and spatial organization (Dyson-Hudson and Smith, 1978; Cashdan, 1983a); (2) foraging-group size (Smith 1981, 1985; Hill and Hawkes, 1983); (3) reciprocal food-sharing (Kaplan and Hill, 1985b); and (4) optimal birth-spacing (Blurton Jones and Sibly, 1978; Blurton Jones, nd, a, b).

Hunter-Gatherer Land Tenure and Spatial Organization

Anthropologists have long recognized the diversity of human systems of land tenure, but usually analyzed this data with an inductive, atheoretical approach. That is, little attempt was made until recently to formulate general models, or test them systematically against the ethnographic and archaeological record. The need for such an effort became quite apparent in the 1960s, as a protracted controversy over the origin and significance of territorial/private property systems arose. On the one hand were a number of popular works making aggressive claims concerning the instinctual basis of territoriality and private property (e.g., Ardrey, 1966; Lorenz, 1966). While anthropologists gave these little credence (Montagu, 1968; Alland, 1972), there remained a division of opinion concerning the universality of human territoriality. One position held that territorial exclusion was characteristic of even the simplest hunter-gatherer societies, and linked this practice to male solidarity in hunting and defense, and thus the practice of patrilocal residence (Radcliffe-Brown, 1930–1931; Service, 1962; Williams, 1974), or to the resource-conservation effects of private property as compared to common property (Speck, 1915; Speck and Eisley, 1939). An opposing perspective argued that patterns of land tenure were responsive to changes in economic and ecological circumstances, and that hunter-gatherers in particular were subject to localized resource fluctuations, and thus needed to exhibit fluid residence and communal access to resources to buffer this fluctuation (e.g., many authors in Lee and DeVore, 1968).

The balance of anthropological opinion has historically shifted from one side to the other, with the fluid group/communal access view holding the upper hand in recent years. But the striking thing about this debate is the tendency of each side to dismiss the arguments of the other, and deny the validity of empirical evidence supporting the opposing view. Thus, universal-territoriality proponents portray cases of fluid group composition and spatial arrangement as products of (often undocumented) colonial disruption or depopulation, while the nonterritorial dogma holds that all of the territorial cases are the product of trade or unusual conditions, or that the systems of exclusive land tenure described by some ethnographers are depictions of native ideology (or even that of the observer) rather than native practice.[7]

Research on territorial behavior in other species (especially birds) was also hampered for many years by an "either/or" opposition over the causes, significance, and range of variation of these phenomena. The elementary but compelling argument by Brown (1964) that territorial aggression is costly and should therefore only be expected to evolve when the fitness benefits to the territory defender exceed these costs reoriented research toward a more productive path. The accumulation of both theory and experimental and natural observations on territorial behavior over the succeeding twenty years has been impressive (Brown and Orians, 1970; Schoener, 1983; Davies and Houston, 1984).

Inspired by these successes (as of 1976), and frustrated by the polemical nature of much of the anthropological literature, Dyson-Hudson and I formulated the basic principles of what had by then become known as the "economic defendability model" of spatial organization in terms that we felt could be readily applied to the existing anthropological data set. Retaining the basic optimization logic and diversity-explaining orientation of the ecological theory, we formulated a simple, qualitative version of the argument (Dyson-Hudson and Smith, 1978). Briefly, we considered two dimensions of resource value (density and predictability), and argued on various grounds that the benefits of territorial exclusion were most likely to exceed the costs when resources were both dense (but still scarce relative to demand—i.e., not "superabundant") and relatively predictable in space and time. Since this was only one of the four possible combinations of resource quality in our 2 × 2 formulation, we went on to predict other optimal patterns of land tenure and spatial organization associated with the three other idealized resource distributions (figure 11.1).

While primitive in execution, the economic defendability model does exhibit the characteristic features of an optimization model: (1) the *actors* consist of groups of varying size and spatial exclusivity; (2) the *currency*, though never formally specified in Dyson-Hudson and Smith (1978), is some measure of the net return of resources per unit time spent in harvest and defense; (3) the *strategy options* consists of the alternative forms of land tenure and resource division considered in figure 11.1; (4) the *constraints* are defined by the local resource qualities (density and predictability) and by the actor's abilities to harvest resources, monitor the movements of others, and defend a locale against trespass.

Although this model only offers qualitative predictions, and is obviously a grossly simplified version of any actual situation, it has the virtue of allowing one to move from rather sterile "either/or" arguments about human territoriality to an attempt to explain cross-cultural, historical, and even synchronic intracultural (resource-specific) variation in land tenure. Provisional applications to a number of foraging and pastoral/agricultural societies indicate substantial qualitative support for the model. For

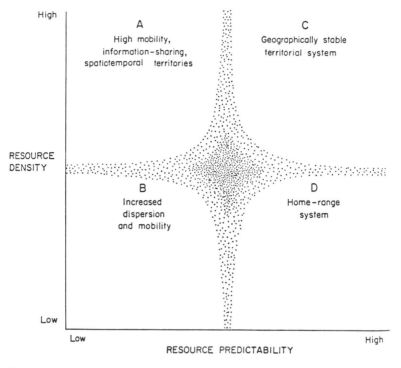

Figure 11.1
The economic defendability model of spatial organization. Resource density and predicta-bility combine to determine costs and benefits of alternative forms of land tenure and sociospatial interaction (from Dyson-Hudson and Smith, 1978).

example, Richardson (1982) found that the degree of territorial exclusive-ness (as codified in rules of ownership, privileged access, and hereditary rights) varied between Indian groups within the Northwest Coast region of North America, in such a way that locales with denser and more reliable resource concentrations were more territorial. This parallels the findings of Steward's (1938) research on variation in land tenure within the Great Basin and that of Bishop on historical shifts in land tenure accompanying changes in resource availability and utilization in the Canadian Subarctic (both cases discussed in terms of the economic defendability model by Dyson-Hudson and Smith, 1978).

In contrast, Cashdan (1983a) has examined four San or Bushman societies, and argues that a pattern opposite to that predicted by the model holds—groups with the scarcest and most unpredictable resources have the tightest controls over access (although none of the four actually exhibit territorial exclusion to any degree). She interprets this as a special pattern of territoriality due to human cognitive and information-sharing abilities. However, her arguments have been challenged on the grounds that control of access to the social group has different adaptive significance and ecological causes than does territorial exclusion (Smith, 1983a; Hill, 1983; cf. Cashdan, 1983b). Specifically, I suggest (1983a, nd) that the systems of controlled access described by Cashdan involve *reciprocal access* to resources on the lands of neighboring bands, and that the social controls on this access are designed to prevent cheating ("free rider" phenomena) as well as to reduce inefficient foraging-area overlap. Further research is clearly needed to explore these issues, as well as to test the economic defendability explanation of territoriality in a more rigorous fashion, following the example of behavorial ecology (reviewed in Davies and Houston, 1984).

Foraging Strategies and Optimal Group Size
The most extensive application of evolutionary/ecological optimization models within anthropology has been in the study of hunter-gatherer production strategies. Here, models developed by evolutionary ecologists under the rubric of optimal foraging theory (OFT) have been borrowed and adapted to the human context.

In both ecology and anthropology, OFT has been used to predict foraging behavior as the outcome of relatively simple "decision rules for predators" (Krebs, 1978). As is characteristic of optimality theory in general, OFT is best viewed as a "shortcut" approach to understanding foraging decisions. First, the details of perceptual and cognitive mechanisms are generally ignored (see Staddon, this volume). Second, it is assumed that foraging outcomes as expressed in operational currencies (e.g., net rate of energy capture) are correlated with fitness, but this assumption is usually not directly tested. Nevertheless, and despite the complexity of actual foraging processes, OFT has been relatively successful both in generating research and in accounting for a substantial portion of relevant empirical data (Krebs, Stephens, and Sutherland, 1983; Pyke, 1984). Anthropological applications, although more limited in number and often less rigorous in method, generally share in these accomplishments (Smith, 1983b; Winterhalder, 1987; Hill et al., 1987).

Standard OFT models are explicit in their optimization logic. The actors are individual foragers (who may sometimes cooperate in groups). The currency in most OFT models is the expected net rate of energy capture while foraging, although more complex currencies involving multiple nutrients (linear programming) or risk-sensitive measures (where both mean and variance are assayed) are sometimes employed. The strategy set varies according to the type of decision being considered; most models fall under one of the following categories: diet choice; patch (foraging area) choice; movement rules (time allocation, searching paths); and foraging group size.

The constraints incorporated vary considerably from one model to the next, even within decision categories; indeed, much of the recent OFT literature is devoted to analyzing the effects of incorporating alternative constraints into a family of models (e.g., perfect information versus information gathering, deterministic versus stochastic outcomes, various perceptual mechanisms, and "rules of thumb"). These "second-generation models" have had little impact on anthropological applications of OFT, but the example discussed here—foraging group size—involves just this element of examining alternative assumptions about the constraints governing individual decisions.

Group foraging activities are conspicuous features among human hunter-gatherers, and are implicated in many widely accepted scenarios of hominid evolution (review in Hill, 1982). By the logic of optimal foraging theory, foraging groups should arise when each member gains an advantage (not necessarily equal) relative to solitary foraging. This advantage may be due to increased mean harvest rates (in detecting or capturing prey), decreased variance in individual food intake, simple aggregation at resource concentrations, or some other benefit of grouping (such as improved predator detection, resource defense, etc.) (reviews in Schoener, 1971; Bertram, 1978; Smith, 1981; Pulliam and Caraco, 1984).

Although many anthropologists have speculated on the selective factors favoring cooperative foraging among hunter-gatherers, relatively few formal models on this topic have been presented, and even less often have empirical tests been attempted (Smith, 1980, 1981; Heffley, 1981; Beckerman, 1983; Hill and Hawkes, 1983). Of the available applications, I shall discuss my own study of Inuit foraging groups (Smith, 1980, 1981, 1985). I choose this example not only because I am most familiar with it, but because it shows how problems with the initial optimization model revealed by empirical tests can lead to further model building in an attempt to uncover factors not considered initially.

The Inuit (Canadian Eskimo) foragers I studied harvest a variety of prey species under varying conditions (Smith, 1980). Because it is the conditions and foraging techniques, not just the prey species, that determine the payoff structure, I refer to the foraging options as "hunt types." If cooperative foraging is undertaken whenever it increases per capita foraging returns, then different hunt types might be characterized by different payoff structures as a function of group size. My initial hypothesis, which I termed the per capita maximization hypothesis, was that foragers should seek to form groups that maximize the per capita net rate of energy capture, defined as

$$\bar{R} = \frac{\sum_{}^{n}(E_a - E_e)}{t \cdot n}, \tag{1}$$

where n is the foraging group size, t is the duration of the foraging period (e.g., a single hunt), and E_a and E_e refer to food energy acquired and metabolic energy expended, respectively, by each member of the foraging group during t.[8] Lacking perfect information, foragers might still develop (or culturally inherit) the ability to predict the expected value of R for different group sizes that pertain to each hunt type, and then choose the optimal group size for each type.

Data from 10 hunt types (361 hunts) revealed that when the optimum is $n = 1$, the prediction is generally met (5 out of 6 hunt types), but that when cooperative foraging is favored, the model group size frequently *exceeds* the optimum (Smith, 1981). In an attempt to explain this finding, and improve upon the predictive power of the simple per capita maximization model, three additional factors have been considered (Smith, 1985): (1) conflicts of interest between individual foragers, given different opportunity costs; (2) kinship structure of foraging groups; and (3) the effect of different sharing rules (governing division of the harvest). Let us now consider some of these factors.

In the best of all possible worlds, an individual would not only know what the optimal group size was under each foraging condition, but would have no trouble finding a place in such a group. But what happens if a forager cannot find a group of $n^* - 1$ other foragers to join (where n^* is the optimal size, i.e, the size associated with R_{max}, the maximum per capita return rate)? An efficiency-maximizing forager should still attempt to maximize his or her own return rate, by choosing from the available options that which yields the highest R. As several analyses have recently shown, this "selfish" choice shifts the solution away from a single "optimal group size" to a range of possible equilibrium group sizes, which will often be larger than that which maximizes per capita return rates (Sibly, 1983; Pulliam and Caraco, 1984; Clark and Mangel, 1984; Smith, 1985).

The exact equilibrium depends on the dynamics of group formation. For simplicity, consider the case where there are only two options: to join a group of $n-1$ foragers (and become the nth member) or to forage alone. Assuming equal division of the harvest at the end of the foraging period, the optimal forager should seek to join the group as long as

$$\bar{R}_n > \bar{R}_1, \tag{2}$$

where R_n is the per capita return rate (as well as the actual rate of each group member if equal sharing occurs) for a foraging group of size n. At the point where this inequality reverses, it will be preferable to forage alone. I have termed this the "joiner's rule" (Smith, 1985). In contrast, once a member of a foraging group, a selfish efficiency maximizer should favor the addition of the nth forager only as long as

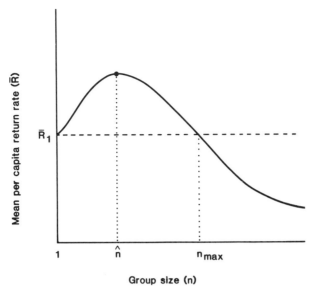

Figure 11.2
Graphical representation of the conflict between the "joiner's rule" and the "members' rule." Per capita returns peak at $\hat{n}$, the size at which members will obtain the maximum share, but foragers faced with the option of solitary foraging will improve their return rate by joining groups as large as n_{max} (the size where the per capita return rate $\bar{R}_n$ is equal to the solitary return rate $\bar{R}_1$). This model can be generalized by substituting $\bar{R}_a$, the expected return rate from *all* available alternatives open to the prospective joiner, for $\bar{R}_1$ (from Smith, 1985).

$$\bar{R}_n > \bar{R}_{n-1}. \tag{3}$$

A conflict between the joiner's rule [equation (2)] and the members' rule [equation (3)] will arise whenever

$$\bar{R}_{n-1} > \bar{R}_n > \bar{R}_1. \tag{4}$$

A graphical version of this conflict of interest (figure 11.2) indicates that whenever the expected returns from solitary foraging are low relative to the per capita returns from group foraging, individuals will attempt to join groups even though this pushes group size above the optimum. If members are never capable of excluding joiners (or if the costs of doing so are too high), the resulting group size will approach the Nash equilibrium (Pulliam and Caraco, 1984, p. 146), whereas complete ability to exclude [Vehrencamp's (1983) "despotism"] will keep the average group size (including those excluded and forced to forage alone) *below* the per capita optimum.

In the Inuit case, the relative ability of "members" versus "joiners" to determine the size of foraging groups varies according to the circumstances of group formation. For example, beluga whale hunts are localized and small groups of hunters arrive independently at the site, form loosely cooperative groups that attempt to encircle the prey, and then divide the catch at the end of the hunt. Here, early arrivals ("members") would find it difficult or impossible to exclude later arrivals ("joiners"), and the data indicate that the result predicted by the joiner's rule [equation (2)] is approximately met (Smith, 1985). Breathing-hole seal hunting, involves different and less clearly understood group-formation dynamics, but the data suggest that the resulting group sizes represent a compromise between the interests of joiners and members (Smith, 1985).

The joiner/member model predicts conflicting optima based on different opportunity costs (forgone opportunities) facing those who already "belong" to a foraging party versus those who are seeking to do so. There are at least two factors that can modify or even eliminate these conflicts of interest, at least in theory. One of these is the increased overlap of interests produced by inclusive fitness considerations where group members are closely related (Rodman, 1981; Smith, 1985). Another is communal sharing at a central place (i.e., camp) by a set of foragers (Hill and Hawkes, 1983; Smith, 1985). Only this second type of situation will be summarized here.

The situation envisaged by the communal-sharing model is one in which foragers, singly or in groups, set out from a central base to forage, and upon returning at the end of a foraging period pool the entire catch and divide this catch equally. This sharing rule differs from that assumed in the joiner/member model, and this altered constraint results in a different optimization rule for foraging group size. Specifically, the optimization rule that can be derived under central-place sharing is to increase the size of any foraging group to n members as long as

$$n\bar{R}_n - (n - 1)\bar{R}_{n-1} > \bar{R}_1 \qquad (5)$$

(Smith, 1983, 1985; Hill and Hawkes, 1983).

Several interesting contrasts with the predictions of the joiner/member model result from communal sharing.[9] First, equation (5) expresses the optimal decision rule for *all* foragers in the sharing network, regardless of their status as "member" or "joiner" of a foraging group. Second, because foragers will benefit by maximizing the per capita share of the entire camp rather than their own personal harvest rates, there is no conflict of interest over size of foraging groups. Third, the optimal (equilibrium) group size under the communal-sharing rule will always be greater than or equal to that which maximizes per capita returns for a foraging group [specified in equation (3)], but less than or equal to the maximum size determined by the joiner's rule [equation (2)]. Finally, as long as the communal sharing rule is strictly adhered to, and foragers attempt to maximize their own share (and hence total harvest for the sharing network), the equilibrium group size will approach Pareto-optimality (maximizing total benefits for the community) rather than the pessimistic Nash equilibrium (selfish maximizing) that might otherwise prevail. This is because the communal-sharing rule results in a payoff structure where the marginal contribution of a foraging group member is equal to the marginal cost of not joining the group (i.e., the expected solitary return rate) (Smith, 1985, p. 52). Obviously, this convenient intervention of the Invisible Hand begs several questions, one of which—the conditions under which a communal sharing rule might evolve—is the next topic examined here.

Reciprocal Food Sharing
The reciprocal exchange of resources is a striking characteristic of human social groups. Furthermore, the extent of such sharing, in terms of its frequency and intensity (proportion of total resources shared), is highly variable from one context to another, within and between societies. Here, I shall focus on reciprocal sharing involving one type of resource—food—and one social context—sharing between (rather than within) family units among human foragers (although the optimization model discussed is sufficiently general that it could be applied to other contexts and resource types with little modification).

Hunter-gatherers are an interesting test case for explanations of food sharing because there is a substantial anthropological literature discussing the extensive sharing practices typical of this mode of subsistence (e.g., Isaac, 1978; Gould, 1981, 1982; Hayden, 1981; Wiessner, 1982). Over the years, anthropologists have advanced various alternative explanations for this. Some of these, such as the argument that foragers possess an ethic of "generalized reciprocity," strike me as tautological, or at least highly limited in explanatory power.[10] But one widely accepted view holds that food-sharing is a device to buffer the fluctuations in the daily food supply of individual foragers that seem to be the typical lot of foragers. This view is plausible and logically coherent, but needs to be stated in a form that can generate precise and varied predictions, to facilitate testing and allow one to account for diversity in the extent of sharing practices from one resource, situation, or society to another.

One useful way to satisfy these requirements is to use an optimization model coupled to the concept of risk aversion developed in economics and recently applied in evolutionary ecology (see note 3). The basic elements of risk-sensitive optimization (where "risk" refers to the effects of stochastic variation in resource income) can be incorporated in a very simple model of individual benefit as a function of resource income—that is, what an economist would term a "utility function," and a biologist might label a "fitness function."

The model as considered here involves the following assumptions (see Schaffer, 1978, for a more general and rigorous treatment, and Kaplan and Hill, 1985b, for an extended discussion and application): (1) Each actor is subject to random variation in harvest rates, as measured over some relevant unit of time (e.g., per day). (2) All actors in some local set experience approximately the same *expected* harvest over the long run. (3) The stochastic variation in harvest rates is unsynchronized between actors (e.g., everyone has good days and bad days, but not on the *same* days, except by chance). (4) The marginal value of resources consumed by any actor over the relevant time unit exhibits diminishing returns; that is, beyond some frequently realized point, additional units of food consumed are worth less in the currency of utility or fitness. This diminishing marginal value assumption (convex-upward value function) is graphed in figure 11.3. (5) The

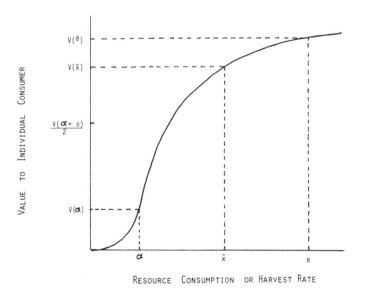

RESOURCE CONSUMPTION OR HARVEST RATE

Figure 11.3
A risk-reduction model of resource sharing. For any actor, the rate of resource harvest is a random variable with a symmetric distribution whose mean is $\bar{x}$ and whose range (or standard deviation) is from α to β. With a diminishing marginal value curve (i.e., reduced utility or fitness to consumption of additional units), those actors who pool their resources and consume equal shares will realize a higher and more certain value $V(\bar{x})$ than those who consume their own resources at a stochastic rate with the same distribution as the harvest rate, since the expected value of the latter strategy is equal to $V(\alpha + \beta)/2$ [i.e., the midpoint between $V(\alpha)$ and $V(\beta)$ on the value axis]. For an accelerating function (i.e., below the inflection point on a sigmoid function such as hypothesized here), the converse results hold.

currency actors seek to maximize is the total expected value obtained from resource consumption over the long run. (Note that the currency thus is not measured directly in resources consumed, but by a measure of value that transforms resource consumption via the utility or fitness function.) (6) Finally, it is assumed that actors do not have any significant alternative sources of the resource(s) is question, nor alternatives to local consumption (i.e., local self-sufficiency prevails).

Given these assumptions, one can generate a number of predictions; further predictions can be obtained by altering or relaxing the assumptions, as shown below. First, actors will reap higher value (greater utility or fitness) if they can somehow avoid or reduce variation in their resource consumption rate. This is because, given a diminishing-returns value function, the mean value of a stochastic consumption rate $[V(\alpha + \beta)/2$ in figure 11.3] is always less than the value of the corresponding mean $[V(\overline{x})$ in same]. In other words, given a diminishing-returns function, an actor should always be risk-averse, preferring a lower-variance option (or a sure bet) to a higher-variance option with the same mean. Of course, the means of different options may *not* be the same, but an actor should be willing to forgo a certain amount of returns [up to $V(\overline{x}) - V(\alpha + \beta)/2$] in order to eliminate risk. One way to do this might be to harvest resources with a lower associated variation in harvest success, even if the overall return rate is also lower; but let us assume here that this option is not available, or has been utilized as much as is optimal, with unwanted variation in the harvest rate remaining. We can then predict that actors who pool their (e.g., daily) catch with a sufficient number of other foragers, then taking an equal share of the total pool (which share, by the law of large numbers, should approximate $\overline{x}$, or at least show a narrower frequency distribution around $\overline{x}$), will reap a higher total value [equal to $V(\overline{x})$ if there is no cost to this sharing].[11]

The most obvious implication of this model for the analysis of food sharing is that food sharing will increase in frequency, extent, and/or intensity as the degree of unsynchronized variation in (e.g., daily) food harvest increases. The comparison implied here could be intracultural, referring to different resource types within a single economic system, or it could be cross-cultural (e.g., hunter-gatherers in environments that differ in the predictability of resource harvest). Despite the various simplifying assumptions (discussed further below), the model strikes me as plausible, and corresponds with my impressionistic assessment of the ethnographic record. For example, most hunter-gatherers are reported to share meat resources far more frequently than they do plant foods, and the former seem to be characterized by greater variability in harvest rates.[12]

But impressions and plausibility can mislead, so careful tests are obviously preferable. The only such test I am aware of is that by Kaplan and Hill (1985b), who collected a wealth of data on foraging activities and sharing practices of Ache Indians in Paraguay (see also Kaplan et al., 1984). These data show that different resource categories differ in the amount of daily variation in harvest rates by individual families, and that the degree of unsynchronized variation is directly correlated with the amount of sharing that occurs between these family units (table 11.2). These results are precisely those predicted by the risk-reduction model.

What is *not* predicted by this model is the finding that individual Ache differ in their long-term foraging success rates. As Kaplan and Hill point out, this violates assumption (2) listed above; and indeed we might expect this assumption to be regularly violated, given the ubiquity of individual differences in foraging abilities. Relaxing this assumption could lead to two different (not necessarily mutually exclusive) outcomes: decreased sharing or "hidden trade" (nonfood compensation for the more productive producers). Decreased sharing, while certainly a possibility, is likely to be less rewarding under most constraints than is compensation, since even the best foragers will find it difficult to avoid substantial stochastic variation. "Hidden trade" could take many forms, but ethnographic data indicate that exceptional producers are usually rewarded with increased political authority, prestige, assistance, access to mates, and ultimately fitness (Kaplan and Hill, 1985a). Further empirical and theoretical work is needed to explore these issues.

Another assumption of the risk-pooling model that may frequently be violated is the last one noted above—that alternative sources of goods, and outlets other than local consumption, are absent. The most likely such alternatives include *storage* (which allows households to buffer daily variation in food income) and *trade* (which serves both as a source of goods and as an outlet for marketing surplus production). Again speaking impressionistically, both of these phenomena do seem to be correlated with decreased

Table 11.2
Relationship between package size, interfamily harvest synchrony, and sharing frequency for different resources among Ache foragers[a]

Resource class	Mean daily standard deviation across families in calories acquired	Percentage of calories consumed outside of acquirer's family	Mean package size (kcal)
Meat resources	9,019	91	2,516
Honey	7,318	83	6,517
Collected resources	2,283	52	1,118
Regression coefficient (log-log)	$r^2 = .61,$ $p < .000001$	$r^2 = .45,$ $p < .0001$	

a. Source: Kaplan and Hill (1985b, tables 2 and 3 and text).

food sharing among hunter-gatherer societies. For example, it is often noted that articulation of foragers with mercantile institutions such as the fur trade (e.g., Leacock, 1954; Balikci, 1964), or adoption of some horticulture allowing increased storage (e.g., Cashdan, 1980), is associated with reduced reciprocity and increased socioeconomic independence of individual households. Again, additional research is needed to examine the extent to which risk reduction versus other factors is responsible for these strategic shifts in social and economic relations. But the model discussed above, simplified as it is, provides a useful starting point for further inquiry.

Optimal Birth Spacing
The examples discussed thus far, since they all utilize material currencies, can with equal validity be viewed as standard economic logic applied to nonmonetized economies or as human evolutionary ecology. But evolutionary theory argues that phenotypic costs and benefits are important only to the extent that they are correlated with reproductive measures. Our final example concerns an application of the optimization approach to human reproduction, where the contrast between economic and evolutionary optima should be clearest. Here, unlike in economic demography, the evolutionary optimization assumption is that children are valued as ends (increased fitness) rather than strictly as means (to such ends as family income, parental security, or the like).[13]

As in previous examples, the optimization approach has been brought to bear on an area of existing anthropological interest, in order to increase the rigor and productivity of both method and theory. On the basis of extensive research by himself and others, Richard Lee (1972, 1980) has described the birth-spacing and foraging practices of !Kung San foragers in the Kalahari region of southern Africa. Lee found that nomadic, bush-dwelling !Kung women had an average interbirth interval (IBI) of nearly four years, while those who settled at cattle posts had much shorter IBIs. He argued that this pattern made sense, given that nomadic !Kung women nurse young children on demand, carry children much of the time through the fourth year of life, and make frequent day-long trips away from camp to collect wild foods, while cattlepost women are much more sedentary and have early-weaning foods available. In fact, Lee's data indicated that for nomadic women, IBIs less than four years long would increase the mother's carrying load dramatically, because of the need to carry two children at a time.

Lee's explanation of !Kung birth spacing is an important contribution to our understanding of hunter-gatherer demography; but like most orthodox ecological anthropology, it remains unclear concerning the definition of satisfactory adjustment and the mechanisms that produce it. On the first point, we can ask, "If wide birth-spacing means less work, why not just have one child, or none at all?" On the second, if we believe that IBIs are adjusted to fit local ecological conditions, what are the selective forces that shape this fit? And if these be a form of natural selection (or its effects as realized through rational choice, physiology, etc.), why is it the !Kung women do not have as many children as they can?

These questions have been systematically tackled within an optimization framework by Nicholas Blurton Jones (Blurton Jones and Sibly, 1978; Blurton Jones nd, a, b). Using a simulation model, Blurton Jones and Sibly tested the basic hypothesis that !Kung women adjust birth spacing to maximize the number of children successfully raised to adulthood. Here, the actors are the mothers (*not* the fathers, the children, etc), and the currency maximized is reproductive success. The strategy set, at least in a simple formulation, consists of the various possible IBIs. The simulation incorporated a large number of constraints (including women's foraging rates, family food requirements, travel distances, children's age-specific weights and survivorship) derived from Lee's research plus information on human physiology, to define the payoff to various IBIs. It assumed that the main selective forces affecting reproductive success (e.g., heat stress, exhaustion, dehydration, food supply for children) are determined by the average weight women carry, not extreme weight (e.g., back injury).

The Blurton Jones and Sibly simulation confirmed that a four-year IBI produces the most even trajectory of average backload throughout a !Kung woman's reproductive career; shorter spacing produces a very sharp upturn in backload, exceeding levels likely to cause heat stress in the dry season (or else insufficient loads of food returned to camp), while longer IBIs lead to lower but fluctuating backloads that can be viewed as "labor underutilization" (lost opportunities for maximizing reproductive success). However, the simulation could not directly test the central prediction of the optimal birth-spacing model: that !Kung women who had IBIs shorter or longer than four years would raise less children. For this, Blurton Jones (nd, a, b) turned to empirical data on individual demographic outcomes collected by Howell (1979 and unpublished field data).

These data confirm the trade-off between IBI and reproductive success postulated in the original simulation. First, calculated backloads (as determined by IBIs) are strongly correlated with offspring mortality; the best fit to the mortality data is provided by a decelerating asymptotic curve (figure 11.4). Second, the optimal IBI predicted by this curve centers on 48 months, which matches the observed IBI frequency distribution.[14] Third, child mortality is *not* affected by IBI length for *first* intervals of women's reproductive careers, nor for *any* intervals of women settled at cattleposts; both of these results are as predicted, given the altered constraints on carrying and food requirements pertaining to these cases. Finally, death of unweaned infants is followed by shortened IBI, indicating "replacement" of

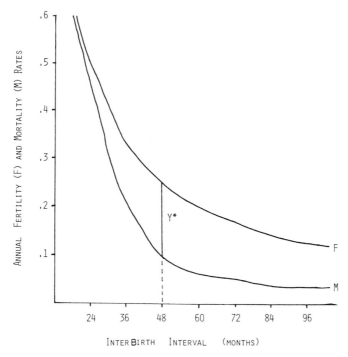

Figure 11.4
Birth-spacing optimization for !Kung women. For lengthening interbirth intervals, annual fertility (curve F) declines by an exponential function of -1 (by definition), while empirical data on mortality as a function of backloads associated with various intervals fits a logistic regression curve with a steeper, but eventually asymptotic shape (curve M, the annual mortality of offspring under ten years of age). The net yield of offspring successfully raised (to age ten) is given by $Y = F - M$, whose highest value occurs at $Y^* = 48$ months (after Blurton Jones nd, a, table 3).

these offspring, whereas death of older children has no effect on IBI— again, as expected given the assumption that carrying children under four is the primary constraint on maximizing reproductive success.[15]

In summary, the optimization model developed by Blurton Jones and Sibly performs remarkably well in predicting details of the reproductive ecology of !Kung foragers. Given the prominent didactic role the well-studied !Kung play in textbooks, generalizations concerning hunter-gatherers, and theoretical treatises on human ecology, the importance of these findings is considerable. Furthermore, it is reassuring that Lee's original insights into the causes of long IBIs are upheld and refined by the optimization approach, which in turn is able to provide precise predictions, suggest numerous empirical tests, and anchor the explanatory argument to a general theory of adaptation.

3 Critiques and Limitations

In terms of several widely accepted criteria for scientific utility—generating new explanations, providing testable hypotheses, linking observations to general theory—optimization theory in biology and the social sciences has been successful. Nevertheless, this approach has been subject to some rather strong criticisms regarding its limitations and potential for abuse. To avoid undue redundancy with other contributions to this volume, I restrict my review primarily to criticisms of the application of optimization models to human social behavior.

Even within this bailiwick, my review is necessarily selective. Issues that are strictly methodological or empirical (e.g., the validity of an energy efficiency currency in studies of human foraging strategies—see Smith, 1983b) are passed over in favor of more general issues. The emphasis is on ecological/evolutionary (rather than strictly economic) topics. The questions reviewed here are arranged in order of increasing specificity to anthropological inquiry, and involve the relation of selection to optimization/maximization, the realism and explanatory sufficiency of optimization models, the constraints placed on individual choice by culture, and the differing currencies in cultural versus genetic evolution.

Does Natural Selection Produce Optimization?
This is obviously a broad issue, and one of much current interest in evolutionary biology and philosophy, as testified by a substantial literature (see references in note 19). The reason for bringing it up here is that critics of anthropological optimization research have challenged the theoretical bases for the optimization postulate. As noted above, there are two such bases: the utility-maximizing assumption of neoclassical economics and the

fitness-maximizing assumption of neo-Darwinism. The former is discussed further in a later section.

The most sustained anthropological critique of attempts to anchor optimization in neo-Darwinism is due to Sahlins (1976a), who argues that selection does not maximize anything, including fitness: "Selection is not *in principle* the maximization of individual fitness but any relative advantage whatsoever .... Nothing is thus asserted about maximization. In the science of economics, it is true that there is only one appropriate answer to any problem of resource allocation: 'the one best answer,' gain *optimus maximus*, the particular distribution of resources which maximizes utilities from the means in hand. But natural selection is not *the* one best; it need be only *one* better" (pp. 74–75; original italics; sequence rearranged). Besides emphasizing the contrast between economic maximization and natural selection, Sahlins (1976a, pp. 71–107) is at pains to derive the neo-Darwinian propensity to postulate fitness maximization from the ideological influence of bourgeois economic theory: "The Darwinian concept of natural selection has suffered a serious ideological derailment in recent years. Elements of the economic theory of action appropriate to the competitive market have been progressively substituted for the 'opportunistic' strategy of evolution .... Darwinism, at first appropriated to society as 'social Darwinism,' has returned to biology as genetic capitalism" (pp. 71–72). In this view, the confusion between selection and maximization is no accident, but a historically specific example of the dialectic between socio-economic structure and ideological superstructure postulated by various "externalist" theories in the sociology of knowledge, especially Marxist varieties.

There is much to be said in favor of Sahlins's arguments. With respect to the linkage between selection and maximization, his critique at least has the virtue of comprehending that the logic of selection involves the reproductive advantage of one unit (be it allele, organism, or lineage) *relative to another*. A surprising number of the critics of evolutionary optimization arguments have confused neo-Darwinian logic with a Panglossian notion that these models assume some form of global optimization at the level of populations or species (as noted by Maynard Smith, 1978, p. 42; for other examples, see Slobodkin and Rapoport, 1974; Slobodkin, 1977; Martin, 1983). Sahlins to his credit avoids this misunderstanding.

Yet he suffers from another: he conflates the *process* of selection with its *results*. The process *is* one of relative advantage only, not of maximization or optimization. But at least since the days of Haldane and Fisher, neo-Darwinists have realized that small relative advantages can have a large cumulative effect, and it is plausible that one of those effects (given sufficient genetic variation and consistence of selection pressures) will often be not just a trajectory of improvement in designs, but a resulting design that can fairly be characterized as "optimal" with respect to the fitness currency, the design problem, and the relevant constraints. Sahlins (1976a, pp. 76ff.) comes close to admitting this possibility, but demurs on the basis that environmental change is ubiquitous, hence selective consistency is untenable. This, of course, is a matter for empirical resolution (Jochim, 1983). But it might also be pointed out that selection could—and in some cases demonstrably has—favor the evolution of capacities for phenotypic adjustment to rapidly shifting environmental conditions. Such abilities are clearly central to behavioral aspects of phenotype.

When behavioral ecologists (including the anthropological variety) invoke optimization arguments, then, they are not granting Panglossian directionality to natural selection; rather, they are postulating that phenotypic capabilities whose outcome is "optimal" in some clearly specified sense will evolve, given sufficient conditions (noted above). Viewed this way, optimization models are merely shortcuts to understanding the outcome of evolutionary history—in Etter's (1978, p. 167) apt phrasing, "These methods investigate the teleologies of evolution, on the assumption that conditions presumed by a model actually hold in the real world."[16] To recognize optimization theory as a shortcut, a simplified and ahistorical approximation to a mechanistic and opportunistic process, does not deny its usefulness to science, although it may serve to alert us to the potential for abuse, and for mistaking the shortcut for the real thing.

As far as the derivation of optimality thinking from neoclassical economic theory, or from the ideology of advanced capitalist society in general, I do not think Sahlins's view is unreasonable. Neither do I think it is very original, sophisticated, nor entirely consistent with his general critique.[17] The glib correlation between the economic interests of capitalist society and the ideological bases of science does not explain why the ideologues of evolutionary optimization are so assailed by critics from all sides—from the left, from the right (e.g., creationists), and from the center (e.g., inductivists). Nor does it account for the uses of evolutionary game theory in subverting the official ideology of utilitarianism ("the greatest good for the greatest number ...") through the irresolvable conflicts of interest and the social dysfunctions of Nash equilibria, as discussed below (and see especially Hirshleifer, 1982); dialectical materialism has no monopoly on contradiction. None of this is meant to support an argument that scientists develop their ideas in a social vacuum, nor to deny that biologists have borrowed many optimization concepts from neoclassical economics. But I see little evidence that this has necessarily been accompanied by a conservative political outlook, or that evolutionary optimization models have regularly been used (wittingly or not) to support the status quo.[18]

Taken to its logical conclusion, the critique of all science as socially conditioned ideology must raise doubts that "we can ever hope to do anything but create a reflection of the current dominant political and economic structure in our reconstructions of the past" (Keene, 1983, p. 148). Accepting this pessimistic, and highly deterministic, view leaves one unable to resolve scientific disputes, except by political sympathies. A less extreme position is that scientific theory and practice is socially conditioned, but not absolutely determined thereby. If so, then the heuristic and explanatory power of optimization theory must be amenable to empirical examination by standard criteria of science. By such criteria, the ideological origins or uses of theory are irrelevant, no matter how interesting (or disturbing) we find them from a sociological or political perspective.

If my arguments are correct, Sahlins's reasons for opposing selection-as-relative-advantage and selection-as-optimization theory are less cogent than they first appear to be. I would submit that this is so even if several other technical objections to evolutionary optimization theory are taken into account.[19] But in the special case of social interactions ("special" to biology, but obviously central to anthropology and the other social sciences), I think there *is* a powerful objection to the optimization viewpoint. This is the realization that strategic interactions characterized by conflicts of interest can lead to evolutionary outcomes quite different from those specified by models of simple individual optimization—a realization first formalized by mathematical economists as "the theory of games" (von Neumann and Morgenstern, 1944; Luce and Raiffa, 1957; etc.) and subsequently given a neo-Darwinian basis in the theory of "evolutionarily stable stategies" or "ESS theory" (e.g., Maynard Smith 1974, 1982; Parker 1984; Parker and Hammerstein, 1985). Put in more ordinary language, when the relative payoffs of different alternative strategies or phenotypic attributes depend on what other individuals in the population are doing, the course of natural selection (or rational choice) cannot be predicted from simple optimization criteria. This is because a strategy that has high payoff when it is rare (and rarely encountered) in the population may have low payoff when common.

The theoretical elaboration of this principle, the counterarguments to it, and the hosts of different types and subtypes of games that can be observed or hypothesized involve complexities that are beyond the scope of this paper. A few simple points can be made here. First, the challenge to optimization theory posed by strategic interaction is fundamental in a way that questions about the details of genetic mechanisms, imperfect information, or cognition and the like (see the previous note) are not—at least to my mind. That is, the results of selection (or rational choice) when there are conflicts of interest cannot usefully be interpreted as "fitness maximization plus some deviation due to constraint x," but rather need to be analyzed in a completely different way (Dawkins, 1980, provides a clear discussion of this). Rather than asking what the optimal solution might be (given a set of options, constraints, and objective function), evolutionary game theory asks what stategy or set of stategies will be *unbeatable* (assuming each actor takes into account what other actors are doing, and "chooses" the feasible payoff that is highest *given that the other actors are equally self-interested*). Of course, it is possible to redefine "optimal" in game-theoretic or frequency-dependent terms—the optimal stategy is then the one that yields the highest payoff in the face of what others are doing—but this is a rather specialized and attenuated meaning of optimal, and it is probably less confusing to call this particular spade by a different name.

Second, ESS/game theory shows that conflicts of interest between "actors" (genes, traits, individuals) structure the payoffs (in fitness or utility) in such a way that the best that actors can achieve is quite often worse than could be achieved if they were (coerced into) cooperating. A simple example of this is the "joiner's rule" for foraging group size discussed above. A population of foragers following such a rule (e.g., join a group as long as the payoff is higher than foraging alone) will *not* usually end up on an adaptive peak in terms of the mean fitness of its individual members, but if the rule is an ESS it will be the best strategy to follow, in the sense that any forager who deviates from it will be worse off. Thus, viewed through the glasses of ESS theory, the simple optimization approach is not a "shortcut"—it is a blind alley (and one I myself wandered up in my initial attempts to explain foraging group size, as noted earlier).

The implications of this disjunction between individual fitness (or utility) maximizing and the evolutionary (or economic) equilibrium are perhaps just as profound as those following from the critique of naive group selectionism raised in the 1960s and 1970s (e.g., Williams, 1966; Dawkins, 1976; Bates and Lees, 1979).[20] The first critique made the common equation between natural selection and "the good of the species" problematic, replacing it with "individual fitness maximization." In turn, the ESS/game theory critique makes fitness or utility maximization problematic, and suggests that many social phenomena are ridden with pervasive or even insoluble contradictions between the best interests of each individual and the interests they can realize in collective interaction.[21] I suspect that ESS theory will eventually force us to rethink not just the pervasive emphasis on functional explanation in the social sciences (including Marxism—see Elster, 1982, on Cohen, 1980), but the rationalist, individual strategizing wing as well. With ESS/game theory, we should no longer be surprised to find that people do not behave in "their own best interest," if the best is defined without benefit of the ESS logic.

Is Optimization Evidence of Adaptation?

The question posed in this subsection, while not quite the inverse of that in the previous, does stand it on its head. Rather than looking at selection and asking whether it produces optimal adaptations, here we find ourselves looking at apparently optimal phenotypes and asking whether their optimality gives us any reason for concluding they have been designed in some way by selection.

There are really two aspects to this epistemological challenge to optimization theory. The first argues that since optimality explanations are normally synchronic demonstrations of a correlation between predicted and observed phenotypic variation, they cannot be direct evidence of an evolutionary (diachronic) process of adaptation. The second critique argues that the link between behavioral trait and adaptation must always pass through some proximate mechanism or set of mechanisms, and that standard optimality analyses that ignore or avoid this necessary linkage are in error.

On the first issue, I find myself in direct agreement with the charge: a synchronic correlation is not a diachronic causality. It should be possible to use optimality theory diachronically, and thus to explore the evolutionary dynamics as a population of traits evolves toward the optimal (or evolutionarily stable) outcome, but because of the extreme time span required this is rarely done. Certainly none of the examples discussed earlier in the paper provide this kind of evolutionary/diachronic analysis (although one empirical case of the evolution of territoriality cited by Dyson-Hudson and Smith begins to do so). Viewed as current end points of some (poorly understood) evolutionary process, these examples indicate that patterns of human behavior do match those predicted by optimality models in particular cases; but to view them as accounts of the evolutionary process that produced these outcomes is to confuse product with process, a state of the world with a "just-so story" about how the world came to be the way it is.

Since a given product could be produced by various alternative processes, the distinction has some significance. But I doubt that it has as much significance as some critics of adaptation have attributed to it (e.g., Gould, 1980; Gould and Lewontin, 1979). For while some adaptationists may make "consistency with natural selection" (i.e., design for fitness maximization) their only criterion for judging the success of adaptive explanations, most recognize that this is a very weak stance. In the case of human behavioral phenotypes in particular, we face a multiplicity of possible causal factors that could account for such consistency, as discussed in the final section of this paper. I certainly agree with the critics of adaptationism that a mere correlation between the optimality predictions and the observed phenotypes is not sufficient evidence that we are looking at an adaptation shaped by natural selection; but I do not agree that until we have all the relevant information on genetics, development, and evolutionary history (a tall order!) we had best stay quiet (cf. Gould and Lewontin, 1979, Gould, 1980, and Kitcher, this volume). The research findings generated by optimal foraging theory, for example, have greatly advanced our understanding of foraging behavior in a wide variety of species (including our own) despite the almost total lack of genetic, developmental, and evolutionary data.

What then *are* the implications of empirical evidence demonstrating consistency between optimization models inspired by neo-Darwinian theory and human behavior? First, that we should *undertake further research* to try and determine the evolutionary forces that led to this consistency. The particular selective forces, accidents of history, cultural or genetic instructions, and cognitive mechanisms that led to this correlation cannot be established through optimization models per se—though these can be helpful in suggesting likely possibilities. Obviously, however, if we continue to find that neo-Darwinian optimization models do an excellent job in predicting real-world phenotypes, and no alternative theory does a better job, we have some reason for *supposing* that there *is* a causal connection between the variables identified as important in that theory (expanded to include possible cultural evolution, as noted below) and the historical processes that may have occurred in the real world. If we can gather the data to test this supposition, we should do so; but if the task is too difficult (e.g., how can we study the past demographic history of small nomadic hunter-gatherer populations?), I see no reason to dismiss the inquiry guided by optimization theory as a fanciful parlor game.

In sum, in seeking and finding consistency between behavioral choices and theoretically optimal phenotypes, I am making no *specific* claim about the historical or evolutionary causes that might have produced this consistency. These must be investigated using additional theoretical and empirical means. The fact that evolutionary hypotheses are particularly difficult to test means that we shall often find ourselves with good evidence for optimizing but little or no evidence for the historical/evolutionary causes of same. This may be an uncomfortable position, but I do not think it is an untenable one.

The second critique examined in this subsection is aimed precisely at the agnostic position about specific causal mechanisms I have invoked in dealing with the first. A number of discussions of human behavior from a neo-Darwinian perspective (particularly several in Chagnon and Irons, 1979) have attempted to blunt charges of genetic determinism by arguing that no assumption about particular proximate mechanisms is being invoked when they search for and find instances of "inclusive fitness maximization" in humans. Several critics have found fault with this strategy; the most detailed argument is that of Kitcher (1985, chapter 9).

Kitcher argues that since patterns of human behavior (we would say, more generally, patterns of phenotypic variation in any species) are expressions of underlying dispositions, learning mechanisms, and the like, and since it is these "proximate mechanisms" (as they are called) that have evolved and that therefore require evolutionary explanation, research strategies that focus directly on the behavioral patterns and sidestep the difficult questions about proximate mechanisms and evolutionary histories are incorrect and "profoundly misguided." In Kitcher's view, this approach "... introduces evolutionary considerations in the wrong place. There is much striving to show that the end products of a complicated process really maximize human inclusive fitness. Usually the striving is in vain. The products should not be expected to maximize inclusive fitness. Yet, even if they were to do so, the proper focus of evolutionary attention is on the mechanisms that drive the process. In the haste to see fitness maximization everywhere, those mechanisms—and the historical process in which they figure—are ignored" (p. 329).

Kitcher's points here are two. First, because proximate mechanisms must serve to map genetic instructions onto a wide variety of environments, we must expect "mistakes" (nonoptimal behavior) to be quite frequent; the mechanisms will maximize fitness (if truly designed by selection) only *on average*. This is actually a conservative reading of Kitcher's position, for at several points he uses stronger language, stating that whether or not the behavioral products of proximate mechanisms maximize fitness is "irrelevant" (pp. 288, 298) and that studies that demonstrate how often they do teach us "little" (p. 307) or (even stronger) "shed no light on what really needs evolutionary explanations—to wit, the proximate mechanisms" (p. 307).

The more cautious reading of Kitcher's argument is one that I have some sympathy with, and will return to in the final subsection of the paper when discussing cultural evolution. The stronger version strikes me as dubious, or even logically incoherent. If we give the hypothesis that proximate mechanisms have evolved by natural selection serious consideration, how can we treat the fitness consequences of much mechanisms (as mediated through their behavioral products) as *irrelevant*? And if, as is often the case, we are relatively ignorant about the possible proximate mechanisms at work and their evolutionary history, what sense does it make to eliminate evidence on these fitness consequences, taken as an average over a set of proximate mechanisms? Surely the evaluation of specified patterns of behavior in terms of their fitness consequences sheds some light on the adaptiveness of the proximate mechanisms that underlie these patterns. More specifically, if the mechanisms evolved and are maintained because of their net fitness-enhancing effects (the primary adaptationist hypothesis), and if the only or main way these effects can be realized is through behavior, then the auxiliary hypothesis that the behavior produced by these mechanisms will have a net fitness-enhancing effect is at least a reasonable, and certainly not an "irrelevant," one.[22] For if a mechanism is fitness-enhancing *on average*, then the behavioral effects of this mechanism must also be so. To determine the average fitness effects, we must collect data on particular instances; hence these cannot be "irrelevant," but must be of the essence to any but Platonists. The problem is, we often do not know which proximate mechanisms are connected to which behavioral outcomes, and here Kitcher's critique (in its weaker form) is valid. But the stronger version does not cohere.

The second point of Kitcher's critique is that evolutionary explanations properly apply only to proximate mechanisms. The stated implication is that adaptive considerations are irrelevant to more distal products of these mechanisms, such as behavior. In what sense is this true? Both behavior and cognitive/neurophysiological mechanisms are aspects of phenotype, so neither can be identified as the units of selection or inheritance; rather it is *information* (genetic and cultural) that is transmitted and exhibits differential fitness (Cloak, 1975; Dawkins, 1982). Interpreted radically, Kitcher's argument would impel us to hold all evolutionary arguments in abeyance until we understand the specific genetic and cultural instructions underlying the aspects of phenotype we are interested in. (Note that this would logically apply as much to proximate mechanisms as to behavior; that is, we would have to trace phenotypic traits all the way back to DNA and the neurophysiology of long-term memory before we could proffer any adaptive argument whatsoever.) If we moderate the argument somewhat, it becomes a claim that analyses that do not identify the proximate mechanisms and evolutionary histories connected to the behavioral patterns of interest are *incomplete*. This is closely analogous to the claim discussed in the first part of this section, and one I agree with; but, as before, it is not sufficient grounds for abandoning optimization hypotheses about behavior, only for *abandoning conclusions that these offer direct evidence of evolutionary history*. And this last caveat is one that applies to proximate mechanisms with equal strength.

Are Optimization Models Realistic?
A third set of criticisms of the optimization approach revolves around the issue of realism. The issue in this case is the simplification or caricature of particular phenomena, rather than of evolution in general. In anthropology, this critique has often been linked to claims that such models might apply to other species (that lack culture) or to certain societies (those with market economies), but not generally. An example of the former is Lee's (1979, p. 434) statement that "mechanical models drawn from animal behavior and animal ecology, however sophisticated, cannot do justice to any but the simplest of cultural ecological phenomena" (see Jochim, 1983, and Keene, 1983 for similar views). The issues of cross-cultural rationality and human uniqueness are taken up below; here I consider the broader issue of simplification versus realism.

This issue is clearly not unique to optimization theory. Any formal model or general law must face it. Galileo's postulate that mass has no effect on the velocity of falling objects does not employ optimization concepts, yet it suffers a loss of realism by ignoring such factors as atmospheric friction. I am persuaded by Levins's (1966) argument that any attempt to construct a model of some facet of nature must face up to the *modeler's dilemma*; while generality, precision, and realism are each highly desirable attributes of models or explanations, we cannot simultaneously maximize all three. Indeed, increasing a given model's position along any one of these dimensions is likely (according to theory and practice) to exact a cost of decline along both of the other axes.[23]

With respect to realism in particular, the trade-off is that an increase in this attribute usually reduces the range of different situations or systems the model applies to, the precision of the predictions it will generate (as more and more factors whose exact effect is unknown are considered), or both. Thus, any criticism of an optimization model as unrealistic is incomplete unless one goes on to ask what will be sacrificed if it is modified or abandoned in order to increase realism. If one is very fortunate, the alternative may yield a large increase in realism at a small cost of reduced generality or precision. But most critics have no alternative model in mind, except some Platonic ideal of pure Realism, unimpaired by declines in generality or precision.

There is probably nothing inherent in optimization theory that make its models less realistic than others; indeed, by fitting utility functions to observed behavior, one could build decision models that mimic human cognition and behavior in very circumscribed areas quite nicely (though the resulting model would be unique to the situation, or even the individual for which it was constructed). In practice, however, simpler models are easier to understand and work with, and are invariably preferred in the early stages of incorporating the optimization approach into a field of research for this reason. This is certainly the case in anthropology, and to a lesser extent evolutionary biology, in comparison to economics and engineering, where a longer history of optimization research has created a greater demand for complex, realistic, situation-specific models.

In a field like anthropology, then, what one sees is a "research frontier" of expanding but still-novel optimization models (of the simple, relatively unrealistic sort) encountering conventional, informal and particularistic research that can often sincerely claim to be more realistic than the upstart optimization models. The short-term result is predictable: the old guard, and all those who favor detailed, realistic analysis (description?) of particular cases as an end in itself, charge optimizationists with being unrealistic and ill-equipped to deal with the complexities of the real world. The upstarts, and all those who favor a strategy of explaining particular cases in terms of general theory, argue for quantitative tests but against abandoning a model unless a more-or-less equally general alternative is available. But if the short term appears at a stalemate, the long term (judging from the experience of other disciplines, and the hints already apparent at this stage in anthropology) promises vigorous hybridization at the frontier, and the proliferation of models exhibiting varying degress of realism, generality, and precision. But judging from the examples of other sciences, natural and social, there will continue to be room for simple, highly stylized and "stripped-down" models of the sort discussed here, though I expect they will be more complex than at present, and better accepted as components of an integrated research strategy.

Before leaving this topic, something should be said about the specific issue of cognition and imperfect information, as this is a key area where anthropological applications of optimization theory lack realism. The simplest and most tractable optimization models are deterministic: the currency is a mean or expected value (with no attention paid to risk or variance) and the actor is assumed to operate with perfect information (complete lack of uncertainty). This is obviously unrealistic. Dealing only with the matter of uncertainty,[24] it is hard to deny that, as one critic of perfect-information models in anthropology has put it, "Ecological optimization models differ drastically from actual decision-making procedures and hence are not likely to predict actual behavior on that basis" (Jochim, 1983, p. 164), or that, as another puts it, "In reality, decisions are based on a mix of information, ignorance, error, and lies" (Moore, 1983, p. 183).

Two responses to these criticisms will be noted here. One is that, while often more realistic, imperfect information models are not necessarily of greater scientific utility. If one is directly concerned with the structure of information and its effects on behavior, then of course the perfect-information assumption is foolish; but in other contexts, especially the initial forays into a field by an optimization approach, simpler models may be preferable. At the least, such models may reveal the degree to which imperfect information affects strategic outcomes. This baseline allows a "piecemeal" adjustment in predictive power and realism to occur at a suitable point, as data and theory accumulate suggesting how uncertainty (as well as other factors) should be incorporated into one's models (cf. Johnson, 1982; Krebs, Stephens, and Sutherland, 1983; Krebs and McCleery, 1984).

A second point is that even if actors are not the "know-it-alls" caricatured in the models, if the strategies they play are heritable (culturally or genetically) and have been shaped by a history of natural selection, actors might come to perform "as if" they had more-or-less perfect information about the long-term probabilities of various outcomes and conditions. This justification is one reason economists have turned to selection to explain phenomena such as profit-maximization in uncertain environments (note 5), and is behind the current interest in "rules of thumb" in areas of evolutionary ecology, such as optimal foraging theory (reviewed in Krebs, Stephens, and Sutherland, 1983). In invoking selection, one must consider the extent to which the currency favored by selection is congruent with that postulated by a simple optimization model. And as Sahlins (1976) reminds us (see above), one must also keep in mind the fact that selective pressures can change, and that selection is opportunistic rather than omniscient (see also Jochim, 1983). But the central point remains: the cognitive or information endowments of foragers should not be uncritically read as defining the compass of optimization models, even "realistic" ones.

Individual Choice, Adaptation, and Cultural Logic

Optimization methods, by themselves, are devoid of explanatory content. Such content is provided by substantive theories, of which two have been discussed in this paper: neoclassical economics and (more fully) neo-Darwinism. I have noted that the former is virtually mute when it comes to answering what actors maximize, and why. All of the models summarized herein, while employing formalisms first developed in economics, have been anchored to the theory of natural selection by the assumption that the currency maximized and the causes of optimal design are the result of selection for increased fitness (probability of genetic replication) in past generations. Our final set of critiques concerns the validity of this assumption, in the face of the presumed role of culture in determining the form and content of human behavior.

This is obviously an extremely broad and complex topic. I shall break it down into three questions: (1) How much genetic determinism is necessarily implied in applying models from evolutionary biology to human behavior? (2) Do optimization models project an egoistic individualism at odds with what we know of cultural tradition? (3) Does culture have a logic and determining force independent from organic evolution? My answers will necessarily be brief and provisional.

The specter of genetic determinism has been especially pronounced with respect to sociobiological assertions regarding human behavior, but some critics have also tarred what they have labeled the "fallback" position of ecological or evolutionary determinism (Gould, 1980; Boucher et al., 1978, contra Alexander, 1978; Emlen, 1980) with the same brush. For these critics, either the hypothesized optimization tendencies are due to genetic evolution of specific propensities to maximize fitness in response to specific stimuli—in which case they partake of genetic determinism and fly in the face of what we know about cultural determination of human behavior—or else they have nothing to do with natural selection (a theory, after all, of genetic evolution) and hence have no basis in evolutionary theory.

Between this rock and hard place, there may be a middle way. Granting that we know surprisingly little about the ontogeny of the sort of behavioral processes that figure in most ecological optimization models, let us accept the conventional anthropological view that very little in the way of *specific* behavioral instructions is encoded in genetic programs. How might genetically adaptive behavior arise? Three main proposals are frequent in the literature: through prepared learning, through fitness-correlated evaluation of consequences, and through a parallel process of cultural evolution. Prepared learning (Seligman, 1981) refers to genetically encoded propensities to learn certain behavioral patterns easily; a paradigmatic, relatively well-studied case is that of language acquisition (e.g., Lenneberg, 1967; Geschwind, 1972). Note that the degree of "preprogramming" need not specify any of the particular content of the behavioral pattern (e.g., English versus Chinese), only the basic form (acquisition patterns, Chomsky's "deep structure").

Though it is debatable, I doubt that prepared learning is important for most areas of ecological adaptation in humans. The remaining two factors are, I would argue. Cultural evolution will be discussed at the end of this section. Fitness-correlated evaluation of consequences (Durham, 1976, 1979, 1987) may arise through natural selection acting on either cultural or genetic variation (Boyd and Richerson, 1985) and refers to a process whereby actors evaluate the outcome of their choices by some measure of success correlated with fitness—what we might term "ethnofitness." The evolutionary programming here does not specify the motor patterns or behavioral propensities of actors, but only the criteria they use to evaluate consequences of their own actions, however originally motivated.

To use a trite but heuristic example, there is nothing "in the genes" to make some people prefer hunting of big game, and others small-game hunting or gathering. Yet the archaeological and ethnographic record clearly reveals a tendency for these preferences to follow regular patterns, and research using optimal foraging models indicates that the pattern may be largely the result of foragers evaluating different options by a simple rule involving opportunity costs and energy return rates (reviews in Smith, 1983b; Winterhalder, 1987; Hill et al., 1987). If so, the selection of alternatives is *by their consequence*, as measured by foraging efficiency. The measure of consequence here presumably has evolved (by genetic and/or cultural evolution); it is the following of this rule, rather than any innate tendencies to engage in one specific foraging tactic or another, that is responsible for the tendency to vary foraging behavior toward the local optimum.

Foraging behavior, or subsistence in general, is of course but a single (some would say marginal) aspect of human social behavior. The further caution might be raised that whereas foraging is a category of behavior humans share in some detail with other species, hence suggesting certain homologous cognitive mechanisms might be at work, kinship and ritual (for example) are unique, or uniquely developed, aspects of our behavior. Is there any reason to suppose that "evaluation by consequence" is as important in these and other areas as it appears to be for foraging, or that the evaluative criteria are as closely correlated with fitness? Empirically, the answer is far from clear (on this point, compare Alexander, 1979, Chagnon and Irons, 1979, and Durham 1987, to Boyd and Richerson, 1985, Kitcher, 1985, and Richerson and Boyd, this volume). This suggests we would do well to take an agnostic position, awaiting further research. But I think there is considerable agreement that some kind of decision-making process is a widespread—though not exclusive—mechanism of behavioral variation. Indeed, that most ubiquitous form of learning, operant conditioning, is best considered a form of selection by consequence, where the selection is by the actor, and the consequence (determined by environmental contingencies) is given a valence by natural selection (Skinner, 1981).

But phrasing the mechanisms of optimization this way, while it may steer us clear of the most prominent shoals of genetic determinism (*sensu strictu*), still yields a very egoistic, individually focused view of human social behavior. In this regard, optimization theory remains true to its source in neoclassical economics, that shrine to social satisfaction of individual needs. The tradition in much of anthropology is different, and could fairly be phrased as an inversion of economics: the individual satisfaction of social needs. Again, our most persistent Jeremiah here is Sahlins: "For the central intellectual problem does come down to the autonomy of culture and of the study of culture. Sociobiology challenges the integrity of culture as a thing-in-itself, as a distinctive and symbolic human creation. In place of a social constitution of meanings, it offers a biological determination of human interactions with a source primarily in the general evolutionary propensity of individual genotypes to maximize their reproductive success" (1976a, p.x). In the extreme form of cultural determinism espoused by Sahlins (see especially 1976b), cultural systems each have their own internal logic, which dominate any individual motives (fitness-maximizing or not) and replace the trajectory of natural selection with that of cultural teleology: "The wisdom of the cultural process consists in putting to the service of its own intentions natural systems which have their own reasons" (Sahlins, 1976a, p. 67).

Metaphor or not, many readers may be impelled to ask what the "intentions" and "reasons" of culture might be, and how they come to exist. Though the tradition of sociological functionalism is venerable, it does not seem to have produced a convincing and widely accepted rationale or generating mechanism. Beyond some vague arguments concerning the social construction of meaning and the logic of semiotics, Sahlins offers no further answer.[25] Yet most anthropologists cling to the conviction that culture determines human behavior, and that individual optimization—whether motivated by rational self-interest or the imperative of fitness-maximization, it does not matter—cannot explain social and cultural patterns, only conform to them. (A recent expression of this view by an ecological anthropologist is presented in Rappaport, 1984, pp. 397–402.)

To a large extent, this disagreement is much older than optimization research, perhaps as old as social philosophy. The methodological individualists have been battling—or talking past—the sociofunctionalists for a long time.[26] It would be immodest to suggest a direct resolution. There is one avenue currently being explored within anthropology and biology that may hold some promise, however: a theory of cultural evolution.

When an actor exhibits strategic behavior conforming to optimization predictions, various proximate causal mechanisms could be responsible: trial-and-error learning, prepared learning, fixed action patterns, and—for humans—rational choice or adherence to cultural tradition. In *all* of these cases, the ultimate values guiding the "choice" of goals or alternatives *must arise by some evolutionary process*. For the last two, characteristically human, mechanisms, it is unlikely that the evolutionary process is limited to changes in gene frequencies. That is, some process of cultural evolution is at least partially responsible for the observed patterns. Even Economic Man acts to maximize status (culturally defined), and exchanges culturally defined goods in socially defined manners; and the accepted means of pursuing individually adaptive ends, even the fitness payoff structure, are socially and culturally conditioned for our species in a way that might make the standard neo-Darwinian optimization approach incomplete.[27]

If constraints, strategies, and even goals sometimes evolve by selection acting on culturally transmitted variation, we may have a partial answer to the paradox posed by cultural determinism. For to stop at the position Sahlins does, postulating a "cultural reason" only loosely constrained by biological (and technoeconomic) possibility, is to indulge in a form of "cultural creationism."[28] We need to explain how cultural elements come to exist and exert such a determining role over human action. Cultural evolution can explain how values and institutions not inscribed in our genes arise. But it can perhaps do much more than this, for the following reason: cultural evolution may not necessarily tend to maximize genetic fitness. This result is preliminary, based on recent quantitative models of the interaction of genetic and cultural evolution (Cavalli-Sforza and Feldman, 1981; Pulliam and Dunford, 1980; Werren and Pulliam, 1981; and especially Boyd and Richerson, 1985). But it seems almost certain that, whatever its quantitative effect, the qualitative effect of any system of cultural transmission not "symmetric" with genetic transmission (i.e., equal inheritance from each biological parent) will cause the evolutionary trajectory of human behavior to deviate from that predicted by fitness optimization.[29]

If this is so, we may have the second answer to Sahlins's paradox of cultural determinism: the source of "cultural reason." Selection acting on cultural variation, whenever it deviates significantly from the genetic fitness optimum, will lead to social traits difficults to interpret in utilitarian, let alone Darwinian, terms. This does *not* mean that culture is maladaptive overall, only that it *sometimes* will be so (see note 29). Of course, this presents an entirely new set of arguments for explaining the evolution of human behavior, and, to quote Boyd and Richerson (1985), "greatly complicates the analysis" of this evolution. The cases reported in this paper would seem to be satisfactorily analyzed using standard Darwinian assumptions (while of course allowing for phenotypic flexibility and selection by consequence, not narrow genetic determinism). But other, less utilitarian aspects of human social behavior may require a new kind of optimization theory, incorporating aspects of the developing theory of cultural evolution.[30]

Notes

1. I use the term "theory" in two senses, a generic sense and a specific one. The generic referent is any nonempirical claim or argument; it is in this sense that I speak of "optimization theory." No sense of unity or consistency is necessarily implied in this use of the term. The more specific referent is any collection of explanatory arguments that does exhibit substantial internal consistency and unity; this second sense is the one referred to in the use of the term noted here. That is, particular *theories* consist of various models linked to each other and to other elements via deductive operations, bridging arguments, and the like. In this second sense, then, there is no "theory of optimization," but rather a large number of optimization models that (while sharing certain formal characteristics) are embedded in a relatively smaller but still diverse set of theories (e.g., the theory of consumer choice and optimal foraging theory).

2. Maynard Smith (1978) provides a somewhat different typology, which includes the strategy set ("phenotype set") as a subset of the "constraints" category (see also Oster and Wilson, 1984). I view this difference between us as semantic rather than substantive. As I have just indicated, the set of feasible strategies is subject to constraints (i.e., not all strategies we can conceive of are necessarily available in ontogenetic or evolutionary time).

3. Some key references in support of my generalizations include the literature on optimal foraging theory (reviewed by Pyke, Pulliam, and Charnov, 1977; Krebs, Stephens, and Sutherland, 1983; Pyke, 1984), life history strategies (reviewed by Horn and Rubenstein, 1984)—especially that utilizing dynamic optimization methods (e.g., Schaeffer, 1983), evolutionary game theory, or ESS models (reviewed by Maynard Smith, 1982; Riechert and Hammerstein, 1983; Parker, 1984; Parker and Hammerstein, 1985), theory concerning risk and uncertainty (e.g., Caraco, 1980, 1981a,b; Real, 1980; Rubenstein, 1982; Stephens and Charnov, 1982), and theory on parental investment—in this case authored by both biologists and economists (e.g., Trivers, 1972, 1974; Maynard Smith, 1977; Hirshleifer, 1978; Rubin, 1979; Samuelson, 1983; Rubin, Kau, and Meeker, 1979).

The convergence of economic and evolutionary optimization models has been reviewed both favorably (Rapport and Turner, 1977; Hirshleifer, 1978) and critically (Sahlins, 1976a), although in neither case do we have a recent or sustained analysis.

4. There is considerable literature on the problematics of "fitness" as a measure of adaptive consequence, as well as on the level at which natural selection is most effective, or effective at all, in producing design (and therefore any approximation of optimal design). Sober (1984) contains many of the key papers from this literature, and Williams (1966), Maynard Smith (1976), Wade (1978), Wilson (1980, 1983), Uyenoyama and Feldman (1980), and Dawkins (1982) should be consulted as well. The point I am making here is that the theory of natural selection provides a framework for examining these questions fairly rigorously, and allows continued attempts to extend and improve matters in this regard; this is in some contrast to the situation in neoclassical economic theory.

5. One of the more striking illustrations of this dependence of economics on evolution is provided by the use Alchian (1950) made of "natural selection" (loosely defined) to rescue the assumption of profit-maximizing as the strategic goal of firms in a competitive capitalist economy. While central to microeconomics, the profit-maximizing assumption encounters two difficulties: (1) A firm is not an individual actor, but rather a collection of individuals, many of whom may have competing goals (i.e., maximizing individual utility may often conflict with maximizing the profits of the firm to which the individual belongs, and detecting such "cheating" or "slacking-off" may often be difficult, or more costly to the firm's profit picture than letting it slide). (2) Imperfect information and rapidly changing market constraints make profit maximization difficult even for dedicated seekers of profit. Empirical evidence indicates that firms do not always make choices that maximize expected profits, although apparently they tend to do so more often than might be expected given the problems of conflicting interests and imperfect information noted above. Alchian's solution to this dilemma was to argue that while these objections are valid, in a competitive marketplace those firms whose members tend to possess utility functions that (for whatever reason) are congruent with maximizing firm profits will tend to outcompete less successful firms, resulting in an evolutionary trend toward the condition previously assumed without sufficient support (i.e., firms are actors that attempt to maximize expected profits) (for further discussion, see Winter, 1975; Hirshleifer, 1977; Nelson and Winter, 1982). Alchian's solution is thus a form of group selection, but raises some of the same issues found in the literature on group selection in organic evolution (e.g., how do firms initially attain the critical frequency of profit-maximizing necessary for group selection to be effective?). Boyd and Richerson (1980) have attempted to fill this lacuna by building theory that specifies plausible individual-level mechanisms of cultural evolution (such as imitation of peers when information on the expected utility of options is costly to obtain).

6. I am not certain which study might lay claim to being the first anthropological application of an optimization model, but perhaps it is Davenport's (1960) application (or misapplication—see Read and Read, 1970) of a game-theory model to analyze the fishing-location strategies of small-scale Jamaican commercial fishermen. In any case, very little work in this tradition occured within anthropology for another decade or so.

7. In recent years, discussions have begun to appear that recognize the variety and ecological context of hunter-gatherer land tenure (e.g., Wilmsen, 1973; Knight, 1965; Binford, 1980; various authors in Williams and Hunn, 1982). And anthropologists studying systems of land tenure among nonforagers have also developed a more sophisticated set of analyses (e.g., Goody, 1976). However, I would still claim that anthropologists have made far too little use of general theory and formal models of land use, such as those developed in geography, economics, and evolutionary biology, and that as recently as five years ago the simple dichotomization discussed in the text still prevailed.

8. Note that the per capita harvest rate is not necessarily equal to the actual or mean rate that each group member gets, unless there is an equal or random distribution of the harvest. Among the Inuit foragers I studied, such an equal division of the harvest does in fact typically occur, but this is not always the case among human foragers, nor is it typical of nonhuman social carnivores.

9. Hill and Hawkes (1983) have done the earliest and most extensive theoretical and empirical work on the effects of central-place sharing on foraging group size. Data on Ache foragers, who approximate the condition of central-place sharing, tentatively support some of these predictions (Hill and Hawkes, 1983).

10. Many (but not all—cf. Gould, 1982) foragers do possess an ethic of widespread, if not quite "generalized," reciprocity. But to point to such an ethic is not to explain its existence, nor the sharing behavior it may help motivate. In other words, the ethic—like any value or belief—is a proximate mechanism or element in a longer causal chain. Even less satisfactory is the frequent argument that sharing rules are a "leveling device" impelled by an "egalitarian ideology." As has been pointed out by others (notably Cashdan, 1980), this view fails to explain variation in sharing rules or the rise and eventual dominance of nonegalitarian, nonreciprocal systems. In addition to these logical and empirical difficulties, the views I criticize here are inconsistent with evolutionary theory, being examples of naive group selectionism or social teleology.

11. The assumption that there is no cost is an important one. Logistical costs are likely to arise for most systems of sharing, but these are relatively easy to measure. More difficult to consider are costs due to cheating on the part of some members of the sharing network, or other costs associated with social relations (such as disputes). Kaplan and Hill (1985b) provide a more extended discussion of these considerations. Even if there are costs, sharing can still be adaptive as long as these costs are less than the net advantage of consuming $V(\overline{x})$ rather than $V(\alpha + \beta)/2$. Whether selection will favor sharing simply because it is adaptive is a more thorny issue, as discussed in the subsection on optimization versus evolutionary equilibrium.

12. A more commonsense explanation of the differential sharing of meat versus plant foods is that the former are more subject to spoilage, and come in larger packages than individuals or households can easily consume. This is empirically correct, but is not an alternative explanation. If the shared resource (e.g., meat) was *not* characterized by variation in individual harvest rates, or did *not* produce diminishing returns if consumed in very large amounts, then there would be no need to share it. These are precisely the conditions assumed to favor sharing in the risk-reduction model, and implicitly assumed in the commonsense view.

13. I am not claiming here that one of these positions is empirically more correct than the other—there has been no direct test of these two assumptions on the same data set—but simply that they are theoretically distinct and that the evolutionary view is presently more theoretically complete than the economic one. It may be possible to use cultural evolutionary theory to provide a more complete theoretical grounding for economic demography, so as to explain *why* actors might make reproductive decisions that maximize economic or status variables rather than fitness [see, for example, Boyd and Richerson's (1985, pp. 199ff.) scenario for the cultural evolution of the demographic transition]. It should also be pointed out that, properly conceived, there is less conflict between children-as-means (economic demography) and children-as-ends (evolutionary biology) than suggested in the text. For one, some economic demographers and economists of the "new household economics" persuasion (e.g., Becker, 1981) are willing to view households as producers—not just passive consumers—that produce such "goods" as children and clothe, feed, and educate them in order to satisfy certain demands [though as Etter (1978) points out, an inherent ambiguity in specifying the

sources of these demands remains]. From the evolutionary side, we must remember that kinship and reciprocity structure family interactions in such a way that the net economic contribution of children to family income, insofar as it may affect parental and sibling survivorship and reproduction, is just as valid a component of fitness calculations of alternative reproductive strategies as is the direct contribution of each child to parental fitness.

14. The optimal IBI is that which maximizes net yield of children surviving. Using the backload/mortality regression and the !Kung demographic parameters, this peaks at 50 months, but shows a fairly broad plateau from 42 through 54 months—hence, the mean IBI for this "optimality plateau" is 48 months. Because of the way in which Howell's data were collected, IBIs cluster at 12-month intervals, making the sample size for the actual optimal IBI (50 months, $n = 2$) too small to compare to that for the mean optimal IBI (48 months, $n = 17$). In any case, the fit is remarkably close (see Blurton Jones, nda, for further details).

15. The exact selective pressures shaping !Kung IBIs cannot be directly ascertained from Blurton Jones's retrospective analysis of demographic rates, as he is quick to admit. From ethnographic accounts by Lee and others, as well as the simulation results of Blurton Jones and Sibly (1978), it seems likely that backload is determined by a complex set of variables, of which the most important are birth spacing and subsistence mobility. Settled women need not forage as widely for food, and they have available weaning foods (in the form of milk and cereals) from the cattle posts that their bush-dwelling sisters lack (Lee, 1980). Bush women who lose an infant are released from backload of both child and food (for lactation requirements), whereas death of an older child reduces only food demand, which is not quantitatively sufficient to allow additional "replacement" reproduction without taking backload above the critical limit (or, alternatively, reducing food carried below the critical limit needed to support herself and her dependents).

16. Similar conclusions are drawn by most proponents of optimization models in evolutionary biology. As examples: "Rather than a grand scheme for predicting the course of natural selection, optimization theory constitutes no more than a tactical tool for making educated guesses about evolutionary trends" (Oster and Wilson, 1984, p. 284). "The role of optimization theories in biology is not to demonstrate that organisms optimize. Rather, they are an attempt to understand the diversity of life" (Maynard Smith, 1978, p. 52).

17. The cultural tradition Sahlins's remarks belong to was established by Marx himself, who even applied it to the topic under discussion here, as in the following passage: "It is remarkable how Darwin recognizes among beasts and plants his English society with its division of labour, competition, opening up of new markets, 'inventions,' and the Malthusian 'struggle for existence'" (Marx to Engels, letter dated 18 June 1862, in McLellan 1977, p. 526; quoted in Sahlins, 1976a, pp. 101ff.). The tradition continues to play a role in the optimization controversy (e.g., Morales and Levins, 1974; Keene, 1983; Lewontin, 1984). As for consistency, Sahlins's antiutilitarian relativism seems at odds with his glib use of historical materialism to account for shifts in intellectual fashion.

18. Certainly economics and evolutionary biology have often been vulgarized to support politically conservative views. But my point here is that these phenomena are not basic to or inherent in optimization approaches, and that liberal or even radical views can just as readily be served by strategic evolutionary and economic thinking (for example, Dyson-Hudson, 1979, and Hrdy, 1981, in evolutionary biology; Elster 1982, and Roemer, 1982, for Marxian political economy).

19. These objections include (1) the possible lack of requisite genetic variability; (2) the

existence of selectively neutral variations; (3) the possibility that various genetic complications (epistasis, pleiotropy, heterozygote superiority, meiotic drive) generate maladaptive genotypes; (4) the multiple selective factors affecting phenotypes, which make atomization into separate adaptive values problematic; (5) developmental constraints that prevent optimal phenotypes from being generated in ontogeny; (6) neurological or cognitive constraints that prevent animals from gathering enough information to behave optimally; and (7) the epistemological difficulties associated with formulating and testing optimality hypotheses. Reviews of these issues from a number of different stances are found in Maynard Smith (1978), Lewontin (1979), Dawkins (1982), Oster and Wilson (1984), Krebs and McCleery (1984), Kitcher (1985, chapter 7), and several chapters in this volume, especially Emlen's contribution. I have not had room (nor expertise) to deal with most of these issues in this paper. While recognizing the validity of these critiques *in principle*, I must record my observation that much of the antiadaptionist literature is far more speculative—pointing to *possible* complications and "just-so stories" about hypothetical voles and poorly understood phenotypic traits—than the bulk of the adaptationist literature (with the possible exception of adaptationist analyses of human behavior, which are often atrociously lacking in evidence and logical rigor— though no more so on average than the rest of social science, I would contend).

20. The "group-selection controversy" is far from dead—or better stated, it continues to mutate and evolve into new forms. The reference in the text is to the original, *naive* formulation that held "good-of-the-species" arguments to be isomorphic with Darwinism, or that attempted to derive group advantage from natural selection theory without use of rigorous mathematical argument (e.g., Dunbar, 1960; Wynne-Edwards, 1962). The more recent mathematically based debates about the form and frequency of selection at various levels of biological organization are a different matter. With reference to human behavior, Boyd and Richerson's (1985, chapter 7) models suggesting that the conditions favoring group selection may be more commonly encountered in the case of cultural evolution than in the case of genetic evolution also offer a more sophisticated and precise basis for explaining the existence of traits with reference to their group-supporting functions. Although as yet relatively untested, this line of inquiry is given tentative support in James Peoples's (1982) provocative reanalysis of Rappaport's (1968, and cf. 1984) functionalist view of intergroup conflict among the Tsembaga Maring of highland New Guinea. Peoples's analysis is also relevant to a question addressed by Hirshleifer (this volume)—to wit, can evolution provide a way out of dysfunctional Nash equilibria that result from individual self-interest? (See also note 21.)

21. Extended discussions of this in terms of human socioeconomic processes can be found in the literature on "collective decision" (e.g., Olson, 1965; Schelling, 1978; Hardin, 1982; Elster, 1978, 1982). An explicit link to evolutionary theory and a direct attack on the wisdom of the Invisible Hand is provided in an extremely stimulating essay by Hirshleifer (1982—see also Hirshleifer, this volume).

22. The argument sketched here depends on at least one additional assumption, that the aspects of the environment relevant to the proximate mechanism(s) in question have not recently changed sufficiently to make products of the mechanism(s) maladaptive. The validity of this assumption, while an empirical issue for any particular mechanism, depends in general on the specificity of the mechanisms involved (as well as on the stability of the environment). I think much evidence and theory favors the view that human cognitive mechanisms are relatively (though not absolutely, whatever that would mean) "general-purpose" or "open" (for futher discussion, see Mayr, 1974; Dyson-Hudson, 1983). If so, then these mechanisms should continue to produce adaptive responses (on average) even in markedly altered or novel environments.

23. If Levins's model of models is approximately correct, then "any use of models involves

some implicit or explicit ranking of these three attributes by the modeler. The optimum toward which we aim our models will be determined—as in any optimization problem—by a combination of goals (what are the strategic objectives of our research? how do we plan to test the model?) and constraints (what relevant theories are available? what kinds of data can we hope to collect?)" (Smith, 1983b, p. 637).

24. Risk is incorporated into optimization models more easily; indeed, it plays a central role in two of the models reviewed in this paper (land tenure and resource sharing). For further discussion of the role of risk in anthropological optimization theory, see Smith (1983b, pp. 638–640) and Winterhalder (1987).

25. Neither do other nonevolutionary cultural determinists, nor biologists influenced by them. As example of the latter, consider the following "explanation" in support of Sahlins's (1978) critique of a (rather dubious, I would admit) cultural-materialist explanation of Aztec sacrificial cannibalism proposed by Harner (1977): "Human cultural practices can be orthogenetic and drive toward extinction in ways that Darwinian processes, based on genetic selection, cannot. Since each new monarch had to outdo his predecessor in even more elaborate and copious sacrifice, the practice was beginning to stretch resources to the breaking point" (Gould and Lewontin, 1979, p. 583). Just how this argument really explains Aztec sacrifices, I fail to see; at best it could account for an escalation of same, *given* some initial reason why sacrifice was practiced, and *given* the motivation of individual monarchs to compete with (the reputation of) their predecessors. But the givens here carry the bulk of the explanatory load, and remain undemonstrated and unaccounted for.

26. This conflict, involving economic optimization models, is well exemplified by the "formalist" (read, neoclassical) versus "substantivist" (read, cultural relativist) debate that occupied economic anthropology for well over a decade, and still flares up in border skirmishes now and then. Many of the key position papers in this dispute are included in the reader edited by LeClair and Schneider (1968; see also Sahlins, 1969, 1972; Godelier, 1972; White, 1973; Donham, 1981).

27. The claim just made does not entail, nor do I subscribe to, the further claim that social institutions or structures are *autonomous* causes of individual behavior. Instead, I hold a view more akin to game theory and other sophisticated versions of methodological individualism that recognize the emergent properties of social interaction and social evolution, while still seeking the causes of these at lower levels of organization (e.g., Dawkins, 1976, p. 89; Elster, 1982).

28. I am indebted to William Durham (1987) for this clever phrase.

29. How *much* of a deviation is subject to various estimations, given the formal assumptions and informal prejudices of the various judges. It is important to note that cultural evolution (as opposed to plain cultural determinism) offers no basis for asserting that the system of cultural transmission as a whole leads to maladaptive (by neo-Darwinian measures) outcomes. Durham (1976) argues that only low-cost low-benefit traits will evolve culturally away from fitness optima, while Cavalli-Sforza and Feldman (1981) and Boyd and Richerson (1980, 1985) obtain much stronger deviations than this under their particular model assumptions. It is also important to note that the only evolutionary force capable of creating sustained deviations away from fitness optima is *natural selection acting on cultural variation* (with asymmetric inheritance, as in horizontal transmission or unequal contribution from parents) (see Boyd and Richerson, 1985). Whether selection acting on cultural variation is actually strong enough to override the effects of biased transmission and guided variation (evaluation by fitness-correlated consequences) programmed into the human brain by genetic evolution remains an empirical question (Flinn and Alexander, 1982; Boyd and Richerson, 1985).

30. Richerson and Boyd (nd) have constructed a model of "runaway selection" involving

cultural transmission that is analogous to runaway models of sexual selection, which (under proper values of model parameters) produces results they interpret as similar to those implied by Sahlins's (1976a,b) views of "cultural reason." They have gone on to suggest the application of this model to an empirical case involving the association of giant yams with prestige in a Micronesian society. It is not clear that one would want to call this an optimization model (they do not), but to the extent that some measure of fitness (combining cultural and genetic components) is maximized, the suggestion may not be completely absurd.

References

Alchian, Armen (1950). Uncertainty, Evolution, and Economic Theory. *J. of Political Economy* 58 : 211−222.

Alexander, Richard D. (1978). Biology, Determinism, and Human Behavior: A Response to Slobodkin. *Michigan Discussions in Anthropology* 3 : 154−156.

Alexander, Richard D. (1979). *Darwinism and Human Affairs*. Seattle: University of Washington Press.

Alland, Alexander (1972). *The Human Imperative*. New York: Columbia University Press.

Ardrey, Robert (1966). *The Territorial Imperative*. New York: Atheneum.

Balikci, Asen (1964). *Development of Basic Socio-Economic Units in Two Eskimo Communities*. Bulletin 202. Ottawa: National Museum of Canada.

Bates, Daniel, and Susan Lees (1979). The Myth of Population Regulation. In *Evolutionary Biology and Human Social Organization*, ed. N. Chagnon and W. Irons, North Scituate, MA: Duxbury Press, pp. 273−289.

Becker, Gary S. (1981). *A Treatise on the Family*. Cambridge, MA; Harvard University Press.

Beckerman, Stephen (1983). Optimal Foraging Group Size for A Human Population: The Case of Bari Fishing. *American Zoologist* 23 : 283−290.

Bertram, Brian C. R. (1978). Living in Groups: Predators and Prey. In *Behavioral Ecology: An Evolutionary Approach*, ed. J. R. Krebs and N. B. Davies, Sunderland, MA: Sinauer, pp. 64−96.

Binford, Lewis R. (1980). Willow Smoke and Dogs' Tails: Hunter-Gatherer Settlement Systems and Archaeological Site Formation. *American Antiquity* 45 : 4−20.

Blurton Jones, Nicholas (nd,a). Bushman Birth Spacing: a Test for Optimal Inter-Birth Intervals. Manuscript, Department of Anthropology, University of California, Los Angeles, California.

Blurton Jones, Nicholas (nd,b). Bushman Birth Spacing: Direct Tests of Some Simple Predictions. Manuscript, Department of Anthropology, University of California, Los Angeles, California.

Blurton Jones, Nicholas G., and R. M. Sibly (1978). Testing Adaptiveness of Culturally Determined Behaviour: Do Bushmen Women Maximize Their Reproductive Success by Spacing Births Widely and Foraging Seldom? In *Human Behavior and Adaptations*, ed. N. G. Blurton Jones and V. Reynolds, Symposium No. 18, Society for the Study of Human Biology, London: Taylor & Francis, pp. 135−157.

Boucher, Doug, Pat Bresnahan, Karl Figlio, Stephen Risch, and Scott Schneider (1978). Sociobiological Determinism: Theme with Variations. *Michigan Discussions in Anthropology* 3 : 169−186.

Boyd, Robert, and Peter J. Richerson (1980). Sociobiology, Culture and Economic Theory. *Journal of Economic Behavior and Organization* 1 : 97−121.

Boyd, Robert, and Peter J. Richerson (1985). *Culture and the Evolutionary Process*. Chicago: University of Chicago Press.

Brown, Jerram L. (1964). The Evolution of Diversity in Avian Territorial Systems. *Wilson Bulletin* 76:160–169.

Brown, Jerram L., and Gordon H. Orians (1970). Spacing Patterns in Mobile Animals. *Annual Review of Ecology and Systematics* 1:239–262.

Caraco, Thomas (1980). On Foraging Time Allocation in a Stochastic Environment. *Ecology* 61:119–128.

Caraco, Thomas (1981a). Risk-Sensitivity and Foraging Groups. *Ecology* 62:527–531.

Caraco, Thomas (1981b). Energy Budgets, Risk and Foraging Preferences in Dark-Eyed Juncos (*Junco hyemalis*). *Behavioral Ecology and Sociobiology* 8:213–217.

Cashdan, Elizabeth A. (1980). Egalitarianism among Hunters and Gatherers. *American Anthropologist* 82:116–120.

Cashdan, Elizabeth A. (1983a) Territoriality among Human Foragers: Ecological Models and an Application to Four Bushman Groups. *Current Anthropology* 24:47–66.

Cashdan, Elizabeth A. (1983b) Reply to Hill and King. *Current Anthropology* 24:536–537.

Cavalli-Sforza, L. L., and M. W. Feldman (1981). *Cultural Transmission and Evolution: A Quantitative Approach.* Monongraphs in Population Biology, No. 16, Princeton: Princeton University Press.

Chagnon, Napoleon, and William Irons (eds.) (1979). *Evolutionary Biology and Human Social Behavior.* North Scituate, MA: Duxbury Press.

Clark, Colin W., and Marc Mangel (1984). Foraging and Flocking Strategies: Information in an Uncertain Environment. *The American Naturalist* 123:626–641.

Cloak, F. T., Jr. (1975). Is a Cultural Ethology Possible? Human Ecology 3:161–182.

Cohen, G. A. (1980). *Karl Marx's Theory of History: A Defence.* Princeton: Princeton University Press.

Davenport, William (1960). *Jamaican Fishing: A Game Theory Analysis.* Yale University Publications in Anthropology, 59.

Davies, Nicholas, and Alastair I. Houston (1984). Territory Economics. In *Behavioural Ecology: An Evolutionary Approach,* ed. J. R. Krebs and N. B. Davies, Oxford: Blackwell, pp. 148–169.

Dawkins, Richard (1976). *The Selfish Gene.* New York: Oxford University Press.

Dawkins, Richard (1978). Replicator Selection and the Extended Phenotype. Zeitschrift fur Tierpsychologie 47:61–76.

Dawkins, Richard (1980). Good Strategy or Evolutionarily Stable Strategy? In *Sociobiology: Beyond Nature/Nurture?,* ed. G. W. Barlow and J. Silverberg, Boulder, CO: Westview Press, pp. 331–367.

Dawkins, Richard (1982). *The Extended Phenotype: the Gene as the Unit of Selection.* San Francisco: W. H. Freeman.

Demsetz, Harold (1967). Toward a Theory of Property Rights. *American Economic Review* 57:347–359.

Donham, Donald L. (1981). Beyond the Domestic Mode of Production. *Man* 16:515–541.

Dunbar, M. J. (1960). The Evolution of Stability in Marine Environments: Natural Selection at the Level of the Ecosystem. *American Naturalist* 94:129–136.

Durham, William H. (1976). The Adaptive Significance of Cultural Behavior. *Human Ecology* 4:89–121.

Durham, William H. (1979). Toward a Coevolutionary Theory of Human Biology and Culture. In *Evolutionary Biology and Human Social Behavior,* ed. N. Chagnon and W. Irons, North Scituate, MA: Duxbury Press, pp. 39–59.

Durham, William H. (in press). *Coevolution: Genes, Culture, and Human Diversity.* Stanford: Standford University Press.

Durkheim, Emile (orig, 1895) (1938). *The Rules of Sociologic Method,* S. Solovay and J. Mueller, trans., New York: Free Press.

Dyson-Hudson, Rada (1979). Sociobiology as a Political Statement. *Cornell Review* 7:48–67.

Dyson-Hudson, Rada (1983). An Interactive Model of Human Biological and Cultural Adaptation. In *Rethinking Human Adaptation*, ed. R. Dyson-Hudson and M. A. Little, Boulder, CO: Westview Press, (pp. 1–22.)

Dyson-Hudson, Rada, and Eric Alden Smith (1978). Human Territoriality: An Ecological Reassessment. American Anthropologist 80:21–41.

Elster, Jon (1978). *Logic and Society*. Chichester: Wiley.

Elster, Jon (1982). Marxism, Functionalism, and Game Theory. *Theory and Society* 11:453–482.

Emlen, Stephen T. (1980). Ecological Determinism and Sociobiology. In *Sociobiology: Beyond Nature/Nurture?*, ed. G. W. Barlow and J. Silverberg, AAAs Selected Symposia, No. 35, Boulder, CO: Westview Press, pp. 125–150.

Engels, Friedrich (orig. 1884) (1942). *The Origins of the Family, Private Property, and the State*. New York: International Publishers.

Etter, Martin A. (1978). Sahlins and Sociobiology. *American Ethnologist* 5:160–169.

Flinn, Mark V., and Richard D. Alexander (1982). Culture Theory: The Developing Synthesis from Biology. *Human Ecology* 10:383–400.

Friedman, Jonathan (1974). Marxism, structuralism, and Vulgar Materialism. *Man* 9:444–469.

Friedman, Jonathan (1979). Hegelian Ecology: Between Rousseau and the World Spirit. In *Social and Ecological Systems*, ed. P. C. Burnham and R. F. Ellen, London: Academic Press, pp. 253–270.

Geschwind, Norman (1972). Language and the Brain. *Scientific American* 226:76–83.

Godelier, Maurice (1972). *Rationality and Irrationality in Economics*. London: New Left Books.

Goody, Jack (1976). *Production and Reproduction: A Comparative Study of the Domestic Domain*. Cambridge: Cambridge University Press.

Gould, Richard A. (1981). Comparative Ecology of Food-Sharing in Australia and Northwest California. In *Omnivorous Primates*, ed. R. S. O. Harding and G. Teleki, New York: Columbia University Press. pp. 422–454.

Gould, Richard A. (1982). To Have and Have not: The Ecology of Sharing among Hunter-Gatherers. In *Resource Managers*, ed. N. M. Williams and E. S. Hunn, Boulder, CO: Westview Press, pp. 69–91.

Gould, Stephen J. (1980). Sociobiology and the Theory of Natural Selection. In *Sociobiology: Beyond Nature/Nuture?*, ed. G. W. Barlow and J. Silverberg, AAAS Selected Symposia, No. 35, Boulder, Co: Westview Press, pp. 257–269.

Gould, Stephen J., and Richard C. Lewontin (1979). The Spandrels of San Marco and the Panglossian Paradigm: A Critique of the Adaptationist Programme. *Proceedings of the Royal Society of London*, B205:581–598.

Hardin, Russell (1982). *Collective Action*. Baltimore: Johns Hopkins University Press.

Harner, Michael (1977). The Ecological Basis for Aztec Sacrifice. *American Ethnologist* 4:117–135.

Harpending, Henry, and Herbert Davis (1977). Some Implications for Hunter-Gatherer Ecology Derived from the Spatial Structure of Resources. *World Archaeology* 8:275–283.

Harris, Marvin (1968). *The Rise of Anthropological Theory*. New York: Crowell.

Harris, Marvin (1979). *Cultural Materialsim: The Struggle for a Science of Culture*. New York: Random House.

Harris, Marvin, and Marshall Sahlins (1979). "Cannibals and Kings": An exchange. *New York Review of Books*, June 28, 1979, pp. 51–53.

Hayden, Brian (1981). Subsistence and Ecological Adaptation of Modern Hunter/Gatherers. In *Omnivorous Primates*, ed. R. S. O. Harding and G. Teleki, New York: Columbia University Press, pp. 344–421.

Heffley, Sheri (1981). Northern Athabaskan Settlement Patterns and Resource Distributions: An Application of Horn's Model. In *Hunter-Gatherer Foraging Strategies*, ed. B. Winterhalder and E. A. Smith, Chicago: University of Chicago Press.

Hill, Kim (1982). Hunting and Human Evolution. J. of Human Evolution 11:521–544.

Hill, Kim (1983). On Territoriality in Hunter-Gatherers. *Current Anthropology* 24:534–535.

Hill, Kim, and Kristen Hawkes (1983). Neotropical Hunting among the Aché of Eastern Paraguay. In *Adaptive Responses of Native Amazonians*, ed. R. Hames and W. Vickers, New York: Academic Press.

Hill, Kim, Hillard Kaplan, Kristen Hawkes, and A. Magdalena Hurtado (1987). Foraging Decisions among Aché Hunter-Gatherers and Implications for Human and Hominid Resource Choice. *Ethology and Sociobiology*.

Hirshleifer, Jack (1977). Economics from a Biological Viewpoint. *Journal of Law and Economics* 20:1–52.

Hirshleifer, Jack (1978). Natural Economy versus Political Economy. *Journal of Social and Biological Structures* 1:319–337.

Hirshleifer, Jack (1982). Evolutionary Models in Economics and Law: Cooperation versus Conflict Strategies. *Research in Law and Economics*, 4:1–60.

Horn, Henry S., and Daniel I. Rubenstein (1984). Behavioural Adaptations and Life History. In *Behavioural Ecology: An Evolutionary Approach*, ed. J. R. Krebs and N. B. Davies, Sunderland, MA: Sinauer Associates, pp. 279–298.

Howell, Nancy (1979). *Demography of the Dobe !Kung*. New York: Academic Press.

Hrdy, Sarah Blaffer (1981). *The Woman That Never Evolved*. Cambridge, MA: Harvard University Press.

Isaac, Glynn Ll. (1978). Food Sharing and Human Evolution: Archaeological Evidence from the Plio-Pleistocene of East Africa. *J. of Anthropological Research* 34:311–325.

Jochim, Michael A. (1983). Optimization Models in Context. In *Archaeological Hammers and Theories*, ed. A. S. Keene and J. A. Moore, New York: Academic Press, pp. 157–172.

Johnson, Allen W. (1978). *Quantification in Cultural Anthropology*. Stanford: Stanford University Press.

Johnson, Allen W. (1982). The Limits of Formalism in Agricultural Decision Research. In *Agricultural Decision Making: Anthropological Contributions to Rural Development*, ed. Peggy F. Barlett, New York: Academic Press, pp. 19–43.

Kaplan, Hillard, and Kim Hill (1985a). Hunting Ability and Reproductive Success among Male Aché Foragers: Preliminary Results. *Current Anthropology* 26:131–133.

Kaplan, Hillard, and Kim Hill (1985b). Food Sharing among Aché Foragers: Tests of Explanatory Hypotheses. *Current Anthropology* 26(2).

Kaplan, Hillard, Kim Hill, Kristen Hawkes, and Ana Hurtado (1984). Food Sharing among Aché Hunter-Gatherers of Eastern Paraguay. *Current Anthropology* 25:113–115.

Keene, Arthur S. (1983). Biology, Behavior and Borrowing: A Critical Examination of Optimal Foraging Theory in Archaeology. In *Archaeological Hammers and Theories*, ed. J. A. Moore and A. S. Keene, New York: Academic Press, pp. 137–155.

Kitcher, Philip (1985). *Vaulting Ambition: Sociobiology and the Quest for Human Nature*. Cambridge, MA: MIT Press.

Knight, Rolf (1965). A Re-Examination of Hunting, Trapping, and Territoriality among the Northeastern Algonkin Indians. In *Man, Culture, and Animals*, ed. A. Leeds and A. P. Vayda. Washington D. C.: Amer. Assoc. Adv. Sci., pp. 27–42.

Krebs, John R. (1978). Optimal Foraging: Decision Rules for Predators. In *Behavioural Ecology, An Evolutionary Approach*, ed. J. R. Krebs and N. B. Davies, Sunderland, MA: Sinauer, pp. 23–63.

Krebs, John R., and Robin H. McCleery (1984). Optimization in Behavioural Ecology. In *Behavioural Ecology: An Evolutionary Approach*, ed. J. R. Krebs and N. B. Davies, Sunderland, MA: Sinauer Associates, pp. 91–121.

Krebs, John R., David W. Stephens, and William J. Sutherland (1983). Perspectives in Optimal Foraging. In *Perspectives in Ornithology*, ed. G. A. Clark and A. H. Brush, Cambridge: Cambridge University Press, pp. 165–216.

Leacock, Eleanor (1954). *The Montagnais "Hunting Territory" and the Fur Trade*. Amer. Anth. Assoc. Memoir No. 78.

LeClair, Edward E., Jr., and Harold K. Schneider (eds.) (1968). *Economic Anthropology. Readings in Theory and Analysis*. New York: Holt, Rinehart, and Winston.

Lee, Richard B. (1972). Population Growth and the Beginnings of Sedentary Life among the !Kung Bushmen. In *Population Growth: Anthropological Implications*, ed. Brian Spooner, Cambridge MA: MIT Press, pp. 329–342.

Lee, Richard B. (1979). *The !Kung San*. Cambridge: Cambridge University Press.

Lee, Richard B. (1980). Lactation, Ovulation, Infanticide, and Women's work: a Study of Hunter-Gatherer Population Regulation. In *Biosocial Mechanisms of Population Regulation*, ed. M. N. Cohen, R. S. Malpass, and H. G. Klein, New Haven: Yale University Press, pp. 321–348.

Lee, Richard B., and Irven DeVore (eds.) (1968). *Man the Hunter*. Chicago: Aldine.

Lenneberg, Eric H. (1967). *Biological Foundations of Language*. New York: Wiley.

Levins, Richard (1966). The Strategy of Model-Building in Population Biology. *American Scientist* 54:421–431.

Lewontin, Richard C. (1979). Fitness, Survival, and Optimality. In *Analysis of Ecological Systems*, ed. D. H. Horn, R. Mitchell, and G. R. Stairs, Columbus, OH: Ohio State University Press, pp. 3–21.

Lewontin, Richard C. (1984). Adaptation. In *Conceptual Issues in Evolutionary Biology*, ed. Elliott Sober, Cambridge, MA: MIT Press, pp. 234–251. (Originally published in *The Encyclopedia Einaudi*, Milan, 1980.)

Lorenz, Konrad (1966). *On Aggression*, trans. M. K. Wilson. New York: Harcourt, Brace and World.

Luce, Robert D., and Howard Raiffa (1957). *Games and Decisions*. New York: Wiley.

Martin, J. F. (1983). Optimal Foraging Theory: A Review of Some Models and their Applications. *American Anthropologist* 85:612–629.

Maynard Smith, John (1974). The Theory of Games and the Evolution of Animal Conflicts: *Journal of Theoretical Biology* 47:209–222.

Maynard Smith, John (1976). Commentary: Group Selection. *Quarterly Review of Biology* 51:277–283.

Maynard Smith, John (1977). Parental Investment: A Prospective Analysis. *Animal Behaviour* 25:1–9.

Maynard Smith, John (1978). Optimization Theory in Evolution. *Annual Review of Ecology and Systematics* 9:31–56.

Maynard Smith, John (1982). *Evolution and the Theory of Games*. Cambridge: Cambridge University Press.

Mayr, Ernst (1974). Behavior Programs and Evolutionary Strategies. *American Scientist* 62:650–659.

McLellan, David (ed.) (1977). *Karl Marx: Selected Writings*. Oxford: Oxford University Press.

Montagu, M. F. Ashley (ed.) (1968). *Man and Aggression*. London: Oxford University Press.

Moore, James A. (1983). The Trouble with Know-It-Alls: Information as a Social and Ecological Resource. In *Archaeological Hammers and Theories*, ed. J. A. Moore and A. Keene, New York: Academic, pp. 173–191.

Morales, Rosario, and Richard Levins (1974). Neither a Borrower Nor a Lender Be. Paper presented at the Smithsonian Conference on Human Biogeography, Washington, D.C., April 30–May 2, 1974.

Nelson, Richard R., and Sidney G. Winter (1982). *An Evolutionary Theory of Economic Change*. Cambridge, MA: Harvard/Belknap.

Olson, Mancur (1965). *The Logic of Collective Action: Public Goods and the Theory of Groups.* Cambridge, MA: Harvard University Press.

Oster, George F., and Edward O. Wilson (1984). A Critique of Optimization Theory in Evolutionary Biology. In *Conceptual Issues in Evolutionary Biology*, ed. Elliott Sober, Cambridge, MA: MIT Press, pp. 271–288. (Originally Published as chapter 8 in *Caste and Ecology in the Social Insects*, by G. F. Oster and E. O. Wilson, Princeton University Press Monographs in Population Biology No. 12, 1978.)

Parker, Geoffrey A. (1984). Evolutionary Stable Strategies. In *Behavioural Ecology: An Evolutionary Approach*, 2nd ed., ed. J. R. Krebs and N. B. Davies, Sunderland, MA: Sinauer Associates, pp. 30–61.

Parker, Geoffrey A., and Peter Hammerstein (1985). Game Theory and Animal Behaviour. In *Evolution: Essays in Honour of John Maynard Smith*, ed. P. J. Greenwood, P. H. Harvey, and M. Slatkin, Cambridge: Cambridge University Press, pp. 73–94.

Peoples, James G. (1982). Individual or Group Advantage? A Reinterpretation of the Maring Ritual Cycle. *Current Anthropology* 23:291–310.

Pulliam, H., Ron Caraco, and Thomas Caraco (1984). Living in Groups: Is There an Optimal Group Size? In *Behavioural Ecology*, 2nd ed., ed. J. R. Krebs and N. B. Davies, Oxford: Blackwell, pp. 122–147.

Pulliam, H. Ronald, and Christopher Dunford (1980). *Programmed to Learn. An Essay on the Evolution of Culture.* New York: Columbia University Press.

Pyke, Graham H. (1984). Optimal Foraging Theory: A Critical Review. *Annual Review of Ecology and Systematics* 15:523–575.

Pyke, G. H., H. R., Pulliam, and E. L. Charnov (1977). Optimal Foraging: A Selective Review of Theory and Tests. *Quarterly Review of Biology* 52:137–154.

Radcliffe-Brown, A. R. (1930–1931). Social Organization of Australian Tribes. *Oceania* 1:34–63, 206–246, 322–341, 426–456.

Rappaport, Roy A. (1968). *Pigs for the Ancestors.* New Haven: Yale University Press.

Rappaport, Roy A. (1984). *Pigs for the Ancestors: Ritual in the Ecology of a New Guinea People*, 2nd ed. New Haven: Yale University Press.

Rapport, David J., and James E. Turner (1977). Economic Models in Ecology. *Science* 195:367–373.

Read, D. W., and C. E. Read (1970). A Critique of Davenport's Game Theory Analysis. *American Anthropologist* 72:351–355.

Real, Leslie A. (1980). Fitness, Uncertainty, and the Role of Diversification in Evolution and Behavior. *American Naturalist* 115:623–638.

Richardson, Allan (1982). The Control of Productive Resources on the Northwest Coast of North America. In *Resource Managers: North American and Australian Hunter-Gatherers*, ed. N. M. Williams and E. S. Hunn, Boulder, CO: Westview Press, pp. 93–112.

Richerson, Peter J. (1977). Ecology and Human Ecology: A Comparison of Theories in the Biological and Social Sciences. *American Ethnologist* 4:1–26.

Richerson, Peter J., and Robert Boyd (1984). Natural Selection and Culture. *BioScience* 34:430–434.

Richerson, Peter J., and Robert Boyd (nd). A Darwinian Theory for the Evolution of Symbolic Cultural Traits. Manuscript, Institute of Ecology, University of California, Davis.

Riechert, Susan E., and Peter Hammerstein (1983). Game Theory in the Ecological Context. *Annual Review of Ecology and Systematics* 14:377–409.

Rodman, Peter S. (1981). Inclusive Fitness and Group Size with a Reconsideration of Group Sizes in Lions and Wolves. *American Naturalist* 118:275–283.

Roemer, John E. (1982). *A General Theory of Exploitation and Class.* Cambridge, MA: Harvard University Press.

Rubenstein, Daniel I (1982). Risk, Uncertainty and Evolutionary Strategies. In *Current Problems in Sociobiology*, ed. King's College Sociobiology Group, Cambridge: Cambridge Univerersity Press, pp. 91–111.

Rubin, Paul H. (1979). The Productivity of Parental Investment. *Journal of Social and Biological Structures* 2:133–140.

Rubin, Paul H., James B. Kau, and Edward F. Meeker (1979). Forms of Wealth and Parent-Offspring Conflict. *J. of Social and Biological Structures* 2:53–64.

Sahlins, Marshall (1969). Economic Anthropology and Anthropological Economics. *Social Science Information* 8:13–33.

Sahlins, Marshall (1972). *Stone Age Economics*. Chicago: Aldine.

Sahlins, Marshall (1976a). *The Use and Abuse of Biology: An Anthropological Critique of Sociobiology*. Ann Arbor: University of Michigan Press.

Sahlins, Marshall (1976b). *Culture and Practical Reason*. Chicago: University of Chicago Press.

Sahlins, Marshall (1978). Culture as Protein and Profit. *New York Review of Books*, Nov. 23, 1978, pp. 45–53.

Samuelson, Paul A. (1983). Complete Genetic Models for Altruism, Kin Selection and Like-Gene Selection. *Journal of Social and Biological Structures* 6:3–15.

Schaffer, William (1978). A Note on the Theory of Reciprocal Altruism. *American Naturalist* 112:250–253.

Schaffer, William (1983). The Application of Optimal Control Theory to the General Life History Problem. *American Naturalist* 121:418–431.

Schelling, Thomas C. (1978). *Micromotives and Macrobehavior*. New York: Norton.

Schoener, Thomas (1971). Theory of Feeding Strategies. *Annual Review of Ecology & Systematics* 2:369–404.

Schoener, Thomas (1983). Simple Models of Optimal Feeding-Territory Size: A Reconciliation. *The American Naturalist* 121:608–629.

Seligman, M. (1971). Phobias and Preparedness. *Behavior Therapy* 2:307–320.

Service, Elman R. (1962). The Social Organization of Bands. In *Primitive Social Organization*, by Elman Service, New York: Random House, pp. 59–109.

Sibly, R. M. (1930). Optimal Group Size is Unstable. *Animal Behaviour* 31:947–948.

Skinner, B. F. (1981). Selection by Consequences. *Science* 213:501–504.

Slobodkin, Lawrence B. (1977). Evolution Is No Help. *World Archaeology* 8:332–343.

Slobodkin, Lawrence B., and Anatol Rapoport (1974). An Optimal Strategy of Evolution. *Quarterly Review of Biology* 49:181–200.

Smith, Eric Alden (1980). Evolutionary Ecology and the Analysis of Human Foraging Behavior: An Inuit Example from the East Coast of Hudson Bay. Ph.D. Dissertation, Cornell University.

Smith, Eric Alden (1981). The Application of Optimal Foraging Theory to the Analysis of Hunter-Gatherer Group Size. In *Hunter-Gatherer Foraging Strategies*, ed. B. Winterhalder and E. A. Smith. Chicago: University of Chicago Press.

Smith, Eric Alden (1983a). Comment on Cashdan. *Current Anthropology* 24:61.

Smith, Eric Alden (1983b). Anthropological Applications of Optimal Foraging Theory: A Critical Review. *Current Anthropology* 24:625–651.

Smith, Eric Alden (1985). Inuit Foraging Groups: Some Simple Models Incorporating Conflicts of Interest, Relatedness, and Central-Place Sharing. *Ethology and Sociobiology* 6:37–57.

Smith, Eric Alden (nd). Environmental Uncertainty and Ecological Risk: Implications for Hunter-Gatherer Social Organization and Demography. Manuscript, Department of Anthropology, University of Washington, Seattle.

Sober, Elliott (ed.) (1984). *Conceptual Issues in Evolutionary Biology*. Cambridge, MA: The MIT Press.

Speck, Frank G. (1915). The Family Hunting Band as the Basis of Algonkian Social Organization. *American Anthropologist* 17 : 289–305.

Speck, Frank G., and Loren C. Eisley (1939). The Significance of the Hunting Territory System of the Algonkian in Social Theory. *American Anthropologist* 41 : 269–280.

Stephens, D. W., and Eric L. Charnov (1982). Optimal Foraging: Some Simple Stochastic Models. *Behavioral Ecology and Sociobiology* 10 : 251–263.

Steward, Julian (1938). *Basin-Plateau Aboriginal Sociopolitical Groups.* Bulletin 120, Bureau of American Ethnology Washington D.C.: Smithsonian Institution.

Trivers, Robert L. (1972). Parental Investment and Sexual Selection. In *Sexual Selection and the Descent of Man, 1871–1971,* ed. B. G. Campbell, Chicago: Aldine, pp. 136–179.

Trivers, Robert L. (1974). Parent-offspring Conflict. *American Zoologist* 14 : 249–264.

Uyenoyama, M., and M. W. Feldman (1980). Theories of Kin and Group Selection: A Population Genetics Perspective. *Theoretical Population Biology* 17 : 380–414.

Vehrencamp, Sandra L. (1983), A Model for the Evolution of Despotic versus Egalitarian Societies. *Animal Behaviour* 31 : 667–682.

von Neumann, John, and Oskar Morgenstern (1944). *Theory of Games and Economic Behavior.* Princeton: Princeton University Press.

Wade, Michael J. (1978). A Critical Review of the Models of Group Selection. *Quarterly Review of Biology* 53 : 101–114.

Werren, John H., and H. Ronald Pulliam (1981). An Intergenerational Model of the Cultural Evolution of Helping Behavior. *Human Ecology* 9 : 465–483.

White, Douglas R. (1973). Mathematical Anthropology. In *Handbook of Sociocultural Anthropology,* ed. J. Honigmann, Chicago: Rand-McNally, pp. 363–446.

Wiessner, Polly (1982). Risk, Reciprocity, and Social Influences on !Kung San Economics. In *Politics and History in Band Societies,* ed. E. Leacock and R. B. Lee, Cambridge: Cambridge University Press, pp. 61–84.

Williams, B. J. (1974). *A Model of Band Society.* Society for American Archaeology, Memoir No. 29.

Williams, George C. (1966). *Adaptation and Natural Selection.* Princeton: Princeton University Press.

Williams, Nancy M., and Eugene S. Hunn (eds.) (1982). *Resource Managers: North American and Australian Hunter-Gatherers.* Boulder, CO: Westview Press.

Wilson, David Sloan (1980). *The Natural Selection of Populations and Communities.* (Series in Evolutionary Biology, Institute of Ecology, University of California at Davis) Menlo Park: Benjamin/Cummings.

Wilson, David Sloan (1983). The Group Selection Controversy: History and Current Status. *Annual Review of Ecology and Systematics* 14 : 159–187.

Wilmsen, Edwin (1973). Interaction, Spacing Behavior, and the Organization of Hunting Bands. *Journal of Anthropological Research* 29 : 1–31.

Winter, S. G. (1975). Optimization and Evolution in the Theory of the Firm. In *Adaptive Economic Models,* ed. R. H. Day and T. Groves, New York: Academic, pp. 73–118.

Winterhalder, Bruce (1987). The Analysis of Hunter-Gatherer Diet: Stalking an Optimal Foraging Model. In *Food and Evolution: Toward a Theory of Human Diets,* ed. M. Harris and E. Ross, Philadelphia: Temple University Press.

Wong, S. (1978). *The Foundations of Paul Samuelson's Revealed Preference Theory.* London: Routledge and Kegan Paul.

Wynne-Edwards, V. C. (1962). *Animal Dispersion in Relation to Social Behaviour.* Edinburgh: Oliver and Boyd.

12

Evolution of a Mesh between Principles of the Mind and Regularities of the World

Roger N. Shepard

As the organ of knowing, the mind must be commensurate with what it knows. The achievements of the physical and biological sciences—from Newtonian, relativistic, and quantum mechanics to current grand unification theories, and from the theory of evolution to the characterization of the genetic code and its double-helical basis—reveal the structural richness and beauty of the physical and biological worlds. But, these same achievements, being achievements of the human mind, also indicate something of the structural richness and beauty of the mental world.

By virtue of this structural richness, psychology, just as much as physics and biology, admits investigation and description at many levels. Moreover, while the most concrete levels primarily manifest diversity, the most abstract levels reveal, in the case of each science, an underlying uniformity. In physical science, the falling of a particular leaf, the braking of a particular wave, or the curling of a particular whiff of smoke, being subject to many undetermined boundary conditions, appears more or less chaotic and unpredictable; yet experiments under suitably controlled conditions reveal that such processes are governed by a few precisely formulatable general laws of physical mechanics. In biological science, the size, morphology, motility, etc, of individuals vary enormously between species; yet biochemical investigations have established that all this diversity results from different sequences of the same four bases in the polynucleotide chain of the helical DNA molecule. Likewise, in the cognitive and behavioral sciences, the language spoken by humans in a particular culture or the reaction of an individual animal in a particular situation seems to be arbitrarily chosen from a large set of possible alternatives, yet Chomsky (1968) has argued that all human languages are based on a common innate schematism and I claim that human and animal reactions are guided by abstract general principles that reflect the invariant properties of the world in which we have evolved (Shepard, 1981, 1984a).

Preparation of this article was supported by National Science Foundation grants BNS 80-05517 and BNS 85-11685 to Stanford University. I thank Leda Cosmides and John Tooby for helping me to understand many puzzling points of evolutionary theory, and for their insightful comments on earlier drafts of this article.

1 A Genetic Basis for Cognition

Until its relatively recent emergence from the strictures of behaviorism, psychology itself failed to appreciate the importance of genetically determined constraints on behavior. In confining themselves to observable responses, behaviorists were not sensitive to the internalized structures and processes that select and guide those responses. Everything was attributed to learning, without recognizing that any principles of learning sufficiently nontrivial to justify the term "principles," being themselves unlearned, must be innate. Correspondingly, the environment was not regarded as something fixed, with properties that might thus be internalized over evolutionary history, but as something variable, to be controlled in shaping an individual animal's behavior through learning.

Of course, studies both of sensory neurophysiology and of the perceptual capabilities of newborns have long revealed the presence of highly developed perceptual mechanisms at birth. Less widely acknowledged is the accumulating psychological and anthropological evidence indicating that even quite abstract processes of thought are also guided by a cognitive predilection for certain types of structures—including those that are

> *linear* (DeSoto, 1960, 1961; Osgood, Suci, and Tannenbaum, 1957, pp. 114–116; Shepard, 1964C),
> *spatial* (Clark, 1973; DeSoto, London, and Handel, 1965; Hutenlocher, 1968; Shepard, 1966, 1982b; Shepard and Hurwitz, 1984),
> *discrete* (Boyd, 1972; Dowling, 1978; Helmholtz, 1862/1954, pp. 252–253; Newport, 1981),
> *hierarchical* (Berlin and Kay, 1969; Greenberg, 1966; Krumhansl, 1983; Krumhansl and Shepard, 1979; Rosch, 1975a, b; Rosch et al., 1976; Shepard and Jordan, 1984; Simon, 1967),
> *balanced* (Abelson and Rosenberg, 1958; Cartwright and Harary, 1956; Heider, 1958),
> *componential* (Bierwisch, 1970; Boyd, 1969; Clark, 1973; Goodenough, 1956, 1967; Lévi-Strauss, 1967; Romney and D'Andrade, 1964), and, hence,
> *shareable* (Freyd, 1983).

True, our processes of thought do not feel constrained to us, and even some contemporary commentators on cognitive science profess to see little discernible structure governing these mental processes (e.g., Fodor, 1983). However, as I once noted (Shepard, 1964b), a spider, too, may not feel constrained as it builds its own characteristic type of web (cf. Fodor, 1980, p. 333). In order to become directly aware of the constraints that govern our processes of thought, we would have, literally, to go out of our minds.

An instructive example of how reasoning processes may be guided by evolutionarily acquired constraints is afforded by the recent doctoral dissertation of Leda Cosmides (1985). She began with the fact, empirically established by Wason and others, that in many reasoning tasks, humans behave in ways that depend on the content reasoned about and in ways that consistently depart from the canons of formal logic (see Evans and Lynch, 1973; Pollard, 1982; Wason and Johnson-Laird, 1982; Wason and Shapiro, 1971). Drawing on joint work with John Tooby, Cosmides argued that long before the laws of formal logic attained what little significance they may now have for human affairs, and extending back into the Pleistocene and even to our primate ancestors, reasoning about social contracts was of primary importance. Success and stability of small groups of hunter-gatherers depended on the general maintenance of reciprocity in which individuals helped each other and relied upon return of favor when it was needed. Under these long-prevailing circumstances, a sensitivity to cheaters—those who accept the benefits without paying the costs—attained a high level of development. Thus even today, nothing is more likely to engender anger than the refusal of any reciprocation by one whom we have repeatedly helped at appreciable cost to ourselves. Cosmides showed how the strategy of identifying cheaters leads to a social contract logic that differs from standard logic in just the ways in which people were found to make the "wrong" responses in the kinds of selection tasks investigated by Wason and others.

Cosmides and Tooby (this volume) indicate why evidence for evolutionary internalization is more likely to be found at the level of underlying cognitive structures than at the level of particular, observable responses issuing from those underlying structures. Obviously, many quite different responses may be compatible with the same underlying structure, and the choice of a particular response on a particular occasion may be dependent on the circumstances peculiar to that occasion.

Nevertheless, the greater accessibility to observation and description of the more concrete levels of behavior has led students of human and animal behavior to be impressed, first, by the diversity evident at that level. Thus ethologists are quick to notice that even relatively closely related species may be diurnal or nocturnal, carnivorous or herbivorous, social or solitary, vocal or mute; aquatic, terrestrial, arborial, or aerial; and primarily receptive to information in the form of visual, acoustic, chemical, mechanical, or electrical stimulation. Likewise, ethnologists tend to emphasize the unique complex of language, beliefs, and practices characteristic of each human culture; and ethnomusicologists may even focus entirely on subtle differences in tuning of the gamelan from one Indonesian village to the next, without taking any notice of the fact that at a more abstract level, all such tunings exhibit certain general structural properties that they share even with our own superficially very different diatonic system (Kessler, Hansen, and Shepard, 1984; also see Castellano, Bharucha, and Krumhansl, 1984; Dowling, 1978; Pressing, 1983; Shepard, 1982a).

2 The Search for General Psychological Laws

As a cognitive scientist, my orientation is in some ways more like that of a physicist than like that of a naturalist or ethnologist. Much as a physicist seeks abstract physical laws that underlie all concrete physical phenomena, including such diverse and seemingly haphazard ones as falling leaves, breaking waves, and curling whiffs of smoke, I seek general psychological laws that underlie all specific mental processes and behaviors, despite their apparent variation between individuals, cultures, or species. Moreover, I seek an evolutionary origin of such general psychological laws in the properties of the world that have been so pervasive and enduring as to be relevant for a broad spectrum of species. I reason that in the evolutionary long run, these general properties of the world would tend to become even more deeply internalized than the more local and transitory properties peculiar to any particular ecological niche. Each individual would then not have to learn about each such property *de novo* by trial and possibly fatal error.

In concluding that the regularities that are the most ubiquitous and long enduring in the environment are the ones that are most likely to become entrenched in such internalized structures, I concur with Cosmides and Tooby (this volume). In my own work, however, I have pushed this idea to the extreme of looking for evidence of internalization of the very most pervasive and enduring properties of the world. Beyond those characteristic of the hominid situation during the Pleistocene, I have looked for properties that have been essentially invariant throughout the entire history of biological evolution on this planet.

The relative neglect by evolutionary theorists of the possible internalization of these very general properties of the world is understandable. Consideration of the evolutionary basis of behavioral predispositions has usually focused on those predispositions that are characteristic of a particular species. The uniqueness of such behavior attracts our attention and motivates us to look for a special property of that species' ecological niche that might have favored genes for that particular behavior.

In contrast, general properties do not call for any particular, easily specified behavior; they merely place abstract constraints on large classes of behaviors serving widely different functions. Because they are so abstract, such internalized constraints cannot be identified simply by observing behavior. Rather, the identification of such constraints requires a combination of theoretical and experimental research that alternates between identifying the relevant invariants in the world and demonstrating that certain patterns of behavior recorded in the psychological laboratory imply that those invariants have in fact been internalized.

As illustrative examples of enduring regularities of the world that appear to have been internalized over the course of biological evolution, I suggest the following:

1. *Terrestrial circadian period.* The earth has, with long continuing isochrony, completed one 360° rotation about its axis every 24 hours. This fact does not itself favor genes for a diurnal or a nocturnal pattern of activity. Nevertheless, in animals commited to either of these two patterns, this external regularity has favored genes for an internal 24-hour clock that enables such animals to emerge, to feed, and to return to the safety of their nests or burrows at appropriate times, despite wide variations in such other circumstances as season, temperature, sunlight, or shade. Hamsters maintained in a laboratory environment of constant illumination and temperature, for example, continue a circadian activity cycle with a period of 24 hours plus or minus no more than a few minutes per day (Rusak and Zucker, 1975). I have previously used this internalization of the invariant period of the earth's rotation as a model for our perceptual and cognitive internalization of the invariants of our world generally (Shepard, 1984a).

2. *Three degrees of freedom of terrestrial illumination.* The complete physical specification of the light reflected from objects requires an essentially unlimited number of degrees of freedom. For each point on the surface of an object, a different number would be required to specify the energy at each wavelength reflected from that point. However, variation in natural illumination of objects has principally had only three degrees of freedom—namely, (1) freedom of variation simply on a light-dark dimension corresponding to the variation between daylight and nighttime or deep shade, (2) freedom of variation on a yellow-blue dimension corresponding to the proportion of the sunlight falling directly on the object versus the proportion of shorter-wavelength light reaching the object indirectly through atmospheric scattering, and (3) freedom of variation on a red-green dimension corresponding both to how low the sun is in the sky (and hence to the amount of short-wavelength sunlight lost by atmospheric scattering) and to the amount of long-wavelength absorbing water vapor in the atmosphere. This fact does not itself confer a decisive advantage on genes for three-dimensional color vision (such as we have) over, say, two- or four-dimensional color vision. The recent work of Maloney and Wandell (1986) does, however, suggest that color constancy, which greatly facilitates the recognition of objects despite variations

in ambient illumination, may be adequately approximated only if the input is analyzed into three color components.

3. *Geometry of three-dimensional space*. Physical space has been locally three-dimensional and Euclidean throughout evolutionary history. This fact does not itself favor genes for hunting, for hiding nuts for the winter, for building a nest, a dam, or a web, or for using tools. However, it does suggest that an animal that engages in any of these spatial activities will do so more effectively if it has genetically internalized some of the basic geometrical properties of three-dimensional Euclidean space—properties such as that a straight line is the shortest distance between two points, a one-dimensional curve will divide a two-dimensional surface but a two-dimensional surface is required to divide three-dimensional space, rigid objects have just six degrees of freedom of motion, and every change of position of such an object has a uniquely associated fixed axis in space (Shepard, 1984a; also, Carlton and Shepard, in preparation).

4. *Metric of functional equivalence*. Exactly the same situation rarely, if ever, recurs in our world, yet similar situations often lead to the same biologically significant consequences. These two facts do not themselves favor genes for eating particular types of animals or plants rather than others, or for avoiding or fleeing from particular animals or situations rather than others. Yet, every animal must have some basis for deciding whether any particular new situation is similar enough to a situation previously found to have a positive or negative outcome, and that it should approach or take flight. In short, every animal must have internalized an appropriate metric of functional equivalence of possible situations and an appropriate principle of generalization with respect to that metric (Shepard, 1984b, 1986).

Of course, such regularities of the world are not equally internalized in all animals. For example, while there is evidence for the internalization of the circadian period in a wide range of organisms from simple to complex, evidence for the internalization of the three degrees of freedom of natural illumination is restricted to those species with highly developed color vision. What accounts for such differences in internalization? As a preliminary list of the principal determiners of how quickly and how deeply regularities of the world will tend to become genetically internalized in an evolutionary line, I suggest the following:

1. *Relevance*—that is, the degree of benefit that would be conferred on the species if it internalized the regularity. The fact that the earth has a uniform 24-hour period of rotation is of great biological significance. It determines a predictable alternation between relative light and warmth and relative darkness and cold, and has been deeply inter-

nalized in a wide variety of terrestrial species. The planet Mars has a different but comparably uniform period of rotation, but that period has virtually no relevance for life on earth and has almost certainly not been internalized by any terrestrial species.

2. *Accessibility*—that is, the simplicity of the minimum biological system needed to pick up that regularity from the environment. This tends to be correlated with the factor (1) just listed, because things more proximal to an organism are often both more significant for it and easier to pick up. Thus the variation of lightness and temperature resulting from the earth's rotation can be and is picked up by the simple sensory transducers of quite primitive organisms, while the period of rotation of Mars was not even detectable on earth until one species invented the telescope. However, the correlation is not perfect. The internalization of the invariant period of the earth's rotation, as opposed merely to the detection of changes in light or temperature, requires the development of a sophisticated biological clock that runs at a rate that is unaffected by temperature (Johnson and Hastings, 1986; Pittendrigh, 1954). Moreover, whereas single-celled animals are largely governed by proximal properties of their fluid environment, such as the local concentration of some protein (Koshland, 1980), humans have come to rely heavily on the intrinsic properties of size, shape, and color of distal objects—properties that (because of variations in distance, orientation, and illumination) can be determined only by much more sophisticated perceptual systems.

3. *Permanence*—that is, the period of time during which the regularity has been invariant in the world. To recur to the example already considered, although tidal friction is expected gradually to decrease the rate of rotation of the earth and although paleontological evidence for such a slowing has recently been reported (Vanyo, Hutchinson, and Awramik, 1986), the period of the rotation has remained sufficiently constant to afford the opportunity for the selectional process of biological evolution to achieve the genetic internalization of its current value. I suggest that other pervasive and enduring regularities of our world that are more abstract and less accessible than this period have also been internalized in humans and in other perceptually sophisticated animals. Such regularities may include those of kinematic geometry entailed by the three-dimensionality of space (Shepard, 1984a). In contrast, properties of our world that have emerged only recently, such as that roads and electrical outlets are hazardous, have not had time to be genetically internalized, as is attested by the flattened remains of small animals and our admonishments to young children.

3 The Evolutionary Trend toward Increasing Internalization

Evolutionary theorists have generally eschewed any notion of an objective progression, hierarchy, or *scala natura* of adaptation. Every living organism, whether a human being, a whale, a worm, or a bacterium, is the product of an unsurpassed success story: Every single one of its ancestors, throughout the more than a billion years of life on this planet, has been clever enough, despite many hazards, to maintain its integrity long enough to reproduce! From a biological perspective, every species that is not undergoing a secular population decline can be regarded as well adapted to its particular niche. Although each such niche has its own peculiar characteristics, what objective criterion could be adduced for declaring any niche to be better or more representative than any other?

This prevailing evolutionary perspective has reinforced the preoccupation with differences between species. If each niche is unique, and if each surviving species is, as its survival attests, well adapted to its specific niche, then it would seem to be the resulting uniqueness of the behavior observed in that species that is of paramount importance. Moreover, because there can be quite different strategies of coping with the same circumstances, different species may, through the vicissitudes of biological history and genetic sorting, achieve comparably successful adaptations to essentially the same ecological niche by means of quite different behavioral predispositions. Thus in two closely related species of bird, living in similar habitats, dependent on the same sources of food, and subject to the same predators, one species may produce songs of great structural complexity, with selection of mates evidently based on subtle variations, while the other species may produce relatively rudimentary songs (Kroodsma and Verner, 1978; Marler and Sherman, 1983; Nottebohm, 1984).

However, there are objective properties of the world, and these properties do objectively differ in degree of generality—from the relatively local and, possibly, transitory ones that characterize a particular niche, to those that are extremely general or even universal and hence characterize, at however abstract a level, all niches. Depending on their abstractness or lack of accessibility, these more general properties are not internalizable in primitive organisms and so have come to be genetically internalized only as more complex forms have emerged through the process of biological evolution.

This is not to say the evolutionary process embodies an inherent force such that any one evolutionary line tends, automatically, toward increasing complexity and internalization. Assortive recombination, mutation, and genetic drift may all be quite random, so that in the absence of external factors, shifts toward greater or lesser internalization within any one breeding population may be at least as likely to be downward as upward. And

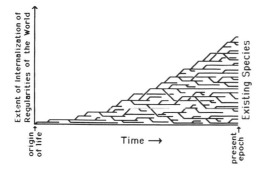

Figure 12.1
Schematic illustration of how random variations lead to an increasing internalization of regularities of the world. [Cf. Jerrison (1985, p. 18) on "encephalization quotient."]

such regressions as the simplification or disappearance of formerly present visual systems in animals adapting to cave dwelling, burrowing, and parasitism is well known. Nevertheless, two considerations suggest that in the evolutionary long run, increasing degrees of internalization of external regularities will arise.

First, the evolutionary process necessarily begins, with the origin of life, at the level of minimum possible complexity and internalization. Even if the ensuing variations are purely random, so that each change is at least as likely to go down as to go up, the maximum and the average of the process being bounded from below, have a statistical expectation of increase. This is illustrated in figure 12.1, where the degree of internalization of external regularities is schematically plotted as a function of time, from the origin of life to the the present epoch. Notice that although any one line, as it is traced from left to right, is as likely to deviate downward as upward, the height attained by whatever is the highest branch at any given time tends to increase monotonically. The same secular trend would emerge for any purely random walk or diffusion process that begins at a fixed barrier—corresponding, in this case, to the barrier of zero internalization.

Second, presumably there is, in addition, an external pressure that biases the otherwise random process toward a generally upward direction. True, random mutations are more likely to result in downward than in upward deviations. However, within a set of competing evolutionary lines, those that have achieved a greater internalization of the regularities of their common world are expected to have some advantage, however slight. Thus, although there is always room near the bottom (as is attested by the continuing survival and replenishment of relatively primitive forms), we might expect, on the average, a differentially higher rate of extinction of downward relative to upward deviators.

Of course the two considerations just given might be applied to many other quantifiable characteristic of living forms. Thus, instead of "degree of internalization," I could as well have labeled the upward pointing axis in figure 12.1 with another quantifiable characteristic, such as size, weight, or speed of locomotion. And, indeed, similar trends are evident with respect to those characteristics: among existing species, the blue whale may well be as large and massive as any animal that has lived on earth, and the cheetah, dolphin, and swift may come close to the speed records for land, water, and air, respectively.

However, whereas there may be limitations of physics and mechanics that ultimately constrain size or speed, no such limitations are evident in the case of internalization of external regularities. Indeed, while increases in size and speed have probably been negligible for many millions of years, internalization has continued apace—as attested, particularly, by advances in the primate and hominid lines.

Indeed, such advances may seem surprisingly abrupt and unprecedented, as in the emergence of an innate competence for language. They may also seem surprisingly complex in relation to the apparently small contribution that they could make to survival or reproduction, as in the emergence of an innate competence for music (which appears to depend upon internal structures that are in some respects comparable to those underlying language—see Krumhansl, 1983; Krumhansl and Shepard, 1979; Shepard and Jordan, 1984). Toward the end of this paper I offer some speculations to the effect that in comparison to major increases in, say, size or speed, increases in mental competence may in the long run be relatively cheap.

In any case, these considerations lead to a view that seems to differ from what I take to be the currently prevailing view in evolutionary biology, namely, a view that holds, first, that all presently thriving species are equal with respect to their adaptation to their ecological niches and, second, that all such niches are equal with respect to their representativeness of the world at large. In contrast I suggest that niches vary enormously and hierarchically in terms of how much of the universe they include. I further suggest that because these niches thus differ in the extent to which their successful occupancy requires the internalization of abstract principles of physics, geometry, and the like, there is no reason to suppose that the currently most successful occupiers are in any sense optimally adapted to these niches.

We know how often an apparently successful species, on an isolated island, say, has been reduced to extinction by a more successful competitor inadvertently introduced by a visiting ship. And countless science fiction stories of alien subjugation of humankind attest to our own insecurities in this regard.

Nevertheless, at the present epoch, humans appear to have taken over the broadest terrestrial niche. Tooby and DeVore (1986) have called it the "cognitive niche." Although we clearly have not fully mastered this niche, we do not currently appear to have any serious terrestrial competitors for it. Indeed, it could come to pass that all advanced forms of life on earth are saved from extinction because one species, having acquired an interest in looking both outward toward the stars and inward toward the atom, is alone capable of detecting the closing trajectory of a massive asteroid or comet and also capable of sufficiently deflecting its course by a strategically launched thermonuclear device. (Unfortunately the same species so far seems to be having a much less salutary effect on the life of this planet.)

Given that a significant part of our world, or of any niche within it, consists of other organisms that are themselves evolving, spreading, or dwindling to extinction, the problem of defining what would be an overall optimal organism seems quite beyond our reach. My own strategy, in the face of this problem, has been to concern myself with the internalization of abstract and general properties of the world that (like the period of the earth's rotation) depend little, if at all, on the particular collection of other species assumed. The four examples of internalized regularities that I listed at the outset seem to be of this kind. I turn now to a closer consideration of the last two of those, which I have been particularly studying of late— namely, those concerning the geometry of three-dimensional space and the metric of functional equivalence.

4 Internalization of Kinematic Geometry of Three-Dimensional Space

Between any two positions of a rigid object in three-dimensional space there are infinitely many ways in which the object could be moved from the one position to the other. Experiments in the psychological laboratory reveal, however, that certain paths are psychologically preferred. There are several ways of demonstrating such preferences. (a) One can present motions over two such alternative paths and ask for a subjective judgment as to which of the two presented motions appears simplest or most natural. (b) One can block out a portion of any one such presented motion and make an objective determination of the accuracy with which the observer can discriminate whether or not the motion was altered in any way during the time that it was being blocked from view. (c) One can simply present the two terminal positions of the object in temporal alternation, without any intervening real motion, and determine the path over which the observer nevertheless experiences an illusion of *apparent motion* between those two positions (for example, by having the oberver adjust the position of a gap or "window" in a partition displayed between the two presented positions so that the object appears to pass through that window). (d) One can ask the observer to judge whether two simultaneously presented objects are the same or different in intrinsic shape and attempt to infer the path over which the the observer imagined the one object moved into congruence with the other in order to make this determination (as in the paradigm of "mental rotation"—see Shepard and Metzler, 1971, and, for an overview, Shepard and Cooper, 1982).

So far, the preferred paths of motion revealed by these quite different techniques are usually the same. I suggest that these preferred paths are determined by internalized principles governing the way rigid objects move in the three-dimensional space in which we have evolved (Shepard, 1981, 1984a). Just which principles these are is, however, a matter for continuing investigation. It turns out that different principles that might be proposed, such as those of kinetic physics or kinematic geometry, make different predictions as to which paths should be considered simplest. Moreover, these predictions are often not obvious in advance—an indication that our knowledge about how objects move in space is internalized at a deep, unarticulated level of automatic perceptual mechanisms and not at the much more recently developed level of articulate introspection and communication.

Because we have evolved in a physical world, one might first be tempted to suppose that our internalized principles for the simplest motions would be the principles of kinetic physics that prescribe the motions of rigid macroscopic objects in physical space. Such motions are determined by a variational (least energy) principle. In the absence of external forces, an object will move so that its center of mass traverses a straight line at a constant velocity. Any rotation, if present, either is of constant angular velocity about one of the principal axes of inertia of the object or is of a more complex, wobbling sort, if the momentary axis of rotation does not coincide with a principal axis of the object.

In simple cases, the psychological data are in agreement with these predictions of kinetic physics. In particular, positions of an object differing by a pure translation or by a pure rotation about a natural axis of the object do seem to be most readily connected, in real, apparent, or imagined motion, by a rigid constant-velocity rectilinear translation or rotation (Shepard and Cooper, 1982).

In more complex cases, in which the starting and ending positions differ by both a translation and a rotation, however, the psychologically preferred motions generally depart from those prescribed by kinetic physics in the absence of forces. Such preferred paths, instead of carrying the center of the object over a straight path, carry that center over a path that is curved (Foster, 1975) and, in the general case, helical (Shepard, 1984a). Such motions might seem more complex than the rectilinar motions prescribed by kinetic physics. In fact, however, they correspond to the still more abstract, general, and in some ways simpler principles of kinematic geometry.

According to Chasles's theorem of kinematic geometry, for any two positions of an object in three-dimensional space, there exists a unique axis in space such that the object can be carried from the one position to the other by a combination of a translation along that axis together with a rotation about it, that is, by a *screw displacement*. The preferred motions that we have determined from experiments on real, apparent, and imagined motion have often conformed with the twisting motions prescribed by Chasles's theorem, indicating that the abstract principles of kinematic geometry have been internalized (Shepard, 1984a).

Moreover, the natural axes of the object that affect the psychologically preferred motions are not the principle axes of inertia (as estimated on the assumption that the visible object is of uniform density) but are, rather, the axes of symmetry of the visual object. This, again, indicates the domination of the relatively more concrete physical principles by still more abstract and general geometrical principles. It also means that the internalized principle based on Chasles's theorem must be elaborated to take account of such axes of symmetry. My associates and I are currently testing the idea that the preferred motion is then one in which the salient axis of symmetry is represented as undergoing the simplest helical motion prescribed by Chasles's theorem, while the object is represented as undergoing the minimum rotation about that moving axis.

What is rather remarkable is the structural richness and elegance of the internalized knowledge implied by these results. Eloise Carlton and I are currently formulating this internalized knowledge in terms of a group structure on the six-dimensional manifold of possible positions of an object in three-dimensional space in such a way that the preferred motions correspond to geodesic paths (the analogues of great circles on the two-dimensional surface of the earth) in this curved manifold (Carlton and Shepard, in preparation; Shepard, 1985). The six-dimensional manifold corresponds to the Euclidean group E^+, which is the semidirect product of the rotation group and the translation group:

$$E^+ = SO(3) * R^3.$$

5   Internalization of a Metric of Similarity and Principle of Generalization

I have argued that if we are to seek a universal psychological law, our first search must be for a law of generalization. Any other proposed law will be general only to the extent that it specifies how it applies under altered conditions; but this is essentially the problem of generalization.

Empirical "gradients of stimulus generalization" specifying how the probability, strength, or speed of a response that had originally been learned to a particular training stimulus falls off with the dissimilarity of the test stimulus to that original training stimulus had been obtained since Pavlov. However, no invariant law was forthcoming. The shape of the gradient depended on the particular sensory continuum and species used. Gradients were not even uniformly monotonic, manifesting augmented generalization between tones separated by an octave in pitch, between the two (red and violet) ends of the spectrum of visible wavelengths, between symmetrical shapes differing by certain angles, and between times of day separated by 24 hours (see Shepard, 1965, 1985). By midcentury, the pessimistic view prevailed that generalization, being determined by the organism as much as by the physical continuum, could not be expected to obey an invariant law (see Bush and Mosteller, 1951; Lashley and Wade, 1946; Razran, 1949).

In 1955, however, I suggested that such a law might after all be obtainable if one separated the psychological problem of determining the way in which generalization falls off with distance in *psychological space* from the psychophysical problem of determining the mapping of the physical parameter space into the corresponding psychological space (Shepard, 1955, 1957). I showed that if the psychological space is taken to be that space in which generalization falls off in accordance with an invariant monotonic function—without making any further stipulation about the form of the function—the function invariably turns out to approximate an exponential decay function (Shepard, 1958a, 1965). My attempt to put this approach on a more secure footing (and to demonstrate that the approach is not, as it first seems, circular) led to the development of nonmetric multidimensional scaling (Shepard, 1962; also see Kruskal, 1964a,b; Shepard, 1980). In this way I have been able to demonstrate a close approximation to an exponential decay for many different sets of generalization data, including a variety of types of stimuli (visual and auditory, unidimensional and multidimensional) and species (including humans and pigeons, see Shepard 1958a, 1965, 1972, 1980, 1984b).

Here, then, is one candidate for a general psychological law: For any sufficiently advanced animal and for any set of stimuli, there exists a unique psychological space of those stimuli such that the probability that a response learned to one stimulus will generalize to another stimulus decreases with the distance between those stimuli according to an invariant monotonic function that is universally concave upward and approximately exponential.

However, from my present perspective, the discovery of a general psychological law takes us only halfway. We must now ask what general property of the world is reflected in this general law. The property that I have proposed is that sets of stimuli having the same important consequence for an organism are not arbitrary point sets in the parameter space of the stimuli. Rather, because the set of objects having a particular consequence will generally be physically similar to each other, the set will constitute a compact region with perhaps additional properties such as convexity or central symmetry in the abstract space of the objects. I call such a region, corresponding to a particular significant consequence for an individual, the *consequential region*. A certain consequential region of a small animal's psychological space might correspond to an edible berry or to a predatory hawk, while neighboring locations in the space would correspond to inedible berries or to harmless birds (cf. Seyfarth, Cheney, and Marler, 1980).

The canonical generalization experiment is conceived as follows: An individual (animal or person) is given a single reinforced trial with a novel stimulus from some domain. The individual is then tested with another stimulus from that domain. The problem faced by such an individual is not the problem of discriminating between the two stimuli. The two stimuli may obviously differ. Indeed, an animal would be ill served by the assumption that just because it can detect a difference between the present and an earlier situation, what it learned in that previous situation has no application to the present one. Rather, the problem that the individual faces is that of deciding whether the new stimulus, even though different from the preceding one, is nevertheless similar enough that it, too, might belong to the class of objects possessing the same reinforcing consequences. I proposed, therefore, that the individual assumes, in effect, that the set of stimuli having this particular reinforcing consequence corresponds to some reasonably shaped, compact region in its psychological space of possible stimuli.

By hypothesis, however, the individual has no knowledge of the size or location of the consequential region in that abstract space. It knows only that the point representing the original training stimulus, by virtue of the fact that it was followed by reinforcement, must fall within this region. The problem, then, is one of considering potential consequential regions of all possible sizes and locations and estimating the probability that the point corresponding to the test stimulus also falls in the consequential region. This estimated probability is obtained by integrating over all such possible regions, each one weighted, if desired, by an a priori probability based, for example, on its size.

The result that I have obtained (Shepard, 1984b, 1985) is that almost independent of the assumed a priori probabilities assumed, the integration yields a function that is concave upward and uniformly approximates an exponential decay function. Indeed, if the probabilities are chosen in accordance with a minimum knowledge (i.e., maximum entropy) assumption, integration yields exactly the exponential decay function. Not only do we seem to have a general psychological law; we seem to have an explanation for this law in terms of a very general and highly abstract property of the world.

In extensions of this work, I have been able to establish two further results: First, integration over possible consequential regions also provides an explanation for the widely supported finding that the metric of psychological space is of the Euclidean (L_2 norm) or "city-block" (L_1 norm) varieties, depending on whether the dimensions of the stimuli are integral or separable (cf Shepard, 1964a, 1984b, 1985, 1986). Second, the same theory also predicts the uniformly reciprocal form found for the function relating discriminative reaction time to distance in psychological space (Shepard, 1985).

6 Concluding Speculations

The Importance of Context

The internalized constraints that embody our knowledge of the enduring regularities of the world are likely to be most successfully engaged by contexts that most fully resemble the natural conditions under which our perceptual/representational systems evolved. Cognitive psychologists are awakening to the importance of context in a variety of human performances. Examples include the powerful effects (a) of content on logical reasoning (Cosmides, 1985; Wason and Johnson-Laird, 1972), (b) of mental models on deductive reasoning (Johnson-Laird, 1983), (c) of semantic interpretation on learning syntactic rules (Moeser and Bregman, 1972), (d) of the way problems are framed on the judgments that are made (Tversky and Kahneman, 1981), (e) of the musical context on the judgment of the relations between tones (Krumhansl, 1979, 1983; Krumhansl and Shepard, 1979), and (f) of the presence of a human infant on the elicitation of the distinctive and cross-culturally uniform prosodic features of "motherese" in adult speech (Fernald, 1984; Fernald et al., 1986; Fernald and Simon, 1984).

The intriguing failures of "intuitive physics" demonstrated by McCloskey and his associates (McCloskey, 1983; McCloskey, Caramazza, and Green, 1980) may be explainable as a failure to supply an effective context. Recent evidence indicates that individuals who give an incorrect answer when asked to draw, for example, the trajectory of a projectile emerging from a curved tube, may respond more accurately when asked to choose between more realistically simulated or actually moving alternatives (e.g., Kaiser, Proffitt, and Anderson, 1984; Shannon, 1976; also Yutaka Sayeki, personal communication, 26 January 1984). (There is also the possibility that the tendency to draw a curved trajectory is an extrapolation based on the extraction of the fixed point of the preceding circular motion and, hence, reflects an internalization not so much of physical dynamics as of the more abstract kinematic geometry—see Shepard, 1984a).

Individuals may also differ in the extent to which they can voluntarily access this deeply internalized wisdom in the absence of relevant external stimulation. Using a cube comparison test, Just and Carpenter (1985) found that individuals of high spatial ability were faster and more accurate because they would spontaneously imagine, where appropriate, a single 120° rotation of a cube about a diagonal axis through opposite corners, whereas individuals of lower spatial ability would imagine only 90° rotations about axes through opposite faces—necessitating a sequence of two or three such operations. My prediction is that in an analogous task of apparent motion, which should more fully engage the underlying perceptual machinery, all of these individuals will extract the invariant diagonal axis implied by kinematic geometry and will experience the simpler 120° rotational motion. This prediction is based on the idea that our deepest wisdom about the world has long ago been built into our perceptual systems at a level that is relatively automatic and unconscious (compare Runeson, 1977). If this is so, we may all be smarter than we "think"—that is, smarter than our more recently acquired processes of articulate thought.

The Sudden Emergence of Complex Competencies
Many "higher" animals have developed some ability to recognize and to manipulate three-dimensional objects. Many more manifest a remarkable ability to orient and to find their ways about in three-dimensional space, including—in addition to humans (Thomson, 1983) and human infants (Gibson and Spelke, 1983; Liben, Patterson, and Newcombe, 1981; Landau, Gleitman, and Spelke, 1981)—primates (Menzel, 1973), rats (Maier, 1929; Tolman, 1932), birds (Emlen, 1975; Kamil and Balda, 1983; Sauer, 1958), and even such invertebrates as ants (Hölldobler, 1980), bees (Gould, 1980, 1986; von Frisch, 1967), wasps (Thorpe, 1950), and spiders (Forster, 1982). But, because the three-dimensional Euclidean nature of our common world has remained invariant, we have had ample time to evolve this competency. More puzzling is the relatively sudden emergence of language competency in humans, and musical competencies in humans, birds, and whales.

The puzzle here is not perhaps very different from the puzzle of the emergence of complex physical structures, such as the wings of insects or birds, that are of such a character that evolutionarily intermediate structures (e.g., something halfway between a leg and a wing) would seem to confer little survival value. However, this puzzle may be somewhat reduced by recognizing that genetic control, like control in complex systems generally (Simon, 1967), is hierarchical. A complex anatomical structure that has already evolved in the service of one function might be moved or transformed as a whole, where in rare cases its already highly developed capabilities might find a new use. In insects, the alteration of a single gene can have the effect of replacing an antenna by a leg (Gehring, 1985; Kaufman, Lewis, and Wakimoto, 1980), and there is evidence that such *homeotic* mutations can result in the transfer of corresponding neural mechanisms as well (Jimenez and Campos-Ortega, 1981; Teugels and Ghysen, 1983). Moreover, the neucleotide sequences (called *homeo boxes*) that are critical for these mutations in insects have more recently been identified in vertebrates, including mammals, where their alteration appears capable of similar transformations or transpositions of neuroanatomical structures (Awgulewitsch et al., 1986; Jackson, Schofield, and Hogan, 1985; Ruddle et al., 1985).

There is, as I already noted, abundant evidence that the brain is not a homogeneous, randomly connected system but possesses a definite structural connectivity at birth. At the same time, the genetic code apparently does not have the informational capacity to specify each connection separately. However, separate specification is not required if the development of the brain is hierarchical, with modules that have evolved to perform certain basic operations duplicated throughout the brain (perhaps especially in parallel spatial arrays). In that case, moreover, a highly evolved hierarchical system might, through mutation, be transformed as a whole or transferred to a new location in the brain where, in the rare case in which it turns out to provide some useful capability, it might take root and undergo further modifications suitable to its new function. Some ten years ago, in a paper that has received insufficiently wide attention, Rozin (1976) proposed essentially this explanation for the emergence of new cognitive capabilities.

Similarly with regard to the emergence of linguistic competence in particular, I have for some time been suggesting that computational resources that had previously evolved to subserve spatial cognition may in this way have been preempted, apparently on one side of the brain, to subserve language (Shepard, 1975, 1982b, 1984a). Because the cost of transferring or transforming a high-level unit in the hierarchy need not be great, the transformation may become entrenched even if the utility it confers is relatively small (as it might be, for example, in the case of competence for music or song).

The Representation of the World by Different Animals
The natural tendency to focus on what is concretely given leads to an emphasis on differences. This partly explains the tendency, which I noted at

the outset, of biopsychologists and cultural anthropologists to focus on the uniqueness of each species or each culture. Similarly, one is naturally struck by obvious differences between the sense organs of different species. One may be tempted to suppose that we, who primarily experience the world through vision, experience a very different world from the worlds experienced by bats or dolphins, who rely more on hearing, dogs or rats, who make greater use of smell, certain fish and eels, who respond primarily to electric fields (Bullock, 1973; Hopkins, 1974, 1981), or spiders or scorpions, who are attuned to mechanical vibrations (Barth, 1982; Brownell, 1984). But at a sufficiently abstract level, our worlds are all the same three-dimensional Euclidean world, similarly populated with enduring three-dimensional objects with six degrees of freedom of global motion. So, although the sense organs are very different, the internal models and internalized constraints on the representation of their transformations may be similar.

In a popular account of the world of insects, I once read that because the butterfly's eyes are composed of arrays of separate ommatidia, the butterfly's mate must appear to it as a constellation of disconnected dots. This is like saying that because our own retinal images are upside down, analyzed by two-dimensional arrays of discrete receptor cells, and, also, are constantly jerking across the retina (as we shift our gaze), we must experience the world as pointillistic, two-dimensional, upside down, and violently jumping about! What we and other animals internally represent are the distal objects and events in the external world—not the proximal energy patterns on our sensory surfaces.

Toward Universal Principles of Mind
I have argued that to the extent that the principles of the mind are not merely arbitrary, their most likely ultimate sources are the abiding regularities in the world (Shepard, 1981, 1984a). Among such external regularities, the most abiding are the ones that in the long run should have the greatest opportunity to become internalized—however abstract those regularities may be. The facts that space is three-dimensional, that objects have six degrees of freedom of global motion, that light and darkness alternate with a fixed period, and that sets of objects having the same significant consequences tend to form a compact region in an appropriate parameter space are expected to hold not just on earth but on the millions of planets that may be capable of supporting life in each of the millions of galaxies within just the observable portion of the (possibly infinite) universe. Accordingly, we might begin to conceive of the most general of the internalized principles of mind not just as human or even terrestrial principles of mind. We might begin to regard them as universal principles of mind.

References

Abelson, R. P., and M. J. Rosenberg (1958). Symbolic Psycho-Logic: A Model of Attitudinal Cognition. *Behavioral Science* 3:1−13.

Awgulewitsch, A., M. F. Utset, C. P. Hart, W. McGinnis, and F. H. Ruddle (1986). Spatial Restriction in Expression of a Mouse Homeo Box Locus within the Central Nervous System. *Nature* 320:328−335.

Barth, F. G. (1982). Spiders and Vibrating Signals: Sensory Reception and Behavioral Significance. In P. N. Witt and J. S. Rovner (eds.), *Spider Communication Mechanisms and Ecological Significance*, Princeton: Princeton University Press, pp. 67−122.

Berlin, B., and P. Kay (1969). *Basic Color Terms: Their Universality and Evolution*, Berkeley: University of California Press.

Bierwisch, M. (1970). Semantics. In J. Lyons (ed.), *New Horizons in Linguistics*, Baltimore: Penguin Books.

Boyd, J. P. (1969). The Algebra of Group Kinship. *Journal of Mathematical Psychology* 6:139−167.

Boyd, J. P. (1972). Information Distance for Discrete Structures. In R. N. Shepard, A. K. Romney, and S. B. Nerlove (eds.), *Multidimensional Scaling: Theory and Methods in the Behavioral Sciences*, Vol. 1 New York: Seminar Press, pp. 213−223.

Brownell, P. H. (1984). Prey Detection by the Sand Scorpion. *Scientific American* 251:86−97.

Bullock, T. H. (1973). Seeing the World through a New Sense: Electroreception in Fish. *American Scientist* 61:316−325.

Bush, R. R., and F. Mosteller (1951). A Model for Stimulus Generalization and Discrimination. *Psychological Review* 58:413−423.

Carlton, E. H., and R. N. Shepard (in preparation). A Geometrical Basis for Preferred Motions of Objects in Space.

Cartwright, D., and F. Harary (1956). Structural Balance: A Generalization of Heider's Theory. *Psychological Review* 63:277−293.

Castellano, M. A., J. Bharucha, and C. L. Krumhansl (1984). Tonal Hierarchies in the Music of North India. *Journal of Experimental Psychology: General* 113:394−412.

Chomsky, N. (1968). *Language and Mind.* New York: Harcourt, Brace & World.

Clark, H. (1973). Space, Time, Semantics and the Child. In T. E. Moore (ed.), *Cognitive Development and the Acquisition of Knowledge*, New York: Academic Press.

Cosmides, L. (1985). Deduction or Darwinian Algorithms? An Explanation of the "Elusive" Content Effect on the Wason Selection Task. Unpublished doctoral dissertation, Harvard University.

DeSoto, C. B. (1960). Learning a Social Structure. *Journal of Abnormal and Social Psychology* 60:417−421.

DeSoto, C. B. (1961). The Predilection for Single Orderings. *Journal of Abnormal and Social Psychology* 62:16−23.

DeSoto, C. B., M. London, and S. Handel (1965). Social Reasoning and Spatial Paralogic. *Journal of Personality and Social Psychology* 2:513−521.

Dowling, W. J. (1978). Scale and Contour: Two Components of a Theory for Melodies. *Psychological Review* 85:341−354.

Emlen, S. T. (1975). Migration: Orientation and Navigation. In D. J. Farner and J. R. King (eds.), *Avian Biology* (Vol. 5), New York: Academic Press.

Evans, J. St. B. T., and J. S. Lynch (1973). Matching Bias in the Selection Task. *British Journal of Psychology* 6:391−397.

Fernald, A. (1984). The Perceptual and Affective Salience of Mothers' Speech to Infants. In L. Feagans, C. Garvey, and R. Golinkoff (eds.), *The Origins and Growth of communication* Norwood, NJ: Ablex, pp. 5−29.

Fernald, A., and T. Simin (1984). Expanded Intonation Contours in Mothers' Speech to Newborns. *Developmental Psychology* 20:104–113.

Fernald, A., J. Dunn, M. Papousek, B. Bardies, L. Camaioni, and T. Taeschner (1986). A Cross-Cultural Study of Parental Speech to Infants. Presented at the International Conference on Infant Studies, Los Angeles, CA (April).

Fodor, J. A. (1980). Reply to Putnam. In *Language and Learning: The Debate between Jean Piaget and Noam Chomsky*, Cambridge, MA: Harvard University Press, pp. 325–334.

Fodor, J. A. (1983). *Modularity of Mind*. Cambridge, MA: The MIT Press.

Forster, L. M. (1982). Vision and Prey-Catching Strategies in Jumping Spiders. *American Scientist* 70:165–175.

Foster, D. H. (1975). Visual Apparent Motion and Some Preferred Paths in the Rotation Group SO(3). *Biological Cybernetics* 18:81–89.

Freyd, J. (1983). Shareability: the Social Psychology of Epistemology. *Cognitive Science* 1:191–210.

Gehring, W. J. (1985). Homeotic Genes, the Homeo Box, and the Genetic Control of Development. *Cold Spring Harbor Symposia on Quantitative Biology* 50:243–251.

Gibson, E. J., and E. S. Spelke (1983). The Development of Perception. In J. H. Flavell and E. M. Markman (eds.), *Handbook of Child Psychology*, Vol. 3: *Cognitive development* New York: Wiley, pp. 1–76.

Goodenough, W. H. (1956). Componential Analysis and the Study of Meaning. *Language* 32:195–216.

Goodenough, W. H. (1967). Componential Analysis. *Science* 156:1203–1209.

Gould, J. L. (1980). The Case of Magnetic Sensitivity in Birds and Bees (Such as It Is). *American Scientist* 68:256–267.

Gould, J. L. (1986). The Locale Map of Honey Bees: Do Insects Have Cognitive Maps? *Science* 232:861–863.

Greenberg, J. H. (1966). *Language Universals with Special Reference to Feature Hierarchies*. The Hague: Mouton & Co.

Heider, R. (1958). *The Psychology of Interpersonal Relations*. New York: Wiley.

Helmholtz, H. von (1862/1954). *On the Sensations of Tone as a Physiological Basis for the Theory of Music*. New York: Dover, 1964 (original German publication, 1862).

Hölldobler, B. (1980). Canopy Orientation: A New Kind of Orientation in Ants. *Science* 210:86–88.

Hopkins, C. D. (1974). Electric Communication in Fish. *American Scientist* 62:426–437.

Hopkins, C. D. (1981). The Neuroethology of Selectric Communication. *Trends in Neurosciences* 4:4–6.

Hutenlocher, J. (1968). Constructing Spatial Images: A Strategy in Reasoning. *Psychological Review* 75:550–560.

Jackson, I. J., P. Schofield, and B. Hogan (1985). A Mouse Homeo Box Gene Is Expressed during Embryogenesis and in Adult Kidney. *Nature* 317:745–748.

Jerrison, H. J. (1985). On the Evolution of Mind. In D. A. Oakley (ed.), *Brain and Mind*, London: Methuen, pp. 1–31.

Jimenez, F., and J. A. Campos-Ortega (1981). A Cell Arrangement Specific to Thoracic Ganglia in the Central Nervous System of the *Drosophila* Embryo: Its Behaviour in Homeotic Mutants. *Wilhelm Roux's Archives of Developmental Biology* 190:370–373.

Johnson, C. H., and J. W. Hastings (1986). The Elusive Mechanism of the Circadian Clock. *American Scientist* 74:29–36.

Johnson-Laird, P. N. (1983). *Mental Models: Towards a Cognitive Science of Language, Inference, and Consciousness*. Cambridge, MA: Harvard University Press.

Just, M. A., and P. A. Carpenter (1985). Cognitive Coordinate Systems: Accounts of Mental Rotation and Individual Differences in Spatial Abilities. *Psychological Review* 92:137–172.

Kaiser, M. K., D. R. Proffitt, and K. Anderson (1984). Sensitivity to Natural Dynamics in Ongoing and Static Displays. Paper presented at the annual Meeting of the Psychonomic Society, San Antonio, TX (November 9).

Kamil, A., and R. Balda (1983). Spatial Memory and Food Cache Recovery by Nutcrackers (*Nucifraga columbiana*). Presented at the meeting of the Psychonomic Society, San Diego, CA (November 17).

Kaufman, T. C., R. Lewis, and B. Wakimoto (1980). Cytogenetic Analysis of Chromosome 3 in *Drosophila melanogaster*: The Homeotic Gene Complex in Polytene Chromosome Interval 84A, B. *Genetics* 94:115–133.

Kessler, E. J., C. Hansen, and R. N. Shepard (1984). Tonal Schemata in the Perception of Music in Bali and in the West. *Music Perception* 2:131–165.

Koshland, B. (1980). *Bacterial Chemotaxis as a Model Behavioral System*. New York: Raven Press.

Kroodsma, D. E., and J. Verner (1978). Complex Singing Behaviors among *Cistothorus* Wrens. *The Awk* 95:703–716.

Krumhansl, C. L. (1979). The Psychological Representation of Musical Pitch in a Tonal Context. *Cognitive Psychology* 11:346–374.

Krumhansl, C. L. (1983). Perceptual Structures for Tonal Music. *Music Perception* 1:24–58.

Krumhansl, C. L., and R. N. Shepard (1979). Quantification of the Hierarchy of Tonal Functions within a Diatonic Context. *Journal of Experimental Psychology: Human Perception and Performance* 5:579–594.

Kruskal, J. B. (1964a). Multidimensional Scaling by Optimizing Goodness of Fit to a Nonmetric Hypothesis. *Psychometrika* 29:1–27.

Kruskal, J. B. (1964b). Nonmetric Multidimensional Scaling: A Numerical Method. *Psychometrika* 29:28–42.

Landau, B., H. Gleitman, and E. Spelke (1981). Spatial Knowledge and Geometric Representation in a Child Blind from Birth. *Science* 213:1275–1278.

Lashley, K. S., and M. Wade (1946). The Pavlovian Theory of Generalization. *Psychological Review* 53:72–87.

Lévi-Strauss, C. (1967). *The Savage Mind*. Chicago: University of Chicago Press, 1967 (original French publication, 1962).

Liben, L. S., A. H. Patterson, and N. Newcombe (eds.) (1981). *Spatial Representation and Behavior across the Life Span*. New York: Academic Press.

Maier, N.R.P. (1929). *Reasoning in White Rats*. Comparative Psychology Monographs 6 (No. 29).

Maloney, L. T., and B. A. Wandell (1986). Color Constancy: A Method for Recovering Surface Spectral Reflectance. *Journal of the Optical Society of America* 3:29–33.

Marler, P., and V. Sherman (1983). Song Structure without Auditory Feedback: Emendations of the Auditory Template Hypothesis. *The Journal of Neuroscience* 3:517–531.

McCloskey, M. (1983). Intuitive Physics. *Scientific American* 248 (4):122–130.

McCloskey, M., A. Caramazza, and B. Green (1980). Curvilinear Motion in the Absence of External Forces: Naive Beliefs about the Motion of Objects. *Science* 210:1139–1141.

Menzel, E. W. (1973). Chimpanzee Spatial Memory Organization. *Science* 182:943–945.

Moeser, S. D., and A. S. Bregman (1972). The Role of Reference in the Acquisition of a Miniature Artificial Language. *Journal of Verbal Learning and Verbal Behavior* 11:759–769.

Newport, E. L. (1981). Constraints on Structure: Evidence from American Sign Language and Language Learning. In W. A. Collins (ed.), *Aspects of the development of Competence. Minnesota Symposia on Child Psychology* (Vol. 14), Hillsdale, NJ: Erlbaum.

Nottebohm, F. (1984). Birdsong as a Model in Which to Study Brain Processes Related to Learning. *The Condor* 86:227–236.

Osgood, C. S., G. J. Suci, and P. H. Tannenbaum (1957). *The Measurement of Meaning.* Urbana, IL: University of Illinois Press.

Pittendrigh, C. S. (1954). On Temperature Independence in the Clock-System Controlling Emergence in *Drosophila. Proceedings of the National Academy of Sciences* 40:1018–1029.

Pollard, P. (1982). Human Reasoning: Some Possible Effects of Availability. *Cognition* 10:65–96.

Pressing, J. (1983). Cognitive Isomorphisms between Pitch and Rhythm in World Musics: West Africa, the Balkans and Western Tonality. *Studies in Music* 17:38–61.

Razran, G. (1949). Stimulus Generalization of Conditioned Responses. *Psychology Bulletin* 46:337–365.

Romney, A. K., and R. G. D'Andrade (1964). Cognitive Aspects of English Kin Terms. *American Anthropologist* 66:146–170.

Rosch, E. (1975a). Cognitive Reference Points. *Cognitive Psychology* 7:532–547.

Rosch, E. (1975b). Cognitive Representation of Semantic Categories. *Journal of Experimental Psychology: General* 104:192–233.

Rosch, E., C. B. Mervis, W. D. Gray, D. M. Johnson, and P. Boynes-Braem (1976). *Cognitive Psychology* 8:382–439.

Rozin, P. (1976). The Evolution of Intelligence and Access to the Cognitive Unconscious. In J. M. Sprague and A. N. Epstein (eds.), *Progress in Psychobiology and Physiological Psychology* New York: Academic Press, pp. 245–280.

Ruddle, R. H., C. P. Hart, A. Awgulewitsch, A. Fainsod, M. Utset, D. Dalton, N. Kerk, M. Rabin, A. Ferguson-Smith, A. Fienberg, and W. McGinnis (1985). Mamalian Homeo Box Genes. *Cold Spring Harbor Symposium in Quantitative Biology* 50:277–284.

Runeson, S. (1977). On the Possibility of "Smart" Perceptual Mechanisms. *Scandinavian Journal of Psychology* 18:172–179.

Rusak, B., and I. Zucker (1975). Biological Rhythms and Animal Behavior. *Annual Review of Psychology* 26:137–171.

Sauer, E. G. F. (1958). Celestial Navigation by Birds. *Scientific American* 199(2):42–47.

Seyfarth,R. M., D. L. Cheney, and P. Marler (1980). Vervet Monkey Alarm Calls: Semantic Communication in a Tree-Ranging Primate. *Animal Behavior* 28:1070–1094.

Shannon, B. (1976). Aristotelianism, Newtonianism and the Physics of the Layman. *Perception* 5.241–243.

Shepard, R. N. (1955). Stimulus and Response Generalization during Paired Associates Learning. Unpublished doctoral dissertation, Yale University.

Shepard, R. N. (1957). Stimulus and Response Generalization: A Stochastic Model Relating Generalization to Distance in Psychological Space. *Psychometrika* 22:325–345.

Shepard, R. N. (1958a). Stimulus and Response Generalization: Deduction of the Generalization Gradient from a Trace Model. *Psychological Review* 65:242–256.

Shepard, R. N. (1958b). Stimulus and Response Generalization: Tests of a Model Relating Generalization to Distance in Psychological Space. *Journal of Experimental Psychology* 55:509–523.

Shepard, R. N. (1962). The Analysis of Proximities: Multidimensional Scaling with an Unknown Distance Function. I. *Psychometrika* 27:125–140; II. *Psychometrika* 27:219–246.

Shepard, R. N. (1964a). Attention and the Metric Structure of the Stimulus Space. *Journal of Mathematical Psychology* 1:54–87.

Shepard, R. N. (1964b). Book Review of E. Feigenbaum and J. Feldman's *Computers and Thought. Behavioral Science* 9:57–65.

Shepard, R. N. (1964c). On Subjectively Optimum Selection among Multiattribute Alternatives. In M. Shelley and G. L. Bryan (eds.), *Human Judgments and Optimality*, New York: Wiley, pp. 257–281.

Shepard, R. N. (1965). Approximation to Uniform Gradients of Generalization by Monotone Transformations of Scale . In D. J. Mostofsky (ed.), *Stimulus Generalization*, Stanford, CA: Stanford University Press, pp. 94–110.

Shepard, R. N. (1966). Learning and Recall as Organization and Search. *Journal of Verbal Learning and Verbal Behavior* 5:201–204.

Shepard, R. N. (1972). Psychological Representation of Speech Sounds. In E. E. David and P. B. Denes (eds.), *Human Communication: A Unified View*, New York: McGraw-Hill, pp. 67–113.

Shepard, R. N. (1975). Form, Formation, and Transformation of Internal Representations. In R. Solso (ed.), *Information Processing and Cognition: The Loyola Symposium*, Hillsdale, NJ: Erlbaum, pp. 87–122.

Shepard, R. N. (1980). Multidimensional Scaling, Tree-Fitting, and Clustering. *Science* 210:390–398.

Shepard, R. N. (1981). Psychophysical Complementarity. In M. Kubovy and J. Pomerantz (eds.), *Perceptual Organization*, Hillsdale, NJ: Erlbaum, pp. 279–341.

Shepard, R. N. (1982a). Geometrical Approximations to the Structure of Musical Pitch. *Psychological Review* 89:305–333.

Shepard, R. N. (1982b). Perceptual and Analogical Bases of Cognition. In J. Mehler, M. Garrett, and E. Walker (eds.), *Perspectives on Mental Representation*, Hillsdale, NJ: Lawrence Erlbaum Associates, pp. 49–67.

Shepard, R. N. (1984a). Ecological Constraints on Internal Representation: Reasonant Kinematics of Perceiving, Imagining, Thinking, and Dreaming. *Psychological Review* 91:417–447.

Shepard, R. N. (1984b). Similarity and a Law of Universal Generalization. Presented at the annual meeting of the Psychonomic Society, San Antonio, TX (November).

Shepard, R. N. (1985). Mental Representations and Psychological Laws. Proposal submitted to the National Science Foundation (February).

Shepard, R. N. (1986). Discrimination and Generalization in Identification and Classification: Comment on Nosofsky. *Journal of Experimental Psychology: General* 115:58–61.

Shepard, R. N., and L. A. Cooper (1982). *Mental Images and Their Transformation.* Cambridge, MA: MIT Press/Bradford Books.

Shepard. R. N., and S. Hurwitz (1984). Upward Direction, Mental Rotation, and Discrimination of Left and Right Turns in Maps. *Cognition* 18:161–193.

Shepard, R. N., and D. Jordan (1984). Auditory Illusions Demonstrating That Tones Are Assimilated to an Internalized Musical Scale. *Science* 226:1333–1334.

Shepard, R. N., and J. Metzler (1971). Mental Rotation of Three-Dimensional Objects. *Science* 171:701–703.

Simon, H. A. (1967). The Architecture of Complexity. *Proceedings of the American Philosophical Society* 106:467–482.

Teugels, E., and A. Ghysen (1983). Independence of the Numbers of Legs and Leg Ganglia in *Drosophila bithorat* Mutants. *Nature* 304:440–442.

Thomson, J. A. (1983). Is Continuous Visual Monitoring Necessary in Visually Guided Locomotion? *Journal of Experimental Psychology: Human Perception and Performance* 9:427–443.

Thorpe, W. H. (1950). A Note on Detour Experiments with *Ammophila pubescens* Curt (Hymenoptera; Sphecidae). *Behaviour* 2:257–264.

Tolman, E. C. (1932). *Purposive Behavior in Animals and Men.* New York: Appleton-Century-Crofts.

Tooby, J., and I. DeVore (1986). The Reconstruction of Hominid Behavioral Evolution through Strategic Modeling. In W. G. Kinzey (ed.), *Primate Models for the Origin of Human Behavior.* New York : SUNY Press.

Tversky, A., and D. Kahneman (1981). The Framing of Decisions and the Psychology of Choice. *Science* 211:453–458.

Vanyo, J. P., R. A. Hutchinson, and S. M. Awramik (1986). *Heliotropism in Microbial Stromatolitic Growths at Yellowstone National Park: Geophysical Inferences.* Elsevier Oceanography Series Transactions (April 1).

von Frisch, K. (1967). *The Dance Language and Orientation of Bees.* Cambridge, MA: Harvard University Press.

Wason, P. C., and P. N. Johnson-Laird (1972). *Psychology of Reasoning: Structure and Content.* London: Batsford.

Wason, P. C., and D. Shapiro (1971). Natural and Contrived Experience in a Reasoning Problem. *Quarterly Journal of Experimental Psychology* 23:63–71.

13

From Evolution to Behavior: Evolutionary Psychology as the Missing Link

Leda Cosmides and John Tooby

Popular wisdom has it that arguments against new ideas in science typically pass through three characteristic stages, from

1. "It's not true," to
2. "Well, it may be true, but it's not important," to
3. "It's true and it's important, but it's not new—we knew it all along."

If the papers in this volume are any indication, then the application of evolutionary biology to the understanding of human behavior has entered the "It's true but not important" stage.

Yet evolutionary theory is important for understanding human behavior, and not everyone knows it—in fact, those most involved in the scientific investigation of "human nature" are generally the most unaware of its implications. We shall argue that the reluctance of many social scientists to appreciate or take advantage of the richness of the evolutionary approach is a direct consequence of a widespread tendency to overlook a crucial link in the causal chain from evolution to behavior: the level of innate psychological mechanisms, described as information processing systems. This level is pivotal, because it describes the mechanisms that actually link the evolutionary process to manifest behavior. It is these mechanisms that evolve over generations; within any single generation it is these mechanisms that, in interaction with environmental input, generate manifest behavior. The causal link between evolution and behavior is made through the psychological mechanism.

Efforts that skip this step in the evolutionary analysis of behavior, as valuable as they may be in other ways, have contributed to an erroneous caricature of the evolutionary approach to behavior as offering nothing more than post hoc compilations of correspondences between behavior and loosely reinterpreted evolutionary theory. But a rejection of the evolutionary approach based on such an incomplete and misleading character-

We would like to thank David Buss, George Cosmides, and Roger Shepard for their very helpful comments on an earlier version of this paper, and Roger Shepard for all the encouragement and support he has given us.

ization of its nature and valid possibilities is mistaken: as we shall discuss, the search for order in human behavior requires the application of the emerging principles of evolutionary psychology. We shall argue that an approach drawn from evolutionary psychology, consistently applied, can repair many of the deficiencies that have hampered progress in the social sciences.

1 Natural Selection Theory Does Not Predict Invariance in the Manifest Behavior of Different Individuals

Sciences prosper when researchers discover the level of analysis appropriate for describing and investigating their particular subject: when researchers discover the level where invariance emerges, the level of underlying order. What is confusion, noise, or random variation at one level resolves itself into systematic patterns upon the discovery of the level of analysis suited to the phenomena under study. The lack of success the behavioral sciences have had since their founding has been explained either by the claim that no such science is possible (e.g., human complexity intrinsically transcends any attempt to discover fundamental patterns) or by the view we share, that progress has been slow because scientific efforts have not yet, for the most part, been framed using concepts and organizing principles suitable to the phenomena under study. Can such an appropriate level of inquiry be found for a science of human behavior? Because humans are the product of the evolutionary process, the explanation for their characteristics must be sought in the evolutionary process: for a science of human behavior, the level of underlying order is to be sought in an evolutionary approach.

However, using evolution as an informing concept is not enough. During the formative period of modern behavioral ecology in the 1970s, many researchers thought that evolutionary biology would revolutionize research in human behavior; this conviction spread after the publication of E. O. Wilson's *Sociobiology* drew widespread attention to the dramatic advances that were taking place in the application of evolution to behavior. Many thought that evolutionary theory would reveal the level of underlying order, that the apparent variation in human behavior would resolve itself into systematic patterns, that invariant relationships would be identified, and that a true social science would emerge. However, after more than a decade, this is a revolution still waiting to happen.

We shall argue that the reason that progress has been slow is that, in the rush to apply evolutionary insights to a science of human behavior, many researchers have made a conceptual "wrong turn," leaving a gap in the evolutionary approach that has limited its effectiveness. This wrong turn has consisted of attempting to apply evolutionary theory directly to the level of manifest behavior, rather than using it as a heuristic guide for the discovery of innate psychological mechanisms.

The attempt to find evolutionary invariants at the level of manifest behavior has created a series of difficulties, from forced typological approaches, to using the "optimality" of manifest behavior (or the lack of it) as the measure of the success of the evolutionary paradigm. The assumption that manifest behavior should be invariant across individuals has invited a brute force, typological approach to variation in, for example, cross-cultural studies and primate behavior. All too often, the researcher would take the observed variation, average it, and typify the species or group by that average (see Tooby and DeVore, 1987, for a more extensive discussion of this problem). The variation itself is considered noise, or an embarrassment to be explained away. Those social scientists skeptical that biology had anything to offer to an understanding of human behavior would dwell on the extraordinary complexity of human behavior, and its enormous and engaging variety, and counterpose this richness to the clear explanatory inadequacy of what they considered to be naive and simplistic typological characterizations.

Yet natural selection theory itself predicts that the manifest behavior of different individuals will vary enormously. Furthermore, it deductively implies that an individual's behavior will often appear far from "optimal," when optimality is defined without respect to the individual's social environment. The reasons why this is so are summarized by Tooby and DeVore (1987), in their discussion of hominid behavioral evolution. They include the following:

1. The interests of different individuals are often in conflict; in fact, much of modern evolutionary theory analyzes the conflicting fitness interests of different categories of individuals [e.g., self versus kin (Hamilton, 1964), parent versus offspring (Trivers, 1974), male versus female (Trivers, 1972)]. An interaction between individuals whose fitness interests conflict cannot, in principle, produce an outcome that is optimal for both individuals. The outcome will either be optimal for one party but not the other, or it will be nonoptimal for both.

2. Therefore, larger patterns of social behavior are not necessarily optimal for any individual or group of individuals, but rather may be the emergent result of the conflicting interests of interacting individuals, each selected to promote its own inclusive fitness. Frequently, therefore, the behavior of an individual cannot be understood in isolation; its behavior will be the mutual result of its interests and the counterstrategies of those with whom the individual is associated.

3. Individuals are selected to be adapted to their individual situation, not simply to their local habitat. For example, an individual's best

behavioral strategy may depend on its size, its health, its aggressive formidability, its facility at accruing resources, or the number of sibs it can rely on for support. This means that organisms may be selected to be facultative strategists (where appropriate) rather than inflexibly committed to the same behavior or morphology. Consequently, individuals with the same psychological programming may manifest different behaviors in response to the different information they derive from assessing their own abilities and resources.

4. For certain social and reproductive behaviors, the favored strategy will depend on the distribution of other behaviors in the population [the prevailing analytic tool for dealing with this is game theory and evolutionarily stable strategies (Maynard Smith and Price, 1973)]. In such situations, selection can produce facultative psychological mechanisms that are sensitive to information indicating the distribution of relevant behaviors in the local population.

5. To be selected for, a trait need not be advantageous under every conceivable circumstance. It need only be of benefit *on balance*. This means it must be advantageous more often than not, or that the frequency with which it is advantageous, times the magnitude of the advantage, outweighs the frequency of disadvantage times the cost. Thus, selection for a trait is always against a background probability distribution of ancestral environmental conditions, and cannot be understood when abstracted from this background.

6. Therefore, natural selection cannot be expected to produce behavioral responses that maximize fitness under every imaginable circumstance. The situational specificity of adaptation depends on the selective history of similar situations. The degree of situational adaptation manifested by individuals will be a matter of (a) how common in the species' evolutionary history that situation has been, (b) how long (in phylogenetic terms) it has been recurring, and (c) how large its fitness consequences are. Organisms will be well adapted to common, important situations, reasonably adapted to common less important situations and uncommon highly important situations, but not adapted to uncommon, unimportant situations.

7. The recognition that adaptive specializations have been shaped by the statistical features of ancestral environments is especially important in the study of human behavior. Our species spent over 99% of its evolutionary history as hunter-gatherers in Pleistocene environments. Human psychological mechanisms should be adapted to those environments, not necessarily to the twentieth-century industrialized world. The rapid technological and cultural changes of the last several thousand years have created many situations, both important and unimportant, that would have been uncommon (or nonexistent) in

Pleistocene conditions. Evolutionary theorists ought not to be surprised when evolutionarily unprecedented environmental inputs yield maladaptive behavior. Our ability to walk fails us hopelessly when we are chased off a cliff.

Consequently, behavioral variation is not an embarrassment to evolutionary theory, it is a prediction of evolutionary theory. Equally, the assumption that individuals pursue strategies that will tend to promote their inclusive fitness deductively entails that (1) an individual's theoretically "optimal" behavioral strategy will vary, depending on the composition of its social group, and (2) an interaction between individuals whose fitness interests conflict cannot, in principle, produce an outcome that is optimal for both individuals. Typological approaches to manifest human behavior, involving attempts to interpret such behavior in terms of evolutionary optimality, violate these deductive implications of natural selection theory. For these and other reasons, the search for invariance on the level of manifest behavior will have very limited success.

When the appropriate level of analysis is found, variation becomes fuel in the search for order: instead of averaging out variation, one looks for systematic relations among the different varying elements. What is variable at one level manifests order—that is, invariance—at another. Instead of lamenting the complex variations in human behavior, researchers can use patterns in behavioral variation positively, as clues to the nature of the psychological mechanisms that produce behavior.

2 Evolution → Psychological Mechanism → Behavior

To speak of natural selection as selecting for "behaviors" is a convenient shorthand, but it is misleading usage. The error is worth belaboring, because the failure to appreciate it has delayed the fruitful application of evolutionary theory to human behavior by years. When used too casually, this shorthand misleads because it obscures the most important level of proximate causation: the psychological mechanism.

Natural selection cannot select for behavior per se; it can only select for mechanisms that produce behavior. There is nothing special about behavior in this regard; the same can be said, for example, of digestion. Natural selection can only rearrange patterns in tissues and molecules; these rearrangements have *effects*, and it is because they have these effects that they are selected for or not. Natural selection gives us teeth, salivary amylase, a peristaltic esophagus, an acid-filled stomach, an absorptive colon: mechanisms that produce digestion. The operation of these mechanisms causes certain molecules to be extracted from plant and animal tissues and incorporated into our own tissues: an effect that we call digestion. Natural selection gives us food processing machinery, and the operation of this machinery results in digestion, which is an effect of the functioning of mechanisms.

Behavior, like digestion, is an effect of the functioning of mechanisms. Natural selection can give you a reflex arc, and the functioning of this arc causes an effect: your leg swings when your knee is tapped. But this effect cannot occur in the absence of a mechanism for producing it. Behavior cannot occur sui generis; behavior is an effect produced by a causal system: proximately, by psychological mechanisms. Although researchers would acknowledge these points as patently obvious, in practice, many simply methodologically leapfrog this level, with unfortunate consequences such as those discussed. Their desire to do this stems, in many cases, from the belief that the exploration of mechanisms means the exploration of the neurophysiological bases of behavior, a difficult endeavor, and one that, at the present state of knowledge, is limited to addressing only very simple kinds of behaviors. However, there exists an alternative approach to the study of psychological mechanisms that does not involve neurophysiology, with its present limitations. This is the characterization of psychological mechanisms in terms of their information processing structure. This approach dovetails smoothly with evolution, because in the adaptive regulation of behavior, information is key.

Behavior is not randomly emitted; it is elicited by information, which is gleaned from the organism's external environment, and, proprioceptively, from its internal states. Natural selection gave us information processing machinery to produce behavior, just as it gave us food processing machinery to produce digestion. This machinery selects—and frequently seeks—particular information from the environment; it manipulates it, extracts inferences from it, stores some of it in memory in altered form; the machinery's output is used to make mental models, to inform other parts of the system, and to instruct the motor neurons responsible for behavior. *The evolutionary function of the human brain is to process information in ways that lead to adaptive behavior*; the mind is a description of the operation of a brain that maps informational input onto behavioral output.

Thus, behavior is one output of our information processing machinery. Behavioral output differs with informational input; the information processing machinery that maps informational input onto behavioral output is a psychological mechanism.

The psychology of an organism consists of the total set of proximate mechanisms that cause behavior. Natural selection, acting over evolutionary time, shapes these mechanisms so that the behavior of the organism correlates to some degree with its fitness. However, in the lifetime of any particular animal, it is the proximate mechanisms that actually cause behavior—not natural selection. If these proximate mechanisms can be understood, behavior can be predicted more exactly; understanding the fitness-promoting strategies studied by evolutionary theorists allows only approximate prediction. Behavior correlates exactly with proximate mechanisms, but only approximately with the fitness-promoting strategies that shaped those mechanisms.

Evolutionary psychology (Tooby, 1985) relates explanations in terms of adaptive strategy to explanations in terms of proximate mechanisms. Correct characterization of adaptive strategies gives precise meaning to the concept of function for proximate mechanisms. Reciprocally, a detailed analysis of the proximate mechanisms of a species gives rich insight into the present and past selective pressures that have acted on it. Psychological mechanisms constitute the missing causal link between evolutionary theory and behavior. Evolutionary theory frequently appears to lack predictive value because most researchers skip this crucial predictive and explanatory level. Yet it is the proximate mechanisms that cause behavior that promise to reveal the level of underlying order for a science of human behavior.

3 The Cognitive Level of Explanation

Psychological mechanisms can be studied on different descriptive and explanatory levels. Most biologically informed studies of proximate mechanisms have described psychological mechanisms in tems of their physiological underpinnings, finding, for example, that birth spacing is mediated by lactation, which suppresses ovulation, that testosterone levels change with shifts in dominance, thereby affecting agonistic behavior, or that one part of the brain controls language while another part controls sexual behavior.

But natural selection theory, so far, has made only limited contributions to the investigation of physiology. Just as different kinds of hardware can run the same computer program, different physiological mechanisms can accomplish the same adaptive function. Both humans and pitcher plants digest animal tissues, but the physiological mechanisms by which humans and pitcher plants accomplish this function are different. And there is another, pragmatic problem: unless you know that a particular information processing system exists and what its function is, it is very difficult to discover its physiological underpinnings. Who would look for the physiological mechanisms responsible for the contraction of the heart unless they first knew that the heart exists and that its function is to pump blood?

Although valuable, physiological studies do not address a crucial *functional* level of explanation, a level that describes what a mechanism does, rather than how it does it. Evolutionarily oriented students of human behavior have neglected what may prove to be the most important level of proximate causation: the cognitive level. *Adaptive behavior is predicated on adaptive thought*: an animal must process information from its environment in ways that lead to fit behaviors while excluding unfit behaviors. The cognitive level of explanation describes psychological mechanisms in functional terms, as programs that process information.[1]

Traditionally, ethologists have studied very simple cognitive programs: a newborn herring gull has a cognitive program that defines a red dot on the end of a beak as salient information from the environment, and that causes the newborn to peck at the red dot upon perceiving it. Its mother has a cognitive program that defines pecking at her red dot as salient information from her environment, and that causes her to regurgitate food into the newborn's mouth when she perceives its pecks.

Note that the descriptions of these simple programs are entirely in terms of the functional relationships among different pieces of information; they describe two simple information processing systems. Naturally, these programs are instantiated in some kind of neurological "hardware." However, knowledge of this hardware would add little to our understanding of these programs as information processing systems—presumably, one could build a silicon-based robot that would produce the same behavioral output in response to the same informational input. The robot's cognitive programs would maintain the same functional relationships among pieces of information, and therefore be identical to the cognitive programs of the herring gull. However, the robot's "neural" hardware would be totally different. The specification of a cognitive program constitutes a complete description of an important level of proximate causation, independent of any knowledge of the physiological mechanisms by which the program is instantiated.

We assume that the cognitive programs of different individuals[2] of a species are essentially the same—that cognitive programs are species-typical traits. However, the parameters fed into them can be expected to differ with individual circumstance. Insofar as individual variation in personal qualities (such as aggressive formidability or sexual attractiveness), in opportunities to engage in particular behaviors (to mate, to threaten, to help), and in the social and physical environment, are all parameters that feed into the same cognitive programs, variations in these parameters will produce variations in manifest behavior across individuals. Therefore, although the cognitive programs of different individuals should be essentially the same, the manifest behavior of different individuals may be different.[3] Cognitive programs constitute the level of invariance for a science of human behavior, not behavior itself.

When applied to behavior, natural selection theory is more closely allied with the cognitive level of explanation than with any other level of proximate causation. This is because the cognitive level seeks to specify a psychological mechanism's function, and natural selection theory is a theory of function. Natural selection theory specifies how an organism should respond to different kinds of information from its environment. It defines adaptive information processing problems that the organism must have some means of solving. Cognitive programs are solutions to information processing problems.

An evolutionary approach to understanding the cognitive level of proximate causation asks, What kind of programming must an organism have if it is to extract and process information about its environment in a way that will lead to adaptive behavior? How does the organism use information from its environment to compute what constitutes the "right" behavior at the right place and the right time (Staddon, this volume)?

4 Evolution and the Cognitive Level

It is nearly impossible to discover how a psychological mechanism processes information unless one knows what its function is, what it was "designed" or selected to do. Trying to map out a cognitive program without knowing what its function is, is like attempting to understand a computer program by examining it in machine language, without knowing whether it is for editing text, accounting, or launching the Space Shuttle. It is possible that a gifted programmer may finally figure it out, but not probable. If, on the other hand, the programmer knows that the program she is trying to map out is a text editor, she can begin by looking for a way of loading text, or for a command that will delete a word, or for a procedure that will move a whole paragraph. It is far easier to understand the architecture of a "black box" if one knows what it was designed to do.

Recognizing this, a number of cognitive scientists, such as Chomsky, Shepard, Fodor, and Marr, recently have argued that the best way to understand any mechanism, either mental or physical, is first to ask what its purpose is, what problem was it designed to solve (e.g., Chomsky, 1975; Shepard, 1981; Fodor, 1983; Marr and Nishihara, 1978).

This is exactly the question that evolutionary theory allows one to address—it allows one to pinpoint the kinds of problems the human mind was "designed" to solve, and consequently should be very good at solving. And although it cannot tell one the exact structure of the cognitive programs that solve these problems, it can suggest what design features they are likely to have. It allows one to develop a "computational theory" for that problem domain: a theory specifying what functional characteristics a mechanism capable of solving that problem must have (Marr, 1982; Marr and Nishihara, 1978).

Many cognitive psychologists assume that the human mind is a general-purpose computer with domain-general, content-independent processes. We shall argue that from an evolutionary point of view, this is a highly implausible and unparsimonious assumption, and logically impossible to sustain. There are domains of human activity for which the evolutionarily appropriate information processing strategy is complex, and deviations from this strategy result in large fitness costs. An organism that relied on the vagaries of trial-and-error learning for such domains would be at a selective disadvantage (see also Shepard, 1981).

Instead, for such domains, humans should have evolved "Darwinian algorithms"—specialized learning mechanisms that organize experience into adaptively meaningful schemas or frames (Cosmides, 1985). When activated by appropriate environmental or proprioceptive information, these innately specified "frame-builders" should focus attention, organize perception and memory, and call up specialized procedural knowledge that will lead to domain-appropriate inferences, judgments, and choices. Like Chomsky's language acquisition device, these inference procedures allow you to "go beyond the information given"—to reason adaptively even in the face of incomplete or degraded information (Bruner, 1973).

There are many domains of human activity that should have Darwinian algorithms associated with them. Aggressive threat, mate choice, sexual behavior, pair-bonding, parenting, parent-offspring conflict, friendship, kinship, resource accrual, resource distribution, disease avoidance, predator avoidance, and social exchange are but a few. The dynamics of natural selection rigidly constrain the patterns of behavior that can evolve in such domains, and therefore provide insights into the structure of the cognitive programs that produce these patterns.

In the remainder of this article we present arguments supporting this perspective.

5 Complex Adaptive Problems Should Be Defined in Computational Theories

The signal lesson lurking beneath the surface of modern evolutionary theory is that adaptive behavior requires the solution of many information processing problems that are highly complex—far more complex than commonly supposed. The cognitive programs that allow the newborn herring gull to gain sustenance from its mother are relatively simple: they directly connect the perception of an environmental cue with an adaptively appropriate behavioral response. But not all adaptive problems are so easily solved, and many complex adaptive problems can be solved only by complex cognitive programs.

Discovering the structure of complex cognitive programs requires a great deal of theoretical guidance. A series of hunt-and-peck experiments may uncover a few simple cognitive programs, but it is unlikely that a research program that is blind to function will ever uncover the structure of a complex information processing system—such as the human mind.

What form should this theoretical guidance take? In his pioneering studies of visual perception, David Marr argued that "computational theories" of each information processing problem must be developed before progress can be made in experimentally investigating the cognitive programs that solve them (e.g., Marr, 1982; Marr and Nishihara, 1978). A computational theory specifies the nature of an information processing problem. It does this by incorporating "constraints on the way the world is structured—constraints that provide sufficient information to allow the processing to succeed" (Marr and Nishihara, 1978, p. 41). A computational theory is an answer to the question, What must happen if a particular function is to be accomplished?

For example, the information processing problem that Marr wanted to understand was how an organism reconstructs three-dimensional objects in the world from a two-dimensional retinal display. As you walk around a table with a square top, for example, light reflected from the tabletop hits your retina, projecting upon it a two-dimensional trapezoid of changing dimensions. Yet you do not perceive an ever-deforming, two-dimensional trapezoid. Instead, your cognitive programs use these data to construct a "percept" of a stable, three-dimensional, square tabletop.

To understand how we compute solid objects from data like this, Marr and his colleagues first examined relevant constraints and relationships that exist in the world, like the reflectant properties of surfaces. They consider the discovery of such constraints the "critical act" in formulating a theory of this computation, because these constraints must somehow be used by and embodied in any cognitive mechanism capable of solving this problem (Marr, 1982; Marr and Nishihara, 1978). Marr calls the specification of such constraints, together with their deductive implications, a "computational theory" of an information processing problem.

Natural selection, in a particular ecological situation, defines and constitutes "valid constraints on the way the world is structured," and therefore can be used to create computational theories of adaptive information processing problems. For example, the cognitive programs of an organism that confers benefits on kin cannot violate the [cost to self < (benefit to kin member) × (coefficient of relatedness to kin member)] constraint of kin selection theory. Cognitive programs that violate this constraint cannot be selected for. Cognitive programs that instantiate this constraint can be selected for. This is inherent in the dynamics of natural selection, true of any species on any planet at any time. A species may lack the ability to confer benefits on kin, but if it has such an ability, then it has it by virtue of cognitive programs that produce behavior that respects this constraint.

The production of behavior that respects constraints imposed by the evolutionary process is a cognitive program's *adaptive function*: the reason it was selected for, the reason it could outcompete other cognitive programs and spread through the population to become a species-typical trait.

The specification of constraints imposed by the evolutionary process—

the specification of an adaptive function—does not, in itself, constitute a complete computational theory. These constraints merely define what counts as adaptive behavior. Cognitive programs are the means by which behavior—adaptive or otherwise—is produced. The important question for a computational theory to address is, What kind of cognitive programs must an organism have if it is to behave adaptively?

Natural selection theorists do not usually think of their theories as defining information processing problems, yet this is precisely what they do. For example, kin selection theory raises—and answers—questions such as, How should the information that X is your brother affect your decision to help him? How should your assessment of the cost to you of helping your brother, versus the benefit to your brother of receiving your help, affect your decision? Will the information that Y is your cousin have a different effect on your decision than if you thought Y were your brother? In general, how should information about your relatedness to X, the costs and benefits to you of what X wants you to do for him, and the costs and benefits to X of your coming to his aid, affect your decision to help X?

As these questions show, an organism's behavior cannot fall within the bounds of the constraints imposed by the evolutionary process unless it is guided by cognitive programs that can solve certain information processing problems that are very specific. To confer benefits on kin in accordance with the constraints of kin selection theory, the organism must have cognitive programs that allow it to extract certain specific information from its environment: who are its relatives? which kin are close and which distant? what are the costs and benefits of an action to itself? to its kin? The organism's behavior will be random with respect to the constraints of kin selection theory unless (1) it has some means of extracting information relevant to these questions from its environment, and (2) it has well-defined decision rules that use this information in ways that instantiate the theory's constraints. A cognitive system can generate adaptive behavior only if it can perform specific information processing tasks such as these.

The fact that any organism capable of conferring benefits on its kin must have cognitive programs capable of solving these information processing problems does not imply that different species will solve each problem via the same cognitive program. There are many reasons why such programs may differ. For example, different environmental cues may have different reliabilities and accessibilities for different species. Moreover, each species occupies a different ecological niche, and hence the value of particular actions will differ across species: the cognitive programs of a baboon will assign a different value to social grooming than will the cognitive programs of a whale. But cognitive programs that perform the same function in different species may differ in more profound ways: the cognitive programs for recognizing kin might operate through phenotype matching in one species, but through early imprinting in another species. Both programs will accomplish the same important adaptive function. Yet they will embody radically different information processing procedures, and they will process different information from the environment.

Natural selection theory can be used to develop computational theories of adaptive information processing problems. As we shall show below, such computational theories are valuable as heuristic guides for psychological research, despite the fact that evolutionary theory does not uniquely specify which cognitive programs will be used to accomplish a given function.

6 The Importance of Computational Theories

The most essential part of a computational theory is a catalog of the specific information processing problems entailed by the constraints of natural selection theory. They should be made explicit, for they are the building blocks of psychological theories. There are two reasons why this is so.

The first is obvious. Knowing, for example, that an organism must have some means of distinguishing kin from nonkin may not uniquely determine the structure of a cognitive program, but it does help narrow hypotheses. The cognitive program responsible must be sensitive to environmental cues that correlate with kin, but do not correlate with non-kin. In most cases, very few cues from the species environment of evolutionary adaptedness will be sufficiently reliable or accessible, and the researcher can very quickly discover which are used by the organism's cognitive programs. Discovering which cues are used will illuminate other of the program's information processing procedures: early exposure suggests an imprinting process, whereas facial similarity suggests phenotype matching procedures. Step by step, deduction by deduction, the cognitive programs responsible for kin recognition can be mapped. In the meantime, the researcher who is blind to function will not even be looking for a program that guides kin recognition, let alone figure out which environmental stimuli it monitors, and how it processes them.

The second reason why a fully elaborated computational theory is essential is less obvious, but far more important. The computational theory allows a test of adequacy that any proposed psychological theory must be able to pass. The test is this: *Is the hypothesized system of cognitive programs powerful enough to realize the computational theory? That is, is the proposed mechanism capable of solving the adaptive problem?*

Any proposed cognitive system must be powerful enough to produce adaptive behaviors while *not* simultaneously producing maladaptive behaviors. Not just any cognitive program will do: our cognitive programs must be constructed in such a way that they somehow lead to the adaptive results specified by evolutionary theory on the basis of the information available. This crucial test of adequacy may allow researchers to eliminate whole categories of hypotheses, for current research in cognitive psychology and artificial intelligence suggests that many of the general-purpose learning theories that were popular in psychology's past are not powerful enough to solve even simple computational problems, let alone the complex problems posed by natural selection theory.

7 The Computational Theory Test

Thirty years ago, the study of the psychology of language took a major stride forward when Noam Chomsky developed a computational theory that allowed him to test whether certain hypothesized learning mechanisms were powerful enough to account for how humans acquire the ability to produce grammatical sentences. By this method, he was able to falsify the hypothesis that humans learn language through operant conditioning. Subsequently, others have used this method as a primary tool in constructing alternative psychological theories of language that are more powerful, and therefore more promising (for review, see Wanner and Gleitman, 1982). This incident shows that the "computational theory test" can provide an enormously effective tool for psychological theory.

Chomsky's (1957, 1959) computational theory was the grammar of the English language: a set of rules that can generate all the grammatical sentences of English, but no ungrammatical sentences. The information processing problem to be solved was, How do we learn this grammar? Can it be learned via the simple, stimulus-response (S-R) information processing mechanisms proposed by the behaviorists of the time, or does the acquisition of a natural language grammar require cognitive programming that is more specialized and complex?

Chomsky demonstrated that the general-purpose, S-R learning mechanisms proposed by the behaviorists were not powerful enough to allow one to acquire English grammar: they were not powerful enough to permit the speaker to produce many grammatical sentences, nor could they prevent the speaker from producing many ungrammatical sentences.

Native speakers of English have internalized its grammar; Chomsky showed that the behaviorists' learning mechanisms could not, in principle, account for this fact. He thereby falsified the hypothesis that we acquire grammar via such mechanisms. In fact, this computational theory test allowed him to eliminate a whole class of hypotheses: those invoking learning mechanisms that embody a "finite state grammar" (Chomsky, 1957).

This demonstration was an important turning point in the development of modern psychology. Up until that point, psychology had been dominated by behaviorism's general-purpose learning theories. These theories were *domain general*: the same process was supposed to account for learning in all domains of human activity, from suckling at the breast to the most esoteric feat of modern technology. Yet by specifying what actually needed to be accomplished in order to produce grammatical utterances, Chomsky showed that a task routinely mastered by two-year-old children was too complexly structured to be accounted for by behaviorist learning theory.

Chomsky's specification of a computational theory convinced many psychologists that no general-purpose learning mechanism would be powerful enough to permit the acquisition of the grammar of a natural language under natural conditions. But what kind of learning mechanism *would* have the requisite power? Chomsky (1980) argued that just as the body has many different organs, each of which is specialized for performing a different function—a heart for pumping blood, a liver for detoxifying poisons—the mind can be expected to include many different "mental organs." A mental organ is an information processing system that is specialized for performing a specific cognitive function. A mental organ instantiates learning theories that are *domain specific*: its procedures are specialized for quick and efficient learning about an evolutionarily important domain of human activity. Chomsky argued that the acquisition of a grammar could be accomplished only through a highly structured and complex "language acquisition device": a functionally distinct mental organ that is specialized for learning a language.

The controversy between Chomsky and the behaviorists has broad applicability. Many psychologists think of it as a controversy about innateness, but, as we shall see below, it was not. "Innate" is not the "opposite" of "learned." Every coherent learning theory—even Hume's associationism—assumes the existence of innate cognitive mechanisms that structure experience.[4] A "blank slate" will stay forever blank: Without innate cognitive mechanisms, learning is impossible (e.g., Hume, 1977/1748; Kant, 1966/1781; Quine, 1969; Popper, 1972). Rather, the controversy in psycholinguistics is important because it highlights the ambiguity of the most central concept in the history of psychology: learning.

8 "Learning" Is Not an "Alternative Hypothesis"

Many common concepts in the social sciences are used as if they are hypotheses and explanations, but in fact are not. "Learning" is a concept that many people believe is fully freighted with meaning; analytically, however, the only meaning to the word "learned" is "environmentally influenced." As a hypothesis to account for mental or behavioral phenomena, it is nearly devoid of meaning. Processes categorized as "learning" are accomplished through information processing mechanisms. Such mechanisms may be simple or complex, domain general, or domain specific. An organism may have many different learning mechanisms, or just a few. The belief that the human mind contains only one, simple, domain general cognitive process that results in "learning"—be it "induction" or "hypothesis testing" or "conditioning"—is nothing but conjecture. It has no basis in fact, and can only be explained as a metatheoretical holdover from the heyday of behaviorism.

In reality, the controversy in psycholinguistics was over whether the innate learning mechanisms that allow humans to acquire a grammar are simple and domain general or complex and domain specific (e.g., Atherton and Schwartz, 1974; Chomsky, 1975; Katz, 1975; Marshall, 1981; Putnam, 1967). The behaviorists thought that the simple, domain general processes of classical and operant conditioning could account for language; Chomsky showed that they could not, and proposed the existence of learning mechanisms that were complex and domain specific. Both camps agreed that language is "learned"; they disagreed about *how* it is learned.

The failure to grasp this point leads to enormous conceptual confusion in the behavioral sciences. The common belief that "learning" is an alternative hypothesis to an evolutionary theory of adaptive function is a category error. Learning is a cognitive process. An adaptive function is not a cognitive process; it is a problem that is solved by a cognitive process. Learning is accomplished through psychological mechanisms (whose nature is not yet understood), and these were created through the evolutionary process, which includes natural selection. Consequently, the issue is not whether a behavior is the result of natural selection "or" learning. The issue is, What kind of learning mechanisms would natural selection have produced?

When models of cognitive programs become sufficiently well specified actually to account for empirical results, they often turn out to be complex and domain specific. When researchers present such well-specified models together with the empirical results that support them, they are often met with the counter-claim that "people might learn to think that way." Yet, the invocation of an unspecified learning process does not constitute a valid alternative hypothesis. Suggesting that "learning" is an alternative hypothesis is comparable to claiming that an alternative hypothesis to a well-specified theory of vision, such as Marr's (1982), is, "Light hits the retina and this causes the organism to see three-dimensional objects." This is not an explanation; it is a description of the phenomenon to be explained. All the intervening steps are missing: it does not count as an "alternative hypothesis" because no one has bothered to specify the nature of the cognitive programs that cause it to happen.

"Learning" designates the phenomenon to be explained. A complex, domain specific cognitive program *is* a learning mechanism; how, then, can "learning" be construed as an "alternative hypothesis"?

The claim that a behavior is the product of "culture" is not an "alternative hypothesis" either. It entails nothing more than the claim that surrounding or preceding individuals are an environmental factor that have influenced the behavior under discussion in some way. It leaves the learning mechanisms that allow humans to acquire and generate culture completely unspecified (Tooby and Cosmides, 1987).

In speaking with evolutionary biologists and evolutionarily oriented anthropologists, we find that many operate from the implicit premise that an organism can "decide" which course of action, however complex, will maximize its inclusive fitness simply by inspecting the environment. These researchers interpret the fact that humans were produced by the evolutionary process to mean that humans must be maximizing their inclusive fitness in all situations—even in evolutionarily unprecedented modern environments. This view makes sense only if one believes that the organism has a "simple" cognitive program that says, "Do that which maximizes your inclusive fitness." Yet this is merely a veiled way of claiming that the organism "learns" what to do to maximize its fitness. It is not a hypothesis. It leaves "learning" a mysterious, omniscient, and utterly unspecified process.

It is improper to invoke an undefined process as an explanation. "Learning" should not be invoked to explain other phenomena at this point in the history of science, because it is itself a phenomenon that requires explanation. The nature of the cognitive processes that allow learning to occur are far from understood.

The tendency to assume that learning is accomplished only through a few simple domain general mechanisms lingers in cognitive psychology. We believe this metatheoretical stance is seriously flawed, and persists only because psychologists and evolutionary biologists have not joined forces to create computational theories that catalog the specific and detailed information processing problems entailed by the need to track fitness under Pleistocene conditions. Below, we join Rozin (1976), Shepard (1981), and Symons (1987) in arguing that a consideration of such problems suggests that natural selection has produced a great many cognitive programs that are complex and highly domain specific.

In this article, cognitive programs that evolved to accomplish important adaptive functions are called "Darwinian algorithms" (Cosmides, 1985).[5] We now turn to the question, Does natural selection theory suggest that most Darwinian algorithms will be domain general, or domain specific?

9 Why Should Darwinian Algorithms Be Specialized and Domain Specific?

> Nature has kept us at a great distance from all her secrets, and has
> afforded us only the knowledge of a few superficial qualities of ob-
> jects; while she conceals from us those powers and principles, on
> which the influence of these objects entirely depends. Our senses
> inform us of the colour, weight, and consistence of bread; but neither
> sense nor reason can ever inform us of those qualities, which fit it for
> the nourishment and support of a human body. (David Hume,
> 1977/1748, p. 21)

Genes coding for psychological mechanisms that promote the inclusive
fitness of their bearers will outcompete those that do not, and tend to
become fixed in the population. The promotion of inclusive fitness is an
evolutionary "end"; a psychological mechanism is a means by which that
end is achieved. Can the human mind be comprised primarily of domain
general and content-independent psychological mechanisms, and yet realize this evolutionary end? We shall argue that natural selection could not
have produced such a psyche, nor could such a hypothetical psyche successfully promote fitness, that is, regulate behavior adaptively.

Consider how Jesus explains the derivation of the Mosaic code to his
disciples:

> Jesus said unto him, "Thou shalt love the Lord, thy God, with all thy
> heart, and with all thy soul, and with all thy mind. This is the first and
> great commandment. And the second is like it, Thou shalt love thy
> neighbor as thyself. *On these two commandments hang all the law and
> the prophets.*" (Matthew 22 : 37–40, emphasis added)

Jesus has given his disciples a domain general, content-independent decision rule to be used in guiding their behavior. But what does it mean *in
practice*? Real life consists of concrete, specific situations. How, from this
rule, do I infer what counts as "loving my neighbor as myself" when, to
pick a standard biblical example, my neighbor's ox falls into my pit? Should
I recompense him, or him me? By how much? How should I behave when I
find my neighbor sleeping with my spouse? Should I fast on holy days?
Should I work on the Sabbath? What counts as fulfilling these commandments? How do I know when I have fulfilled them?

In what sense does all the law "hang" from these two commandments?

These derivations are not obvious or straightforward. That is why the
Talmud was written. The Talmud is a "domain specific" document: an
interpretation of the "law" that tells you what actions fulfill the injunctions
to "love God" and "love your neighbor" in the concrete, specific situations
you are likely to encounter in real life. The Talmud solves the "frame

problem" (e.g., Boden, 1977; Fodor, 1983) posed by a "domain general" rule like Jesus'.

A domain general decision rule such as "Do that which maximizes your inclusive fitness" cannot guide behavior in ways that actually do maximize fitness, because what counts as fit behavior differs from domain to domain. Therefore, like the Talmud, psychological mechanisms governing evolutionarily important domains of human activity must be domain specific.

The easiest way to see that Darwinian algorithms must be domain specific is to ask whether the opposite is possible: In theory, could one construct a domain general, content-independent decision rule, that, for any two courses of action, would evaluate which better serves the end of maximizing inclusive fitness?

Such a rule must include a criterion for assessing inclusive fitness: there must be some observable environmental variable against which courses of action from any domain of human activity can be measured. As the maximization of inclusive fitness means differential representation of genes in subsequent generations, the time at which the consequence of an action can be assessed is remote from the time the action is taken. For simplicity's sake, let us assume that number of grandoffspring produced by the end of one's life is an adequate assessment of inclusive fitness. Using this criterion, the decision rule can be rephrased more precisely as, "Choose the course of action that will result in more grandoffspring produced by the end of one's life."

But how could one possibly evaluate alternative actions using this criterion? Consider a simple, but graphic example: Should one eat feces or fruit?

Clearly, no individual has two parallel lives to lead for purposes of comparison, identical except that he or she eats feces in one life and fruit in the other. Will trial and error work?[6] The individual who eats feces is far more likely to contract parasites or infectious diseases, thereby incurring a large fitness cost. And if this individual instead eats fruit and leaves a certain number of grandoffspring, he or she still does not know whether eating feces would have been better: for all that individual knows, feces could be a rich food source that would greatly increase fecundity.

Does learning from others constitute a solution to the problem? Imitation is useless unless those imitated have themselves solved the problem of the adaptive regulation of behavior. If the blind lead the blind, there is no advantage in imitation. However, if others are monitored not as role models for imitation but instead as natural experiments, such monitoring does allow the comparison of alternative courses of action. However, each individual life is subject to innumerable uncontrolled and random influences that the observer would have to keep track of to make valid inferences. If the observer watches some people eat fruit, and others eat feces, and waits to see which have a larger number of grandoffspring, how would the observer know whether these individuals' differential fitness was caused by their diet or by one of the many other things they experienced in the course of their lives? Of course, perhaps the major problem is that of time delay between action and the cue used to evaluate the action: grandoff-spring produced. It is fundamentally impractical to have to wait two generations to determine the value of choices that must be made today.

Moreover, why would *others* choose to learn through trial and error while the observer does not? The population of self-experimenters would be selecting themselves out, compared to the observers who parasitize their risky experiments.

Can the use of perceptual cues solve the problem? The individual could decide to eat what smells good and avoid what smells bad. However, this method violates the assumption that the information processing system is domain general, and side-steps the "grandoffspring produced" criterion entirely. Nothing smells intrinsically bad or good; the smell of feces is attractive to dung flies. Moreover, what establishes the knowledge that foul-smelling entities should not be eaten? Admitting smell or taste preferences is admitting domain specific innate knowledge. Admitting the inference that foul-smelling or foul-tasting entities should not be ingested is admitting a domain specific innate inference.

Without domain specific knowledge such as this, what kind of mechanism could result in learning to avoid feces and ingest fruit? Even if it were possible, an individual with appropriate domain specific knowledge would enjoy a selective advantage over one who relied on "trial and possibly fatal error" (Shepard, this volume). The tendency to rely on trial and error in this domain would be selected out; domain specific Darwinian algorithms governing food choice would be selected for, and become a species-typical trait.

There is also the problem of deciding which courses of action to evaluate. The possibilities for action are infinite, and the best a truly domain general mechanism could do is generate random possibilities to be run through the inclusive fitness decision rule. When a tiger bounds toward you, what should your response be? Should you file your toenails? Do a cartwheel? Sing a song? Is this the moment to run an uncountable number of randomly generated response possibilities through the decision rule? And again, how could you compute which possibility would result in more grandchildren? The alternative: Darwinian algorithms specialized for predator avoidance, that err on the side of false positives in predator detection, and, upon detecting a potential predator, constrain your responses to flight, fight, or hiding.

The domain general "grandchildren produced" criterion fails even in these simple situations. How, then, could it work in more complicated learning situations—for example, when an action that increases your inclusive fitness in one domain decreases it in another? Suppose the hypothetical domain general learning mechanism somehow reached the inference that sexual intercourse is a necessary condition for producing offspring. Should the individual, then, have sex at every opportunity?

According to evolutionary theory, no. There are large fitness costs associated with, for example, incest (e.g., Shepher, 1983). Given a potential partner with a physique, personality, or resources that would normally elicit sexual desire, the information that the potential partner is close kin must inhibit sexual impulses.

How could this be learned? Again, if a female engages in incest, then loses her baby after a few months, how would she know what caused the miscarriage? Each life is a series of many events (perhaps including sex near the time of conception with nonkin as well as kin), any one of which is a potential cause. Why conclude that sex with one individual, who physically and psychologically resembles other members of his sex in many respects, caused the loss of the baby?

The need to avoid incest implies the ability spontaneously and automatically to acquire the category "kin versus nonkin" by merely observing the world—even if it were possible to learn it by engaging in incest, the fitness costs would be too high. But the "number of grandoffspring produced" decision rule cannot be used to acquire evolutionarily crucial categories through mere observation: unless a categorization scheme is used to guide behavior, it has no consequences on fitness.

Kin recognition requires Darwinian algorithms tuned to environmental cues that are correlated with kin but not with nonkin. These cues must be used in a particular way: either they must be used to match self to other, as in facial or olfactory phenotype matching, or they must categorize others directly, as when one imprints during a critical period on those with whom one was raised. There are an infinite number of dimensions that could be used to carve the environment into categories; there is no assurance that a general-purpose information processing system would ever isolate those useful for creating the kin/nonkin categorization scheme, and the "grandchildren produced" criterion cannot guide such a system toward the appropriate dimensions.

Additionally, there is the problem of generalization. Suppose the psyche somehow had correctly inferred that avoiding sex with kin had positive fitness consequences. How could one generalize this knowledge about the kin/nonkin categorization scheme to other domains of human activity? Would one, for example, avoid any interaction with kin? This would be a mistake; selectively avoiding sex with kin has positive fitness consequences, but selectively avoiding helping kin has negative fitness consequences (given a certain envelope of circumstances—Hamilton, 1964).

Thus, not only must the acquisition of the kin/nonkin categorization scheme be guided by domain specific Darwinian algorithms, but its adaptive use for guiding behavior is also domain specific. In the sexual domain, kin must be avoided; in the helping domain, they must be helped; when one needs help, kin should be among the first to be asked (Hamilton, 1964); when one is contagiously ill, kin should be selectively avoided (Tooby, 1982). The procedural knowledge governing how one behaves toward kin must differ markedly from domain to domain. Only Darwinian algorithms with procedural knowledge specific to each of these domains can assure that one responds to kin in evolutionarily appropriate ways. Simply put, *there is no domain general criterion of fitness that could guide an equipotential learning process toward the correct set of fit responses.*

Trial-and-error learning is inadequate, not only because it is slow and unreliable, but because there is no domain-independent variable for signaling error. In the sexual domain, error = sex with kin. In the helping domain, error = not helping kin given the appropriate envelope of conditions. In the disease domain, error = infecting kin.

Consequently, there are only two ways the human mind can be built. Either

1. All innate psychological mechanisms are domain general, and therefore do not track fitness at all,

or

2. Some innate psychological mechanisms are domain specific Darwinian algorithms with procedural knowledge specialized for tracking fitness in the concrete situations hominids would have encountered as Pleistocene hunter-gatherers.

Clearly, the first alternative is no alternative at all. Unguided plasticity is evolutionarily fatal: there are an infinite number of unfit courses of action, and only a narrow envelope of fit behaviors. A psyche without Darwinian algorithms is incapable of keeping the organism within this narrow envelope. The idea that humans evolved from cognitively constrained ancestors into general problem solvers, now nearly devoid of adaptive specializations but equipped instead with generalized learning mechanisms, cannot be sustained. No one has yet been able to specify a general learning mechanism or general cognitive problem solver that has the power to solve the complex array of adaptive problems faced by humans, either in principle or in practice. Moreover, not only are more general sets of decision procedures less likely to provide correct guidance, but also they tend to be slower than sets of procedures designed to take advantage of the recurrent features of defined adaptive problems. In sum, advocates of the idea that the human mind is comprised predominantly of a set of domain general learning procedures has to explain how genes that code for such a maladaptive system could outcompete genes that code for existing successful adaptive specializations.

10 Darwinian Algorithms Solve the "Frame Problem"

Darwinian algorithms can be seen as schema- or frame-*builders*: as learning mechanisms that structure experience along adaptive dimensions in a given domain. Positing them solves the "frame problem"—which is the name artificial intelligence researchers gave to the family of problems with domain general mechanisms that emerged in their own work, and that parallel those raised in the discussion above.

Researchers in artificial intelligence have found that trial and error is a good procedure for learning only when a system already has a well-specified model of what is likely to be true of a domain, a model that includes a definition of what counts as error. Programmers call this finding the "frame problem" (e.g., Boden, 1977; Fodor, 1983). To move an object, make the simplest induction, or solve a straightforward problem, the computer must already have a sophisticated model of the domain in question: what counts as an object or stimulus, what counts as a cause, how classes of entities and properties are related, how various actions change the situation, what goal is to be achieved. Unless the learning domain is severely circumscribed and the procedures highly specialized and content-dependent —unless the programmer has given the computer what amounts to vast quantities of "innate knowledge"—the computer can move nothing, learn nothing, solve nothing. The frame problem is a concrete, empirical demonstration of the philosophical objections to the *tabula rasa*. It is also a cautionary tale for advocates of domain general, content-independent learning mechanisms.

Unfortunately, the lesson has been lost on many. Although most cognitive psychologists realize that their theories must posit some innate cognitive architecture, a quick perusal of textbooks in the field will show that these still tend to be restricted to content-independent operating system characteristics: short-term stores, domain general retrieval and storage processes, imagery buffers. Researchers who do insist on the necessity of positing content-dependent schemas or frames (e.g., Minsky, 1977; Schank and Abelson, 1977) seldom ask how these frames are built. Their approach implicitly presumes that frames are the product of experience structured only by domain general learning mechanisms[7]—yet the building of frames must also be subject to the frame problem. Even Fodor (1983), a prominent exponent of the view that the mind's innate architecture includes specialized, content-dependent modules, restricts these to what he calls "input systems": perceptual or quasi-perceptual domains like vision, hearing, and language. He doubts the existence of modules governing "central" processes like reasoning and problem solving. Yet one wonders: Without domain specific inference processes, how can all these perceptual data be expected to guide our behavior in adaptive directions?

Restricting the mind's innate architecture to perceptual systems, a content-independent operating system, a domain general concept learning mechanism, a content-independent hypothesis testing procedure, and a small ragbag of dimensions for construing similarity might be sufficient if it did not matter what a person learned—if, for example, learning that E is the most frequently used letter in the English language were as critical to one's inclusive fitness as learning that a hungry tiger can leave a sizable hole in one's life plan. But what a person learns does matter; and not only what, but when, how reliably, and how quickly. Even more important is what a person *does* with that knowledge. The purpose of learning is, presumably, to guide behavior. Should one eat gravel? Should one engage in incest? How willing should a person be to give up the last remaining food available for feeding one's own children? Natural selection theory provides definite answers to questions like these, because the wrong decision can be shown to result in large fitness costs. How can an equipotential learning system that simply looks for relations in the world provide information about the relative value, in inclusive fitness terms, of alternative courses of action? It cannot; it has no standard for assessing it.

Cognitive psychologists can persist in advocating such systems only because they are not asking what problems the mind was designed, by natural selection, to solve. The Darwinian view is that humans have innately specified cognitive programs that allow them to pursue goals that are (or once were) correlated with their inclusive fitness. These innately specified programs cannot all be domain general. Behavior is a transaction between organism and environment; to be adaptive, specific behaviors must be elicited by evolutionarily appropriate environmental cues. Only specialized, domain specific Darwinian algorithms can ensure that this will happen.[8]

11 The Frame Problem and So-Called "Constraints" on Learning

Biologists and psychologists have an unfortunate tendency to refer to the properties of domain specific (but not domain general) mechanisms as "constraints." For example, the one-trial learning mechanism, discovered by Garcia and Koelling (1966), that permits a blue jay to associate a food taste with vomiting several hours later is frequently referred to as a "biological constraint on learning." Books reporting the existence of domain specific learning mechanisms frequently have titles like *Biological Boundaries of Learning* (Seligman and Hager, 1972) or *The Tangled Wing: Biological Constraints on the Human Spirit* (Konner, 1982). This terminology is seriously misleading, because it incorrectly implies that "unconstrained" learning mechanisms are a theoretical possibility; it implicitly denies the existence of the frame problem.

All constraints are properties, but not all properties are constraints. Calling a property a "constraint" implies that the organism would have a wider range of abilities if the constraint were to be removed.

Are a bird's wings a "constraint on locomotion"? Birds can locomote by flying or hopping. Wings are a property of birds that enables them to locomote by flying, but wings are not a "constraint on locomotion." On the contrary. Wings expand the bird's capacity to locomote—with wings, the bird can fly *and* hop. Removing a bird's wings reduces its capacity to locomote—without wings, it can hop, but not fly. Wings cannot be a constraint, because removing them does not give the bird a wider range of locomoting abilities. If anything, wings should be called "enablers," because they enable an additional form of locomotion. Having them expands the bird's capacity to locomote.

A thick rubber band placed in such a way that it pins a bird's wings to its body is a constraint on the bird's ability to locomote: With the rubber band the bird can only hop; without it the bird can both fly and hop.

Similarly, there is no evidence that the domain specific mechanisms that permit one-trial learning of an association between taste and vomiting are "constraints on learning." Removing the specific properties that allow the efficient learning of this particular association would not expand the bird's capacity to learn; it would reduce it. Not only would the blue jay be unable to associate a food taste with an electric shock; it would also be unable to associate a food taste with vomiting.

The tendency to refer to such innate knowledge as "constraints on learning" is perhaps the result of the mistaken notion that a *tabula rasa* is possible, that learning is possible in the absence of a great deal of domain specific innate knowledge. If true, then a property that "prepares" an organism to associate a taste with vomiting might preclude it from associating a taste with an electric shock. However, if an organism with this prepared association also had a domain general associative mechanism, there is no a priori reason why that mechanism should not work to pair taste with electric shocks. In order to call the prepared association a "constraint" on the learning caused by the general purpose mechanism, one would have to demonstrate empirically that the activation of the prepared association by the presence of food somehow causes the general-purpose mechanism to shut down.

Rozin and Schull (1987) have pointed out another way in which the terminology of constraint is misleading: it implies that the human mind was "built down" from a more general-purpose cognitive system present in our ancestors. Yet such a phylogenetic history seems far from likely: it presumes that our primate ancestors had a capacity to learn that was broader and more powerful than our own.

12 Conclusions

Many evolutionary biologists seem to think that once they have identified an adaptive function, their job is done: specifying how the organism accomplishes the function is a trivial matter. This is comparable to thinking that once Einstein had shown that $E = mc^2$, designing a nuclear power plant was a trivial matter. Understanding what properties a cognitive program must have if it is to accomplish an adaptive function is far from trivial—it is one of the most difficult and challenging problems of this century.

There is emerging a new method, here called evolutionary psychology, which is made possible by the simultaneous maturation of evolutionary biology, paleoanthropology, and cognitive psychology. Together, these disciplines allow the discovery and principled investigation of the human psyche's innate cognitive programs. We propose that they be combined according to the following guidelines:

> 1. Use evolutionary theory as a starting point to develop models of adaptive problems that the human psyche had to solve.
> 2. Attempt to determine how these adaptive problems would have manifested themselves in Pleistocene conditions, insofar as this is possible. Recurrent environmental features relevant to the adaptive problem, including constraints and relationships that existed in the social, ecological, genetic, and physical situation of early hominids, should be specified; these constitute the conditions in which the adaptive problem arose, and further define the nature of the adaptive problem. Such features and relationships constitute the only environmental information available to whatever cognitive program evolved to solve the adaptive problem. The structure of the cognitive program must be such that it can guide behavior along adaptive paths given only the information available to it in these Pleistocene conditions.
> 3. Integrate the model of the adaptive problem with available knowledge of the relevant Pleistocene conditions, drawing whatever valid and useful implications can be derived from this set of constraints. Catalog the specific information processing problems that must be solved if the adaptive function is to be accomplished.

> This constitutes a computational theory of the adaptive information processing problem. The computational theory is then used as a heuristic for generating testable hypotheses about the structure of the cognitive programs that solve the adaptive problem in question.

4. Use the computational theory to (a) determine whether there are design features that *any* cognitive program capable of solving the adaptive problem must have and (b) develop candidate models of the structure of the cognitive programs that humans might have evolved to solve the adaptive problem. Be sure the model proposed is, in principle, powerful enough to realize the computational theory.

5. Eliminate alternative candidate models with experiments and field observation. Cognitive psychologists have already developed an impressive array of concepts and experimental methods for tracking complex information processing systems—these should be used to full advantage. The end result is a validated model of the cognitive programs in question, together with a model of what environmental information, and other factors, these programs take as input.

6. Finally, compare the model against the patterns of manifest behavior that are produced by modern conditions. Informational inputs from modern environments should produce the patterns of manifest behavior predicted by the model of the cognitive programs already developed.

As previously discussed, some who adopt the evolutionary perspective attempt to leap directly from step one to step six, neglecting the intermediate steps, searching only for correspondences between evolutionary theory and modern manifest behavior.

Attempts to finesse a precise characterization of the cognitive programs that cause human behavior have led to a series of roadblocks in the application of evolutionary biology to the behavioral sciences. Because they leave the causal chain by which evolution influenced behavior vague and unspecified, such attempts have sown the widespread confusion that hypotheses about economics, culture, consciousness, learning, rationality, social forces, etc., constitute distinct alternative hypotheses to evolutionary or "biological" explanations. Instead, such hypotheses are more properly viewed as proposals about the structure of evolved cognitive programs and the kinds of information they take as input.

Cognitive psychology and evolutionary biology are sister disciplines. The goal of evolutionary theory is to define the adaptive problems that organisms must be able to solve. The goal of cognitive psychology is to discover the information processing mechanisms that have evolved to solve them. Alone, each is incomplete for the understanding of human behavior. Together, applied as a unified research program, they offer the promise that by using their organizing principles, the level of analysis appropriate for describing and investigating human behavior has, at last, been found.

Notes

1. See, for example, Block (1980) or Fodor (1981) for more discussion of the nature of cognitive explanations.
2. At least of the same sex and age.
3. Of course there can be individual variation in cognitive programs, just as there is individual variation in the size and shape of stomachs: this can be true of any structure or process in a sexually recombining species, and such genetic variation constitutes the basis for "inherited" or "constitutional" psychological differences. However, because even simple cognitive programs or "mental organs" must contain a large number of processing steps, and so must have complex polygenic bases, they necessarily evolve slowly, leading to variation being mostly "superficial." There is a large amount of variation among humans concerning single or quantitative characteristics of specific organ systems, but there is almost *no variation* among humans in what organs exist, or the basic design of each organ system. Everyone has a heart, and a liver, and so on, and everyone's heart and liver function in much the same way. We expect that this pattern holds for "mental organs" as well. Such variation, whether it is of "physical" or "mental" organ systems, can modify the functioning of these systems between individuals—sometimes drastically. Phenylketonuria is the result of a single gene modification. Nevertheless, such variation must be recognized as modifications of a design whose integrity is largely intact, and is not likely to consist of a wholly different design, differing "from the ground up." We find implausible, on the basis of population genetics considerations, the notion that different humans have fundamentally different and competing cognitive programs, resting on wholly different genetic bases.

    For these and other reasons, we believe such variation can be better detected and understood if behavioral scientists devote most of their early research effort to elucidating the most commonly shared and basic design features of human cognitive programs.

    A more likely kind of phenomenon is one in which wholly different cognitive programs become *activated* in different individuals, but exist latently in all individuals, based on a species-typical genetic basis. Such facultative programs can be differentially activated early in the life cycle (setting individuals along different developmental tracks), by short-term situational elicitation, or even as the result of superficial (in the sense discussed above) genetic differences in other parts of the genome (e.g., constitutional differences or gender). Gender is the most dramatic example of this facultative latency: although the profound differences between male and female have a large genetic basis, each gender has the full genetic specification for both genders. Which set of simultaneously coexisting genes becomes activated in any particular individual depends on the presence or absence of a single gene, the H-Y antigen, on the Y chromosome.
4. Herrnstein (1977) points out that Skinnerian learning theorists were able to avoid discussion of the cognitive mechanisms governing generalization and discrimination only by ignoring the problem. Available in the environment are an *infinite number* of dimensions that could be used for generalization and discrimination—but which does the organism actually use?
5. They have been called "adaptive specializations" by Rozin (1976), "modules" by Fodor (1983), and "cognitive competences" by Chomsky (1975). In our view, such mechanisms have two defining characteristics: (1) they are most usefully described on the cognitive level of proximate causation and (2) they are adaptations. We prefer "Darwinian algorithms" to the other terms because it emphasizes both characteristics.
6. The argument holds whether you characterize the process as trial and error, induction, or hypothesis testing.
7. Recently, this belief was stated explicitly by Cheng and Holyoak (1985), who cite

"induction" as the process that builds their content-dependent "pragmatic reasoning schemas."

8. We would like to direct the reader to Rozin (1976), Herrnstein (1977), Staddon (1987), and Symons (1987) for similar arguments from slightly different perspectives.

Bibliography

Atherton, M., and R. Schwartz (1974). Linguistic Innateness and Its Evidence. *The Journal of Philosophy* LXXI:6.

Block, N. (1980). What Is Functionalism? In N. Block (ed.), *Readings in Philosophy of Psychology*, Cambridge, MA: Harvard University Press.

Boden, M. (1977). *Artificial Intelligence and Natural Man.* New York: Basic Books.

Bruner, J. S. (1973). *Beyond the Information Given* (J. M. Anglin, ed.). New York: Norton.

Cheng, P. W. and K. J. Holyoak (1985). Pragmatic Reasoning Schemas. *Cognitive Psychology* 17:391–416.

Chomsky, N. (1957). *Syntactic Structures.* The Hague: Mouton.

Chomsky, N. (1959). Review of Skinner's "Verbal Behavior." *Language* 35:26–58.

Chomsky, N. (1975). *Reflections on Language.* New York: Random House.

Chomsky, N. (1980). *Rules and Respresentations.* New York: Columbia University Press.

Cosmides, L. (1985). Deduction or Darwinian Algorithms?: An Explanation of the "Elusive" Content Effect on the Wason Selection Task. Doctoral dissertation, Department of Psychology and Social Relations, Harvard University.

Fodor, J. A. (1981). The Mind-Body Problem. *Scientific American* 244(1):124–133.

Fodor, J. A. (1983). *The Modularity of Mind.* Cambridge, MA; MIT Press.

Garcia, J., and R. A. Koelling (1966). Relations of Cue to Consequence in Avoidance Learning. *Psychonomic Science* 4:123–124.

Hamilton, W. D. (1964). The Genetical Evolution of Social Behavior. *Journal of Theoretical Biology* 7:1–52.

Herrnstein, R. J. (1977) The Evolution of Behaviorism. *American Psychologist* 32:593–603.

Hume, D. (1977/1748). *An Enquiry Concerning Human Understanding* (E. Steinberg, ed.). Indianapolis: Hackett

Kant, I. (1966/1781). *Critique of Pure Reason.* New York: Anchor Books.

Katz, J. J. (1975). Innate Ideas. In S. P. Stich (ed.), *Innate Ideas*, Berkeley: University of California Press.

Konner. M. (1982). *The Tangled Wing: Biological Constraints on the Human Spirit.* New York: Holt, Rinehart, & Winston.

Marr, D. (1982). *Vision: A Computational Investigation into the Human Representation and Processing of Visual Information.* San Francisco: Freeman.

Marr, D., and H. K. Nishihara (1978). Visual Information Processing: Artificial Intelligence and the Sensorium of Sight. *Technology Review* October: 28–49.

Marshall, J. C. (1981). Cognition at the Crossroads. *Nature* 289:613–614.

Maynard Smith, J., and G. R. Price (1973). The Logic of Animal Conflict. *Nature (London)* 246:15–18.

Minsky, M. (1977). Frame-System Theory. In P. N. Johnson-Laird and P. C. Wason (eds.), *Thinking: Readings in Cognitive Science.*, Cambridge: Cambridge University Press.

Popper, K. R. (1972). *Objective Knowledge: An Evolutionary Approach.* London: Oxford University Press.

Putnam. H. (1967). The "Innateness Hypothesis" and Explanatory Models in Linguistics. *Synthese* 17:12–22.

Quine, W. V. O. (1969). *Ontological Relativity and Other Essays.* New York: Columbia University Press.

Rozin, P. (1976). The Evolution of Intelligence and Access to the Cognitive Unconscious. In J. M. Sprague and A. N. Epstein (eds.), *Progress in Psychobiology and Physiological Psychology*, New York: Academic Press.

Rozin, P., and J. Schull (1987). The Adaptive-Evolutionary Point of View in Experimental Psychology. In R. C. Atkinson, R. J. Herrnstein, G. Lindsey, and R. D. Luce (eds.), *Handbook of Experimental Psychology*.

Schank, R., and R. P. Abelson (1977). *Scripts, Plans, Goals, and Understanding*. Hillsdale, N. J.: Lawrence Erlbaum Associates.

Seligman, M. E. P., and J. L. Hager (1972). *Biological Boundaries of Learning*. New York: Meredith.

Shepard, R. N. (1981). Psychophysical Complementarity. In M. Kubovy and J. R. Pomerantz, *Perceptual Organization*, Hillsdale, N.J.: Erlbaum.

Shepard, R. N. (1984). Ecological Constraints on Internal Representation: Resonant Kinematics of Perceiving, Imagining, Thinking, and Dreaming. *Psychological Review* 91: 417–447.

Shepard, R. N. (this volume). Evolution of a Mesh between Principles of the Mind and Regularities of the World. In J. Dupré (ed.), *The Latest on the Best*, Cambridge, MA: MIT Press.

Shepher. J. (1983). *Incest: A Biosocial View*. New York: Academic Press.

Staddon, J. E. R. (1987). Learning as Inference. In R. C. Bolles and M. D. Beecher (eds.), *Evolution and Learning.*, Hillsdale, NJ: Erlbaum.

Staddon, J. E. R. (this volume), Optimality Theory and Behavior. In J. Dupré (ed.), The Latest on the Best, Cambridge, MA: MIT Press.

Symons, D. (1987). If We're All Darwinians, What's the Fuss About? In C. Crawford, D. Krebs, and M. Smith (eds.), *Sociobiology and Psychology*, Hillsdale, NJ: Erlbaum.

Tooby, J. (1982). Pathogens, Polymorphism and the Evolution of Sex. *Journal of Theoretical Biology* 97:557–576.

Tooby, J. (1985). The Emergence of Evolutionary Psychology. In D. Pines (ed.), *Emerging Syntheses in Science*, Santa Fe: Santa Fe Institute.

Tooby, J., and L. Cosmides (1987). Evolutionary Psychology and the Generation of Culture. Part I: Theoretical Considerations. *Ethology and Sociobiology*.

Tooby, J., and I. DeVore (1987). The Reconstruction of Hominid Behavioral Evolution through Strategic Modeling. In W. G. Kinzey (ed.), *Primate Models for the Origin of Human Behavior*, New York: SUNY Press.

Trivers, R. L. (1972). Parental Investment and Sexual Selection. In B. Campbell (ed.), *Sexual Selection and the Descent of Man 1871–1971*, Chicago: Aldine.

Trivers, R. L. (1974). Parent-Offspring Conflict. *American Zoologist* 14:249–264.

Wanner, E., and L. R. Gleitman (1982). *Language Acquisition: The State of the Art*. Cambridge: Cambridge University Press.

Wilson, E. O. (1975). *Sociobiology: The New Synthesis*. Cambridge, MA: Harvard University Press.

14

On the Emotions as Guarantors of Threats and Promises

Jack Hirshleifer

The role of the passions or emotions in supporting civil society has been discussed by social theorists and moral philosophers since earliest times. Adam Smith, in particular, whose name is more usually associated with the claim that an economic system may function effectively even when men act only in accordance with calculated self-interest, was actually very concerned with aspects of human nature that set limits upon the pursuit of self-interest: "Nature, when she formed man for society, endowed him with an original desire to please, and an original aversion to offend his brethren. She taught him to feel pleasure in their favourable, and pain in their unfavourable regard. She rendered their approbation most flattering and most agreeable to him for its own sake; and their disapprobation most mortifying and most offensive."[1] More intriguing than his appreciation of the force of "positive" emotions like benevolence and sympathy are Smith's insights into how even the more dubious passions—pride, vanity, and ambition—may promote the interests of society.[2] This point had of course already been made by Mandeville in *The Fable of the Bees* (1714). But Smith comes closer to my theme here in his argument that these "negative" sentiments can be most socially useful precisely when they drive people to undertake activities *beyond the bounds of pragmatic self-interest*. Thus, of a "poor man's son ... visited with ambition" Adam Smith says,

> For this purpose he makes his court to all mankind; he serves those whom he hates, and is obsequious to those whom he despises. Through the whole of his life he pursues the idea of a certain artificial and elegant repose which he may never arrive at, for which he sacrifices a real tranquillity that is at all times in his power, and which, if in the extremity of old age he should at last attain to it, he will find to be in no respect preferable to that humble security and contentment which he had abandoned for it.[3]
>
> And it is well that nature imposes upon us in this manner. It is this deception which arouses and keeps in continual motion the industry of mankind. It is this which first prompted them to cultivate the ground, to build houses, to found cities and common-wealths, and to

invent and improve all the sciences and arts, which ennoble and embellish human life.[4,5]

The point I shall be making is somewhat different, however. The emotions, positive or negative, can indeed be socially useful in driving a person to act beyond the bounds of pragmatic self-interest. But paradoxically the consequence is not necessarily adverse for himself. A person can sometimes best further his self-interest by *not* intending to pursue it. Methodologically speaking also, I shall be advancing somewhat beyond the classical discussions referred to above, in providing a systematic *analysis* of the precise ways in which different emotional sets may promote or subvert socially advantageous arrangements. My discussion follows a lead by Becker (1976), who demonstrated how "altruism" can, in effect, force cooperation upon a completely selfish partner (the "Rotten-Kid Theorem"). I shall try to show more generally here how, and up to what limits, positive or negative emotions can serve a constructive role as guarantors of *threats* or *promises* in social interactions.

If a mutually desired objective is to be achieved, it is often necessary that one or more of the parties forgo the opportunity to reap a self-interested gain. Intelligence permits reasoning beings to "look around the corner," to visualize the advantages of *not* pursuing immediate self-interest. But the problem of securing the necessary coordination of actions remains. A meeting of the minds—a contract, to use that term in its broadest sense— does not generally suffice; some method of *enforcing* (or otherwise guaranteeing) performance is generally required.[6]

The most obvious method of enforcement is through the legal-judicial system. But it has long been appreciated that in some cases contracts may be self-enforcing (Macaulay, 1963), the key point being that fear of losing profitable future business with a trading partner may suffice to deter defection here and now. This topic has recently been studied by Telser (1980), using the analytical model of the repeated-play Prisoners' Dilemma ("supergame" theory, in the standard jargon). The difficulty is the well-known incentive to defect at the last round of play. This obstacle can be overcome, so that the contract becomes self-enforcing, when the number of rounds is infinite or at least if there is a sufficiently high probability of play always continuing for another round (see also Luce and Raiffa, 1957, p. 102).

In contrast with this line of discussion, I shall be dealing solely with single-round games. But my analysis will not be limited to Prisoners' Dilemma, which is only one of a number of distinct payoff environments combining a mutual gain from cooperation with a self-interested motive to defect. In the situations to be considered the possibility of enforcement stems from an assumed asymmetric game protocol, such that one of the players "has the last word" (Hirshleifer, 1977) and thus is potentially in a position to confer reward or punishment. Since offers of reward or punishment are contingent strategies, we are in the realm of "metagames" in the jargon of the trade (Howard, 1971; Thompson and Faith, 1981).

In what follows I shall first briefly discuss the nature of threats versus promises in different payoff environments. Then I shall provide an explicit analysis for several different categories of emotions. Finally, I shall speculate upon the possible reasons why emotions, and other limitations upon "rationality," have survived as part of the human constitution.

1

An individual who makes a threat or promise is pledging to respond in a contingent way to another's actions, with the goal of influencing the other party's choice. The intended effect would presumably always be to the threatener's advantage, though not necessarily to the other's disadvantage. The only other point worthy of special note is that a promise or threat must be *to do something that the individual would not otherwise be motivated to do*. That is what distinguishes these pledges from mere forecasts, however informative, of one's likely responses to another's actions (see also Schelling, 1960, chapter 2).

Matrix 1 illustrates a Prisoners' Dilemma payoff environment, where 4 represents the highest and 1 the lowest of the ordinally ranked returns to each of the players (see figure 14.1). Here and throughout, unless indicated to the contrary, the Column player moves first so that it is the Row player who "has the last word." It is then possible to define *contingent* strategies

	Matrix 1			Matrix 1A	
	Prisoners' Dilemma			Expanded Prisoners' Dilemma	
	LOYAL	DEFECT		LOYAL	DEFECT
LOYAL	3,3 #	1,4	LOYAL	3,3	1,4
DEFECT	4,1	2,2*	DEFECT	4,1	2,2
			TIT FOR TAT	3,3	2,2
			REVERSAL	4,1	1,4

	Matrix 2	
	Chicken	
	DOVE	HAWK
DOVE	3,3 #	2,4*
HAWK	4,2**	1,1

Figure 14.1

for Row. Let the two elementary strategies available to each player be LOYAL and DEFECT. Row's additional contingent strategies can be termed TIT FOR TAT (play LOYAL in response to LOYAL, and DEFECT in response to DEFECT) and REVERSAL (play DEFECT in response to LOYAL, and LOYAL in response to DEFECT). It is standard to represent these contingent strategies by additional rows in the game's normal form, as in the "expanded" Matrix 1A. However, for my purposes it suffices to deal directly with the underlying Matrix 1, where it is easy enough to visualize the effects of threats or promises on the part of the Row player.

With Column having the first move, suppose that Row—even though he may contemplate or even intend a contingent strategy like TIT FOR TAT—cannot *guarantee* to Column that he will be following it. Then, returning to Matrix 1, Column will surely choose DEFECT. (For, his choice of LOYAL would be responded to by Row's DEFECT, leaving Column with his worst payoff of 1.) Row will of course answer Column's DEFECT with his own DEFECT. Thus the parties end up at the cell of Matrix 1 marked with a star; the payoffs are 2 each—their next-to-worst outcomes in each case.[7] This is of course the traditional "trap" equilibrium of Prisoners' Dilemma,[8] a seemingly paradoxical result since, by cooperation, the parties could have reaped their next-to-best payoff of 3 each.

This Pareto-superior 3,3 outcome (marked with a # in Matrix 1) would indeed be achieved if Row could guarantee abiding by a *promise* to play LOYAL in response to LOYAL on Column's part. Column, if he could rely upon that promise, then would play LOYAL on the first move. What makes Row's utterance a promise (rather than a forecast) is that he offers *not to do* what he is in fact motivated to do when his turn comes up. In promising LOYAL, Row engages himself to confer a benefit upon Column, at a cost to himself, should the latter first choose LOYAL himself. But that Row will play DEFECT in response to DEFECT is only a forecast and not a threat, since Row would be doing that anyway.

To illustrate an actual *threat*, consider the almost equally famous payoff environment known as the game of Chicken (Matrix 2). Holding to the ornithological metaphor, the two strategies can be called HAWK and DOVE. If Row cannot guarantee performance of a contingent strategy, then Column, having the first move, must inspect Row's response to each of his choices. Evidently, Column's best first move is the "less cooperative" HAWK strategy, leading to an asymmetrical 2,4 outcome in his favor (starred in the matrix). In order to influence Column to change his strategy, Row would have to guarantee execution of a *threat* to play HAWK in response to HAWK. Once again, that is an engagement to do something at a cost to himself, but now the action imposes a *loss* on Column. If Column bows to the threat and plays DOVE instead, Row now plays HAWK leading to the reversed payoff outcome 4,2 in Row's favor (double-starred in the matrix).

On the other hand, Row might sweeten the deal by issuing a *threat-and-promise*. That is, in addition to the aforesaid threat to play HAWK in response to HAWK, he could promise to forgo part of his gain and respond to DOVE with DOVE. Then, the parties could achieve the symmetrical 3,3 outcome (marked # in Matrix 2). It might seem puzzling that, if Row's threat is solid enough to work, he would ever choose to reduce his gain by combining a threat and a promise. But throughout this paper we are contemplating the possibility that parties might, owing to emotional limits upon self-interested rationality, *not* necessarily do what it is in their material advantage to do. In such circumstances, threat-and-promise might conceivably trigger a less hostile response than threat alone.

2

In this section I shall examine the consequences of two different scaled classes of emotion: (1) the malevolence/benevolence spectrum and (2) the anger/gratitude spectrum. The first category is *action-independent*, the second is *action-dependent*. I shall continue to employ the assumption throughout that one player always has the first move; in fact, let us call him First. The other player, Second, is therefore the one who may be in a position to confer reward or punishment.

Benevolence/Malevolence

Figures 14.2a and 14.2b illustrate benevolence and malevolence *on the part of the last mover*, Second. Thus it is Second's indifference curves that are being pictured, on axes representing the two parties' material incomes Y_S and Y_F. In figure 14.2a Y_S and Y_F are both *goods* for a benevolent Second, so his indifference curves have the familiar negative slope. In figure 14.2b his own income Y_S remains of course a good for Second, but now Y_F is a *bad* from his point of view. Hence the abnormal indifference curve map in figure 14.2b.

I shall also be assuming that Second always has the power to transfer income to First, or else to deprive him of income, if he chooses—in each case, at a cost to himself. Specifically, in the transfer mode Second can increase First's income Y_F by giving up his own income Y_S on a 1:1 basis. (Note the dashed 135° "transfer lines" *TT* in figure 14.2a, where the arrows attached indicate the direction of movement.) In the deprivation mode, Second can reduce First's income but again only by incurring an assumed equal cost himself—indicated by the dashed 45° "deprivation lines" *DD* in figure 14.2b. (Once again, the arrows indicate the possible direction of movement.)

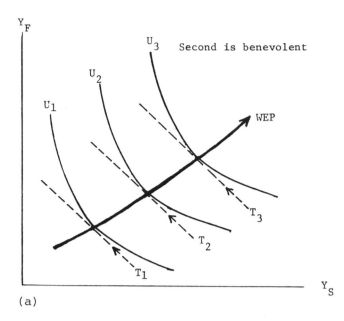

(a)

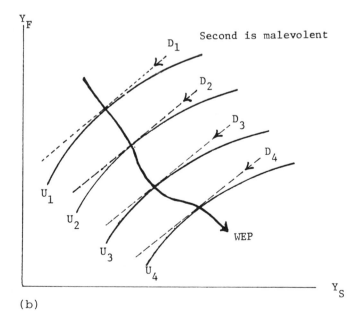

(b)

Figure 14.2
Benevolence versus malevolence.

In figure 14.2a the *WEP* curve (a "Wealth Expansion Path") connects all the tangencies of Second's benevolent indifference curves with the 135° transfer lines. It follows immediately that, provided the starting position is to the *southeast* of the *WEP* curve (that is, provided he is relatively well off and First relatively poorly off to begin with), Second will always transfer exactly that amount of income leading him to a final solution along *WEP*. Similarly, in figure 14.2b the *WEP* curve connects all the tangencies of Second's malevolent indifference curves with the 45° deprivation lines. Here Second will always impose enough deprivation to end up along *WEP*, provided the starting position is to the *northeast*. (That is, provided both parties are relatively well endowed with income to begin with. Second must be reasonably wealthy in order to afford the cost of inflicting the deprivation, while First must be well off to begin with else the initial situation would not be intolerable to a malevolent Second.)

Another property of the *WEP* curves will be important in what follows. In figure 14.2a *WEP* has positive slope throughout. This indicates that, as a benevolent Second grows wealthier, he will want to choose positions involving greater Y_S and greater Y_F *both*. That is, as he becomes richer, he wants to end up with more income for himself and more income for the object of his benevolence. This represents a special, though reasonable, assumption, that Y_S and Y_F are both "superior" goods from Second's point of view.[9] By a corresponding argument, in figure 14.2b the curve *WEP* has negative slope. As Second becomes richer, he prefers to so arrange matters as to have more income himself while leaving the target of his malevolence worse off.

Now we turn to the decisions available to the first mover. It will be assumed that a joint productive opportunity boundary like *QQ'* in figure 14.3 always exists, and that First has the sole choice of the productive arrangements to be made—i.e., he determines the point to be chosen along *QQ'*. Furthermore, for simplicity First is assumed throughout to be merely self-interested, neither benevolent nor malevolent.[10] It then follows that, in the absence of any anticipated reaction from Second, First would always simply prefer the most northerly position along *QQ'*—point *M* in the diagram. As it happens, the joint productive arrangements represented by point *M* do generate some income for Second as well, but this is a merely incidental fact from First's selfish point of view.

But now note the position of Second's (solid) Wealth Expansion Path *WEP* in figure 14.3. This indicates that, beyond point *X*, where *WEP* cuts *QQ'*, Second regards himself as wealthy enough to display some benevolence toward First. Thus, First, should he choose his short-sightedly selfish optimum, *M*, would end up doing better than this—since Second would benevolently transfer enough income to him along the transfer line $T_1 T_1$ to end up at point *N* that lies to the north of *M*. But that is still not the best

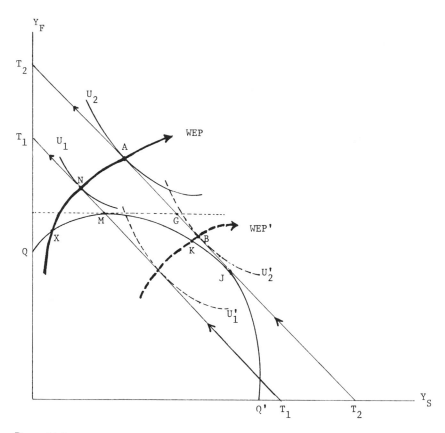

Figure 14.3
The Rotten-Kid Theorem—benevolence as guarantor of a promise.

that a *far-sightedly* selfish First could achieve. In fact, it will be evident from the diagram that First should choose point *J*, where *QQ′* is tangent to the highest attainable 135° transfer line $T_2 T_2$. True, in the short run, First will have sacrificed income on behalf of Second. But the latter will then benevolently transfer enough of his enlarged income to First so as to achieve a final indifference-curve tangency at point *A*. From the selfish First player's point of view, *A* is better than (north of) *N*. In fact, *A* represents the largest income attainable by First under the conditions assumed.

That, however, is not the surprising part of this result. The real point is, not only does "enlightened self-interest" lead the selfish first mover to a better outcome thanks to a predictable benefit from Second's benevolence, but the latter gains as well! And the gain to Second is not merely in terms of his psychic satisfaction from seeing First better off. Even in the crassly material sense, the benevolent second mover himself has gained from his generosity. His own material income Y_s is greater at point A than it would have been otherwise, i.e., had the selfish First player chosen point M along QQ'.

What has happened here is that Second's benevolence guaranteed an implicit "promise" to reward First, a necessary condition for securing cooperation from a merely self-interested individual. The second mover's "hard-core altruism" has served to elicit the first mover's pragmatic or "soft-core altruism." [11]

Another aspect of the constructive role played by benevolence is brought out if we look at the alternative (dashed) Wealth Expansion Path WEP' in figure 14.3. This curve is associated with a different possible set of preferences for Second, suggest by the dashed indifference curves U'. These alternative preferences are *qualitatively* similar in that they also represent benevolent tastes, but now to a *quantitatively* lesser degree. In these altered circumstances, if First were to choose the jointly cooperative position J along QQ' as before, Second would then transfer a smaller amount to him— so that the parties would end up at position B along WEP' rather than at A along WEP. But, for the selfish First player, position B is inferior to his short-sightedly selfish optimum, M. The conclusion: far-sighted or enlightened self-interest may not suffice to achieve mutual improvement, in the absence of a *sufficiently strong degree* of benevolence on the part of the player having the last move.

Of course, in the latter situation Second could still *promise* to provide First with a sufficient reward to induce cooperation—say, by pledging to choose position A if First selects J along QQ'. But by assumption there is nothing to guarantee Second's promise—save his own benevolence, which is here inadequate. In fact, there is a critical threshold degree of benevolence on the part of Second needed to elicit cooperation from First. To wit, to provide enough inducement for a far-sightedly selfish First to choose point J, Second's benevolent Wealth Expansion Path must cut the transfer line $T_2 T_2$ north of its intersection with the dotted line through M. Thus, lots of love may do the trick where a little love achieves nothing at all!

If benevolence can serve as guarantor of a *promise* by the party having the last word, can malevolence serve as a guarantor of a *threat?* It surely can, but the overall effect is not to elicit cooperation, if we hold to the assumption that the WEP curve in figure 14.4 (compare figure 14.2b) has negative slope throughout. (That is, the richer Second gets, the more he can afford to and want to spend on depriving First.) In figure 14.4 then, should the first mover short-sightedly choose the most northerly position M along QQ', he will have empowered a malevolent Second to impoverish him to the degree represented by the final position L. If First were instead to choose the efficient productive point J, he would end up still worse off at

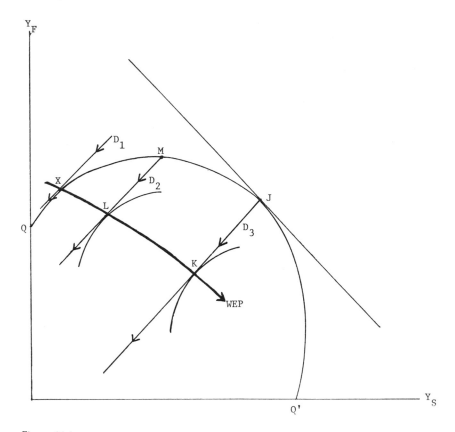

Figure 14.4
Malevolence and threat.

K. Evidently a selfish First does best to choose point X, where he is initially poorer but where Second is also so poor that he cannot afford (or at least does not care) to incur costs to impose any further deprivation upon him. Thus malevolence guarantees execution of a threat, but the consequence is that *both* parties are worse off—in terms of psychic satisfaction and in terms of material income as well.

Gratitude/Anger

I now turn to the *action-dependent* emotional scale ranging from gratitude at the positive end to anger at the negative end of the spectrum. The question as before will be whether these emotions can guarantee execution of threats or promises and thereby promote achievement of mutually beneficial solutions.

Allowing for the possibility that malevolence and benevolence represented a departure from the economist's standard assumption of self-interested behavior, but did not otherwise do violence to the picture of economic man as a rational utilitarian calculator. An individual who values other people's income (positively or negatively) as well as his own can nevertheless coolly go about his business of calculating a preferred final outcome in the light of his given preferences and opportunities.[12] But I am now introducing a much more serious departure from the standard assumptions of the economist—to wit, the idea that an individual can be *passionate*, in the sense of "losing control" and doing what he does not really want to do (on this see Schelling, 1980). Or an alternative (and my preferred) interpretation would be that what he wants to do need not depend only upon the final outcome in the utilitarian sense—i.e., strictly upon the ultimate distribution of incomes between the two parties—but rather may be *action-dependent*. An income distribution that could be tolerable as an accidental or random event, for example, might lead to violent revolt if seen to be the result of conscious choice on the part of another economic agent. Common observation tells us that, whatever the textbooks assume, such behavior is in fact very important in the makeup of normal human beings. I shall be showing that, at least in certain circumstances, such nonutilitarian behavior[13] makes ultimate utilitarian sense!

Since preferences are now assumed action-dependent, we can no longer postulate a fixed preference map defined simply over the parties' incomes Y_F and Y_S. Nevertheless, it is possible to place plausible restrictions upon how a second mover influenced by anger/gratitude motivations would respond to choices by a first mover. (By analogy with the foregoing, I assume here that only Second is subject to anger/gratitude emotions, First remaining throughout a coolly calculating and self-interested economic man.) In figure 14.5, Second's responses to First's choice along QQ' are summarized diagrammatically by his Anger/Gratitude Response (AGR) curve. This curve might take on a number of possible shapes, subject to the restrictions that (1) increasing wealth empowers Second to spend more either on transferring income to or else withdrawing income from First, but (2) the more "cooperative" is First's behavior (i.e., the more his choice along QQ' approaches point J), the less is Second's anger and/or the greater is Second's gratitude—with the obvious implication for his willingness to confer benefit or injury upon the other.[14]

In figure 14.5 the "effective anger" region of Second's AGR curve extends from point X to point M along the opportunity boundary QQ'. (If First were to choose any point to the west of X along QQ', Second might be even angrier still, but too impoverished to do anything about it.) As First's choice hypothetically shifts to the east of X so as to provide Second with more income, the latter can *increasingly afford to* react in an angry way but becomes *decreasingly inclined* to do so. Beyond the crossover at M,

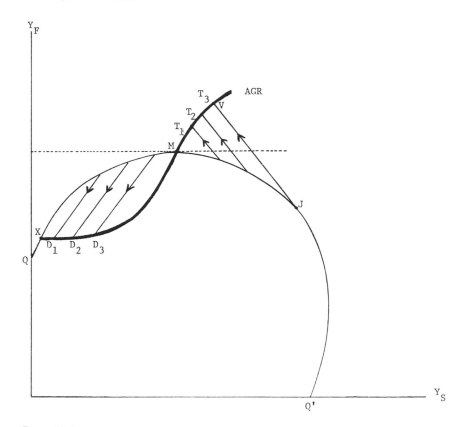

Figure 14.5
The Anger/Gratitude Response (AGR) curve—threat and promise.

Second enters his "effective gratitude" region. Here as his income grows thanks to First's making a more cooperative productive decision, Second is increasingly more able to react (now in a positive grateful way) and is also increasingly inclined to do so. Thus in the effective anger region, between X and M, the gap between QQ' and AGR first widens and then narrows. But in the effective gratitude region beyond the crossover at M the gap increasingly widens as Second's income increases. This type of situation, it may be noted, corresponds to the *threat-and-promise* contingent behavior mentioned in section 1.[15]

The outcome of the pattern pictured in figure 14.5 is at point V. The efficient productive solution is achieved (at J on QQ') plus a redistribution thereafter in such a way that both parties are better off in comparison with First's simple selfish solution at point M. But this is only one of quite a number of possible consequences of an anger-gratitude scaled reaction pattern.

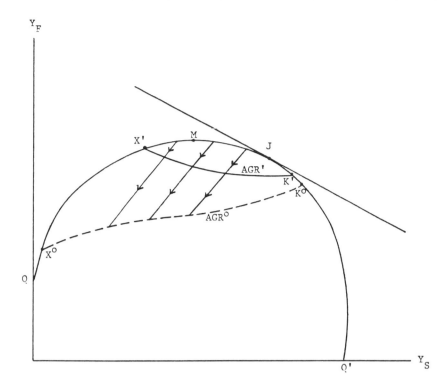

Figure 14.6
Effective and ineffective *AGR* curves.

Two other possibilities are pictured in figure 14.6. Here, in contrast to figure 14.5, anger is the dominant emotion influencing Second's behavior. However, this can have very different implications, as illustrated by the alternative *AGR* curves pictured—the (dashed) *AGR*° versus the (solid) *AGR*'. In each case, by assumption here the crossover point along *QQ*' lies to the east of the efficient productive solution *J*; Second does not give up his wrath until he is very well treated indeed. If Second's emotional set corresponds to *AGR*°, the best choice for First along *X*°*K*° is at point *K*°. Second's threat has worked so effectively as to force First to make a big sacrifice—going not merely beyond First's simple selfish optimum, *M*, but even beyond the jointly efficient outcome. If Second's *AGR*' curve is applicable, on the other hand, First will prefer point *X*'. Second's threat does not work at all. Or rather it works *to the disadvantage* of both parties, in view of the steps First will take to escape the threat. *X*' is inferior for both, not merely in comparison with what could have been achieved by Second's making a transfer after First chooses the jointly efficient outcome *J*, but even in comparison with First's simple selfish outcome *M*.

What is the difference between the two cases? AGR' represents a relatively "small" threat in comparison with $AGR°$—it does not take hold at all until point X' rather than $X°$, and it inflicts smaller punishment throughout the relevant range. This feature is not the essential, however. The important feature is the overall *slope* of the AGR curve. That is, no matter whether the magnitude of the threat is large or small, its effectiveness depends upon the "appeasing" effect of each increment of compliance. A sufficient appeasing effect would be reflected by a positively sloped AGR curve, like $AGR°$ in figure 14.6. Here a coolly calculating First can always do better by complying, up to the limit of feasibility at point $K°$. But if Second's anger is never sufficiently appeased, as reflected by the negatively sloped AGR' in the diagram, First can minimize the loss to himself by non-compliance—to the disadvantage of Second as well.

While many other pictures can be drawn illustrating interesting possibilities, the following points summarize the key considerations:

1. The rationally selfish first mover will want and (assuming that he has the relevant information) be able to achieve the most northerly point along the AGR curve that represents Second's scaled emotional response to his behavior.

2. Second's AGR curve will typically take off at some interior point X *along QQ'*, where he begins to have income enough to be able to indulge his anger. The AGR curve may have positive or negative slope, but will eventually cross QQ' again at a point where First's move has become generous enough to appease Second's anger.

3. If *anger* is Second's dominating emotion, reflected by an AGR curve that does not cut QQ' until some point K to the east of the efficient point J, then the solution for First—the most northerly point along AGR (unless M is higher still)—will tend to be toward one extreme or the other, depending upon whether the slope of the AGR curve is predominantly positive or negative. If the slope is predominantly positive, there are typically positive *marginal* payoffs to First of appeasement, of bowing to the threat. It does not matter how heavy a punishment Second might impose in aggregate, but only how he reacts, on the margin, to First's concessions. A positively sloped AGR function thus tends toward an excellent outcome for Second, with First appeasing him heavily. If, on the other hand, the slope of the AGR curve is predominantly negative, First typically suffers negative marginal payoffs from making concessions. Here the typical outcome is toward the other extreme, at point X where Second is left too poor to inflict punishment. Of course, here First will end up poor as well.

4. But if *gratitude* is Second's dominating emotion, reflected by an AGR crossing QQ' to the west of point J, the efficient solution tends

to be achieved—provided again that the *AGR* curve has positive slope. Both parties then end up better off than at First's simple selfish optimum.

3

Biologists and anthropologists have been long concerned with explaining the great gap between human intellectual capacities and those of the nonhuman primates, an advance that appears to go beyond the adaptive environmental requirements of primitive man (Washburn, 1960; Rose, 1980; Staddon, 1981). But equally mysterious, perhaps, is the survival of those *limitations* upon self-interested rationality we term the passions or emotions. In *The Expression of the Emotions*, Charles Darwin emphasized the universality of these emotions over the human species, and also their continuity with behaviors visible among animals. Of course, there would be no special need to explain survival of the passions if they are only "imperfections." Since the development of any trait involves some energetic cost, or at least some opportunity cost in terms of other capacities that have to be sacrificed, we do not need to explain why all living beings are not unlimitedly fecund, powerful beyond measure, or as speedy as light. But we ought not prejudge the question as to whether the observed limitations upon the human ability to pursue self-interested rationality are really no more than imperfections—might not these seeming disabilities actually be functional?

The thrust of the argument here has been that certain patterns of environmental payoffs to interpersonal cooperative opportunities can make retention of a capacity for emotion materially profitable. In this paper I distinguished between the *action-independent* versus the *action-dependent* passions. The first category was illustrated by non-self-interested motivations (the malevolence/benevolence spectrum), the second by impairment of the ability to calculate owing to reactive "loss of control" (the anger/gratitude spectrum). Given that one party in a social interaction is a selfish and perfectly rational calculator, it turns out that there are circumstances in which it is indeed profitable for the other to diverge from self-interested rationality—in accordance with one or both of these emotional scales.

As a related point, evolutionary biologists have also been concerned to explain the survival of "altruism" on the one hand and "spite" on the other. Despite the psychological connotations of these terms, the interpretation in the standard literature has been entirely operational rather than motivational: "altruism" is taken to mean acting so as to help another organism, at a cost to oneself, while "spite" refers to incurring a cost so as to injure another. Since evolutionary success is a selfish criterion,[16] the biological literature has attempted to explore the different patterns by which proximate sacrifice, the cost incurred to benefit or to injure another organism, can ultimately pay off through some indirect route [for example, in the case of "altruism," if one's beneficiaries are kin (Hamilton, 1964) or if an other-benefiting act leads to adequate reciprocation (Trivers, 1971)]. This paper, in contrast, directly attacks the problem of motivation. (Hence it is not applicable to lower organisms lacking the capacity for emotions.) What it examines are possible mechanisms whereby individuals may be led to supply the reward or punishment (the positive or negative reciprocation) that make certain forms of social cooperation possible. The vague terms "altruism" and "spite" are inadequate to describe the subtly different forms that these reciprocations may take.

In summary, the models analyzed here represent a special but illuminating case. It was assumed that, in a given payoff environment, a merely self-interested and accurately calculating party has the first move, after which a possibly emotion-influenced agent makes his choice in response. When it comes to the action-independent emotions—the malevolence/benevolence spectrum—*benevolence* can serve to guarantee a promise, but *malevolence* is not generally effective in guaranteeing execution of a threat. (A curious yet important point is that just a little benevolence may not work either—a generosity threshold must be overcome.) As for the action-dependent reactions, the anger/gratitude scale, *gratitude* has effects rather parallel with benevolence, but *anger* tends to be more effective than malevolence in securing cooperation. The key reason for the difference is that malevolence becomes a more powerful force as the responding party's wealth increases, a factor that strongly inhibits any desire on the part of the first mover to enrich the other by cooperation. But anger tends to erode as the first mover's choice shifts toward cooperation, hence may provide the needed inducement for achieving a mutually beneficial arrangement. The most general and interesting conclusions are that (i) absence of self-interest can pay off *even measured in terms of material selfish gain*, and, a parallel but quite distinct point, (ii) the loss of control that makes calculated behavior impossible can be more profitable than calculated optimization. (It follows that a coolly calculating individual might more or less successfully *pretend* to be driven by passion-dominated responses. Furthermore, in this pretense he need not be seeking a merely selfish goal!)

Analytically, this paper demonstrates the not-so-paradoxical fact that it is possible to analyze, in terms of effects upon rationally calculated self-interest, the consequences of non-self-interested motivations and of limitations upon the ability to calculate. The economist must go beyond the assumption of "economic man" precisely because of the economic advantage of *not* behaving like economic man—an advantage that presumably explains why the world is not populated solely by economic men.

I would like also to indicate some of the limitations of the analysis, which suggest directions for generalization:

1. The analysis here does not pretend to explain *all* the behaviors and attitudes we think of as emotions, but only certain of these, which are alleged to help guarantee the execution of contracts. Other types of emotions also serve important functions—for example, fear, which makes us flee danger, or romantic love, which helps us win mates—but are not relevant to the purpose at hand. Coming closer to the topic here, there are still other sentiments that bear upon the kinds of interpersonal transactions a group of individuals can arrive at, but which I have not studied—envy, pride, and shame are among them.

2. I have dealt only with one-time interactions. There is already a considerable body of literature dealing with repeated interactions, in which refusal to continue a business relationship with a defecting trading partner may alone suffice to enforce a contract. Nevertheless, I suspect the anger/gratitude response pattern is an important additional factor, providing a degree of extra support where mere refusal of future business cannot carry all the weight of maintaining a social relationship.

3. The postulated division of responsibility, whereby the first mover has free choice of productive arrangements while the second mover can only react by a reward or deprivation response, is of course a special assumption. But I do not believe it is unduly restrictive. We could equally well imagine the first mover as making some preliminary choice that narrows down the productive or other options available, after which the second mover makes a "finalizing" decision, possibly including productive aspects as well. The assumed special shapes of the functions could also be easily generalized. If the productive opportunity locus were to become less concave-downward (i.e., if QQ' in the diagrams were to approach a linear or even a convex-downward shape), the potential mutual gain via productive coordination would be reduced. Cooperation will then, other things being equal, become less likely.[17] And similarly, one could allow for different "exchange rates" in the second mover's ability to transfer or to deprive the other party, with predictable consequences for the efficacy of the second mover's ability to exert influence upon the other.

4. I considered only interactions between a self-interested coolly calculating party on the one hand, and an emotion-driven individual on the other, where the latter has the last move. If the time sequence were reversed, what I have called "threat" and "promise" would evidently not be successful.

5. Finally, the analysis here hints at a more daring suggestion. *Leader-*

ship involves to a significant extent the function of conferring reward or punishment upon other members of the society, i.e., serving as second mover in many social interactions. While the role of leader is often simply seized by the strongest and/or cleverest, there also is commonly some degree of popular consent involved. Might it not be the case that the "inspirational" or "charismatic" quality that we look for in leaders is an extraordinary capacity to transcend self-interested motivations, to be passionately driven by action-dependent, non-utilitarian goals? There are of course merely self-interested, calculating princes who would follow Machiavelli's advice: "Therefore, a prudent ruler ought not to keep faith when by so doing it would be against his interest, and when the reasons which made him bind himself no longer exist" (*The Prince*, XVIII). But such a ruler would likely find it difficult to elicit from citizens that extra measure of devoted cooperation upon which the survival of his regime may depend. So, even the most Machiavellian of princes is likely at least to *simulate* the possession of genuine action-independent or action-dependent passions—what Boulding (1969) has called the heroic ethic.

Notes

1. Smith, *Moral Sentiments*, p. 212.
2. On this, see especially Coase (1976), pp. 536, 542–543.
3. *Moral Sentiments*, p. 300.
4. Ibid., p. 303.
5. Compare also the Talmudic argument that even the evil impulse instilled by God in man is "very good": "Were it not for that impulse, a man would not build a house, marry a wife, beget children or conduct business affairs" (Cohen, 1949).
6. Sometimes a meeting of the minds can suffice, as in adoption of a convention that no one has any incentive to violate. Agreeing to drive on the right (left), or to meet under the clock at Grand Central Station, are possible examples (on this see Schelling, 1978a, chapter 3). I have shown that such coordination tends automatically to emerge under particular types of social environments (Hirshleifer, 1982, p. 14).
7. It might be thought that this analysis is over-elaborate in that DEFECT is by inspection a "dominant" strategy for each player given the payoffs of Matrix 1. But dominance arguments must be used with great care in sequential-play protocols. It is easy to demonstrate underlying payoff matrices where the *first* mover would want to emply a "dominated" strategy, since he can thereby influence the other player's responding choice. Schelling (1978b) provides a number of illustrations: for example, to keep you from kidnapping my children I may give away all my wealth.
8. The starred cell is also the unique "Nash equilibrium" of the usual (simultaneous move) Prisoners' Dilemma. However, we are dealing here with a sequential-move rather than a simultaneous-move game. It would be possible, using the appropriate expanded matrix in each case, to expand the Nash equilibrium idea to cover sequential-move games, but I shall not in fact be using that solution concept.
9. While superior goods are the normal pattern, standard economic models allow for the possibility of "inferior" goods—i.e., goods of which less is chosen as the consumer

becomes richer. This possibility can, however, be excluded here. Note that if Y_F were an inferior good for Second, then First would be motivated to impoverish his benefactor! Even if this were infeasible, First would also be motivated to impoverish himself. If First throws away $10, Second would then rationally compensate him by more than the $10 lost. If Y_F were inferior over any range, this process would continue until Y_F entered a range where it was no longer inferior, unless Second became bankrupt before this point was reached (see Becker, 1981, Chapter 8).

10. The proposition of this section can easily be extended to cover a benevolent or male-volent First. In particular, there can be instances where Second's benevolence can induce cooperation even from a malevolent First, to their mutual gain.

11. The terminology is due to E. O. Wilson (1978). However, the point made here diverges from Wilson's. He was concerned to contrast the weakness of "hard-core altruism" (benevolence) *compared* to "soft-core altruism" (enlightened self-interest) as organizers of cooperation in large social units. The analysis here indicates that the two factors may sometimes *complement* one another in a socially useful way.

12. Such models of interpersonal consumption preferences have been employed by a number of economists, including Boulding (1962, chapter 2), and Becker (1971).

13. It would be possible, by a somewhat forced twist of terminology, to interpret passionate behavior as rational choice—for example, by having the individual's preferences (as to benevolence or malevolence) be responsive to the other's actions. But passionate behavior, the essential character of which involves loss of control and heedlessness of consequences, cannot be fitted smoothly into the utilitarian mold.

14. While there is some diagrammatic similarity between the *AGR* and the previous *WEP* curves, they stand logically on quite a different footing. An *AGR* curve *could* also be interpreted as a locus of tangencies of transfer lines (or deprivation lines) with the second mover's indifference curves. But, the crucial point is, owing to the emotional action-dependent effects, Second's entire indifference curve map changes in response to First's choice along QQ'.

15. Of course a person capable *only* of anger can only guarantee execution of threats; a person capable only of gratitude is similarly restricted to promises. Having such a narrow repertoire of behaviors may be less costly, but restricts the contingent strategies available.

16. "Natural selection will never produce in a being any structure more injurious than beneficial to that being, for natural selection acts solely by and for the good of each" (Darwin, *Origin of Species*, chapter 6).

17. See Friedman (1980).

References

Becker, Gary S. (1971). A Theory of Social Interactions. *J. Polit. Econ.* 82:1063–1093.

Becker, Gary S. (1976). Altruism, Egoism, and Genetic Fitness: Economics and Sociobiology. *J. Econ. Lit.* 14:817–828.

Becker, Gary S. (1981). *A Treatise on the Family.* Cambridge, MA: Harvard University Press.

Boulding, Kenneth E. (1962). *Conflict and Defense.* New York: Harper & Row.

Boulding, Kenneth E. (1969). Economics as a Moral Science. *Am. Econ. Rev.* 59.

Coase, R. H. (1976). Adam Smith's View of Man. *J. Law & Econ.* 19.

Cohen, A, (1949). *Everyman's Talmud*, New American ed. New York: E. P. Dutton.

Darwin, Charles (1872/1859). *The Origin of Species by Means of Natural Selection*, 6th ed. (1st ed., 1859).

Darwin, Charles (1872). *The Expression of the Emotions in Man and Animals.*

Friedman, David (1980). Many, Few, One: Social Harmony and the Shrunken Choice Set. *Am Econ. Rev.* 70.

Hamilton, W. D. (1964). The Genetical Evolution of Social Behavior, I. *J. Theor. Biol.* 7:1–17.

Hirshleifer, J. (1977). Shakespeare vs. Becker on Altruism: the Importance of Having the Last Word. *J. Econ. Lit.* 15:500–502.

Hirshleifer, J. (1982). Evolutionary Models in Economics and Law: Cooperation versus Conflict strategies. *Res. In Law & Econ.* 4:1–60.

Howard, Nigel (1971). *Paradoxes of Rationality.* Cambridge, MA: MIT Press.

Luce, R. Duncan, and Howard Raiffa (1957). *Games and Decisions.* New York: Wiley.

Macaulay, Stewart (1963). Non-Contractual Relations in Business. *Am. Sociol. Rev.* 28:55–67.

Rose, Michael (1980). The Mental Arms Race Amplifier. *Human Ecology* 8:285–293.

Schelling, Thomas C. (1960). *The Strategy of Conflict.* London: Oxford University Press.

Schelling, Thomas C. (1978a). *Micromotives and Macrobehavior.* New York: Norton.

Schelling, Thomas C. (1978b). Altruism, Meanness, and Other Potentially Strategic Behaviors. *American Economic Review* 68:229–230.

Schelling, Thomas C. (1980). The Intimate Contest for Self-Command. *The Public Interest* 60.

Smith, Adam (1969). *The Theory of Moral Sentiments,* ed. E. G. West. Indianapolis: Liberty Classics.

Staddon, J. E. R. (1981). On a Possible Relation between Cultural Transmission and Genetical evolution. In P. P. G. Bateson and P. H. Klopfer (eds.), *Advantages of Diversity,* vol. 4, New York: Plenum, pp. 135–145.

Telser, L. G. (1980). A Theory of Self-Enforcing Agreements. *J. of Bus.* 53:27–45.

Thompson, Earl A., and Roger L. Faith (1981). A Pure Theory of Strategic Behavior and Social Institutions. *Am. Econ. Rev.* 71:366–380.

Trivers, Robert L. (1971). The Evolution of Reciprocal Altruism. *Quart. Rev. Biol.* 46:35–58.

Washburn (1960). Tools and Human Evolution. *Sc. Am.* 203:63–75.

Wilson, Edward O. (1978). Altruism. *Harvard Mag.* 81.

15

Human Kinds

John Dupré

---

1 Introduction

A critical dimension of debate about any large-scale scientific theory is the question of the scope of its generalizations. It is this issue, with respect to the application of evolutionary theory to behavior, particularly human, that I want to address in this paper.

Many very disparate academic disciplines claim relevance to the understanding of human behavior, and these disciplines vary very widely in their pretensions to scope. At one extreme are the main humanistic disciplines (though excluding most of philosophy). Historians may or may not imagine universal processes or laws emerging from the narratives they construct, but they have not primarily achieved fame for the vindication of such generalizations. Literary critics may have general theories about the social functions of texts, but their main professional activity is the study of the most idiosyncratic of cultural artifacts. Among the social sciences, cultural and symbolic anthropology, and much of sociology, is equally focused on such cultural specifics. In such disciplines, discussion that is not so concretely focused almost always concerns methodology rather than the postulation of universal laws.

Uncontroversially at the other extreme are the medical sciences, especially those concerned with behavioral pathology, and a large part of psychology. Since only the most ignorant of racists deny that *Homo sapiens* is a respectable biological species, it is to be expected that strictly physiologically based studies should claim species—or often wider—scope. The psychology of perception, or much of learning theory, can clearly be conceived of in this way. There is no reason to doubt that there are commonalities among humans about the way information is collected and processed. Shepard (this volume) suggests ways in which evolutionary ideas may be applied to such very general aspects of the mind.

This paper has benefited greatly from some extremely thoughtful and pertinent comments on an earlier version by Peter Richerson. I am also very grateful to the Stanford Humanities Center, where this paper was written.

Studies of these two kinds generally avoid conflict with one another. This is because the studies with the broad scope do not generally claim to explain behavior in anything like the detailed way possible for theories of the first kind. The mechanisms of perception, for instance, while obviously necessary for much human behavior, would hardly be expected to determine very much behavior on their own. Relative to the explanation of behavior, then, we might distinguish between those disciplines that aim at breadth but not depth, and those that sacrifice breadth for depth.

Conflict is likely to arise when a theory attempts to claim both breadth and depth. Economics has sometimes, though generally cautiously, tended to make claims of both these kinds. Forthright and unambiguous is E. O. Wilson's notorious manifesto at the beginning of *Sociobiology* (Wilson, 1975). Less aggressively, sociobiologically inclined anthropologists have argued that the potentially universal scope of evolutionary arguments gives an evolutionary methodology a fundamental synthetic role linking the more parochial approaches traditional in the social sciences with each other and with biology.[1]

I want to approach the question of the scope and depth of evolutionary explanations of human behavior by way of an analogy with the explanation of nonhuman behavior. As a partly heuristic device, it will be useful for this purpose to introduce the notion of a "cultural species." I do not mean this concept to be taken wholly seriously, though it does effectively dramatize a major part of the argument I want to present. At the end of the paper I shall indicate one point at which, I believe, the analogy implicit in it breaks down.

2 Culture and Human Behavior

The attempt to apply evolutionary ideas to human behavior has constantly elicited the protest that any such project must disregard the centrality of culture to human life, and is either hopelessly naive or even malicious. Evolutionists retort that human culture is merely an admittedly unique biological phenomenon that appeared at a particular point in the evolution of a particular species of primate, and should be amenable to the same general treatment as any other biological phenomenon. In particular, it is argued, it could not have evolved if it had not been adaptive. And so, subject to whatever limitations may be recognized in the general assumption of optimal adaptation, human behavior, whether culturally or genetically transmitted, should be subject to the standard kind of evolutionary analysis. Some account of the source of the allegedly independent causal force of culture seems at least a reasonable demand. To a considerable extent, participants in this debate, for want of any agreement about adequate standards of explanation, have simply argued at cross purposes to one another.

The chances of genuine progress have been greatly augmented by recent theoretical studies of the possibility of autonomous[2] processes of cultural evolution (Cavalli-Sforza and Feldman, 1981; Boyd and Richerson, 1985). Such studies start from the observation that culture might evolve in a way closely analogous to, but also quite distinct from, standard Darwinian evolution. It is generally agreed that an evolutionary process will occur whenever a class of organisms displays heritable variation in fitness. It is highly plausible that cultural variation should satisfy such a condition. On the other hand, the details of such a process may be very different from those of the familiar Darwinian one. First, the transmission of culture occurs through different channels; there is no reason to assume that it will primarily, or anyway solely, occur from biological parents to offspring, and it may occur laterally, within rather than across generations. Second, it will presumably be Lamarckian; one would expect acquired cultural variation to be transmitted. And third, there is no reason to assume that the appropriate concept of fitness will coincide with the equivalent Darwinian notion. Presumably the appropriate concept of fitness will depend on some measure of the tendency of different cultural variants to be transmitted to other individuals. Though arguments have been proposed purporting to show that, at least in the long term, the two concepts of fitness will tend to coincide (Durham, 1978, 1981), Boyd and Richerson show in considerable detail why this may not be the case.

The great achievement of this work is that it shows precisely what kinds of processes can lead to an independent role for culture in the determination and explanation of behavior. Rather than blankly confronting evolutionists, or sociobiologists, with incompatible ways of approaching human behavior, and asserting their superiority, it confronts them precisely on their own ground. Culture is shown to be fully amenable to integration within a broad evolutionary perspective, and also to have a potentially important role in evolution. On the other hand, while Boyd and Richerson are prepared to argue that some autonomous processes of cultural evolution have been significant in human evolution and offer some specific if tentative instances, they are generally agnostic about the relative importance of genetic transmission and cultural transmission in the determination of human behavior, and leave open the possibility that genetically determined biases with respect to the transmission of culture may have led cultural evolution predominantly to converge on the results that would be predicted by more conventional sociobiology. In this paper I want to argue that cultural variation, very probably the product of divergent cultural evolution, should be seen as the primary focus for the explanation of human behavior.

3   Cultural Species

It will be useful to introduce this argument by recalling a fundamental explanandum of the Darwinian theory of evolution, the diversity of life, or, in a well-known phrase, the origin of species. Note that the diversity in question is that between, not within, species. The latter is an essential part of the explanation of the former. Of course, the details of the process of speciation remain highly controversial to this day. But that it is a primary goal of the theory of evolution to explain it, and that no such explanation would be possible without the existence of intraspecific variation, is not in dispute. And this indicates a striking disanalogy with the theory of cultural evolution as it has mainly been developed. As so far described, the theory is largely concerned with anagenetic evolution within one lineage, *Homo sapiens*.[3] My suggestion is that the full import of the theoretical development only becomes apparent when human evolution is considered as a cladogenetic process involving the generation of many different (cultural) species. It is to explore this suggestion that I want to consider the significance of treating distinct cultures as genuine taxonomic entities, what I am calling "cultural species."[4]

The importance of this perspective, however, derives not so much from the role of evolution in explaining diversity as from the role of taxonomy, or the description of diversity, in evolutionary explanations. This role may best be understood by adverting to another fundamental issue in evolutionary theory, the problem of holism. A central difficulty in adaptationist methodology is the existence of crucial limitations on the atomistic approach generally characteristic of this methodology. These limitations have been identified at various levels of organization. Beginning at the genetic level, probably the least serious difficulty is the phenomenon of genetic linkage, the fact that Mendelian independent assortment breaks down when genes are close together on a chromosome. More significant is pleiotropy, the observation that genes may affect a variety of apparently quite distinct phenotypic properties. And perhaps most important is the phenomenon of epistasis, the dependence of the expression of genes on the action of genes at distinct loci. While these phenomena have mainly been emphasized as showing the limitations of models of single locus selection, they are symptomatic of a much more fundamental fact, the enormous degree of integration of a biological organism.[5] What I want to emphasize here is that the way that a particular kind of organism is integrated, the way its parts and characteristic forms of behavior fit together, while certainly a product of past evolution, is also the most fundamental constraint on the evolutionary process. Thus to whatever extent general laws can be formulated about the course of evolution, their consequences cannot be understood in any concrete way without an account of the nature, past and present, of the particular lineage to which they are to be applied. And this kind of account can only be derived from a descriptive taxonomy of the organisms concerned. The elaboration of this claim, and its relevance to the study of both human and other animal behavior, will be the central task of this essay.

4 Animal Behavior and Taxonomy

To defend the centrality of cultural taxonomy to the explanation of human behavior, I want now to develop an analogy with a case of nonhuman behavior. Consider the question of understanding the behavior of a fairly diverse group of animals, say the mammals, relevant to the acquisition of food. The question I want to ask is to what extent such explanations can be universal, and to what extent they must rest on quite specific aspects of the physiology and ecology of the particular species.

One obvious aspect of such an explanation that will be quite universal will be the most general function attributed to it. Animals seek food because they need energy for survival, reproduction, and whatever other activities they engage in. Almost equally universal, at least in general outline, are the physiological processes leading from the capture of food to the utilization of energy from that food. All mammals have mouths into which items of food are placed, most have some kind of teeth with which these items are physically degraded, all have stomachs and intestines in which the items are chemically degraded and absorbed, and all have anuses from which the unused components are excreted. Of course the exact processes of physical and chemical degradation are significantly differentiated, but I shall ignore those here.

Much more promising attempts at general explanation with prospects for addressing the specifics of behavior are provided by evolutionary optimality theorists—in particular, by what has become known as "optimal foraging theory" (Charnov, 1976). This theory addresses questions such as how long an animal will persist in a particular episode of foraging, how many different kinds of food item it will seek, and whether it will share pieces of food with other conspecifics. My interest here is not in the adequacy of such analyses (though see Emlen, this volume), but in what is involved in their application. And what is clear is that even if the theory were to apply perfectly to every possible case, no predictions about behavior could be made without considering the details of the ecology and physiology of the type of organism concerned.

To begin with, it is a clear feature of such models that the optimal searching behavior is a function of characteristics of the kind of food being sought. If the food consists of small items concentrated in particular areas, such models can give quite precise predictions, as a function of the density of food in these patches, about when the animal will abandon one patch and move on to look for another. On the other hand, if the food is uniformly distributed in small portions, or randomly distributed in large bundles, this particular type of model will have no application. Thus, however successful the model is in describing the decision procedure of an anteater deciding to move on to the next termite mound, it will tell us nothing about a horse grazing in a cultivated field or a tiger stalking through the forest.

Similarly, there is a very elegant analysis of what variety of food items a particular animal will be prepared to eat. And while this may be extremely illuminating in explaining why a shrew eats beetles but shows no interest in spiders, say, it will clearly have no application to anteaters—for the obvious reason that they are entirely specialized at the eating of termites. Moreover, even when we know that the animal is an omnivore, or a generalized carnivore, unless we know a good deal about its physiology, we are still in no position to draw any behavioral conclusions from such a model. If we knew merely that shrews were generalized carnivores, we might well predict that they would eat nothing but elephants. Slightly less absurdly, we might anticipate that grizzly bears should live mainly on deer or other large ungulates if we did not find out that they could not run fast enough to catch them.

A further point, emphasized by Emlen (this volume), is that the way an animal looks for food may very well depend also on what other types of behavior it engages in. A very general example might be the question whether the animal is nocturnal or diurnal. The prey species selected by a nocturnal carnivore that hunts at water holes will evidently differ from those selected by a diurnal carnivore. A nocturnal way of life will require a whole complex of adaptations, such as suitable sensory equipment and mode of locomotion, which may well provide constraints on the sources of nutrition available to it. And of course there is no reason to assume that the method of foraging will be the decisive determinant in the evolutionary selection of a nocturnal life.

The point that is perhaps being labored here is just that an atomistic treatment at a quite abstract level of one general aspect of behavior generates no behavioral conclusions whatever. Even if the optimality analysis proved to be exceptionlessly true, it would have no application to a particular species without detailed understanding of how the possible modes of acquisition of food are integrated with the many other behavioral and physiological peculiarities of the species in question. The question that is then crucial for considering the human analogy is the following. How far must one pursue a process of taxonomic analysis before one arrives at a sufficiently homogeneous group of organisms for a meaningful application of abstractly conceived optimality analyses? And the rhetorical point of introducing the notion of "cultural species" is to argue that for *Homo sapiens* this process must be pursued to a much finer level than merely the biological species.

5 Human Behavior and Cultural Taxonomy

I want now to show why the application of such general adaptationist arguments to humans not only faces the same sorts of limitations as would apply to a general account of mammalian foraging behavior, but does so in an even more severe form. And the problem is more severe primarily because even if it is defensible to consider the behavior of nonhuman animals as involving the reconciliation of a very small number of goals derived from the general postulate of fitness maximization—feeding, reproduction, predator avoidance, perhaps—this does not seem to be at all plausible for the human case. I put this more cautiously than I would wish, because a major tendency in sociobiology, supported by sympathetic anthropologists and some economists, is committed to just this prima facie implausible thesis. I shall argue, however, that it is not only implausible, but also false. And consequently, the variation in the context into which a particular aspect of behavior has to be integrated may actually be greater within the human species than even that across somewhat related animal species.

Let us again focus on behavior involved in the acquisition of food, and again begin by asking what aspects of this behavior may fairly be treated as human universals. Clearly, the ultimate, though by no means exclusive, function of such behavior is common to all humans, and indeed is the same as in other animals. Equally clearly, the physiological context is much more homogeneous than that considered in the previous case, and this may reasonably be extended to include general features of the neurological processing involved. Perhaps some of these general features may be amenable to the kind of evolutionary approach suggested by Cosmides and Tooby (this volume).

Leaving aside for the moment that a large proportion of the world's human population "forages" by carrying pieces of paper of purely conventional significance to the supermarket or village store, let us focus only on the hunter-gatherer societies to which evolutionary analysis seems most readily applicable. Despite the physiological homogeneity, it is obvious that the geographic variability of human populations will be sufficient to require one crucial environmental constraint. One cannot select the same items of food in the Arctic as in a tropical forest or in a desert; so, no behavioral predictions follow from the general analysis, at least by itself. This problem may be considered relatively superficial, analogous to the common observation that no predictions follow merely from Newton's laws without detailed specification of the initial conditions to which they are to be applied. But even if we take a description of the environment as providing the necessary initial conditions for application of optimality analyses, there are much more serious obstacles to be faced. And these again involve the integration of one aspect of behavior into a much broader pattern.

One basic difficulty that emerges here may best be expressed as a difficulty in determining what is being optimized. The great strength of optimality theory in biology is that for all the doubts about whether optimal solutions will in fact be achieved, or even wholly determinable, it is roughly clear what, if anything, is being optimized. In the standard Darwinian conception, even when there are conflicting objectives, so that one goal must be treated as a constraint on the behavior appropriate for achieving the other, at least a common currency exists for evaluating such trade-offs, namely, inclusive fitness. That such a resource is available in analyzing human societies is much less clear. The problem may be analyzed in two stages. First, ecological analysis of human behavior will generally begin with assessing not fitness, but something treated as a promising proxy. Divergence of the proxy from actual fitness consequences has been recognized by ecological anthropologists, and causes great complications. But second, and ultimately more serious, other facts about the social organization of a society may provide constraints that are not even analyzable into competing determinants of fitness. (The analysis in the first part of Lewontin's paper in this volume suggests that problems of the kind indicated here may become unmanageable even apart from the special complexities in the human case.)

The difficulties of the first kind are fairly evident in the literature on optimal foraging theory. The simplest assumption is that hunter-gatherers should adopt a foraging strategy that maximizes the rate of energy acquisition. Presumably the adoption of such a strategy is to be seen as an adaptation, achieved either by group or individual selection, with an undetermined mix of genetic and cultural inheritance (Durham, 1981, pp. 228–229). Since even "primitive" peoples have many goals other than the avoidance of starvation, and foraging strategies may have relevance to some of these other goals, the plausibility of assuming that energy intake maximization will be a successful predictor of foraging strategy must depend on the assumption that energy acquisition is a dominant constraint on the survival or reproduction of either individuals or groups. But even apart from any other goals that may be directly served by particular foraging techniques, average rate of energy intake may well not be the appropriate variable to consider. If energy shortages are a recurring problem for hunter-gatherer groups (Winterhalder, 1981, p. 67), it may well be that minimizing the variance of energy acquisition rather than maximizing the mean rate will be crucial (Smith, 1981). Again, energy may not be the crucial constraint on the success of foraging. Linear programming models analyzing the various goods and dietary constituents that can be important consequences of foraging suggest that much more specific factors may be important at different times (Keene, 1981). While these complications do not show that this approach to anthropological explanation is hopeless, they do illustrate well the difficulties encountered by optimization in the absence of the clear definition of currency provided in evolutionary theory (difficulties, of course, in addition to the limitations of optimization within evolutionary theory).

The preceding difficulties show that human foraging is a very much more complex activity than, say, feeding gasoline into a car. But the fundamental difficulty is not so much this complexity but, again, the question of integration. Durham (1978, 1981) has argued that whether the determinants of optimal foraging behavior are cultural or genetic, ultimately selection within and between groups will guarantee that this optimum is approached. Presumably this would be true if there were infinite variation and sufficient selection. But a general point lying behind the subordination of optimality to taxonomic fact is that there is far from infinite variation. The available options on which selection can work are both highly restricted and—which has been my main point so far—highly integrated. In both the human and the general cases, the integration, by presenting only a relatively small number of structured packages of features, is a primary explanation of the limitations on evolutionary possibility. The force of the analogy I have been trying to develop is that the integration of organisms with a specific physiology and a specific behavioral repertoire quite generally provides an extremely powerful set of constraints on the optimal adaptation of a particular domain of behavior. The further point in considering human behavior is that specific cultures are also highly structured systems. My purpose in considering the notion of cultural species is to emphasize that this is a level of organization quite as significant as the specific adaptation of an animal species as a constraint on behavior.

I do not mean to imply that ecological anthropologists typically ignore constraints of these kinds. On the contrary, and in contrast at least to what Philip Kitcher (1985) has called "pop sociobiology," most evolutionary anthropologists aim only to describe quite local fitness maxima. My worry, however, is not merely that local circumstances will determine different fitness maxima, but rather that aspects of the overall social integration of human groups may constrain behavior in such a way that no optimum in terms of any remotely simple features even of the local environment will be attainable.

Let me illustrate the kind of thing I have in mind with two crude examples. Suppose that a certain species of lobster proves to be one of the most efficient sources of energy and nutrients in the environment of a particular tribe. However, age-old tradition has it that only the aristocracy is permitted to eat lobsters (as, for instance, in England the consumption of swans is the prerogative of the royal family and the fellows of St. John's College, Cambridge). Hence lobsters, from an optimal point of view, are greatly underutilized. Or perhaps monkeys would be an ideal food source, but the local religion considers them unclean (miscreants are supposed to be reincarnated as monkeys, for example). Historical experience does not suggest any overwhelming tendency for such arbitrary conventions to collapse in the cause of efficiency; and there may well be strong functional reasons, again to be understood in terms of the particular articulation of a particular culture, why they are maintained. Assume, also, that the tribes in question get by quite well without eating lobsters or monkeys, though perhaps with a slightly lower equilibrium population. The point about infinite variation should now be clear enough. There may be no other groups competing in the same territory; and if they are, they are not likely to differ only in respect to whether lobsters or monkeys are part of the diet. The determinants of competitive success may be quite unrelated to diet— the monkey shunners, for instance, have invented the bow and arrow. There is no relevant individual selection, since anyone found illegally eating a lobster is summarily executed.

To summarize the preceding argument, my main thesis is that very little in the way of a behavioral conclusion can come from a general evolutionary argument. This is not an argument against the legitimacy of abstract optimality arguments in evolutionary theory, but a point about their place in a general theory of behavior. The analogy mentioned above, between evolutionary theory and Newtonian mechanics, indicates a starting point for my contention: general theories have no consequences without specifying initial conditions or constraints. The situation in evolutionary theory is worse, however, because an abstract optimality argument can only indicate one among many possible evolutionary forces (see Richerson and Boyd, this volume, and Sober, this volume). As the complexity of an organism increases, so will the number of relevant forces that may come into play. Not only do we need a detailed description of the particular organism to understand what the significance of a particular force, *ceteris absentibus*, would be, but we need such information to understand how various such forces have interacted in the organism's evolutionary history, and now determine its mode of existence in its current environment. The analogy with mechanics would begin to be appropriate only if we add to the determination of initial conditions the stipulation that the bodies concerned were additionally endowed with various degrees of electric charge and magnetism [the point thus parallels part of Nancy Cartwright's (1983, essay 3) argument for the falsity of the laws of physics].

The specific claim about humans is that part of the information we need is the detailed environmental parameters of a particular human being. I am suggesting that cultural evolution, in relation to this explanatory problem, has provided variation quite comparable to the physiological variation generated by Darwinian evolution; and features of the cultural environment that exhibit this variation are indeed among the decisive determinants of human behavior. Moreover, there is little basis for the assumption that these determinants can even approximately be reduced to genetic fitness. I have tried to indicate some general considerations that show why this is so; Boyd and Richerson have examined some specific processes with this consequence in a much more rigorous way. These points go a long way toward justifying the appeal to the notion of a cultural species.

The point of all this is not, of course, that *Homo sapiens* is in any way an inadequate *biological* species. The question is rather whether the biological species category is an adequate one for analyzing human behavior. My answer, evidently, is in the negative. The claim that I have been trying to defend is only that cultural distinctions within the (biological) species should play a role in our understanding analogous to that played by distinctions between species in biology generally. Obviously this is not an attempt to identify the one concept with the other. It would thus be glaringly irrelevant to point out that there is substantial gene exchange— or even, for that matter, cultural exchange—between human groups. (I do not know how the pattern even of *gene* interchange between human cultural groups would compare with, say, that between various species of *Compositae* or *Rosaceae*. But as I have just said, this question is of no relevance to the present discussion.)

Let me finally put the issue in a rather broader philosophical context. Biologists (such as Ernst Mayr, 1963) and philosophers of biology (such as David Hull, 1965) have been arguing for many years against essentialist thinking in biology. One aspect of essentialist thinking that is particularly difficult to eradicate is the idea that *if* one has identified the fundamental taxonomic entity to which an object is to be assigned, then it is by reference to properties characteristic of that class that ultimate explanations of the behavior of the object must be constructed. But first, there is no reason to believe that there is such a thing as a "fundamental taxonomic entity." And even if there were, good empiricism requires that we in no way prejudge the issue of how much of the behavior of the entities belonging to such a class is uniform within it. [I have discussed the latter point at some length elsewhere (Dupré, 1986)]. Thus the undoubted fact that the species is the fundamental level of distinction among biological organisms (arguably the controversy about how species should be defined reflects the fact that this is taken as true by definition) tells us nothing about what range of generalizations will hold within a particular species. Thus there is at least no conceivable a priori objection to my claim that within the particular biological species *Homo sapiens*, behavioral generalizations usually fail. For this purpose a finer taxonomy is essential. The claim that humankind encompasses many human kinds is, I believe, a perspicuous statement of the objection that has so often been entered against human sociobiology on behalf of the importance of culture.

6 Cultural Species and Forces

I have been arguing that it is unprofitable to approach the study of human behavior with a search for universal principles. Though there will certainly be rough universals about such matters as the general ways in which humans process information, or acquire language, specific dispositions to behavior will be dependent on a much more detailed description of the cultural context in which the particular human is situated.

I have also suggested that cultural diversity should be understood in many respects in the same way as biological diversity—that is, as the result of an evolutionary process. In particular, individual variation, and processes analogous to selection, should be seen as providing a historical basis for the present existence of various internally articulated and integrated cultural forms. I shall also make some tentative suggestions later about one important possible source of such variation. But first, I want to emphasize in another way the appropriateness of this way of thinking about these issues.

Part of the significance of an adequate taxonomy for understanding biology might be put in the following way: The species to which an organism belongs will be an excellent and indispensable predictor of its susceptibility to the various environmental forces that impinge on it. For example, the appearance or introduction of a certain parasite might have devastating effects, including even extinction, on certain species, while having none at all on most others. A drought might have very little effect on suitably adapted plants, while being fatal to whole species that are adapted to higher water consumption. I shall suggest, analogously, that the major forces that have an impact on humans are cultural rather than biological, and that their impact is similarly susceptible to the cultural contexts of individuals.

Consider, for instance, a very biological-looking force, a food shortage. In some societies it might happen that this would provide selection for the capacities to produce food efficiently: hunting, gathering, raising produce, etc. But clearly this is not at all the impact of such an occurrence on most of the societies with which we are familiar. Consider the great Irish famines of the nineteenth century. Presumably the Irish peasants were actually more skillful in the production of food than the English landowners (mainly noted, in this context, for the spectacularly inefficient pursuit of highly unpalatable small animals); but it was certainly the former, not the latter, who suffered the effects of the famine. The general point of this example is simply that it is aspects of the cultural phenotype that determine not only behavior, but also susceptibility to extracultural forces.

The next logical step in this exposition is to point out that there are many forces impinging on humans (political, ideological, and, perhaps above all, economic) that are wholly cultural in origin. The impact of these forces, I suggest, is almost entirely mediated by the cultural rather than the biological phenotype of the individual. However, before developing this point, I want to consider a line of objection to my argument so far implicit in the contribution to this volume by Cosmides and Tooby.

7 Levels of Explanation

The general drift of my argument has been to claim that specifics of the cultural environment in which an individual is situated will provide determinants of behavior that will tend to overwhelm any tendency toward biological optimality. But, as Cosmides and Tooby (this volume) argue, the level of manifest behavior is not the appropriate one upon which to conceive of natural selection as operating. It is rather that selection will optimize the structure and characteristics of the information processing systems that mediate between environmental cues and behavioral responses. Thus they deny that there is any genuine conflict between cultural explanations of behavior and an evolutionary theory of adaptive function. "The claim that a behavior is the product of culture ... entails nothing more than the claim that surrounding or preceding individuals are an environmental factor that has influenced the behavior under discussion in some way. It leaves the learning mechanisms that allow humans to acquire and generate culture completely unspecified" (p. 293).

This is surely quite unobjectionable. In particular, it would be foolish to deny, and is probably important to assert, that the physiological mechanisms that enable us to lead the behaviorally complex, culturally varied, lives that we do, are a product of the evolutionary process. But despite their emphasis on the evolution of learning and information processing mechanisms, as opposed to behaviors, Cosmides and Tooby do want to insist on the importance of this evolutionary perspective to the understanding of behavior. The question that this raises, then, is to what extent the specifics of behavior are best explained by appeal to the details of such cognitive mechanisms. I take it that Cosmides and Tooby do think that these mechanisms are highly relevant to behavior, and that this is a major part of the force of their insistence on the domain specificity of cognitive mechanisms.

Cosmides and Tooby are clearly right to emphasize the necessity of an intervening level between evolution and behavior. Evolution can only act on the physiological mechanisms that are proximate causes of behavior. And they are therefore right to insist that the evolutionary approach to behavior does not entail either uniformity of behavior or uniformly adaptive behavior. The conception of the mind as an all-purpose genetic fitness calculator is rightly derided, but its absurdity is no criticism of the evolutionary approach to behavior. However, the problem that Cosmides and Tooby's approach raises, but does not, I think, fully answer, is to what extent the more complex picture they present really does substantiate a systematic connection between evolution and behavior.

I shall, at least for the sake of argument, accept the following claims: First, that understanding the human mind requires functional analysis, and evolutionary theory is the most promising way of approaching such analysis. (The methodological issues here are admirably analyzed by Kitcher in this volume. No one could object to the use of evolutionary optimality analyses as a means of generating hypotheses about the functional organization of the mind; and with sufficient caution, the derivation from such analyses may provide additional weight in favor of such hypotheses.) And second, even less controversially, understanding the function and functioning of the human mind is an essential component of the explanation of human behavior.

The reason that, in spite of these concessions, I remain skeptical about the relevance of evolution to human behavior is that I do not believe, in general, that explanation is transitive. That is, from the fact that A is an essential ingredient in the explanation of B, and B in the explanation of C, it does not follow that A has a comparable importance in the explanation of C. And so, the explanatory relevance of evolution to cognitive mechanisms, and cognitive mechanisms to behavior, does not imply that evolutionary theory has much explanatory relevance to behavior.

Space will not permit an adequate treatment of this issue here (the position I have stated is defended in more detail in Dupré, 1983). An example should give some sense of the underlying issue. Levels of, and changes in, populations of various animals can be explained, to some extent, by models that reflect interactions with other predator and prey species (see, e.g., May, 1973). A standard case concerns the populations of lynx and hare in Northern Canada. It is a presupposition of this model that lynxes are physiologically equipped to consume hares; and parameters in the model that measure their efficiency at doing so may be thought of as reflecting such things as the relative speeds of the two animals.

In this case, it is certainly true to say that these physiological properties of lynxes have an important influence on the prevalence of hares. However, in explaining the frequency of hares, such properties would not naturally be appealed to. The sort of property that one would rather want to know would be the propensity of lynxes to eat hares, presumably as a function of the frequency of hares (strictly a population level property). That there is such a propensity at all certainly depends on lynxes having the appropriate physiological characteristics. But it is very questionable whether the required propensity could be inferred from physiological facts about the two animals; and even if it could, it is unclear what this would add to the explanatory project at the population level. I am inclined to put the point in the following, perhaps contentious, way: The abstract conception of a lynx appropriate for constructing population models has no tight theoretical connections with the conception derived from physiological studies of lynxes. The assumption of transitivity of explanations rests on the erroneous assumption that the models of an entity that are constructed for distinct theoretical purposes can be identified with one another. I suggest that they cannot.

Returning, then, to the specific topic under discussion, I do not take it as obvious that the model of the human mind derived from an evolutionarily based functional analysis can be identified with that appropriate to the correlation of information absorbed from the environment with behavior emitted by the organism. As in the ecological case just discussed, I suspect that the structure of the mind as conceived in the former project will provide important constraints on the possible accounts of the latter. Human physiology will limit what kinds of information can be absorbed, and what kinds of behavior are possible for the organism. Evolutionary considerations may be highly relevant to the formation of plausible hypotheses about such matters. It might, for instance, turn out that people really do have very sophisticated capacities for distinguishing degrees of relatedness to themselves. If so, possibilities for patterns of social behavior would exist that otherwise would not.

In sum, I agree with Cosmides and Tooby that evolution has structured the mind, but has not done so in a way that can be expressed in terms of behavior. But I do not think this is simply because the mind determines behavior in response to a variable environment. Rather, and this brings us back to the main theme of this essay, behavior is a phenomenon that must be understood at the social level. The social cannot be constructed out of the psychological dispositions of individuals any more than the ecological can be constructed from the physiological. In both cases, the relevant properties at the more complex level of organization are, at least in part, constructed from phenomena at that level.

8 The Breakdown of Cultural Species in Modern Society

If the human species were divided into the relatively isolated tribal groups that are the classical subject matter of anthropology, I believe that the analogy I have been proposing between biological and cultural species would be almost exact. The adaptation of such groups to their environments is highly varied, and primarily varied with respect to culturally transmitted modes of behavior. And such groups may well be as *culturally* isolated from their neighbors as, say, species of a typical genus of flowering plants are genetically.[6]

However, in the modern world things are not so simple. To begin with, modern societies are stratified in ways that suggest that the taxonomy must be applied within, not just across, what are generally considered as cultures. For a paradigmatic class society, such as nineteenth-, and to some extent twentieth-, century Britain, such a classification may provide plausible cultural species; certainly such classes can be culturally distinct and very effectively isolated from one another.[7] But when we move to the contemporary United States it is doubtful whether such an analysis is useful. American society can be divided by economic class, ethnic background, religious belief, geographic region, and no doubt many other factors, all of which carry a number of behavioral propensities, and all of which more or less cross-classify the population. Perhaps a biological analogue could be constructed by finding a large area of land, temperate, fertile, and well irrigated, and introducing a few thousand fairly similar species of *Compositae*. I doubt whether, in ten years' time, a very useful taxonomy, or anyhow a unique taxonomy useful for all purposes, could be constructed for the consequences of such a scheme.

Since most of the human species lives in pluralistic rather than tribal societies, it may well be asked what the point of all this fuss about cultural species can be. But of course if contemporary culture is seen as historically resulting from the gradual hybridization of many earlier cultural species, it should be clear that this only emphasizes the importance of culturally transmitted properties. The point is rather that to whatever extent such primitive cultural species may have been natural kinds, there may be no such natural taxonomy for contemporary society.

How, then, does this illuminate the appropriate way of understanding contemporary human behavior? Presumably, in the first place, we should recognize that the appropriate typology for modern humankind is going to vary according to the context of inquiry (it can be argued that the same is true for biological taxonomy generally, but that is not my present concern). And what this means is that what we need to consider are cultural properties, and the forces to which such properties make their bearers more or less susceptible. A suitable typology may of course be very helpful in understanding the distribution of such properties.

One example may suffice to illustrate the general point. A person's susceptibility to advertising might turn out to be a function of the amount of time spent watching television. One could then describe a pattern of consumption (behavior, presumably) characteristic of the ideal advertising victim. This would approximately correspond to the amount of money spent advertising various products on television. It might turn out that the more time a person spent watching television, the closer their consumption approximated this pattern. It might even be possible to correlate the disposition to watch television with distinguishable cultural groups, perhaps religious affiliation. In this, obviously hypothetical, example, the disposition to watch television is an aspect of the cultural phenotype, and advertising is a cultural force the influence of which depends on that aspect of the cultural phenotype. It is also conceivable that there is a human typology that provides a good predictor of the relevant phenotypic feature. Whether or not this is probable in the present case, it is evident that such a taxonomy would be fairly specific to the particular problem in view. I take it that, hypothetical though it be, this is a fairly typical pattern of behavioral determination in complex modern societies.

A final complication is that in modern times there exist culturally generated forces that have intercultural and international dimensions. Consider, for instance, the recent precipitous halving of the price of oil.[8] This constitutes an enormous change in the flow of wealth between the producers and consumers of oil. Presumably it will eventually have profound effects on great numbers of people. Citizens of those relatively poor countries that depend heavily on income from oil-production will on average become poorer, and consume less. Californians will probably drive their cars more, and Minnesotans keep their houses a few degrees warmer. The ramifications of such a phenomenon will at any rate be extremely complex, but in the end will be manifested in behavioral changes of numerous kinds. Cultural isolation, it would appear, is even less prevalent than might be imagined.

In the end, then, I suspect that the significance of the concept of cultural species is more historical than contemporary. But historical significance is hardly to be demeaned when the underlying topic is evolution. If cultural speciation has the conceptual role in human evolutionary history that I am suggesting, then it should be no surprise that cultural properties and forces should now be the major determinants of human behavior.

9 The Significance of Culture

I hardly intend to say everything that could be said about the topic at the head of this section. However, by way of conclusion, I would like to say something about why the emphasis on cultural forces and properties over biological analogues makes some very significant differences to the understanding of human behavior. In particular, supposed political implications have figured very prominently in the debate over sociobiology, but I do not think that the issues have always been correctly conceived. I shall say very briefly here how I do think some of these issues should be treated. But before making some rather general comments on this topic, I want to address a more specific worry that might be raised about my present approach to this topic.

What I have in mind is the possibility that the concept of cultural species that I have advocated may be thought open to all kinds of disastrous political abuse. To assert fundamental differences between different human groups, it may be said, may provide ammunition for racist propaganda. Now of course, as I have emphasized, cultural species are not biological species, so no support is offered for the traditional form of racism that claims fundamental biological differences between human geographical variants. Indeed, to the contrary, it should be clear that cultural species will often cut across racial divisions. In the contemporary United States there are many, though perhaps deplorably few, people of African or Asian origin who are fully assimilated into contemporary American culture, or one of its predominantly Caucasian variants.

On the other hand, sophisticated xenophobes are inclined to talk more about cultural differences than about biological differences. Contemporary anti-immigration rhetoric, in particular, tends to appeal to fears of the local culture being swamped or overwhelmed by alien introductions. I do not believe, however, that the way to respond to such claims is to deny, in the face of the facts, the existence of cultural differences. Part of the response, on the other hand, should be to emphasize the actual nature of cultural diversity. Such diversity, particularly within pluralistic societies, will only be amenable to a very loose and probabilistic typography. The topology of such a typography will be a good deal flatter than that of typical biological variation. Certainly an essentialist conception of cultural groups would be even more glaringly inappropriate than it is for biological species.

But one crucial response to xenophobia is to make clear exactly what threat is supposed to be involved in the interaction of different cultures. This is the kind of consideration for which relatively simple models of cultural evolution may have considerable significance. For example, with respect to the question of immigration, it is difficult to see why the introduction of fairly low levels of unfamiliar cultural traits should be likely to spread through the population unless they prove to be both very attractive to the indigenous population and also consistent with the central themes and values of the existing culture. For instance, the introduction of a significant population of Indians and Pakistanis to the British Isles has no doubt led to a great increase in the consumption of the cuisines of these parts of Asia—a great boon to a gastronomically impoverished culture. I take it that only the most rabid cultural conservative would consider this kind of innovation objectionable. On the other hand, as far as I know there has been little tendency for the natives to adopt the Hindu or Moslem religions. (I do not, of course, wish to imply that these would be any less desirable than those presently dominant.) If cultural variants spread solely to the extent that they prove both attractive to the indigenous population and compatible with their antecedent cultural values, then such innovations would appear, prima facie, to be an unqualified benefit.

The most interesting possibilities perhaps arise from the consideration of density-dependent phenomena. It is certainly plausible that there will be a tendency for a culture to spread purely as a consequence of the numerical superiority, or power and wealth, of its adherents. I take it that in the United States, to whatever extent there has been assimilation of members of cultural and ethnic minorities, it greatly exceeds any reverse assimilation into the minority cultures. Insofar as it is felt that cultural diversity is a good thing, certainly a reasonable claim, the real danger is in the excessive cultural assimilation of minorities—and perhaps, on an international scale, deliberate cultural imperialism—and not in the subversion of a culture by immigrants and minorities.

Turning now to the more traditional debate about the political significance of evolutionary arguments, much of the trouble derives from confusion over notions of determinism. Sociobiologists are widely accused of being biological determinists, or even genetic determinists, and respond with understandable puzzlement that they recognize many other forces, including environmental conditions that interact with the alleged biological determinants of behavior, apart from the purely biological. Moreover, the objection to determinism of whatever kind has to do with worries about the lack of human autonomy. It is often not at all clear how postulating cultural rather than biological forces has any effect on this problem.

However, the real problem here has not to do with any wholly implausible suggestion that all human behavior is determined by some simple and homogeneous collection of forces. The point is rather the extent to which forces of particular kinds are susceptible to any kind of deliberate manipulation. And in this respect there is a great divide between cultural and biological forces. To whatever extent biological causes, genetically based, play a role in determining behavior, they are susceptible to manipulation only in the very long term by behavioral eugenics. (I do not mean to deny, again, the dependence on the actual expression of such forces on other contextual factors. That is a quite different point.) Cultural causes, on the other hand, are, in principle at least, much more malleable. Lamarckianism, lateral transmission (within a generation), and asymmetric transmission are features of cultural evolution that suggest that, under favorable circumstances, change may be rapid.

But more even than just the pace of change, cultural evolution suggests no obstacle to the idea that change may be directed, and may even be directed in the service of objectives such as freedom and justice—or, of course, as may be historically more typical, oppression and injustice. (There is a philosophical line of thought, deriving from Kant, that asserts that this possibility is the only intelligible ground for human autonomy.) It is sometimes implied that such notions are only products of our particular cultural traditions or even, occasionally, of our biological evolutionary history. But, though there is something in this, since many of the most pressing, or depressing, contemporary examples of injustice have to do precisely with the way accidents of cultural history are taken as adequate grounds for unequal treatment, there are surely aspects of justice that can, and indeed must, be seen in a genuinely transcultural way. The deep truth that lies behind the political suspicions of sociobiology is that a biological explanation of the human condition may seem to explain what is wrong with the world, but does so in a way that suggests that this wrong is inevitable. Cultural explanation holds out the possibility not only of explaining, but also of changing the world. I do not mean to suggest that cultural forces are any less determinative of their good or bad causal upshots. It is rather that if we understood sufficiently how they operated, it would seem that they would be the kind of forces that should be susceptible to interactions with, and redirections by, deliberate acts of public policy. Of course, this is not an argument that such explanations are correct. That was the aim of the earlier sections of this paper.

The preceding remarks lead to a concluding thought on the role of the concept of optimality. Evolutionists (and some economists), despite increasingly numerous reservations, are still inclined to treat optimality as providing a methodology for describing the world. But given the way the world strikes most reflective people, there is much to be said for preferring to see optimality as concerned rather with a normative description of how the world should be. Although I do not mean to imply that economists or sociobiologists who defend the importance of optimality as a tool for descriptive analysis of human society typically confuse this with a normative conception of optimality, there is nevertheless a serious danger that the descriptive concept will seem much more significant—since more causally efficacious—than the normative. Emphasis on cultural determinants of behavior, regardlesses of the extent to which they are usefully analyzable by appeal to a descriptive concept of optimality, has the great virtue of showing how a normative conception of society might also have importance, and even causal weight, in our reflections on society.

Notes

1. See Smith (this volume) for such a claim and further references; a philosopher with a similar, but even stronger, position is Alexander Rosenberg (1980).
2. Peter Richerson (personal communication) has expressed some concern about my use of the word "autonomous," pointing out that he and Boyd model cultural evolution as a process intimately linked to genetic evolution. I certainly do not mean to take a stand against this claim. What I do mean to stress is that, first, culturally driven processes have major weight as partial contributors to the course of human evolution, and second, for many aspects of human evolution they may be the most significant forces at work.
3. The apparent rarity of cultural transmission in nonhuman species is briefly discussed by Boyd and Richerson (1985, pp. 130–131); see also Pulliam and Dunford (1980). I shall not be concerned here with this fascinating and important question.
4. A similar suggestion can be found in Lorenz (1977, chapter 9). A specific application of such an attempt to the Indian caste system has been attempted by Gadgil and Malhotra (1983), though they concentrate almost exclusively on ecological factors. (I am grateful to Peter Richerson for this reference.)
5. I take it that this is a central point of the much discussed critique of adaptionism by Gould and Lewontin (1979). Peter Richerson has pointed out to me that there is no necessary connection between the complexity of genetic interactions and the integration of organisms at the macroscopic level. Both phenomena, however, will give rise to analogous constraints on evolutionary possibility.
6. Which is to say, not very. No doubt cultural traits have always been fairly readily transferable across cultures. The important point is not so much the extent of isolation as the extent to which particular groups, at particular times, exhibit distinctive and reasonably homogeneous forms of social organization.
7. Bourdieu (1984) provides a fascinating and detailed analysis of this kind for contemporary France. It appears from this example that a detailed cultural topography, at least, is feasible for some modern societies.
8. There are still, I suppose, some who would like to include such a phenomenon with biological evolution in a more generalized doctrine of optimality. That this particular change reflects a change in some ideal market, in any but the narrowest sense, would be a difficult case to make. That the independent decisions of buyers and sellers should be coordinated so as to clear the market may be an admirable thing, but is hardly a sufficient achievement for constituting Utopia.

Bibliography

Bourdieu, P. (1984). *Distinction: A Social Critique of the Judgement of Taste*. Cambridge, MA: Harvard University Press.

Boyd, R., and P. J. Richerson (1985). *Culture and the Evolutionary Process*. Chicago: University of Chicago Press.

Cartwright, N. (1983). *How the Laws of Physics Lie*. Oxford and New York: Oxford University Press.

Cavalli-Sforza, L. L., and M. W. Feldman (1981). *Cultural Transmission and Evolution: A Quantitative Approach*. Princeton: Princeton University Press.

Charnov, E. L. (1976). Optimal Foraging, the Marginal Value Theorem. *Theoretical Population Biology* 9:129–136.

Dupré, J. (1983). The Disunity of Science. *Mind* 92:321–346.

Dupré, J. (1986). Sex, Gender, and Essence. *Midwest Studies in Philosophy* 11:441–457.

Durham, W. (1978). Toward a Coevolutionary Theory of Human Biology and Culture. In *The Sociobiology Debate*, ed. A. Caplan, New York: Harper and Row, pp. 428–448.

Durham, W. (1981). Overview: Optimal Foraging Analysis in Human Ecology, In Winterhalder and Smith (1981).

Gadgil, M., and K. C. Malhotra (1983). Adaptive Significance of the Indian Caste System: An Ecological Perspective, *Annals of Human Biology* 10:465–478.

Gould, S. J., and R. C. Lewontin (1979). The Spandrels of San Marco and the Panglossian Paradigm: A Critique of the Adaptationist Programme. *Proceedings of the Royal Society of London* 205:581–598.

Hull, D. L. (1965). The Effect of Essentialism on Taxonomy: 2000 Years of Stasis. *British Journal for Philosophy of Science* 15:314–326, 16:1–18.

Keene, A. (1981). Optimal Foraging in a Nonmarginal Environment. In Winterhalder and Smith (1981).

Kitcher, P. (1985). *Vaulting Ambition: Sociobiology and the Quest for Human Nature.* Cambridge, MA: MIT Press.

Lorenz, K. (1977). *Behind the Mirror: A Search for a Natural History of Human Knowledge.* London: Methuen.

May, R. M. (1973). *Stability and Complexity in Model Ecosystems.* Princeton: Princeton University Press.

Mayr, E. (1963). *Animal Species and Evolution.* Cambridge, MA: Harvard University Press.

Pulliam, H. R., and C. Dunford (1980). *Programmed to Learn: An Essay on the Evolution of Culture.* New York: Columbia University Press.

Rosenberg, A. (1980). *Sociobiology and the Preemption of Social Science.* Baltimore: Johns Hopkins Press.

Smith, E. (1981). Optimal Foraging Theory and the Analysis of Hunter-Gatherer Group Size. In Winterhalder and Smith (1981).

Wilson, E. O. (1975). *Sociobiology: the New Synthesis.* Cambridge, MA: Harvard University Press.

Winterhalder, B. (1981). Optimal Foraging Strategies and Hunter-Gatherer Research in Anthropology. In Winterhalder and Smith (1981).

Winterhalder, B., and E. Smith (eds.) (1981). *Hunter-Gatherer Foraging Strategies.* Chicago: University of Chicago Press.

Name Index

Subject Index